QUESTION EVERYTHING

QUESTION EVERYTHING

—

A STONE READER

—

Edited by

PETER CATAPANO
AND SIMON CRITCHLEY

LIVERIGHT PUBLISHING COMPANY
A Division of W. W. NORTON & COMPANY
Independent Publishers Since 1923

For information about permission to reproduce selections from
this book, write to Permissions, Liveright Publishing
Corporation, a division of W. W. Norton & Company, Inc.,
500 Fifth Avenue, New York, NY 10110

For information about special discounts for bulk purchases,
please contact W. W. Norton Special Sales at
specialsales@wwnorton.com or 800-233-4830

Manufacturing by Lakeside Book Company
Production manager: Julia Druskin

ISBN 978-1-324-09183-7

Liveright Publishing Corporation, 500 Fifth Avenue, New York,
N.Y. 10110
www.wwnorton.com

W. W. Norton & Company Ltd., 15 Carlisle Street, London W1D 3BS

1 2 3 4 5 6 7 8 9 0

CONTENTS

———

V. WHAT IS HAPPINESS?

VI. DOES LIFE HAVE MEANING?

VII. WHY CAN'T WE ALL JUST GET ALONG?

VIII. WHAT IS THE DIFFERENCE BETWEEN RIGHT AND WRONG?

IX. WHAT IS IT LIKE TO BE A WOMAN?

X. WHY DOES ART MATTER?

XI. IS THIS THE END OF THE WORLD AS WE KNOW IT?

XII. DO WE NEED GOD?

XIII. NOW WHAT?

INTRODUCTION

Plato, the Priest, and the Bottle

W HEN I WAS A YOUNG, IMPRESSIONABLE LAD ATTENDING high school in Staten Island, New York, in the 1970s, I had a memorable teacher in a course called Humanities. Father Julius was a Jesuit priest, an imposing man with a booming voice who possessed an air of philosophical and theological gravity that my other teachers, with their kindly post–Vatican II mannerisms, did not. He had been a promising theologian as young man, having studied in Rome, but had somehow landed here in this small parish in the city's Forgotten Borough, the reasons for which were never quite clear.

Whatever the case, this priest's humble assignment was my good fortune. To be sure, Father Julius was not an easy teacher. He was mercurial—sometimes genial, other times gruff and dismissive. But he never talked down to us. He challenged us intellectually and, most importantly, he introduced us to philosophy and the literature of thought. I'll never forget his drawing of Plato's Cave on the school blackboard—my first exposure to the ancient Greeks—with its subterranean prisoners, enchained and thereby condemned to witness shadows while real life unfolded above them in the sunlight. I was fascinated, even moved, by this stunning lesson on perception, illusion, and the ascent toward knowledge. I realize now that it was the first time that anyone had even vaguely hinted at the possible source of the teenage angst I had been feeling. My growing dissatisfaction with everything around me—my hometown, my family, my friends, and my school—was justified in this ancient allegory. I was in chains, witnessing mere shapes and shadow-play, the appearances of appearances, but there was a truer, blazing, light-filled reality awaiting me outside, if I could only escape.

My classmates and I were typical teenagers. We traded gossip and rumors and devised outlandish backstories to explain the mysterious personalities of our teachers. One of those stories was that Father Julius liked to drink. We had no evidence of this, of course. He "looked like a drinker"—large, often red-faced—and that was enough for us. Those rumors must have reached Father Julius's ears, because one day, he entered our classroom with an unusually stern expression. Settling in front of us, he reached into his bag and pulled out a large vodka bottle—a fifth, about half full—opened it, took a long swig, screwed the cap back on, placed it on his desk, and promptly began the day's lesson. Our eyes widened with disbelief. No one said a word. We sat there in utter silence, furtively side-eyeing the bottle until we could no longer bear to look at it, and we buried our heads in our notebooks. We discussed "A Modest Proposal" that day.

In the cruel adolescent gossip of the hallways, we condemned our teacher to this vice and even mocked him—but always half-admiringly. Whatever we had witnessed in class, it was clear that he had acted without fear of punishment or earthly authority, and to a group of aspiring teenage rebels, that was the definition of "cool."

Later, as I thought more about the Allegory of the Cave, I began to see the flaw in our understanding of what we had witnessed. After all, what had we seen? A bottle. The label said "vodka." There was clear liquid inside. He drank from it. All of that had been verified. But one important fact hadn't been. Was the liquid in the bottle really vodka? Or was it water? Was Father Julius confirming the rumors we had spread or performing a clever philosophical trick, reinforcing the lesson of the cave? Were we listening to echoes? Looking at shadows? None of us had the courage to ask—and so we drifted on in a sort of semidarkness about what we had seen until the whole incident faded from memory.

As I learned more about philosophy over the years, both in and out of school, and as the work of thinkers from Pascal to Nietzsche to Arendt became integral to my understanding of the world, I couldn't help but think of Father Julius. He was our Socrates—at least, the closest we could get to Socrates in our little Catholic school—sticking a finger in the eye of authority, rankling the complacent, and sharpening the minds of those around him in the process. Although I've long forgotten most of what we read that year in Humanities, I learned an important lesson: that it is not always enough in life to rely on what you see and what you are told. In fact, there is a danger, both individual and social, in passively accepting information. You must interrogate not only others, but yourself, your thoughts, the very evidence of your senses. We may never reach absolute certainty, but we should still aspire to it. And to do that we must question what we see, what we hear, and what we feel. We must question our beliefs. We must question everything.

Many years later, in my day-to-day work as an editor at the *New York Times*, "question everything" became a sort of mantra. It is a catchy phrase, yes, but also a fundamental principle of both journalism and philosophy. For more than a decade, it has been the unifying theme of this endeavor, and it is now the title of this book.

IT'S THE SAME, ONLY DIFFERENT

Question Everything: A Stone Reader is a brand-new collection of essays from the *New York Times* philosophy series The Stone. The idea for the series was born over a beer, some twelve years ago, conjured up in an Irish bar in Brooklyn by myself and Simon Critchley—the British American philosopher, prolific author, New School professor, incurable David Bowie and Liverpool Football Club fan, and coeditor of this volume. For more than a decade, Simon and I have collaborated on hundreds of philosophical arguments and essays published in the *Times*, discussing themes, fielding dozens of submissions each month, and searching for thinkers engaging issues that we believed would matter to readers in their everyday lives. Through our partnership, we cleared a space in the cluttered media landscape, a rigorous but wide and welcoming platform, for philosophers and the philosophically inclined to voice their ideas. The essays appeared weekly, and The Stone became a leading force in reviving what is often called "public philosophy," in which professional and academic philosophers step out of their usual precincts to engage larger audiences. In this way, the series was not an innovation; it was a throwback. The ancient Greeks roaming the agora were nothing if not public.

Question Everything follows two previous volumes, *The Stone Reader: Modern Philosophy in 133 Arguments* and *Modern Ethics in 77 Arguments*, both of them, like this one, published by Liveright. Readers of those two books will find something familiar here: philosophical commentary written in an engaging and accessible style, free of academic jargon, on almost every imaginable topic, from free speech, human nature, happiness, and art to religion, power, politics, climate change, and the possibility of hope in a time of plague. It may be read as a companion to the previous books, or as an account of philosophical thinking that stands entirely on its own. *Question Everything* reliably delivers the contrarian views, sound arguments, occasional humor, and creative approaches to traditional opinion-writing that loyal readers of The Stone have come to expect. Its appeal, we hope, is still wide, to be read and enjoyed by the philosophically curious; by those who believe that the wisdom and folly of the past can shine light on the present; by lovers of original thinking and writing; by students and teachers looking for thoughtful and accessible ways into the discipline; by corporate and business leaders looking to integrate philosophical and ethical thinking into their workplaces; or by mainstream readers who want an accessible compendium of philosophy that is not too dense or academic for a place on their bookshelves or nightstands.

So, what's new, then? Well, *Question Everything* does differ from its predecessors in some important ways. Notably, the essays collected here are organized not by traditional categories like ethics, political philosophy, or epistemology, but thematically by question, thirteen of them, to be exact—the first twelve like the hours of a clock, ticking us through the tumultuous time in which these pieces were written, from late 2015 to 2021, and the last speculating its way into an uncertain future. As Hegel once wrote, "Philosophy is its own time comprehended in thoughts," and so these essays are not mere experiments in logic or reason. They are real-time arguments, meditations, and responses to events that cannot be glossed over with disinterested philosophical detachment: political and social upheavals, crises of war and human migration, climate-driven catastrophes, and, of course, the terrifying global pandemic that consumed, controlled, and stole so many of our days. In this time, nearly all of us were forced to reassess parts or even the whole of our lives. Some of us found our old beliefs and priorities upended; others found theirs reinforced and strengthened. As crisis after crisis unfolded, whether in a distant land or on our doorsteps, the questions at the root of philosophy took on a renewed urgency. True, they were never far away to begin with. Yet we sought to ask them again, not as an intellectual exercise, but with the number and quality of our remaining days on earth in the balance.

Like any anthology, *Question Everything* is designed both for immediate gratification and long-term use. Its essays can be read in any order, at any pace, over any period of time. But it is by design that the thematic questions that give the book its shape also create a sort of unity, a narrative arc that mirrors a philosophical journey. The book's first question is fundamental: What does it mean to be human? There, contemporary thinkers—Martha Nussbaum, Bernard-Henri Lévy, Pico Iyer, and Ai Weiwei among them—explore the essence of who we are as a species. With the next question—Is democracy possible?—we examine the notion of patriotism, the plausibility of our social and political ideals, and the limits of our systems of government with essays by an international group of thinkers. Faced with new, Orwellian technologies, we ask ourselves, Can we believe our eyes? As we descend into increasingly violent disagreements: Should speech be free? And onward, with more timeless struggles: What is happiness? Does life have meaning? Why can't we all just get along? What is the difference between right and wrong? What is it like to be a woman? Why does art matter? And in the whirl of our growing anxieties, we ask, Is this the end of the world as we know it? Do we need God? And, at last—Now what?—a contemplation of our future.

Careful readers will also notice something else new to this volume—a more pronounced expression of our belief that philosophy is a human activity that is advanced and enriched by the academy but not confined to it. While the book's foundation and core consist of the work of professional scholars and philosophers, it also features prominent artists and thinkers who will most likely never appear on a philosophy syllabus, including the novelist Elena Ferrante (on women and storytelling); the filmmaker Errol Morris (on the "insidious nature of belief"); the actor Cate Blanchett (on art as a thread in the social fabric); the chess master Garry Kasparov (on propaganda and reality); and the jazz colossus Sonny Rollins (on the permanence of the artistic act). What do we gain from these contributors, these so-called non-philosophers? A little celebrity, sure, and a little pizzazz—but the real value lies in the insights these masters share, shaped not by the scholarly tradition but by decades of devotion to and practice of their crafts. Academic philosophy is just one way of asking questions that we all face, and the difference between philosophers and artists is often only a different angle of approach, another and perhaps more immediately felt form of conceptual articulation.

WHY ASK WHY?

You'd think, with all this talk of the ancient ideas and eternal principles that fortify this book, that I'd be thinking about the wisdom that comes with age, but what I actually keep coming back to is the relentlessly inquisitive energy of youth. No doubt, part of this owes to the fact that I am a father. I have a daughter, and she is in college now, but like many children, she was a rigorous questioner at a very young age. This is only appropriate; questions are a function of childhood, of burgeoning minds, and questioning is an essential activity in maintaining that childlike quality in older minds.

When, as a typically curious child, you asked your parents a hundred times why the sky is blue, you were at the beginning of a process of probing the nature of knowledge, of coming to know the world. And if you found out why the sky is blue—from your parents, a teacher, or a book—you learned something fascinating about the scattering of light waves. Maybe you got yourself a prism, or thought twice the next time you saw a rainbow. But receiving the answer to an already settled question isn't philosophy. You just absorbed what is considered reliable information worked out by others over the course of centuries. (We can call that learning.) Maybe, though, after you learned why the sky was blue, you found yourself asking another question: Why does a blue sky make me feel happy? To even begin to answer that one, you had to look up not only to the sky and the infinite space above, but within, inside yourself, and the infinite spaces there. That is the spirit of philosophy, the same one guiding us to question everything. Carrying that spirit into adolescence and young adulthood can cause problems—the "troubled teen" is often the one who resists authority, or asks too many questions—but in our view, they are the good kind of problems.

I recently listened to a conversation, recorded on my old computer, that I had with my daughter when she was about seven years old. I quote it here with her permission.

I remember we were sitting on the couch. She was telling me about the different religions she had learned about in school from her classmates who were Muslim, Christian, Hindu, and Jewish. They had talked about the holidays they celebrated, and about God. (For what it's worth, our family is held together by something of a mongrel faith—an aggregate of lapsed but well-intentioned Catholics, decidedly unorthodox Jews, and Chinese Buddhists, all compassionate and learned but more devoted to family gatherings and meals than formal worship.) She didn't quite understand the idea of a creator, a being who existed before time and from whom all arose. So I asked her what it was about God that she didn't understand. She answered my question with another question, putting her hand on a small cushion.

This pillow, it's handmade, right? she said.

Yes, I said.

And if you go back to the past, who made the wool?

It came from the sheep.

Who made the sheep? The earth did, right? Not the universe.

But the universe made the earth.

(Pause) *I know.*

So go back one more, I told her. Who made the universe?

And then a longer pause, as she seemed surprised to have just accidentally walked up to an answer.

God, she said quietly.

Yes, I said. That's what people believe.

We had wandered into our own little infinite regress problem and come out with an answer—not *the* answer, not even *ours.* But now she had a sense of why her classmates could come to believe what they believed. It was the questions that got us that far.

In childhood we are often given an idealized image of learning as a gentle, exploratory process. We are told that "curiosity is good" and that "learning isn't just memorization" or "failure is part of success." But it doesn't always seem that way. Questions—and the people who ask them—can complicate things, and are often treated with impatience, even contempt. They can interrupt the flow of information and its absorption—the act of memorization that serves as the pedagogical foundation of many schools preparing young people for standardized tests and a world driven by data. And all that continual asking can make others frustrated, annoyed. What was Socrates, with his constant interrogations, if not annoying? He was so annoying, in fact, that he was sentenced to death by the city of Athens.

It would be nice to think that paying for your truth-seeking with your life was merely a brutal ancient practice that snuffed out Socrates, but it's not. At the end of 2020, the Committee to Protect Journalists reported that at least thirty journalists—question-askers as courageous as any Socrates—were killed worldwide, with twenty-one of those killings carried out as a direct response to the reporters' work. Yes, sometimes asking questions can be deadly. Thankfully, for most of us the stakes are not so high.

But in some sense, the cost of not asking them can be even higher.

This seems especially true of the group who will likely be the youngest readers of The Stone. I'm talking about those born near the time of the attacks of September 11, 2001, when both the national and geopolitical landscapes were violently and permanently altered. They have found themselves in a world more fraught, broken, and perilous than the one their parents inherited—fractured by war and racial violence, divided and inflamed by social media, hurtling headlong into climate change, ravaged by hunger, illness, and global pandemics. In a recent interview about the climate crisis with the plant scientist Stan Cox, Noam Chomsky, one of the world's most influential thinkers, was asked whether there was anything that still gave him hope. His answer was, "Young people." It's not outlandish to suggest that the change that their inheritance has forced them to seek might begin with philosophy, now that everything is being questioned again.

Question Everything is a product of the spirit of agitation and inquiry that has been integral to the human enterprise from the beginning of recorded history—the persistent, skeptical questioning of authority, of clichés, misinformation, propaganda, prejudice, the material conditions of our world, and the state of our existence as individuals and as a species. It embraces all those acts of resistance appropriate to our childhood and teenage years—appropriate even to that confused boy in a classroom in Staten Island, staring at the bottle and the prisoners in the cave—and crucial to our life as freethinking adults. This constant process of interrogation, along with a belief in the transformative potential of ideas, and a sheer delight in clear prose, has been the guiding principle of The Stone. And both Simon and I believe passionately in the importance of sharing this work in our times.

—Peter Catapano
New York, New York
2021

I

WHAT DOES IT MEAN TO BE HUMAN?

We Are Merging with Robots. That's a Good Thing.

The old boundaries of the human self are being blurred by technology. The risks are real, but the potential is astounding.

Andy Clark

H ERE ARE SOME THINGS THAT ARE TRUE TODAY:

- Artificial intelligences already outperform us at many tasks and are now able to train themselves to reach competencies (in restricted domains such as chess or Go) that we can barely comprehend.
- The controlled use of hallucinogenics and other drugs may soon be part of mainstream therapy for depression, loss, anxiety, and other conditions.
- Sex and companionship robots are already here.
- Entirely new forms of sensory perception, such as the North Sense, are becoming possible, and human brains look fluid enough to make use of just about any reliable stream of information and control opportunity.
- The human genome itself is now an object of control and intervention.
- Gender is becoming more visibly fluid than ever before, and there is emerging a place in human society for a wonderfully wide spectrum of ways of being (personally, politically, and sexually).

- One new tool for exploring some of that spectrum will be the use of immersive interactive virtual realities, such as the BeAnotherLab.
- Technological devices like cell phones and tablets are being used to help offset types of biological damage, such as a highly impaired memory, that just a few decades ago would have condemned victims to constant care.
- Sports for people with disabilities, whether adaptive or para-sports, are positively expanding our images of health and fitness in ways that would have been hard to imagine just a few decades ago.
- Neuro-enhancement, the improvement by drugs, practices, or implants of normal mental functioning, is possible and may soon become the norm.

What does it mean to live in this kind of emerging world? It is to live in a world marked more by possibility, fluidity, change, and negotiability than by outdated images of fixed natures and capacities. This is a world of remarkable personal and social possibility. Sharing and group solidarity are now easier than ever before, and the communal mapping of new electronic trails is enabling multiple once-hidden demographics to command social, commercial, and political respect. It's a world where human intelligence itself is poised for repair and reinvention. And one whose bedrock nature is itself becoming fluid, as digital overlays augment reality with personalized pointers (the information-rich cousins of the contemporary elves and pixies of Pokémon Go). It's also a world permeated by a growing swath of alien intelligences (just ask Alexa, although she won't really admit it).

All this blurs the boundaries between body and machine, between mind and world, between standard, augmented, and virtual realities, and between human and post-human. At the cusp of these waves of change, this is also the moment at which, increasingly, inclusivities of one kind (extensions of personal, social, and sexual freedom) bump up against the threat of new forms of exclusivity, as the augmented, fluid, connected cyber-haves increasingly differentiate themselves from the unaugmented, less connected, cyber-have-nots. Perhaps this is part of the price of all that laudable loosening?

This is a moment to be savored, even as we sound new notes of care and caution about the speed, nature, and range of these changes. Part of this process involves getting used to the alien nature and pervasive reach of the many new subintelligences that now surround us. These are the algorithms that talk with us, that watch us, that trade for us, that select dates for us, that suggest what we might buy, sell, or wear. They are the algorithms that pool information about us, and that will slowly permeate the full range of human-built environments, from bridges to roads to cities and more minor intelligent devices.

These are not yet intelligences like our own. But some of their greatest potential lies in the ways we humans might cooperate with them to form new hybrid systems that deliver the best of each. On top of all this, new understandings of the mind and brain are helping to break down the old boundaries between the psychological and the physical, as we learn not just how deeply the body matters to the mind, but also how the brain helps predict and construct the world of human experience.

We now glimpse the next steps in human cultural and cognitive evolution, continuing the trend that started with the arrival of human language and the (much later) invention of writing and the external storage and transmission of ideas. The new steps herald an age of fluidity and demand answers to a host of questions and issues that need to be addressed in conversations like this one. The two most important such questions are simply: How should we negotiate this dauntingly large space of human possibility? And what costs are we willing to tolerate along the way?

Ethically speaking, we need to ask what new costs and inequalities the freedoms and augmentations of some may mean for others. We need to ask if we are willing to tolerate some inequality as part of the rollout process for a more fluid and interconnected world. Issues of privacy and the right to control (including to trade or sell) our personal information are vividly with us. Not knowing quite where we as protected selves stop and the world around us begins, law and policy struggle to decide if (for example) information stored on our phones is enough like information stored in our heads to warrant the same protections. Law, education, and social policy currently lag behind many interacting waves of change. What is up for grabs is what we humans are, and what we will become.

AUGUST 13, 2018

What Does It Mean to Be Human? Don't Ask

We don't see the problem with our self-importance
because our narcissism is so complete.

Martha Nussbaum

OVER TIME, THE IDEA OF "BEING HUMAN" HAS SURELY meant—and will continue to mean—many things. There is not and never has been just one answer. But surely one thing it ought to involve today is the ability to recognize that the question itself is a problem.

We humans are very self-focused. We tend to think that being human is somehow very special and important, so we ask about that, instead of asking what it means to be an elephant, or a pig, or a bird. This failure of curiosity is part of a large ethical problem.

The question, "What is it to be human?" is not just narcissistic, it involves a culpable obtuseness. It is rather like asking, "What is it to be white?" It connotes unearned privileges that have been used to dominate and exploit. But we usually don't recognize this because our narcissism is so complete.

We share a planet with billions of other sentient beings, and they all have their own complex ways of being whatever they are. All of our fellow animal creatures, as Aristotle observed long ago, try to stay alive and reproduce more of their kind. All of them perceive. All of them desire. And most move from place to place to get what they want and need. Aristotle proposed that we should strive for a common explanation of how animals, including human animals, perceive, desire, and move.

We know Aristotle as a philosopher, but he also was a great biologist who studied shellfish and other creatures large and small. He encouraged his students not to turn away from studying animals that don't seem glamorous, since there is something wonderful in all of them, not least the sheer fact that they all strive for continued life.

This sense of wonder, which should lead us to a fuller ethical concern, is a deep part of our humanity. But wonder is on the wane, and we humans now so dominate the globe that we rarely feel as if we need to live with other animals on reciprocal terms.

Domesticated animals occupy a privileged sphere, but even they are often treated cruelly (think of puppy mills, or abandoned feral cats). The factory farming of pigs, chickens, and other animals is a relatively new form of hideous brutality. As for the creatures in the "wild," we can see that our human crimes are having a devastating effect on them: the damages that come from lab research using animals; the manifold harms endemic to the confinement of apes and elephants in zoos; the depletion of whale stocks by harpooning; the confinement of orcas and dolphins in marine theme parks; the poaching of elephants and rhinoceroses to benefit the international black market; the illicit trafficking of African elephants to American zoos; the devastation of habitat for many large mammals that is resulting from climate change. It is now estimated that human activity has contributed to the extinction of more than eighty mammalian species.

New issues arise constantly. The world needs an ethical revolution, a consciousness-raising movement of truly international proportions. But this revolution is impeded by the navel-gazing that is typically involved in asking, "What is it to be human?"

Let's rekindle and extend our sense of wonder by asking instead: "What is it to be a whale?" Then let's go observe whales as best we can, and read the thrilling research of scientists such as Hal Whitehead and Luke Rendell. Let's ask about elephants (my own most beloved species), and if we can't go on safaris, let's watch films of elephants simply living their lives, exhibiting communal devotion, compassion, grief, and a host of other complex attitudes that we humans tend to believe belong to us alone.

And let's do much more philosophical and legal work on theoretical approaches to protecting other animals and developing more reciprocity with them. We have gathered so much scientific information about the complexities of animal lives. Now let's put it to use philosophically. Will Kymlicka and Sue Donaldson have already done wonderful work on reciprocity and community with domesticated animals, but there's more to do.

In the world of philosophy-influenced policy, the most significant general approach to animal entitlements until now has been that of the British utilitarian Jeremy Bentham, courageously and ably developed by the philosopher Peter Singer. This approach continues to have great importance because it focuses on animals' suffering. If we were to simply stop inflicting gratuitous pain on animals, that would be a huge step forward.

We now know that animals need many things that don't always cause suffering when they are absent: the chance to associate with others of their kind in normal groupings; the chance to sing or trumpet in their characteristic ways; the chance to breed; the chance to move freely through unobstructed space; the chance to pursue curiosity and make new discoveries. So we also need, I believe, an approach that focuses on a plurality of distinct "capabilities," or freedoms, that each species requires to live a flourishing life.

I'm now writing a book that will use my prior work on the "capabilities approach" to develop a new ethical framework to guide law and policy in this area. But mine is just one approach, and it will and should be contested by others developing their own models. Lawyers working for the good of animals under both domestic and international laws need sound theoretical approaches, and philosophers should be assisting them in their work. And there is so much work to do.

So let's put aside the narcissism involved in asking only about ourselves. Let's strive for an era in which being human means being concerned with the other species that try to inhabit this world.

AUGUST 20, 2018

We Are Not Born Human

Our humanity is a process that begins with negation.

Bernard-Henri Lévy

WHAT DOES IT MEAN TO BE HUMAN? THE IMMENSITY OF THIS question can be boiled down to an old principle proposed by the German philosopher G. W. F. Hegel, which he attributed to fellow philosopher Baruch Spinoza: "Determination is negation."

But negation of what?

First, of God. In the beginning there was God—the source of infinite action. In the Western tradition, man has no purpose without God. For Christians, man was created in God's image; for Jews, God is a good worker who lends a hand. For atheists (who, let's not forget, are Judeo-Christians in their own way), man's purpose is in part to topple God from his throne. If this isn't a complete negation of God, then it at least limits his power, as humans come to occupy the space formerly reserved for God alone.

Determination is also a negation of nature. Nobody will deny—most of all not Spinoza—that a human is "natura naturata," a thing among things, a nature among natures, a figure of the world woven from the same fiber as all other ordinary figures. But to be human is also to desire transcendence, to aspire to be more than merely a sliver of nature.

In his day, the philosopher René Descartes pondered the difference between humans and machines. Today, on the cusp of a revolution in artificial intelligence, we are pondering a similar question: How will we be able to tell a real human from a synthetic one?

A real human is "res cogitans," a thinking thing, as Descartes put it. A source of "intentionality," as the philosopher Edmund Husserl wrote. Being human means taking a leap out of the natural order. To be human requires an escape, in one way or another, from that mass of atoms, cells, and particles from which you and I and everything else is composed. It is to be endowed with a soul, which—even if it is immaterial, without expanse or density, even if it is perfectly invisible, impalpable, and inconsistent—acts as a passport out of nature and into our human essence.

This systematic denaturalization, this confidence that a piece of oneself can escape from the natural order of the world, is akin to a second birth. Nature is the first stage of humanity; but it can, under no circumstance, be its horizon.

But there is also a third birth. To be human, of course, is to be part of another entity that we call society. With all due respect to the "Rousseauism" of those who have never truly read Jean-Jacques Rousseau, man has never existed entirely on his own, with no attachment to a community of others.

But here, we must be very careful. To idolize the social sphere, to passively accept the constraints that result from the imposition of social laws and norms, can prove fatal for human striving. Here lies the bleak realm of Martin Heidegger's "we." Here are the nameless, faceless mobs prophesied by Edgar Allan Poe and who today have been unleashed on social media.

To be human is to preserve, inside oneself, against all forms of social pressure, a place of intimacy and secrecy into which the greater whole cannot set foot. When this sanctuary collapses, machines, zombies, and sleepwalkers are sure to follow.

This private power may not be accessible to us at first. We aren't born human; we become it. Humanity is not a form of being; it is a destiny. It is not a steady state, delivered once and for all, but a process.

To be human also means knowing that one can win battles, but never the war. Death will have the final say. If this seems all too tragic, if we are troubled by the sense that the inhuman is the rule and the human the exception, we must come to understand it as a source of salvation.

Ultimately, I am sure of nothing. Philosophy is strictly concerned with the field of the possible, not the knowable, so I can only wager on what may be.

But I do know one thing: The history of this past century teaches us that when we place our bets on nostalgia—when we dedicate ourselves to the search for some lost native land, for something pure—we only pave the way for totalitarianism. We trigger the machines to clean, purge, and wash us away.

When we instead commit ourselves to moving forward, to diving into the unknown and embracing our humanity in all its uncertainty, then we embark on a truly beautiful and noble adventure—the very road to freedom.

This essay was translated from the French by Emily Hamilton.

AUGUST 22, 2018

A Road Trip to the Origins of Our Species

Along which brain science, stone tools, and scotch appear.

Michael S. Gazzaniga

I.

It was on an all-night Capitol Air flight to Brussels, sitting in the back smoking rows with Leon Festinger, playing endless backgammon and consuming scotch at an alarming rate, that I realized that, whether I liked it or not, I was about to learn a lot about human origins and uniqueness.

The year was 1981. Leon, the ingenious and intellectually adventurous social psychologist responsible for the theory of cognitive dissonance, had once again switched fields, this time from visual perception into what amounted to archaeology, and I was his sidekick.

We'd had extensive discussions in New York, secured a small study grant from the Alfred P. Sloan Foundation, and were off to France to learn more about lithic technology (the production of tools from stone) from a master of the discipline, the archaeologist Jacques Tixier. We wanted to know what on earth had happened roughly one million years earlier when humankind started to make stone tools. As we exited the cigarette-fouled cabin after the long flight, Leon calmly observed, "You know when they outlaw smoking on planes, I am not going to be able to make these trips anymore."

We made our way by train to Paris and found ourselves in meetings with others interested in our quest, like the psychologists David Premack and Serge Moscovici. David's deep knowledge of the chimp mind and its inventiveness was always challenging to simple notions of what makes humans so vastly superior to other species in the acquisition of complex skills. Serge, in his work in the social domain, emphasized the dynamics of groups in human activity and how revolutionary and innovative ideas sped humankind along.

This rich discourse was always considered over good food, which found us at Allard in the Sixth Arrondissement. I can vividly remember a dinner when, over Canard de Challans aux olives, after taking a bite of bread, Leon complained to a stunned waiter, "This is the morning's baguette, not the afternoon's." Our French host calmly took a bite of the baguette in question and confirmed the observation. The duck, on the other hand, was out of this world.

Paris may be the most beautiful place on the planet where humankind comes at you at every turn. There is nothing subtle about it, nothing to suggest that some sort of gradual evolution occurred to create it. Even the trip over, in which 220 animals calmly accepted their shared use of the hugely complex technology of a jet plane, revealed the special capacities of humankind: We are inventive and we thrive in groups. And we all want to know what flipped the switch in our ancestors. What made us this way?

Leon thought clues were to be found in how stone tools came to be—and so, we were soon back on the train, this time to Antibes to visit Jacques Tixier, who welcomed us to his studio. While I don't think Leon ever used a tool in his life, there was no one on earth who could have been more attentive. Watching the master make stone tools, Leon wrote in his 1983 book *The Human Legacy*, was far more instructive than anything he had learned from his considerable reading on the subject. He observed: "The ringing sound that came from a good piece of flint and the dull sound from a poor piece; watching him decide where to prepare the striking platform; seeing how he held the stone and how he struck it; my surprise to realize that the flake came off the bottom of the stone as he held it; the certainty with which he knew the size and shape of the flake that was to be produced."

Tixier also narrated as he worked, explaining in clear language what he was doing. He was telling the story of this particular tool as it was made. Luckily for me it was in English.

It was soon evident that Leon and I were considering two different aspects of this magical afternoon. On his large canvas of the evolution of humankind, he was taken with the incredible insight of early humans both to use the power of external objects (technology) for work and to be persistent in its development. It was, and still is, the inventive human mind producing technologies, and then teaching them to others, as David Premack pointed out, that pushes humankind ahead.

What fascinated me was the million-year plateau, the long period that passed when not much changed in stone-tool sophistication. Then suddenly, about a hundred thousand years ago, all the complexity we witnessed in Tixier's tools began to appear. We estimate that human language emerged about a hundred thousand years ago as well. This is the point when language quickly becomes almost essential to complex thought. For decades, scholars have sought to link the appearance of language to all the grand things we humans do. I recalled that it was when Tixier provided the verbal narrative to the toolmaking process that it became so clear to us. A word says a lot, and the resulting savings on the mind's resources is huge.

Yet to dwell on the role of language misses Leon's underlying insight. It is the more primitive inventiveness of humans—technology and its role as the engine that powered humankind to dazzling heights of accomplishment—that pushed the slow grind of advancement into the fast lane of evolution. And Leon, being a social psychologist at his core, began to see how technology could be used to control human life. Technologies are not only physical things. They can be social forces as well, like philosophical or religious beliefs.

II.

Some years before our Paris trip, my own work in split-brain science had taken a new turn. In 1976, my student Joseph LeDoux and I were studying a teenage boy, known in the scientific literature as P.S. He had undergone split-brain surgery, which severed the pathways between the left and right hemispheres of his brain in an effort to curb his epilepsy. We were in the business of cataloging which mental functions were located in the left and right brains.

We had long known that language and speech processes were located in the left hemisphere, but absent from the right hemisphere, where various nonverbal skills are carried out. In normal, nonsplit brain cases, the two sides work together by integrating the information each receives. But in split-brain patients like P.S., that communication between hemispheres is cut off.

Here, visual perception plays an important role. Normally when a person focuses on a point in space, all visual information to the right of the fixated point is projected to the left brain and all visual information to the left of the point is projected to the right hemisphere. So by positioning images in certain places in relation to the patient's focal point we can deliver visual information to either side of the brain. Images or words perceived by the left hemisphere can be easily described with language, but those perceived by the right cannot.

In the classic test for split-brain subjects, we flashed a picture of a snow scene to the right-half brain, while at the same time we flashed a picture of a chicken claw to the left-speaking brain. When asked afterward what they saw, they could name only the claw. They knew nothing of the snow scene seen only by the disconnected right brain. The right brain does not speak.

We devised a slightly more interesting test for P.S. Instead of asking him what he saw, we presented him with two groups of picture cards and had him point to the one that best matched what he had seen. In quick fashion, his right hand (controlled by the left half of the brain) correctly pointed to a picture of a chicken, and the left hand (controlled by the right) correctly pointed to a snow shovel—meaning both sides of the brain had done their processing.

At this point in the test, the left brain actually didn't see the snow scene and in fact should have no idea why the left hand pointed to the shovel. Of course, the left brain knew why the right hand pointed to the chicken, since all of the brain processes involved in such act were part of the left brain.

Then we stumbled on something very new. After twenty-five years of doing this test we finally asked a different question. "Why did you do that?"

At that moment, his left brain was immediately confronted with a puzzle. Again, it knows why the right hand pointed to the chicken, but why did the left hand point to the shovel? So, on the spot the left brain said, "Oh, the chicken claw goes with the chicken, and you need a shovel to clean out the chicken shed."

That one simple observation, now repeated dozens of times on several patients, revealed another special capacity of the dominant left brain. We called this device the "interpreter" and have come to realize it is the storyteller, the system that builds our narrative and gives our many actions that pour out of us, frequently outside of our conscious control, a centrality, a story—our personal story. It is so powerful an addition to humankind that it masks the reality: We are, in fact, a confederation of relatively independent agents, each struggling to be part of our narrative that is our story. It turns out the left brain has another capacity potentially more important than language itself. The interpreter is the thing that sticks all of those parts together.

It has been almost thirty-seven years since we first made these observations, which is about a microsecond in evolutionary time. Still, it has allowed me to see connections with other ideas about humankind.

III.

In Graham Swift's novel *Waterland*, the narrator, a history teacher named Tom Crick, defines the human as "the storytelling animal" who "wants to leave behind not a chaotic wake, not an empty space," but the "comforting trail signs of stories: As long as there's a story, it's all right." Even at the moment of death, he says, we see our life rush before us as a story.

Our ability to group events into a narrative could certainly help us feel better, could help us store the events as a single episode for later use, or could help us interact in a complex social setting. My threaded interpretation, however, could be different from yours. For stories (beliefs) to be useful as a technology to control groups of people, it is necessary to standardize our interpretations, something we know has occurred almost from the beginning of recorded human history.

This is why the historian Yuval Harari, in his book *Sapiens: A Brief History of Humankind*, has proposed that in addition to our personal narratives, we produce collective fictions that are a uniquely human capacity. "We control the world basically because we are the only animals that can cooperate flexibly in very large numbers," he writes. "And if you examine any large-scale human cooperation, you will always find that it is based on some fiction like the nation, like money, like human rights. These are all things that do not exist objectively, but they exist only in the stories that we tell and that we spread around. This is something very unique to us, perhaps the most unique feature of our species."

Leon used to tell me he didn't believe visual imagery existed because he didn't get it. He hated scientific graphs and instead loved the densest mode of scientific presentations, a table of data. He was the most rationally driven man I have ever met and yet he could turn it off on a dime and talk about recipes for potato pancakes. When he was in his scientific mode, few could keep up with him. His capacity for abstraction was special and rare.

Yet when Yuval Harari is talking about gaining control of people by the use of fictions, he is talking about the kinds of abstractions and ideas everybody can understand—money, religion, politics, and preferences, the kinds of things an interpreter is at work on all day long. As the novelist captures the personal, the historian captures the social story within which most of us are embedded and uniquely thrive. It is the inventive interpretive mind first applying itself to our personal life and then to our social existence that is our core skill. Once humankind realized it possessed this technology, we seized on it to thrive in and control our niche on earth.

Back to Brussels to catch the return flight home. Another eight hours of Camels, backgammon, and scotch, but this time feeling a sense of success. In the taxi from Kennedy Airport we were going through Lower Manhattan and Leon suddenly said, "Have you ever had pickles from Katz's Delicatessen?" The driver quickly doped out what was to follow. I waited in the taxi idling on Ludlow Street while Leon went in to buy two containers of pickles.

It is that big canvas of human history we had experienced on our trip, and this ever so small one, existing at once, that makes humankind so wonderful.

FEBRUARY 20, 2016

The Beast in Me

We tend to forget we are animals, until we become prey.

Maxim Loskutoff

MISSOULA, MONT.—IN THE SUMMER OF 2012, THE SAME year that scientists fully decoded the genome of the bonobo, the last great ape, my partner and I were stalked by a female grizzly bear. We first saw her high above us in a field of huckleberry bushes as we hiked along Grinnell Lake on the east side of Glacier National Park in Montana.

It was the perfect distance to see a grizzly: close enough to make out the rolling power of her gait and the light gold fur on her back, and far enough away for us to feel safe. We watched her for several minutes, remarking on her beauty, then continued up the trail into a stand of stunted, high-altitude pine, the trunks just tall enough to obscure our vision. When we emerged, the bear had traversed and descended along our path and was now only a hundred yards away. A football field. A quick sprint. Several things happened in my mind at once: I realized the bear was following us, I realized she wanted to eat us, and I realized that I was an animal.

It was a strange epiphany. To be human today is to deny our animal nature, though it's always there, as the earth remains round beneath our feet even when it feels flat. I had always been an animal, and would always be one, but it wasn't until I was prey, my own fur standing on end and certain base-level decisions being made in milliseconds (in a part of my mind that often takes ten minutes to choose toothpaste in the grocery store), that the meat-and-bone reality settled over me. I was smaller and slower than the bear. My claws were no match for hers. And almost every part of me was edible.

My partner looked at me. I looked at her. We turned and sprinted back into the trees the way we'd come.

In the pounding of our footsteps, below the wild panic, I remember a distinct thrill of pleasure. Not in a suicidal sense (I was too frightened to look back, and certainly didn't want to feel the bear's jaws on my neck), but as a matter of perspective. The feeling was tied most closely to relief. Every other thing I'd been worrying about that day, from whether I'd worn enough sunscreen to whether my partner really loved me, fell aside. I had one concern: to get us away without being eaten.

Civilization itself is an attempt to protect us from this feeling. From its earliest iterations in fire-starting and cave-dwelling to its current zenith in the construction of megalopolises, as well as the careful documentation of every birth and the methodical laying bare of each strand in every helix, civilization is a way of setting ourselves apart from the prey we once were. Building walls, both physical and informational, to keep out the bears.

Yet even atop the highest tower in the most prestigious university we remain animals, directed by the same base-level needs and emotions that motivate living creatures from bonobos to rats. I've seen flashes of our animal selves in the most unlikely places: genius professors reduced to grunting rage, and overweight shut-ins catching a falling object with sudden, instinctive grace.

We were only halfway through the pine stand when a park ranger met us, running full speed from the other direction holding the largest gun I'd ever seen. He told us to get behind him. His neck shone with sweat. We peeked around his shoulders (and gun) at the bear, which was now lingering at the edge of the trees. "She's almost twelve," he said, catching his breath as we backed along the trail. "It gets harder for them to find food at that age. She's been displaying increasingly aggressive behavior." I hardly noticed the fact that he seemed to know this particular bear intimately (I'd later learn that rangers track many of the grizzlies in the park), and instead had the strange image of my own grandmother in her last days, hunting game with desperate, bloody abandon, rather than living in the guest room of our house.

Of course there are aspects of our communal society—caring for the old, the domestication of livestock, the cultivation of crops—that link us to only a few other species, and other aspects, such as the written word, that link us to none as yet discovered, but in no place but our own minds have we truly transcended our animal brethren. In bonobo societies, both the best and worst aspects of humanity have been documented: from a complex language of facial expressions, to helping the disabled, to the adoption of orphans, to the manipulative and violent pursuit of power. As the anthropologist Clifford Geertz famously said, "Man is an animal suspended in webs of significance he himself has spun."

Most days, I remain fully entangled in this web, cursing at my smartphone while rolling across the earth in four thousand pounds of steel. Yet there is something of the experience with the bear that remains inside me, a gift from my moment of pure terror. It's the knowledge of my animal self. That instinctive, frightened, clear-eyed creature beneath my clothes. And it brought with it the reassuring sense of being part of the natural world, rather than separated from it, as we so often feel ourselves to be. My humanity, one cell in the great, breathing locomotion spreading from sunlight to leaves to root stems to bugs to birds to bears.

All of us fragile, all of us fleeting, all of us prey.

AUGUST 17, 2018

Our Delight in Destruction

We were surprised by Donald Trump because we assumed
both humans and history were driven by reason.

Costica Bradatan

"I, FOR EXAMPLE," SAYS THE NAMELESS NARRATOR IN FYODOR
Dostoyevsky's *Notes from Underground* (1864), "would not be the least
bit surprised if suddenly, out of the blue, amid the universal future
reasonableness, some gentleman of ignoble or, better, of retrograde
and jeering physiognomy, should emerge, set his arms akimbo, and
say to us all: 'Well, gentlemen, why don't we reduce all this reasonableness to dust with one good kick, for the sole purpose of sending
all these logarithms to the devil and living once more according to
our own stupid will!' That would still be nothing, but what is offensive is that he'd be sure to find followers: that's how man is arranged."

The musings of Dostoyevsky's hero certainly seem pertinent
now—not just because of Donald Trump's rise to the White House
but also in light of the populist sentiment and politics emerging in
other parts of the world. But for all their mocking, jovial tone, the
underground man's observations have more serious and far-reach-
ing implications. For, after all, what he tells us here is the story of a
disastrous historical blindness.

For quite a while now we in the West have been operating under
certain cultural assumptions about what it means to be human: that
human beings are driven by a rational "pursuit of happiness," that

they choose—again, rationally—what is best for them and what contributes to their well-being, both individual and collective. Thanks in part to this Enlightenment heritage, we've come to assume that history is a progression toward more inclusion, mutual understanding and respect, tolerance and acceptance, and that bigotry, xenophobia, intolerance, and racism are doomed to disappear as a matter of "historical necessity." For history, Hegel has taught us (and we've rarely challenged this teacher), is nothing but the gradual unfolding of rationality in the world.

These assumptions are reflected in the way mainstream philosophy has come to construct the human subject. What defines us is primarily our capacity for rational thinking; we always use our reason to make decisions, to relate to the others and the world around us, to conduct our lives. Granted, we still have our emotions, we are capable of feelings and passions, but somehow, in our pursuit of the philosophical project, these aspects of our makeup are given a backseat. They are not really what we are; we are fundamentally "rational agents."

This presumption has its benefits. For the economic and social behavior of such agents can be predicted—indeed, it can be shaped, stimulated, even engineered. Not only is it possible to know that rational agents will buy a product, but thanks to certain marketing devices they will be compelled to do so. If modern capitalism is to be considered successful, it's because, at its core, it relies heavily on a hyper-rationalistic understanding of the human subject.

And yet what if this is all wrong and we've been caught in a blind spot? What if reason is not the driving force of human history and, just as often, we act irrationally, out of resentment, anger, spite, frustration, envy, even out of self-destructive impulse? What if there is even such a thing as the pursuit of unhappiness? Or, in the underground man's own words, "What if it so happens that on occasion man's profit not only may but precisely must consist in sometimes wishing what is bad for himself"? What if we in fact take delight in destruction? "I'm certain that man will never renounce real suffering, that is, destruction and chaos," proclaims Dostoyevsky's hero in one of his more philosophical moments.

In reality, the hyper-rationalism we inhabit and embrace relies on an extreme simplification of what we really are. It is more a caricature than an actual description. And philosophy should have known better: From Diogenes of Sinope and Augustine to Pascal, from Dostoyevsky, Schopenhauer, and Leopardi to Nietzsche, Mishima, and Cioran, there has been a long tradition of philosophizing on the human abyss. If man is a complex animal, mankind is an even more complicated beast, with many layers and regions, one more irrational than the next.

The human is a knot of contradictions and opposing drives: reason and unreason; wisdom and recklessness; faithlessness and mysticism; logic and imagination. We feed on exact science as much as we do on myths, on fictions and fabulations. We can die for others or let them perish in the cold; we can create extraordinary things, only to enjoy their utter destruction; human society can be paradise and hell at one and the same time.

In the past century, philosophy has mostly abandoned the effort to account for this complexity, and so has the data-driven age that has blossomed in its wake. We've become masters of conformity, empirical evidence, and science. We read the books of Pascal, Nietzsche, Dostoyevsky, and the other thinkers of the abyss, if we ever do, in the way we look at ancient coins: as curiosa, interesting remnants from times past, not as something that can feed us today. They have no value when it comes to helping us make better sense of ourselves.

It's as though we have become more Cartesian than Descartes; we refuse to have anything to do with that which is not exceedingly clear and distinct; if something defies the usual explanations and seems mysterious, then it "smacks of religion." If a problem unsettles us, but it's not solvable in strictly linguistic, logical, or empirical terms, we deem it a "false problem" and move on. Today, it is considered unrigorous and unprofitable to talk of matters of the human heart— that obscure little thing that, more than logic or arguments, makes people act and live and die.

The main reason we don't engage with the abyss, however, is not necessarily mental laziness. Most of the time, it is sheer fear. For, as Nietzsche warned, if you look intently into an abyss, the abyss will start looking back. Dostoyevsky—socialist, political prisoner, addicted gambler, epileptic, reactionary thinker, and visionary artist—did plenty abyss-gazing and his testimony is overwhelming. It is clear "to the point of obviousness," he confesses in *A Writer's Diary*, that "evil lies deeper in human beings than our socialist-physicians suppose; that no social structure will eliminate evil; that the human soul will remain as it has always been; that abnormality and sin arise from that soul itself; and, finally, that the laws of the human soul are still so little known, so obscure to science, so undefined, and so mysterious, that there are not and cannot be either physicians or final judges."

When the hyper-rationalist model fails, it fails spectacularly. In the American election, reason gave way to fear, resentment, hate, and spite. For the most part, "rational agency" was nowhere to be found. What seemed to drive the support for Trump was darker and more complicated—the heart. And what makes this event particularly significant is not necessarily its political aspect (though that's serious enough), but the fact that we find ourselves so poorly equipped to comprehend it. Thanks to the clumsy way in which we've been imagining ourselves, we are unprepared to digest it. Rarely has a failure of imagination been more humiliating.

Dealing with the human abyss used to be the province of religion, but ever since God died we haven't really been able to find a good replacement. (Not that there are any serious candidates.) Yet if we are to remain human, ignoring the problem, looking elsewhere, is not an option. The humanities can reinvent themselves only to the extent that they will be able to chart, as adequately as humanly possible, the full depth of the human abyss. Unless we will find a way to account for the whole human subject, without self-flattery and self-delusion, we will move in circles, unable to overcome the blinding hyper-rationalism under which we currently slave.

MARCH 27, 2017

The Humanity We Can't Relinquish

Searching for a shared humanness in North Korea.

Pico Iyer

ARA, JAPAN—WE'D JUST EMERGED FROM A LONG AND rather liquid dinner on a barge along the Taedong River, in the heart of North Korea's showpiece capital of Pyongyang. Two waitresses had finished joining our English tour guide, Nick, in some more than boisterous karaoke numbers. Now, in the bus back to the hotel, one young local guide broke into a heartfelt rendition of "Danny Boy." His charming and elegant colleague, Miss Peng—North Korea is no neophyte when it comes to trying to impress visitors—was talking about the pressures she faced as an unmarried woman of twenty-six, white Chanel clip glinting in her hair. Another of our minders—there were four or five for the fourteen of us, with a camera trained on our every move for what we were assured was a "souvenir video"—kept saying, "You think I'm a government spy. Don't you?"

But I was back in North Korea because nowhere I'd seen raised such searching questions about what being human truly involves. Nowhere so unsettled my easy assumptions about what "reality" really is. The people around me clearly wept and bled and raged as I did; but what did it do to your human instincts to be told that you could be sentenced, perhaps to death, if you displayed a picture of your mother—or your granddaughter—in your home, instead of a photo of the Father of the Nation? Did being human really include not being permitted to leave your hometown, and not being allowed to say what you think?

I've never doubted that humanity is a privilege, even if we, as the animals who think, are also the creatures who agitate, plot, and fantasize. Governments try to suppress this at times, and many of us in the freer world now imprison ourselves by choosing to live through screens, or to see through screens, like the Buddhist demagogue Ashin Wirathu, who, in defiance of the shared humanness that the Buddha worked so hard to elucidate, compares his Muslim neighbors in Myanmar to wolves and jackals. More and more of us these days seem to be living at post-human speeds determined by machines, to the point where we barely have time for kids or friends. But if we're feeling less than human—or pretending we can engineer mortality away—for most of us it's a choice we're making, and can unmake tomorrow.

In my home of more than thirty years, Japan, nobody thinks twice about being married by a robot or apologizing to a pencil after you throw it across a room. My neighbors rattle on cheerfully about "two-point-five-dimensional characters" and "demi-humans;" their government has appointed the mouthless cartoon cutie Hello Kitty and a twenty-second century blue robotic cat named Doraemon as cultural ambassadors. Lines between animate and inanimate run differently in an animist Shinto universe where—you see this in the beautiful films of Hayao Miyazaki—every blade of grass or speck of dust is believed to have a spirit.

In Japan, as in its neighbor North Korea, a human is often taken to be part of a unit, a voice in a choir; her job may be to be invisible, inaudible, and all but indistinguishable from those around her. At the Family Romance company in Tokyo, twelve hundred actors stand ready to impersonate, for a price, a child's absent father, for years on end, or a wife's adulterous lover. The Henn-na Hotel in Nagasaki describes itself as the world's "first hotel staffed by robots."

But all this means only that the boundaries of what it is to feel human emotion are stretched, to the point of including motes of pollen or the railway carriages people bring presents for. Even the dead are treated as human in Japan. After my mother-in-law passed away in February, her closest relatives never stopped chattering to her, setting out a glass of her favorite beer next to her coffin, applying blush to her waxen cheeks. My wife still puts food out for her father five years after he was placed into the earth; this month our son will return home because his departed grandfather and grandmother are believed to be visiting for three days then as well.

To me this only confirms the visceral sense many of us have that holiness and humanness may be more closely entwined than we imagine. Speaking to the Dalai Lama for forty-four years now, I'm often most touched when he stresses how mortal he is, sometimes impatient, sometimes grieving, just like all the rest of us. I keep returning to the novels of Graham Greene because he reminds us that a "whisky priest" can get drunk, neglect every duty, even father a child, yet still rise to a level of kindness and selflessness that a pious cardinal might envy. It's in our vulnerability, Greene knew, that our strength truly lies (if only because our capacity to feel for everyone else lies there too).

For more than thirty years now I've been traveling—to Yemen, to Easter Island, to Ethiopia—to see what humanness might be, beneath differences of custom and circumstance and race. I've watched young mothers dodging bullets, children living in garbage dumps, those whom disease has left far from most of the capacities and restraints we associate with being human. If circumstances change, however, I never doubt that the humanness of just about everyone can be recovered.

The first time I visited North Korea, twenty-four years before my evening on the barge, my guide led me, during my last afternoon in the city, up a hill. It was just the two of us. Below were the cutting-edge (if often uninhabited) skyscrapers, the amusement parks, and spotless, wide boulevards his government had created out of what, only thirty-five years before, had been rubble, a demolished city in which, North Koreans claim, only two buildings remained upright.

My guide wasn't unworldly; he'd studied for three years in Pakistan and spoke Urdu and English. He knew that his sense of what it is to lead a human life was very different from mine. But what he said was, "Don't listen to my propaganda. Just tell your friends back in America what you've seen here."

Was he going off script for a moment—or only offering an even craftier set of lines his directors had given him? I couldn't tell. But I could feel that he was appealing to something human in me and whatever understanding two humans can share, even if they come from opposite worlds. Official Pyongyang seems the last word in inhumanity to me, but as my guide kept waving and waving goodbye while I passed through immigration, I felt with fresh power how no one can fully deprive us of our humanity but ourselves.

AUGUST 11, 2018

The Question We Must Keep Asking

We can only define ourselves by continually
reevaluating our humanness.

Ai Weiwei

M ANY OF THE PROBLEMS IN THE WORLD TODAY, WHEN ONE reflects upon them, call for an answer to an ancient question: What is it to be human?

I believe there is no single immutable answer. We humans are what we conceive ourselves to be, by which I mean two things: what we will ourselves to be and what we say we are. Our self-conceptions are, in turn, responses to conditions that we encounter in our environments, and those conditions constantly change with time and place. The only way to answer this question is to examine how a person sees himself or herself and others within the social, cultural, economic, and political conditions of their times.

There is no such thing as a human being in the abstract. Only when we see people as embedded in their experiences—their own social positions, their educations and memories, in pursuit of their own ideals—can the question "What is a human being?" fully make sense.

Everyone seems to agree that we live today in a completely distinctive time. We may use different labels for it—the era of globalization, of the internet, of late capitalism, of the collapse of Cold War ideology—but all such terms seek to describe the world's new situation. The most striking feature of that situation is that we are much freer than ever before in our access to information, knowledge, and the assistance of technology. At the same time, the forces that tend to constrict our personal freedoms—states, religions, ethnic identities, economic interest groups, and others—are both dissolving and reorganizing. Some are dying, while others are growing extraordinarily strong.

Such changes can be mind-boggling. They can make it hard to remember where home is, to recognize language and customs that we once took for granted, and to figure out where we now belong. The question "What is a human being?" or "What does it mean to be human?" gets an entirely new face. The answers today will have to be different from the answers of the past.

Our resources for seeking answers to this question also vary inevitably with our personal experiences. To me, for example, it is obvious that my passage through different social, political, cultural, and economic backgrounds—as an artist in China, as a political prisoner, and now as an expatriate—has obliged me several times to alter and adjust my understandings of what a human being is.

Simply to avoid the question is a terrible mistake. We must ask it, and we must do so repeatedly. The debates and judgments that led to human wisdom in the past were responses, each in its time, to essentially the same question, asked in the political and social context of that time, and it is relevant at every social level: individual, community, family, and nation. Many of the political and cultural disagreements that we see in the world today arise from a reluctance to face this key question squarely, and to arrive at clear definitions with regard to it.

Humankind includes every single one of us. No matter how fearsome the political and cultural affronts that history produces might become, our last, irreducible possession, which would be plain to us if we were suddenly placed upon a barren desert, is respect for human dignity.

Everything hangs on how we define ourselves and how we treat those with whom we share our surroundings, which are teeming with different ethnicities, religions, and cultures. We are doomed if we lose independent thinking, lose the ability to freely evaluate and define ourselves.

In my view, self-definition must be each individual's final and most sturdy principle. It is the iron undergirding of morality, aesthetics, and practical philosophy. If it slips away, even for a moment, then the answer to the question "What does it mean to be human?" will be: "Nothing."

AUGUST 23, 2018

II

IS DEMOCRACY POSSIBLE?

Rethinking Our Patriotism

There is no shared American ideal. Clashing visions and
political conflict are at the core of our national being.

Gary Gutting

A LTHOUGH ABSTRACT LOGIC AND CONCEPTUAL ANALYSIS ARE
among philosophers' primary tools, they must, as John Dewey
emphasized, use these tools to "clarify the social and moral strife of
their day." In particular, surprising political events, like those currently unfolding on both sides of the Atlantic, can call for some serious rethinking. In my case, this has led me to reconsider my views
about patriotism.

In 2012, halfway through Barack Obama's presidency, I wrote a
Fourth of July piece trying to explain my patriotic feelings for this
country. My focus was an apparent contradiction in the idea of patriotism as a moral virtue. Patriotism seemed to require a commitment
to the good of this particular country, even when its good was at odds
with the greater good of everyone ("America First," you might say).
Love of a particular country appeared to conflict with the universal demands of ethics. I found a solution in the idea, expressed in
our Declaration of Independence, that the American commitment to
freedom was a commitment to the freedom of all people, not just of
our citizens. My patriotism, I concluded, was a love of my country's
shared project of promoting freedom for all.

This ideal solves the logical problem of reconciling patriotism with ethics, but it looks bizarrely irrelevant against the current reality of American politics. The ideal implies that we are all somehow working for the same ultimate goal, which should provide a core respect for the views of our political opponents that will serve as a basis for cooperation and compromise in the name of our shared ideal. And, indeed, a ruling platitude of our day says we need to get beyond the politics of acrimony and division that obstructs decisive progress toward this guiding ideal. Viewed this way, the primary patriotic duty today would be to find some way to restore civil political discourse and a spirit of mutually respectful compromise.

But looking back at the last eight years and forward, with trepidation, at those coming, I've concluded that this desire for political civility is wishful thinking. In fact, our major political divisions rest on radically different conceptions of "freedom."

In the broadest terms, those on the right cherish a nostalgic dream that hopes for a return to a golden past of traditional values and individual responsibility, whereas those on the left project a utopian future in which we reject our history of oppression and create new values of diversity and collective action. More specifically, some think freedom is essentially the right to seek wealth and happiness with minimal governmental restraint, whereas others say freedom requires governmental guarantees of basic economic security and full respect for the rights of marginalized groups.

At the extremes, some see our salvation only as a newborn Christian nation, whereas others call for a thoroughly secular post-capitalist society. Of course, there can be short-term tactical alliances that are mutually useful for opposing sides. But we deceive ourselves if we think there are some substantive shared political values that we are all seeking.

This point came home to me when I sought refuge from the trumperies of the recent election by reading *American Revolutions* by Alan Taylor, a masterful survey of the colonies' break with British rule. I suppose I was hoping to find in our nation's origin the shared ideals and high-minded political engagement so lacking in today's politics.

But the history of the Revolution provided no such solace. Taylor's narrative emphasized "the multiple and clashing visions pursued by the diverse American peoples of the continent," contrary to traditional accounts, which apply "a singular purpose and vision to the conflict and its legacy. The revolutionary upheavals spawned new contradictions and tensions rather than neat resolutions."

In principle, the founders opposed all political parties on the grounds that, as George Washington put it, they are likely "to become potent engines, by which cunning, ambitious and unprincipled men will be enabled to subvert the power of the people and to usurp for themselves the reins of government." But from the very beginning bitter party divisions defined American politics.

Describing the clash between Jeffersonian Republicans and Hamiltonian Federalists under the new Constitution, Taylor says: "Claiming exclusively to speak for the American people, each party cast rivals as insidious conspirators bent on destroying freedom and union. Referring to 'the parties of Honest men and Rogues into which every country is divided,' Jefferson insisted that 'the Republicans are the nation.' Federalists agreed with the polarity but reversed it." Taylor concludes, "Both parties believed that the fate of their republic hung in the balance."

These revolutionary divisions set the tone for the subsequent history of the United States. The roughhouse of party conflict, not judicious civil debate, has been the norm. But our struggles for power were not only conflicts of self-interest but also of rival understandings of freedom. Should full freedom reside only in a governing elite of educated and property-owning men? Was slavery consistent with the "self-evident" rights of all human beings? Did the distinctive biological and social roles of women forbid an equal place with men?

We may think that we've decisively answered all these questions, but every answer has led to further questions about, for example, the role of wealth and privilege, the rights of minorities, and the meaning of gender equity. And as America moved to a position of world leadership, these questions exploded into quarrels about what counted as liberation and what as colonization.

I would suggest that today our fundamental political conflict is over the place of the capitalist economic system in a democracy. The right sees capitalism as the paradigm of freedom: entrepreneurs creating the wealth that enriches both themselves and the nation. The left acknowledges an essential economic role for capitalism—at least for the time being—but also sees it as a fundamental danger to freedom, a constant push away from democracy and toward an oligarchy of the wealthy. Our task is to continue with vigor the arguments about freedom that our founders began.

The founders not only initiated our disputes about freedom. They also framed a Constitution designed to prevent our vigorous conflicts from leading to a tyranny that suppresses the political process. The idea was to have a variety of power sources—a president, two houses of Congress, the courts, the separate states, regular elections—each capable of taking the lead when necessary, but none so powerful that it could preempt the others. For the most part, these devices have proved effective. But recent events, here and elsewhere, revive the worry, expressed by Plato, that populist democracy can readily pave the way to dictatorship. Resisting this threat (and this temptation) is the first duty of today's patriots.

The Bill of Rights, sometimes taken as a definitive statement of what freedom means, was in fact a hasty appendix to the Constitution and provided only a rough starting point subject to further amendment and continuous interpretive disputes. Instead of a vision of freedom, the founders gave us a framework for an indefinite continuation of their revolutionary struggle over what freedom should mean to Americans.

My proposal is that this endless, rancorous struggle for the soul of America is precisely what we should love about this country. Patriotism is not sharing with our fellow citizens some anemic idealization of what freedom means. It is a matter of engaging them—with everything short of physical violence, from compelling argument to deft political maneuvers—in the rough-and-tumble of political conflict over how we should understand freedom. This conflict remains our only way of working toward the "life, liberty and pursuit of happiness" our revolution sought. True patriotism now requires not reaching across the aisle; it demands mounting the political barricades.

FEBRUARY 6, 2017

What We Believe About Our Institutions

When we stop questioning the systems we
share, they become open to misuse.

Malka Older

INSTITUTIONS ARE SHARED FICTIONS, DEPENDENT ON A COLLEC-
tive suspension of disbelief to make the structure of modern life
possible. Society agrees that pieces of printed paper have value,
a fiction that lets us avoid the inconveniences of barter. Most of us
cede authority to the government and abide by the principle that
the declared winner of an election is legitimate, therefore saving
ourselves the death, disruption, and destruction of armed conflict.
Every year on a designated day, part of the world adjusts its clocks to
pretend that dawn is one hour earlier than the day before, and this
effectively becomes true because enough of us believe it.

These and other institutions—formal organizations, as well as
processes and procedures, patterns of behavior, and unwritten social
mores—order and standardize our lives, allowing people to work
together on a macro scale. But while our ability to believe in shared
fictions has its benefits, too much belief can be problematic. Loyalty
can veer into unquestioning allegiance as we fixate on the symbolic
auras that institutions amass over time. While a shift in belief can
be a troubling jolt, threatening an order so ingrained we took it for
granted, it's probably a sign that we should be challenging these systems. Loss of faith is a signal to pause, step back, and carefully look at

what we believe: Are we upholding an institution because we believe that it serves a legitimate function? Or are we venerating a flawed tradition for its own sake?

As a science fiction writer, part of my job is to reimagine institutions for the future worlds I create. To do this, I peel off layers of embedded assumptions and reverence, and pinpoint what the institutions we live by are supposed to do and how they might do it differently.

Institutions begin as new ideas, often controversial ones that not everyone believes in. If they have enough adherents, they get put into practice. If an institution works, many more people will start to believe in it, and then act accordingly. At some point, the institution becomes "real" in a de facto sense; it simply becomes the way things are done. Hopefully, the establishment of this institution makes things better for most people, but there is a degree of inertia involved too. At some point, the institution passes a legitimacy horizon: It becomes not just the way things are done, but the way things should be done. Some institutions grow even more powerful as they accrete a halo of symbolic value well beyond their actual function. The sports world is full of championship competitions, but the Olympics are different. They have a cultural influence—built on an ancient tradition with only a tenuous resemblance to the modern games, tied to nationalistic fervor, and carefully cultivated by the television companies that broadcast the events—that far outweighs the athletic competition involved.

But when the symbolic meaning of something can't be measured or defined and gets disconnected from its original purpose, our belief in institutions becomes something closer to an unquestioning allegiance. This is why cities are willing to make vast investments in order to host the Olympics, even when those investments are both ethically dubious and unlikely to be profitable by any measure. When we stop critiquing our institutions, they become opportunities for misuse, appropriation, and even corruption.

Consider the institution of the American presidency. It started as a new idea: a form of leadership that wasn't a monarchy. Not everyone believed it would work; many feared that the presidency would eventually transform itself from an elected position into a type of monarchy, which of course was exactly what it was meant to replace.

But George Washington turned down a third term, and America's nascent democracy stayed independent and kept electing leaders. The presidency clearly existed by this point; to not believe in it would be absurd. And that was when the magic started. After many generations, speeches, election campaigns, official portraits, history books, hagiographies, and political caricatures, the presidency became more than its function or its incumbent. It came to embody the country's growing clout—the president became known as "the most powerful man [sic but not really] in the world." The presidency took on aspects of democracy and meritocracy, so that, "You could grow up to be president," became shorthand for anyone being able to do anything.

These days, belief in the presidency doesn't mean believing the idea will work, or believing that the office exists. Instead, the concept of the presidency encompasses a vague and diverse set of connotations, drawn from half-remembered history lessons and picture books, news montages and Hollywood movies. Exaggerated symbolism obscures the reality of how the institution functions. For decades, our media coverage and common discourse have been about the idea of the presidency, rather than the critical, real-world role it plays in our government. Voters choose a president based on what they think the job is, rather than what it actually requires. That's why we've ended up with candidates who want to be president in order to be thought of as powerful and important, instead of candidates who want to do a job in the government that makes the country better.

The monarchy is another example. What started as a validation of military might was exaggerated into a tradition of divine right and inherited nobility, until a combination of particularly awful incumbents, local grievances, and the possibility of something different made the institution untenable. This allowed it to be replaced, in some countries, by the presidency.

If our politicians praise democracy while passing bills that make it more difficult to vote, then it's no wonder that we would start to doubt our most critical institutions. And while that can leave a dangerous opening for apathy and conspiracy theories, it is also a reminder for us to look beyond the glossy trappings of power and tradition, and fix whatever isn't working.

Losing faith in our institutions is a sign that, at a minimum, we need to reassess the exaggerations of our faith; we probably also need to reassess the institutions themselves. Are we really as democratic as we claim to be? Does what we call our justice system actually enact justice? Does our vaunted economic system do what it claims?

Institutions offer us powerful hope that when we work together we can create abstractions that order and coordinate our efforts, amplify our potential, and outlast individuals. But they are a means, not an end. We don't owe them our belief or our allegiance. Institutions, and the societies they delineate, are ours, to make and remake. Like fiction writers, we control the narrative for our institutions. With critical thinking, imagination, and collaboration, we can change them. Our collective responsibility—to ourselves and to future generations—is to make each institution better than the last.

MAY 19, 2021

Democracy Is for the Gods

It should be no surprise that humans cannot sustain it.

Costica Bradatan

"WHY DO DEMOCRACIES FAIL?"

We've heard that question a lot in the past few years, in books, on opinion pages and cable news shows, and in an increasingly anxious public debate. But I almost always find myself answering the question with another question: Why shouldn't they?

History—the only true guide we have on this matter—has shown us that democracy is rare and fleeting. It flares up almost mysteriously in some fortunate place or another, and then fades out, it seems, just as mysteriously. Genuine democracy is difficult to achieve and, once achieved, fragile. In the grand scheme of human events, it is the exception, not the rule.

Despite democracy's elusive nature, its core idea is disarmingly simple: As members of a community, we should have an equal say in how we conduct our life together. "In democracy as it ought to be," writes Paul Woodruff in his 2006 book *First Democracy: The Challenge of an Ancient Idea*, "all adults are free to chime in, to join the conversation on how they should arrange their life together. And no one is left free to enjoy the unchecked power that leads to arrogance and abuse." Have you ever heard of anything more reasonable? But who says we are reasonable?

Fundamentally, humans are not predisposed to living democratically. One can even make the point that democracy is "unnatural" because it goes against our vital instincts and impulses. What's most natural to us, just as to any living creature, is to seek to survive and reproduce. And for that purpose, we assert ourselves—relentlessly, unwittingly, savagely—against others: We push them aside, overstep them, overthrow them, even crush them if necessary. Behind the smiling facade of human civilization, there is at work the same blind drive toward self-assertion that we find in the animal realm.

Just scratch the surface of the human community and soon you will find the horde. It is the "unreasoning and unreasonable human nature," writes the zoologist Konrad Lorenz in his book *On Aggression*, that pushes "two political parties or religions with amazingly similar programs of salvation to fight each other bitterly," just as it compels "an Alexander or a Napoleon to sacrifice millions of lives in his attempt to unite the world under his scepter." World history, for the most part, is the story of excessively self-assertive individuals in search of various scepters.

It doesn't help matters that, once such an individual has been enthroned, others are only too eager to submit to him. It is as though, in his illustrious presence, they realize they have too much freedom on their hands, which they find suddenly oppressive. In Dostoyevsky's *The Brothers Karamazov*, the Grand Inquisitor says: "There is no more ceaseless or tormenting care for man, as long as he remains free, than to find someone to bow down to as soon as possible." And what a sweet surrender! Alexander the Great, Julius Caesar, Napoleon, Hitler, and Mussolini were all smooth talkers, charmers of crowds, and great political seducers.

Their relationship with the crowd was particularly intimate. For in regimes of this kind, whenever power is used and displayed, the effect is profoundly erotic. What we see, for instance, in *The Triumph of the Will* (thanks, in good measure, to Leni Riefenstahl's perverse genius) is people experiencing a sort of collective ecstasy. The seducer's pronouncements may be empty, even nonsensical, but that matters little; each one brings the aroused crowd to new heights of pleasure. He can do whatever he likes with the enraptured followers now. They will submit to any of their master's fancies.

This is, roughly, the human context against which the democratic idea emerges. No wonder that it is a losing battle. Genuine democracy doesn't make grand promises, does not seduce or charm, but only aspires to a certain measure of human dignity. It is not erotic. Compared to what happens in populist regimes, it is a frigid affair. Who in his right mind would choose the dull responsibilities of democracy over the instant gratification a demagogue will provide? Frigidity over boundless ecstasy? And yet, despite all this, the democratic idea has come close to embodiment a few times in history—moments of grace when humanity almost managed to surprise itself.

One element that is needed for democracy to emerge is a sense of humility. A humility at once collective and internalized, penetrating, even visionary, yet true. The kind of humility that is comfortable in its own skin, one that, because it knows its worth and its limits, can even laugh at itself. A humility that, having seen many a crazy thing and learned to tolerate them, has become wise and patient. To be a true democrat, in other words, is to understand that when it comes to the business of living together, you are no better than the others, and to act accordingly. To live democratically is, mainly, to deal in failure and imperfection, and to entertain few illusions about human society. The institutions of democracy, its norms and mechanisms, should embody a vision of human beings as deficient, flawed, and imperfect.

Ancient Athenian democracy devised two institutions that fleshed out this vision. First, sortition: the appointment of public officials by lot. Given the fundamental equality of rights that all Athenian citizens—that is, free male adults—enjoyed, the most logical means of access to positions of leadership was random selection. Indeed, for the Athenian democrats, elections would have struck at the heart of democracy: They would have allowed some people to assert themselves, arrogantly and unjustly, against the others.

The other fittingly imperfect Athenian institution was ostracization. When one of the citizens was becoming a bit too popular—too much of a charmer—Athenians would vote him out of the city for ten years by inscribing his name on bits of pottery. It was not punishment for something the charmer may have done, but a preemptive measure against what he might do if left unchecked. Athenians knew that they were too vulnerable and too flawed to resist political seduction (their complicated affair with Alcibiades gave them ample proof of that), and promptly denied themselves the pleasure. Man-made as it is, democracy is fragile and of a weak constitution—better not to put it to the test.

After Athens' radical experiment in equality, democracy has resurfaced elsewhere, but often in forms that the ancient Athenians would probably have trouble calling democratic. For instance, much of today's American democracy (one of the best versions on the market right now) would by Athenian standards be judged "oligarchic." It's the fortunate wealthy few (hoi oligoi) who typically decide here not only the rules of the political game, but also who wins and who loses. Ironically, the system favors what we desperately wanted to avoid when we opted for democracy in the first place: the power-hungry, arrogant, oppressively self-assertive political animal.

Yet we should not be surprised. "If there were a people of gods, it would govern itself democratically," Jean-Jacques Rousseau wrote. "So perfect a form of government is not for men." Democracy is so hard to find in the human world that most of the time when we speak of it, we refer to a remote ideal rather than a fact. That's what democracy is ultimately about: an ideal that people attempt to put into practice from time to time. Never adequately and never for long—always clumsily, timidly, as though for a trial period.

Yet democracy is one of those elusive things—happiness is another—whose promise, even if perpetually deferred, is more important than its actual existence. We may never get it, but we cannot afford to stop dreaming of it.

The Tragedy of Democracy

The immigrants, women, and slaves who were silenced
in Athenian democracy were given life onstage.

Simon Critchley

ATHENS—OUR NEXT LOCATION IS A MERE ONE HUNDRED
steps from where I'm writing this essay. I pass it every day on my
way to and from the library. It is the Monument of Lysicrates, built
around 334 BCE, just about the time Aristotle returned to Athens to
found his Lyceum. I always pause there, take in the view, and watch
the many seemingly well-fed and contented cats scattered around the
place. If you let your eyes drift up from the monument, your vision
is seized by the vast sacred rock of the Acropolis. It is skin-pinch-
ingly sublime.

Indeed, New Yorkers might experience a feeling of déjà vu or double vision with this monument because you can find not one, but two
copies of it atop the San Remo apartment building on Central Park
West, just north of the Dakota, where John Lennon lived and died.
The monument was also widely copied elsewhere.

The original Monument of Lysicrates is composed of a 9.5-foot-
square limestone foundation topped with a thirteen-foot-high
cylindrical edifice. There are six Corinthian columns, thought to be
the earliest surviving examples of that style, made from marble from
Mount Pentelicus, about fifteen miles northeast of Athens. These
support a sculpture divided into three bands that carry an inscrip-

tion commemorating Lysicrates—a wealthy patron of the arts of whom little else is known—and a frieze depicting the adventures of the god Dionysus and some pirates whom he transformed into dolphins. The god sits caressing a panther as some satyrs serve him wine, while others, with torches and clubs, drive the pirates into the sea.

Above is a shallow dome that is the base for three rather mutilated scrolls in the shape of acanthus leaves that stand about three feet high. This was designed to hold a large bronze trophy or "tripod," which has long since disappeared. To my eyes, what remains resembles a rather lovely, large broken flower vase.

What does this all mean? And why is it important?

The monument is a trophy to commemorate Lysicrates's triumph in the dramatic contest, or agon, of the world's first theater festival: the City or Great Dionysia, first established in Athens deep in the sixth century BCE. As with theater and opera today, there was patronage of the arts in classical Athens. To be asked to perform a tragedy was, in ancient Greece, to be granted a chorus. Tragedians were sponsored by a choragus, a chorus bringer, a wealthy or important Athenian citizen who would recruit choristers and pay for everything: This was Lysicrates.

We do not know how tragic poets and choragi were matched. But the oldest piece of theater that we possess, *The Persians* by Aeschylus from 472 BCE, was sponsored by the young Pericles, the great champion of Athenian democracy. When a tragic tetralogy won (that's three plays, plus a satyr play, where the preceding dramas would be openly ridiculed), then the sponsor and not the playwright was declared the victor and a memorial or trophy was erected to display the bronze tripod of the winning choragus. These were displayed in the Hodos Tripodon, or Street of the Tripods.

The street still bears this name. It would once have been littered with tripods, but all except for that of Lysicrates have now disappeared. The City Dionysia began with a procession along this street, with all the citizens, foreigners, visiting dignitaries, and choragi dressed in their finery. At the front of the procession, a wooden effigy of Dionysus was carried aloft. The Dionysus that was honored at the festival was the local patron god of Eleutherae, a village on the border between Attica and the neighboring region of Boeotia. But the place name also recalls the Greek word for freedom, eleutheria, and the link between the theater festival and experience of liberation would have been hard to miss.

So, let's liberate our minds for a moment and imagine that you and I could take a walk right now together along the Street of the Tripods. We could follow the road as it extends eastward from the agora of the ancient city and then bends around the southeast corner of the Acropolis. We might pass clusters of slow-moving tourists and groups of schoolchildren, past the bars and tavernas vying for custom on a slow winter's afternoon, past Lulu's Bakery and Deli, and perhaps stopping—in honor of Dionysus, god of the vine and intoxication—for a glass of overpriced and rather routine red wine from Café Diogenes (the locals call the monument the Lamp of Diogenes, alluding to the light that the first of the Cynics was reputed to carry in order to try to find an honest man in Athens).

Then we could set down our glasses, leave the café, and make a sharp right and ascend the steep steps of the narrow Hodos Epimenidou, named after Epimenides, source of the famous liar paradox. We might see a pair of young lovers lost in an embrace, and two old gentlemen distractedly gambling with scratch cards. But then, at the top of the steps, we would find ourselves directly facing the sweeping south slope of the Acropolis. Spreading out before us is the Theater of Dionysus.

It was here, and nowhere else, that theater began almost three millennia ago. I find this thought a continuous source of astonishment. It was here that possibly around fourteen thousand people sat in late March or early April each year and watched plays all day, including the thirty-one tragedies by Aeschylus, Sophocles, and Euripides that survive.

It is tempting to lose oneself, like the young Nietzsche, in Dionysian revelry. And it is always nice to take a walk. But it is also crucially important to remember that the City Dionysia was one of the key institutions in that astonishing Athenian political invention that Nietzsche detested: democracy. The first reference to democratic assembly voting procedure occurs in Aeschylus's early tragedy *The Suppliant Maidens*, from 470 BCE.

But ancient tragedy is not just a celebration or vindication of democracy or Athenian glory (although Athens does come off quite well in some of the plays). Rather, theater is the place where the tensions, conflicts, and ambiguities of democratic life are played out in front of the people. It is the place where those excluded from Athenian democracy are presented onstage: foreigners, women, and slaves. Theater is the night kitchen of democracy.

Let's return to our monument. In June 2016, the Greek press reported that the Monument of Lysicrates had been daubed with graffiti by "anarchists." The green spray-painted uppercase lettering read "YOUR GREEK MONUMENTS ARE CONCENTRATION CAMPS FOR IMMIGRANTS." A little extreme, perhaps, but I was intrigued. Although the offending words were quickly removed, when I looked closely in clear sunlight last weekend, the words were still partly legible.

Rather than simply be outraged, I suggest we think about these words. If ancient monuments simply serve some ideology of Hellenism that is then identified with the defense of the Greek state against immigrants, or Fortress Europe against the infidel hordes, then I think we are misunderstanding something very significant about ancient Athens in general and tragedy in particular.

Consider the Aeschylus play I mentioned above, *The Suppliant Maidens*. The plot is very simple: A group of some fifty women from Egypt seek refuge in Argos in Greece to avoid being forced into marriage to an equal number of young Egyptian men. The women, called the Danaids, claim refuge on the basis of their ethnicity, their bloodline, which they insist is Greek.

Their father, Danaus, says to King Theseus, "Everyone is quick to blame the alien / Who bears the brunt of every evil tongue." But Theseus insists that even if the maidens can prove their Greek ancestry, this is entirely irrelevant to whether they can be admitted into the city, which is something that has to be debated and decided in a democratic vote. In this play, ethnic claims to blood legitimacy are subordinated to democratic procedure and the due process of law.

Questions of refuge, asylum seeking, immigration, sexual violence, and the duties of hospitality to the foreigner reverberate across so many of the tragedies. Theater is that political mechanism through which questions of democratic inclusion are ferociously negotiated and where the world of myth collides with law. Think of *Antigone*, a play about rival claims to the meaning of law, or nomos. Or the *Oresteia* trilogy, whose theme is the nature of justice and which even ends up in a law court on the Areopagus, the Hill of Ares, just next to the Acropolis. Tragedy does not present us with a theory of justice or law, but with a dramatic experience of justice as conflict and law as contest.

To be sure, classical Athens was a patriarchal, imperialist society based on slaveholding. Yet the figures who are silenced in the public realm are represented in the fictions of the theater, as if the democracy that was denied to those figures publicly is somehow extended to them theatrically. As the classicist Edith Hall rightly writes, tragedy is polyphonic: It legitimizes the chauvinism of Athenian power and glory, and at the same time gives voice to that which undermines it.

If we fail to understand the polyphony of antiquity, then we also might be tempted to pick up a can of spray paint and begin daubing monuments with graffiti.

FEBRUARY 27, 2019

Why We Still Need Walt Whitman

With our democracy in crisis, the poet and prophet
of the American ideal should be our guide.

Ed Simon

WHEN WALT WHITMAN ARRIVED IN WASHINGTON AT THE END
of 1862 to take up residence in the city and serve as a hospital volunteer, the construction of the Capitol dome was not yet complete.
In a dispatch published in the October 4, 1863, edition of the *New
York Times*, Whitman described this "vast eggshell, built of iron and
glass, this dome—a beauteous bubble" that "emerges calm and aloft
from the hill, out of a dense mass of trees." The poet recounted how
a "few days ago, poking about there, eastern side" he found the yet-
to-be-hoisted *Statue of Freedom* that now crowns the Capitol dome
"all dismembered, scattered on the ground, by the basement front."
In retrospect it's a rather on-the-nose metaphor, this personified
representation of liberty "standing in the mud" while the nation
immolated itself in civil war, yet still visible to our greatest poet and
prophet of democracy, perhaps signifying the incomplete task of the
American project.

When the war began, Whitman was despondent, but the violence
of those years seemed to strengthen and clarify his faith in democracy, a faith that would take on a transcendent dimension. For the
poet, democracy wasn't simply the least bad form of government, it
wasn't reducible to dreary policy and endless debate, but it was rather

a vital, transformative, and regenerative ethos. Even as the survival of what President Abraham Lincoln called the "last, best hope of earth" was in doubt, Whitman's belief in the philosophical and political foundation of the nation flourished.

If the war against illiberalism takes place on many fronts, including the economic and the cultural, then one domain where the revanchists are clearly gaining power is in the realm of the transcendent. In the delusions of "blood and soil" there is for many the attraction of a deeper meaning. Authoritarians claim that they offer their nations (or at least a segment of the population) unity and purpose. The twentieth century German philosopher (and victim of the Nazis) Walter Benjamin warned how fascism engages an "aestheticization of politics," where spectacle and transcendence provide a type of ecstasy for its adherents. Watch clips of fevered crowds, from today or the past, chanting against "enemies of the people"; they are malignant scenes, but ones that in no small part mimic religious revivals.

Critics of democracy often claim that it offers no similar sense of transcendence. The nineteenth century German philosopher Friedrich Nietzsche castigated democracy as a system of "quarantine mechanisms" for human desires, and as "such they are . . . very boring." If the individual unit of democracy is the citizen, authoritarian societies thrill to the Übermensch, the superman promising that "I alone can fix it." Yet I would argue that all of the hallmarks of authoritarianism—the rallies and crowds, the marching and military parades, the shouting demagogue promising his followers that they are superior—are wind and hot air. What fascism offers isn't elevation but cheap transcendence, a counterfeit of meaning rather than the real thing.

Whitman understood that democracy wasn't "very boring" but rather a political system that could deliver on the promises that authoritarianism only pretended it would. For the poet, democracy wasn't just a way of passing laws or a manner of organizing a government; democracy was a method of transcendence in its own right.

Human beings are meaning-making creatures. A politics that is unable to translate its positions into some sort of transcendent language, pointing to something greater than the individual, is a politics that will ultimately fail. Whitman understood this. Though political theorists of democracy routinely speak of Jefferson's Declaration of Independence or Hamilton and Madison's Federalist Papers, Whitman's poetry of a half century later explicates the metaphysical underpinnings of transcendent democracy. Where Nietzsche would offer the illusions of the Übermensch, Whitman would sing a song of the "divine average."

Such was Whitman's description of Lincoln in a March 1863 letter to two New York friends. The president, wrote Whitman, had a face "like a hoosier Michael Angelo, so awful ugly it becomes beautiful, with its strange mouth, its deep cut, criss-cross lines, and its doughnut complexion." The essence of the "divine average" is that Lincoln was great not necessarily in spite of his supposed ugliness but in part because of it—that all of us have a divine greatness because we share in the common foibles of our humanity. A king, a dictator, an Übermensch will pretend that his lot is above the least of his subjects, but as Whitman would counter in "Song of Myself," his most celebrated poem, "every atom belonging to me as good belongs to you," whether from the slave or slave master, the refugee migrant or the president.

In Whitman's understanding of democracy, we're bound to one another in the experience of being finite creatures with bodies that will one day die. The scholar Kevin J. Hayes explains that in Whitman's estimation, people must "feel the humanity within the self. Deep personal understanding can broaden individual perspective, creating a sense of humanity large enough to include everyone." A demagogue may whip his admirers into a hateful frenzy and impart the illusion of unity, but the loving work of democracy actually provides that unity with others who may be very different from ourselves. Hayes describes Whitman in "Song of Myself" "going from the personal to the national" and finally "to the universal."

What democracy requires is mutual affection over that shared predicament; what it needs is not just politics but also transcendence, enchantment, grace, and love. We mustn't be against transcendence, but against the wrong kind of transcendence. Meaning is not to be found in the cheapness of "blood and soil" but in the mystic chains that connect every woman and man to one another.

Today democracy is imperiled not by civil war but by a citizenry torn apart by warring ideologies, in part because of the compelling, if nihilistic, story that authoritarians have told about nationality. An authoritarian promises a shallow union with others who look like you; the true democrat ensures that such a union is possible with everyone. In democracy there is the reconciliation of opposites, the elevation of the vernacular, the transcendence of the individual through the equality of humanity.

Writing about the *Statue of Freedom*, Whitman noted that the pieces "are at present all separated, ready to be hoisted to their place. On the Capitol generally, much work remains to be done." Sadly, at the end of a tumultuous year and decade, this observation still rings true. All the more reason amid today's national rancor to revisit Whitman's open embrace of the democratic ideal, his declaration that "every atom as belonging to me as good belongs to you," no matter where you were born.

DECEMBER 30, 2019

How Democracy Can Survive Big Data

We can blame Facebook and Cambridge Analytica for the
damage they've done, but the responsibility lies with all of us.

Colin Koopman

ONLY A FEW YEARS AGO, THE IDEA THAT FOR-PROFIT COMPA-
nies and foreign agents could use powerful data technologies to disrupt American democracy would have seemed laughable to most,
a plotline from a Cold War espionage movie. And the idea that the
American system would be compromised enough to allow outside
meddling with the most basic of its democratic functions—the election of its leaders—would have seemed even more absurd.

Today we know that this is not fiction but fact. It is a secret so open
that even its perpetrators seem half-hearted about hiding it.

"Data drives all that we do." That is the motto emblazoned on
the website of Cambridge Analytica, the consulting firm that was
employed by the Trump campaign to influence voters and that is now
under scrutiny for its unauthorized harvesting of data from at least
fifty million social media users.

The heart of Cambridge Analytica's power is an enormous information warehouse—as many as five thousand data points on each of
more than 230 million Americans, according to recent reporting,
a fact the company proudly confirms on its website. Its promise of
elections driven by data ultimately implies a vision of government

steered not by people but by algorithms, and by an expanding data-mining culture operating without restrictions.

That such threats to democracy are now possible is due in part to the fact that our society lacks an information ethics adequate to its deepening dependence on data. Where politics is driven by data, we need a set of ethics to guide that data. But in our rush to deliver on the promises of Big Data, we have not sought one.

An adequate ethics of data for today would include not only regulatory policy and statutory law governing matters like personal data privacy and implicit bias in algorithms. It would also establish cultural expectations, fortified by extensive education in high schools and colleges, requiring us to think about data technologies as we build them, not after they have already profiled, categorized, and otherwise informationalized millions of people. Students who will later turn their talents to the great challenges of data science would also be trained to consider the ethical design and use of the technologies they will someday unleash.

Clearly, we are not there. High schoolers today may aspire to be the next Mark Zuckerberg, but how many dream of designing ethical data technologies? Who would their role models even be? Executives at Facebook, Twitter, and Amazon are among our celebrities today. But how many data ethics advocates can the typical social media user name?

Our approach to the ethics of data is wholly reactive. Investigations are conducted and apologies are extracted only after damage has been done (and only in some instances). Mr. Zuckerberg seemed to take a positive step on Wednesday, when he vowed to take action to better protect Facebook's user data. "We also made mistakes, there's more to do, and we need to step up and do it," he said in, unsurprisingly, a Facebook post.

This is like lashing a rope around the cracking foundation of a building. What we need is for an ethics of data to be engineered right into the information skyscrapers being built today. We need data ethics by design. Any good building must comply with a complex array of codes, standards, and detailed studies of patterns of use by its eventual inhabitants. But technical systems are today being built with a minimal concern for compliance and a total disregard for the downstream consequences of decades of identifiable data being collected on the babies being born into the most complicated information ecology that has ever existed.

Mr. Zuckerberg and other Silicon Valley chiefs admitted in the wake of the election that their platforms needed fixing to help mitigate the bad actors who had exploited social media for political gain. It is not Mr. Zuckerberg's fault that our society has given him a free pass (and a net worth of $67 billion) for inventing his platform first and asking only later what its social consequences might be. It is all of our faults. Thus, however successful Mr. Zuckerberg will be in making amends, he will assuredly do almost nothing to prevent the next wunderkind from coming along and building the next killer app that will unleash who knows what before anybody even has a chance to notice.

The challenge of designing ethics into data technologies is formidable. This is in part because it requires overcoming a century-long ethos of data science: Develop first, question later. Datafication first, regulation afterward. A glimpse at the history of data science shows as much.

The techniques that Cambridge Analytica uses to produce its psychometric profiles are the cutting edge of data-driven methodologies first devised a hundred years ago. The science of personality research was born in 1917. That year, in the midst of America's fevered entry into war, Robert Sessions Woodworth of Columbia University created the Personal Data Sheet, a questionnaire that promised to assess the personalities of Army recruits. The war ended before Woodworth's psychological instrument was ready for deployment, but the Army had envisioned its use according to the precedent set by the intelligence tests it had been administering to new recruits under the direction of Robert Yerkes, a professor of psychology at Harvard at the time. The data these tests could produce would help decide who should go to the fronts, who was fit to lead, and who should stay well behind the lines.

The stakes of those wartime decisions were particularly stark, but the aftermath of those psychometric instruments is even more unsettling. As the century progressed, such tests—IQ tests, college placement exams, predictive behavioral assessments—would affect the lives of millions of Americans. Schoolchildren who may have once or twice acted out in such a way as to prompt a psychometric evaluation could find themselves labeled, setting them on an inescapable track through the education system.

Researchers like Woodworth and Yerkes (or their Stanford colleague Lewis Terman, who formalized the first SAT) did not anticipate the deep consequences of their work; they were too busy pursuing the great intellectual challenges of their day, much like Mr. Zuckerberg in his pursuit of the next great social media platform. Or like Cambridge Analytica's Christopher Wylie, the twentysomething data scientist who helped build psychometric profiles of two-thirds of all Americans by leveraging personal information gained through uninformed consent. All of these researchers were, quite understandably, obsessed with the great data science challenges of their generation. Their failure to consider the consequences of their pursuits, however, is not so much their fault as it is our collective failing.

For the past hundred years we have been chasing visions of data with a singular passion. Many of the best minds of each new generation have devoted themselves to delivering on the inspired data science promises of their day: intelligence testing, building the computer, cracking the genetic code, creating the internet, and now this. We have in the course of a single century built an entire society, economy, and culture that runs on information. Yet we have hardly begun to engineer data ethics appropriate for our extraordinary information carnival. If we do not do so soon, data will drive democracy, and we may well lose our chance to do anything about it.

MARCH 22, 2018

The Making of a Non-Patriot

*American exceptionalism is at best an innocent mistake
that uninformed patriotism makes difficult to surrender.*

Alex Rosenberg

BEST TO START WITH A SMALL BOY, PREFERABLY AN IMMI-
grant, a stateless refugee from a war-torn continent. Place the child
in an environment that makes it obvious he owes his family's pros-
perity, freedom, and even its survival to the generosity of the American nation.

Eager to assimilate completely, the child will embrace the patriotic
symbols—the flag, the president, the military, the national pastime.
Develop in the child a sustained and sincere interest in the trium-
phal progress of the nation's history, from Valley Forge to the Halls of
Montezuma, from the Emancipation Proclamation to the Progressive
Era, from the War to End All Wars through VE and VJ days, to what
President John F. Kennedy called "the long twilight struggle" of Cold
War containment. Encourage the teenager to see Vietnam not as a
military stalemate but a vindication of our democracy.

Instill a reverence for the Declaration of Independence, but only
the good parts. Suppress, for instance, its chilling description of "the
inhabitants of our frontiers, the merciless Indian Savages whose
known rule of warfare is an undistinguished destruction of all ages,
sexes and conditions." The words go well with the iconic narrative
of cowboys and Indians and with John Wayne movies of the 1950s,

like John Ford's *The Searchers* (movies are an especially effective way to foster devotion in the young; they should appear frequently through this process). Don't let the child learn how Oklahoma went from "Indian Territory"—an arid Bantustan in which Native Americans were herded for the better part of a century—to being the forty-sixth state in 1907, owing to the discovery of vast petroleum deposits under its hardscrabble prairie.

Raise the child's sights from his model trains to the spectacular construction of the Transcontinental Railway, completed in 1869. (Cecil B. DeMille's *Union Pacific*, with Joel McCrea, will help do the trick.) Omit any mention of the roughly thirty thousand Chinese "coolies" who actually built the western half of the railway and then, no longer needed for the killing work, were denied citizenship by the Chinese Exclusion Act of 1882. Make sure to extol Teddy Roosevelt, the Bull Moose president, who built the Panama Canal. Do not mention that much of the heavy lifting was done by some fifty thousand black men from the Caribbean islands, also disposed of when they were no longer needed.

Paint a vivid picture of Woodrow Wilson as the great progressive precursor to Franklin Delano Roosevelt, the president whose dream of a League of Nations was destroyed by a narrow-minded vindictive senator from Massachusetts. (The Oscar-winning 1944 film *Wilson* should work well here.) Don't tell the boy the real story of Wilson's egotism and intransigence. It would spoil the way the narrative culminates a quarter century later in the United Nations. And never, never let on that Wilson endorsed D. W. Griffith's *The Birth of a Nation* with a White House screening that personally invited the defunct Ku Klux Klan back into American life. Don't remind him that Wilson resegregated the federal Civil Service—the only domain in which African Americans hadn't been forced to abide by "separate and equal."

While you're at it, when raising FDR to demigod status (*Sunrise at Campobello*, 1960, is a start), be silent about how his administration excluded African Americans from the two most important progressive victories of the New Deal—Social Security and the Wagner

Act, the latter of which protected unionization from strikebreakers. It wasn't hard, once the Dixiecrat senators in Roosevelt's coalition showed him how: just drop "domestics" and "farm labor" from the coverage of the two laws, as sixty percent of these workers were black, more like ninety-five percent in the South. "Domestics" were excluded from Social Security for the next twenty years. Along with agricultural workers, they're still excluded from the (now toothless) Wagner Act that used to protect union rights.

Remember also to hide the tricks used to keep black soldiers out of World War II. Do not tell him that the convoy system used to supply United States forces in Europe, dramatized in the postwar movie *Red Ball Express*, with a mainly white cast and a cameo by Sidney Poitier, was roughly seventy-five percent African American.

Trumpet to the child the Warren Court's overthrow of "separate but equal" in 1954. But don't mention that this was the same Earl Warren who demanded the Supreme Court endorse concentration camps for Japanese American citizens in the Korematsu decision of 1944, never overturned to this day. As your patriot grows to adulthood he will read about how, the very next year after *Brown v. Board of Education* (1954), the same court let Southern state governments off the hook with the requirement that desegregation be completed "with all deliberate speed." He will find that twenty years after *Brown*, school segregation was even worse.

The most effective tools in the making of a non-patriot are time, honesty, and a truthful self-education. Allow the boy, as he becomes an adult, to learn about the injustice and unfairness glossed over before. The process of increasing historical consciousness will make American exceptionalism untenable.

After extolling for years the genius of the United States Constitution, begin to point out the impediments to democratic government that it has imposed upon the American nation itself, and the other countries on whom we have forced it.

Be clear that the Constitution is soiled with the stain of slavery—the three-fifths clause, the requirement that fugitive slaves be returned, the clause allowing the international slave trade to persist for a generation after its ratification. The hypocrisy of our Constitution's wording, in which euphemisms must be found every time the institution of slavery is protected, reveals the founding fathers' chagrin. Once the student of American history discovers what the euphemisms mean, he cannot help reading the Constitution as an inexact copy of George III's regime, not a set of truths requiring centuries of fealty.

Of course, watching Henry Fonda in *Young Mr. Lincoln* (1939) and Raymond Massey in *Abe Lincoln in Illinois* (1940) will have resulted in the boy's "increased devotion" to the American ideal, but disillusion will eventually set in. By the time he's seen Steven Spielberg's *Lincoln* (2012) it will be evident that, given our Constitution, the only way the country could have abolished slavery was by a civil war that took a million lives from both sides. Every other nation—even the autocratic Tsarist Russia and the Empire of Brazil—managed to abolish slavery without a war. How were they able to do it? Because they were not blessed with a constitution intentionally designed, as the Federalist Papers reveal, to make effective government difficult.

The youthful patriot has been raised to admire the United States Senate as "the world's greatest deliberative body" by watching *Mr. Smith Goes to Washington* (1939) or *Advise & Consent* (1962). By the turn of the twenty-first century he'll realize that the Constitution condemned the nation to a Senate in which ten percent of the population of his country controls forty percent of seats. It's an arrangement that does exactly what Madison designed the Senate to do: "protect the minority of the opulent against the majority."

The child may not notice that the Constitution explicitly made the equal representation of each state uniquely unamendable. He will, however, grow up to discover that, as its irremediable result, one citizen of Wyoming has about sixty-five times the representation in the Senate as every Californian.

When he digs into history, the boy will learn of the aberration that, just twice in American history, way back in 1824 and 1876, the popular vote for president was thwarted by the Constitution's Electoral College (the second time "incidentally" ushering in the reign of Jim Crow). But that was ancient history, wasn't it? Alas, no. By the time he's grown, our child patriot will have found the Electoral College flouting the will of the majority in two of the first five elections of the twenty-first century.

Eventually the adult will appreciate why all fully developed nations have given up on the American Constitution as model. They know what we should have learned: that history long ago revealed its defects, anachronisms, hostility to democracy, and unsuitability to life after the eighteenth century. Abroad, no one wants the United States Constitution anymore. But we're stuck with it, Second Amendment and all.

It's not as though other countries are better than ours. Every nation bears the healed scars and the still-open wounds of its history. The lesson our refugee boy will learn as he grows up and old is that American exceptionalism is at best an innocent mistake that uninformed patriotism makes difficult to surrender.

Once the process of disillusionment is completed, so is the making of the non-patriot.

JULY 3, 2017

What We Believe About Freedom

We have a moral obligation to others. Refusing
to recognize that endangers all of us.

Mike Schur and Todd May

F REEDOM, PERHAPS THE MOST SACROSANCT CONCEPT IN AMERI-
can life, is under attack. We've heard this drumbeat for some time,
but it's been especially loud this past year, when requests for tiny
sacrifices of freedom (like wearing masks) were repeatedly met with
anger, scorn, or calls for some kind of nebulous revolution.

For Americans, the concept of freedom is and has always been a
third rail; it cannot be touched without sparks flying. Recently, this
freedom has too often been interpreted as the limitless ability to
believe what one likes, regardless of where the facts lie. This in itself
might not pose much of a problem except for the fact that our beliefs
don't merely lie dormant inside the belief cabinet in our minds; they
give rise to action. What we believe and how we act are intertwined.

Philosophy requires us to interrogate our own beliefs in addition
to the beliefs of others. But before we begin that interrogation, we
need to locate an "ur-belief," a principle that underlies or informs all
the beliefs that come after. This is ours: As members of a society, we
have obligations to others.

Why do we need to believe in obligations to others in order to
adequately approach many of our other beliefs? Because to believe

adequately, we must first understand that our beliefs are inseparable from our responsibility for the safety and happiness of those with whom we share our planet. Without that, we will lose the possibility of a common social existence. We will fulfill Margaret Thatcher's infamous quip: "There is no such thing as society."

Consider this: What we believe about the climate matters because we have an obligation to future generations. What we believe about masking during a pandemic matters because we're obligated to protect the vulnerable. What we believe about elections matters because we have an obligation to our fellow citizens. And what we believe about the beliefs of those who disagree with us matters because we're obligated to respect them, just as they're obligated to respect us. As Gandhi said, nobody has access to all of the truth.

We hasten to add here that although many of our beliefs are bound to obligation, not all of them are. We can all believe that a peanut-butter-and-jelly sandwich is best made with raspberry jam, or that Marvel movies are overrated (or underrated) without any reflection on what this means for other people. Huge parts of our lives can be lived in unfettered freedom.

But other times the ripples of our choices will collide with the lives of others, and our freedom to do and believe what we want needs to be tempered. When we act or commit to a belief, we often consciously or unconsciously run through a checklist of reasons for why we're doing so, and to what end. If the first item on that checklist is always: "Because I have a right to do and believe whatever I want," then Thatcher is right. There is no such thing as society. There is only Steve, Jamel, Selena, and 332 million other siloed ego-states; a confederacy of individuals for whom freedom, safety, and the ability to flourish are zero-sum competitions.

But if instead the first item on that checklist is: "Because I care about the lives of those around me and understand that they have the same right to flourish as I do," then we acknowledge that we are not alone on earth, and that our freedom isn't any more important than anyone else's. If we do that, society holds.

It will be pointed out—and rightfully so—that "obligations to others" is a nebulous concept. How much should we consider those around us before we decide how to act and what to believe? To what extent should we limit our own freedom in consideration of those around us? Is there a calculation we can do? A scale we can use? An app we can download?

In short, there isn't. But there are benchmarks that can serve as guides to belief. For instance, we can trust scientists about scientific matters and doctors about medical matters instead of relying only on ourselves and other nonexperts. But even these benchmarks have their limits (which we can capture with a single word: economists).

There are other areas in which the benchmarks are unclear. What, for instance, should we believe about the proper constraints on free speech? Here we must feel our way, using Gandhi's dictum and recognizing the various others who are affected by our speech. And in feeling our way, we recognize that we often fail. Perhaps this is why believing in absolute freedom is so tempting—if we follow that path, we are always "right," which is easy.

One of the authors, in designing the TV show *The Good Place*, came to the conclusion that a key ethical concept is that of trying. (Which author this was—the professional TV show runner or the other guy—we will leave as an exercise for the reader.) We try to believe rightly about choices and actions that affect other people. Then, when we fail, we try to do better. It's not as easy a path, but it's certainly a more compassionate one, and importantly a more human one.

This is what we think of as our ur-belief: Before we decide what to believe, we have to believe that other people matter. If we act with this obligation in mind and we fail to get it right, then we have to reconsider, learn more, aim to improve, and try again. Our inevitable failures will mean more, and be more productive, if they are grounded in what we might simply call "consideration for other people"—the notion that there are people around us who are affected, directly and indirectly, by so much of what we believe and say and do.

Conversely, if we act only out of a sense of unlimited personal freedom, our failures will mean nothing. The refusal to recognize that we have obligations to others and that our beliefs and our behavior should respond to that recognition, is one we allow ourselves at our peril.

MAY 24, 2021

III

CAN WE BELIEVE OUR EYES?

Consciousness Isn't a Mystery. It's Matter.

*We don't know enough about the nature of physical stuff
to know that conscious experience can't be physical.*

Galen Strawson

E VERY DAY, IT SEEMS, SOME VERIFIABLY INTELLIGENT PER-
son tells us that we don't know what consciousness is. The nature
of consciousness, they say, is an awesome mystery. It's the ultimate
hard problem. The current Wikipedia entry is typical: Consciousness "is the most mysterious aspect of our lives"; philosophers "have
struggled to comprehend the nature of consciousness."

I find this odd because we know exactly what consciousness is—
where by "consciousness" I mean what most people mean in this
debate: experience of any kind whatever. It's the most familiar thing
there is, whether it's experience of emotion, pain, understanding
what someone is saying, seeing, hearing, touching, tasting, or feeling. It is in fact the only thing in the universe whose ultimate intrinsic nature we can claim to know. It is utterly unmysterious.

The nature of physical stuff, by contrast, is deeply mysterious,
and physics grows stranger by the hour. (Richard Feynman's remark
about quantum theory—"I think I can safely say that nobody understands quantum mechanics"—seems as true as ever.) Or rather, more
carefully: The nature of physical stuff is mysterious except insofar
as consciousness is itself a form of physical stuff. This point, which
is at first extremely startling, was well put by Bertrand Russell in

the 1950s in his essay "Mind and Matter": "We know nothing about the intrinsic quality of physical events," he wrote, "except when these are mental events that we directly experience." In having conscious experience, he claims, we learn something about the intrinsic nature of physical stuff, for conscious experience is itself a form of physical stuff.

I think Russell is right: Human conscious experience is wholly a matter of physical goings-on in the body and in particular the brain. But why does he say that we know nothing about the intrinsic quality of physical events except when these are mental events we directly experience? Isn't he exaggerating? I don't think so, and I'll try to explain. First, though, I need to try to reply to those (they're probably philosophers) who doubt that we really know what conscious experience is.

The reply is simple. We know what conscious experience is because the having is the knowing: Having conscious experience is knowing what it is. You don't have to think about it (it's really much better not to). You just have to have it. It's true that people can make all sorts of mistakes about what is going on when they have experience, but none of them threaten the fundamental sense in which we know exactly what experience is just in having it.

"Yes, but what is it?" At this point philosophers like to give examples: smelling garlic, experiencing pain, orgasm. Russell mentions "feeling the coldness of a frog" (a live frog), while Locke in 1689 considers the taste of pineapple. If someone continues to ask what it is, one good reply (although Wittgenstein disapproved of it) is, "You know what it is like from your own case." Ned Block replies by adapting the response Louis Armstrong reportedly gave to someone who asked him what jazz was: "If you gotta ask, you ain't never going to know."

So we all know what consciousness is. Once we're clear on this we can try to go further, for consciousness does of course raise a hard problem. The problem arises from the fact that we accept that consciousness is wholly a matter of physical goings-on, but can't see how this can be so. We examine the brain in ever greater detail, using increasingly powerful techniques like fMRI, and we observe extraordinarily complex neuroelectrochemical goings-on, but we can't even begin to understand how these goings-on can be (or give rise to) conscious experiences.

The German philosopher Gottfried Wilhelm Leibniz made the point vividly in 1714. Perception or consciousness, he wrote, is "inexplicable on mechanical principles, i.e. by shapes and movements. If we imagine a machine whose structure makes it think, sense, and be conscious, we can conceive of it being enlarged in such a way that we can go inside it like a mill"—think of the 1966 movie *Fantastic Voyage*, or imagine the ultimate brain scanner. Leibniz continued, "Suppose we do: visiting its insides, we will never find anything but parts pushing each other—never anything that could explain a conscious state."

It's true that modern physics and neurophysiology have greatly complicated our picture of the brain, but Leibniz's basic point remains untouched.

His mistake is to go further, and conclude that physical goings-on can't possibly be conscious goings-on. Many make the same mistake today—the Very Large Mistake (as Winnie-the-Pooh might put it) of thinking that we know enough about the nature of physical stuff to know that conscious experience can't be physical. We don't. We don't know the intrinsic nature of physical stuff, except—Russell again—insofar as we know it simply through having a conscious experience.

We find this idea extremely difficult because we're so very deeply committed to the belief that we know more about the physical than we do, and (in particular) know enough to know that consciousness can't be physical. We don't see that the hard problem is not what consciousness is, it's what matter is—what the physical is.

We may think that physics is sorting this out, and it's true that physics is magnificent. It tells us a great many facts about the mathematically describable structure of physical reality, facts that it expresses with numbers and equations ($e = mc^2$, the inverse-square law of gravitational attraction, the periodic table, and so on) and that we can use to build amazing devices. True, but it doesn't tell us anything at all about the intrinsic nature of the stuff that fleshes out this structure. Physics is silent—perfectly and forever silent—on this question.

This point was a commonplace one a hundred years ago, but it has gotten lost in the recent discussion of consciousness. Stephen Hawking makes it dramatically in his book *A Brief History of Time*. Physics, he says, is "just a set of rules and equations." The question is what "breathes fire into the equations and makes a universe for them to describe?" What is the fundamental stuff of physical reality, the stuff that is structured in the way physics reveals? The answer, again, is that we don't know—except insofar as this stuff takes the form of conscious experience.

We can say that it is energy that breathes fire into the equations, using the word "energy" as Heisenberg does when he says, for example, that "all particles are made of the same substance: energy," but the fundamental question arises again—"What is the intrinsic nature of this energy, this energy-stuff?" And the answer, again, is that we don't know, and that physics can't tell us; that's just not its business. This point about the limits on what physics can tell us is rock-solid, and it arises before we begin to consider any of the deep problems of understanding that arise within physics—problems with "dark matter" or "dark energy," for example—or with reconciling quantum mechanics and general relativity theory.

Those who make the Very Large Mistake (of thinking they know enough about the nature of the physical to know that consciousness can't be physical) tend to split into two groups. Members of the first group remain unshaken in their belief that consciousness exists, and conclude that there must be some sort of nonphysical stuff: They tend to become "dualists." Members of the second group, passionately committed to the idea that everything is physical, make the most extraordinary move that has ever been made in the history of human thought. They deny the existence of consciousness: They become "eliminativists."

This amazing phenomenon (the denial of the existence of consciousness) is a subject for another time. The present point—it's worth repeating many times—is that no one has to react in either of these ways. All they have to do is grasp the fundamental respect in which we don't know the intrinsic nature of physical stuff in spite of all that physics tells us. In particular, we don't know anything about the physical that gives us good reason to think that consciousness can't be wholly physical. It's worth adding that one can fully accept this even if one is unwilling to agree with Russell that in having conscious experience we thereby know something about the intrinsic nature of physical reality.

So the hard problem is the problem of matter (physical stuff in general). If physics made any claim that couldn't be squared with the fact that our conscious experience is brain activity, then I believe that claim would be false. But physics doesn't do any such thing. It's not the physics picture of matter that's the problem; it's the ordinary everyday picture of matter. It's ironic that the people who are most likely to doubt or deny the existence of consciousness (on the grounds that everything is physical, and that consciousness can't possibly be physical) are also those who are most insistent on the primacy of science, because it is precisely science that makes the key point shine most brightly: the point that there is a fundamental respect in which the ultimate intrinsic nature of the stuff of the universe is unknown to us—except insofar as it is consciousness.

MAY 16, 2016

Do We Really Understand "Fake News"?

We think we are sharing facts, but we are really
expressing emotions in the outrage factory.

Michael P. Lynch

G IVEN HOW MUCH IT'S TALKED, TWEETED ABOUT, AND WOR-
ried over, you'd think we'd know a lot about fake news. And in some
sense, we do. We know that false stories posing as legitimate journalism have been used to try to sway elections; we know they help spread
conspiracy theories; they may even cause false memories. And yet we
also know that the term "fake news" has become a trope, so widely
used and abused that it no longer serves its original function.

Why is that? And why, given all our supposed knowledge of it, is
fake news—the actual phenomenon—still effective? Reflection on our
emotions, together with a little help from contemporary philosophy
of language and neuroscience, suggests an answer to both questions.

We are often confused about the role that emotion plays in our
lives. For one thing, we like to think, with Plato, that reason drives
the chariot of our mind and keeps the unruly wild horses of emotion
in line. But most people would probably admit that much of the time,
Hume was closer to the truth when he said that reason is the slave of
the passions. Moreover, we often confuse our feelings with reality
itself: Something makes us feel bad, and so we say it is bad.

As a result, our everyday acts of communication can function as
vehicles for emotion without our noticing it. This was a point high-

lighted by mid–twentieth century philosophers of language often called "expressivists." Their point was that people sometimes think they are talking about facts when they are really expressing themselves emotionally. The expressivists applied this thought quite widely to all ethical communication about right or wrong, good or bad. But even if we don't go that far, their insight says something about what is going on when we share or retweet news posts—fake or otherwise—online.

When sharing or retweeting, we like to think of ourselves as engaging in what philosophers would call an act of testimony—trying to convey or endorse knowledge. Not always, of course; happily, irony still exists. Yet insincere sharing or retweeting is not the norm—as evidenced by the fact that most people feel obligated to signal that retweets aren't endorsements. That wouldn't make sense if the default wasn't that shares and retweets are endorsements.

But what if we are just confused about the way communication actually functions online? Clues can be found in both what we do and don't do when sharing content online.

Let's start with what we don't do. Current research estimates that at least sixty percent of news stories shared online have not even been read by the person sharing them. As an author of one study summed up the matter, "People are more willing to share an article than read it." On the other hand, what we do is share content that gets people riled up. Research has found that the best predictor of sharing is strong emotions—both emotions like affection (think posts about cute kittens) and emotions like moral outrage. Studies suggest that morally laden emotions are particularly effective: every moral sentiment in a tweet increases by twenty percent its chances of being shared. And social media may just pump up our feelings. Acts that don't elicit as much outrage offline, for example, elicit more online, perhaps because the social benefits of outrage still exist without the normal risks.

This should tell us that conveying knowledge isn't the primary reason news stories are shared. As the influential contemporary philosopher Ruth Millikan puts it, the stabilizing function of a communicative act is whatever explains why that act continues to persist. The stabilizing function of yelling, "Air ball!" at a basketball player trying to make a free throw is to distract him. It may do other things too—amuse people, or even describe what, in fact, turns out to be an air ball. But the reason people continue to yell, "Air ball!" it is that it is distracting. Someone new to the game could conceivably get this backward. They might think that people are warning the player or predicting how the shot is going to fall. Such interpretations would be a misunderstanding of the act's stabilizing function.

Something like this is happening on a massive scale on social media. We are like the person just described, new to the game of basketball. We think we are sharing news stories in order to do one thing, like transfer knowledge, but much of the time aren't really trying to do that at all—whatever we may consciously think. If we were, we would presumably have read the piece that we're sharing. But most of us don't. So, what are we doing?

I think it is plausible that the stabilizing function of the practice of sharing content online is to express our emotions. In particular, when it comes to sharing political news stories, we often are signaling our outrage and thereby hoping that others will share it. That's one way that tribes are built and social norms enforced. Social media is an outrage factory. And paradoxically, it works because most folks aren't aware, or don't want to be aware, of this point.

Yet it is just this lack of awareness that trolls and other workers in the misinformation industrial complex find so useful. Purveyors of deliberate but disguised falsehoods are keenly aware that when we share, we're doing something different from what we think we're doing. Our confusion is what makes us such easy marks.

The expressivists' insight also nicely explains why the term "fake news" itself has changed its use. It has become a vehicle for expressing our hostility, similar to yelling, "Boo," at a sports game. That's an irony all too representative of our age of absurdity. Even our attempts to distinguish truth from falsity turn into screams of outrage.

SEPTEMBER 23, 2019

What We Believe About Reality

Amid an onslaught of misinformation, is it possible to
discard bad ideas if we cannot discuss and refute them?

Garry Kasparov

PEOPLE WHO WERE BORN BEHIND THE OLD IRON CURTAIN ARE
often described as having paranoid tendencies. As a member of this
group, I can only say we had a lot to be paranoid about.

Growing up in Baku, in what is now Azerbaijan, I watched as the
all-powerful Soviet state lied right to our faces, every morning in the
paper and every night on the news. As I began my climb up the chess
Olympus, I realized that every sports official, fan, or neighbor was a
potential informant; perceived disobedience could result in the loss
of your job, your freedom, or your life.

As the doomed Communist economy slowed in the 1980s and our
standard of living fell further behind that of the free world, domestic repression and propaganda only increased. The contrast between
what the authorities said and our observable reality became absurd.
"There's no news in the Truth and no truth in the News," went the
line about the leading Soviet newspapers *Pravda* ("Truth") and *Izves-
tia* ("News").

It's easy to connect an all-powerful state—be it the Soviet Union,
the current Chinese Communist Party, or Big Brother in George
Orwell's *1984*—to the dissemination of false narratives with the
goal of social control. Dictatorships have the means and motive to

twist reality into whatever serves their purpose, and a track record of doing so.

Some individuals living under such a regime truly believe the official story, despite what their eyes may tell them. Others pretend to believe, out of fear. Then you have those who may or may not believe, but who are nonetheless ambitious, bent on not only surviving, but thriving. Demonstrating what a good believer in false narratives you are can provide a ladder up in those environments, especially if you rush to display your purity and conformity by accusing others.

In writing *1984*, Orwell was inspired, if that's the right word, by a novel called *We*, a futuristic portrait of a totalitarian state by the Russian writer Yevgeny Zamyatin. Banned in the Soviet Union, *We* had first been published in English, in 1924. In the novel, Zamyatin took precise aim at the true goals of ideological zealots and their endless pretexts for centralizing control of every aspect of society.

"The way to rid man of criminality is to rid him of freedom," says D-503, the loyal, but increasingly conflicted, spaceship-building protagonist of *We*, pleased by his own mathematical logic. The same logic can easily be applied to speech: You cannot spread prohibited thoughts if you cannot speak. In such a world, the heretic is to be burned, jailed, or lobotomized. Or at least deplatformed.

In Western countries today, there is no state monopoly on misinformation. Falsehoods spread instead from every nook of society. Thanks to the power of the internet, anyone—elected politician, businessman, or private citizen—can be a propaganda minister from the comfort of home. Social media can quickly fan errant sparks into raging wildfires. Online tribes of conspiracy theorists can influence and even merge with political parties, often encouraged by hostile foreign state actors that appreciate the potential damage such groups can inflict.

It's well established that fake news and outrageous lies spread faster than boring truths. Everyone enjoys the idea of being the holder of a secret others don't know. And facts are outnumbered in this fight. There are a million ways to lie, exaggerate, and elide, but still only one lonely truth.

The democratization of misinformation holds fewer obvious dangers than the control of information under a dictatorship, but the consequences are real. Today, false narratives often thrive in communities that are fragmented and difficult to reach by conventional means. Membership in such groups is a potent substitute for loyalty to a political party, and far less predictable in terms of outcome.

I have personal experience with authoritarian rule that has no respect for human freedom or human life. My own news site, Kasparov.ru, has been blocked in Russia for years. And I have closely followed as thousands of my fellow Russians were beaten and jailed in recent months for peacefully protesting the Putin regime. Having witnessed how easily dissent can be criminalized, I am always quick to point out the absurdity of American pundits and politicians decrying censorship after someone loses a book deal or Twitter account for sharing hateful views.

My life experience, however, is also why I am so concerned about a phenomenon that more subtly threatens the free flow of ideas in Western societies: the rise of an unchallengeable majority view, able to turn regular people into silent witnesses, informants, and ambitious zealots like the ones I grew up with in the Soviet Union.

Such intellectual orthodoxy doesn't have the authority of a state behind it, but online platforms such as Facebook and Twitter can be just as effective in enforcing adherence to the new "party" line. Consider the conversation around the origins of the Covid-19 virus.

Earlier in the pandemic, some experts—including Luc Montagnier, a Nobel Prize—winning virologist—suggested that the virus might have been the result of an accidental leak in a Chinese laboratory. The theory, however, was soon enveloped by an increasingly polarized discourse. In attempting to sharpen his rhetoric against China, President Donald Trump and his supporters openly promoted the possibility of the leak, while critics of his administration reflexively rejected it as a false narrative. Silicon Valley titans swiftly removed news articles amplifying the theory; mainstream media labeled them as misinformation.

Yet, at the time little information was available to confirm or contest the validity of the argument. The theory's dismissal was not the result of a thorough scientific investigation; it was a move based on politics and driven by the dominant voices shaping the conversation in the public square. (In recent months, with Mr. Trump out of the picture, the World Health Organization and several scientists have stated that the laboratory leak hypothesis calls for further investigation.)

Disloyalty to intellectual orthodoxy in our free world doesn't bear the grim consequences it does under totalitarian regimes. No one will be sent to the gulag for failing to toe the line. But we cannot successfully fight misinformation without the ability to think and speak without fear. How can we discard bad ideas if we cannot discuss and refute them? It is all an attempt to rid us of crime by ridding us of freedom.

As Zamyatin wrote, "There are ideas of clay and ideas molded of gold, or of our precious glass. In order to know the material of which an idea is made, one needs only to let fall upon it a drop of strong acid."

Our metaphorical acids are education, the free exchange of ideas, and the freedom to think, speak, be wrong, and learn without fear. Protecting these principles does not mean putting up with intolerance or promoting hatred, but it does require courage—courage to admit doubt, to challenge others and be challenged.

JUNE 2, 2021

Deepfakes Are Coming.
We Can No Longer Believe What We See.

It will soon be as easy to produce convincing fake
video as it is to lie. We need to be prepared.

Regina Rini

O N JUNE 1, 2019, THE *DAILY BEAST* PUBLISHED A STORY exposing the creator of a now-infamous fake video that appeared to show House Speaker Nancy Pelosi drunkenly slurring her words. The video was created by taking a genuine clip, slowing it down, and then adjusting the pitch of her voice to disguise the manipulation.

Judging by social media comments, many people initially fell for the fake, believing that Ms. Pelosi really was drunk while speaking to the media. (If that seems an absurd thing to believe, remember Pizzagate; people are happy to believe absurd things about politicians they don't like.)

The video was made by a private citizen named Shawn Brooks, who seems to have been a freelance political operative producing a wealth of pro-Trump web content. (Mr. Brooks denies creating the video, though according to the *Daily Beast*, Facebook confirmed he was the first to upload it.) Some commenters quickly suggested that the *Daily Beast* was wrong to expose Mr. Brooks. After all, they argued, he's only one person, not a Russian secret agent or a powerful public relations firm; and it feels like "punching down" for a major news organization to turn the spotlight on one rogue amateur. Seth

Mandel, an editor at the *Washington Examiner*, asked, "Isn't this like the third Daily Beast doxxing for the hell of it?"

It's a legitimate worry, but it misses an important point. There is good reason for journalists to expose the creators of fake web content, and it's not just the glee of watching provocateurs squirm. We live in a time when knowing the origin of an internet video is just as important as knowing what it shows.

Digital technology is making it much easier to fabricate convincing fakes. The video that Mr. Brooks created is pretty simple; you could probably do it yourself after watching a few YouTube clips about video editing. But more complicated fabrications, sometimes called "deepfakes," use algorithmic techniques to depict people doing things they've never done—not just slowing them down or changing the pitch of their voice, but making them appear to say things that they've never said at all. A recent research article suggested a technique to generate full-body animations, which could effectively make digital action figures of any famous person.

So far, this technology doesn't seem to have been used in American politics, though it may have played some role in a political crisis in Gabon earlier this year. But it's clear that current arguments about fake news are only a taste of what will happen when sounds and images, not just words, are open to manipulation by anyone with a decent computer.

Combine this point with an insight from epistemology—the branch of philosophy dealing with knowledge—and you'll see why the *Daily Beast* was right to expose the creator of the fake video of Ms. Pelosi. Contemporary philosophers rank different types of evidence according to their reliability: How much confidence, they ask, can we reasonably have in a belief when it is supported by such-and-such information?

We ordinarily tend to think that perception—the evidence of your eyes and ears—provides pretty strong justification. If you see something with your own eyes, you should probably believe it. By comparison, the claims that other people make—which philosophers call "testimony"—provide some justification, but usually not quite as much as perception. Sometimes, of course, your senses can deceive you, but that's less likely than other people deceiving you.

Until recently, video evidence functioned more or less like perception. Most of the time, you could trust that a camera captured roughly what you would have seen with your own eyes. So if you trust your own perception, you have nearly as much reason to trust the video. We all know that Hollywood studios, with enormous amounts of time and money, can use CGI to depict almost anything, but what are the odds that a random internet video came from Hollywood?

Now, with the emergence of deepfake technology, the ability to produce convincing fake video will be almost as widespread as the ability to lie. And once that happens, we ought to think of images as more like testimony than perception. In other words, you should only trust a recording if you would trust the word of the person producing it.

Which means that it does matter where the fake Nancy Pelosi video, and others like it, come from. This time we knew the video was fake because we had access to the original. But with future deepfakes, there won't be any original to compare them to. To know whether a disputed video is real, we'll need to know who made it.

It's good for journalists to start getting in the habit of tracking down creators of mysterious web content. And it's good for the rest of us to start expecting as much from the media. When deepfakes fully arrive, we'll be glad we've prepared. For now, even if it's not ideal to have amateur political operatives exposed to the ire of the internet, it's better than carrying on as if we can still trust our lying videos.

JUNE 10, 2019

Knowledge, Ignorance, and Climate Change

Philosophers have been talking about skepticism for
a long time. Some of those insights can shed light on
our public discourse regarding climate change.

N. Ángel Pinillos

NO MATTER HOW SMART OR EDUCATED YOU ARE, WHAT YOU
don't know far surpasses anything you may know. Socrates taught us
the virtue of recognizing our limitations. Wisdom, he said, requires
possessing a type of humility manifested in an awareness of one's
own ignorance. Since then, the value of being aware of our ignorance
has been a recurring theme in Western thought: René Descartes said
it's necessary to doubt all things to build a solid foundation for science; and Ludwig Wittgenstein, reflecting on the limits of language,
said that "the difficulty in philosophy is to say no more than we know."

Awareness of ignorance appears to be common in politics as well.
In a recent *60 Minutes* interview, President Trump said of global
warming, "I don't know that it's man-made." The same sentiment
was echoed by Larry Kudlow, the director of the National Economic
Council. Perhaps Trump and Kudlow, confident in their ignorance on
these important issues, are simply expressing philosophical humility and wisdom. Or perhaps not.

Sometimes, when it appears that someone is expressing doubt,
what he is really doing is recommending a course of action. For
example, if I tell you that I don't know whether there is milk in the

fridge, I'm not exhibiting philosophical wisdom—I'm simply recommending that you check the fridge before you go shopping. From this perspective, what Trump is doing is telling us that governmental decisions should not assume that global warming is caused by humans.

According to NASA, at least ninety-seven percent of actively publishing climate scientists think that "climate-warming trends over the past century are extremely likely caused by human activities." Americans overwhelmingly agree that the federal government needs to take significant action. In a recent poll conducted by Stanford University, ABC News, and Resources for the Future, sixty-one percent of those surveyed said that the federal government should take a great deal or a lot of action to curb global warming. And an additional nineteen percent believe that the government should take moderate action.

As a philosopher, I have nothing to add to the scientific evidence of global warming, but I can tell you how it's possible to get ourselves to sincerely doubt things, despite abundant evidence to the contrary. I also have suggestions about how to fix this.

To understand how it's possible to doubt something despite evidence to the contrary, try some thought experiments. Suppose you observe a shopper at the convenience store buying a lottery ticket. You are aware that the probability that he will lose the lottery is astronomically high, typically above 99.99 percent, but it's hard to get yourself to sincerely say you know this person will lose the lottery. Now imagine your doctor screens you for a disease, and the test comes out negative. But consider the possibility that this result is one of those rare "false negative" cases. Do you really know the result of this particular test is not a false negative?

These scenarios suggest that it's possible to feel as though you don't know something even when possessing enormous evidence in its favor. Philosophers call scenarios like these "skeptical pressure" cases, and they arise in mundane, boring cases that have nothing to do with politics or what one wants to be true. In general, a skeptical pressure case is a thought experiment in which the protagonist has good evidence for something that he or she believes, but the reader is reminded that the protagonist could have made a mistake. If the story is set up in the right way, the reader will be tempted to think that the protagonist's belief isn't genuine knowledge.

When presented with these thought experiments, some philosophy students conclude that what these examples show is that knowledge requires full-blown certainty. In these skeptical pressure cases, the evidence is overwhelming, but not one hundred percent. It's an attractive idea, but it doesn't sit well with the fact that we ordinarily say we know lots of things with much lower probability. For example, I know I will be grading student papers this weekend. Although the chance of this happening is high, it is not anything close to one hundred percent, since there is always the chance I'll get sick, or that something more important will come up. In fact, the chance of getting sick and not grading is much higher than the chance of winning the lottery. So how could it be that I know I will be grading and not know that the shopper at the convenience store will lose the lottery?

Philosophers have been studying skeptical pressure intensely for the past fifty years. Although there is no consensus about how it arises, a promising idea defended by the philosopher David Lewis is that skeptical pressure cases often involve focusing on the possibility of error. Once we start worrying and ruminating about this possibility, no matter how far-fetched, something in our brains causes us to doubt. The philosopher Jennifer Nagel aptly calls this type of effect "epistemic anxiety."

In my own work, I have speculated that an extreme version of this phenomenon is operative in obsessive compulsive disorder, a condition that affects millions of Americans. In many cases of OCD, patients are paralyzed with doubt about some fact—against all evidence. For example, a patient might doubt whether she turned off her stove despite having just checked multiple times. As with skeptical pressure cases, the focus on the possibility that one might be wrong plays a central role in the phenomenon.

Let's return to climate change skepticism. According to social psychology, climate change deniers tend to espouse conservative views, which suggests that party ideology is partly responsible for these attitudes. I think that we should also think about the philosophical nature of skeptical reactions, an apolitical phenomenon.

The standard response by climate skeptics is a lot like our reaction to skeptical pressure cases. Climate skeptics understand that ninety-seven percent of scientists disagree with them, but they focus on the very tiny fraction of holdouts. As in the lottery case, this focus might be enough to sustain their skepticism. We have seen this pattern before. Anti-vaccine proponents, for example, aware that medical professionals disagree with their position, focus on any bit of fringe research that might say otherwise.

Skeptical allure can be gripping. Piling on more evidence does not typically shake you out of it, just as making it even more probable that you will lose the lottery does not all of a sudden make you feel like you know your ticket is a loser.

One way to counter the effects of skepticism is to stop talking about "knowledge" and switch to talking about probabilities. Instead of saying that you don't know some claim, try to estimate the probability that it is true. As hedge fund managers, economists, policy researchers, doctors, and bookmakers have long been aware, the way to make decisions while managing risk is through probabilities. Once we switch to this perspective, claims to "not know," like those made by Trump, lose their force and we are pushed to think more carefully about the existing data and engage in cost-benefit analyses.

Interestingly, people in the grips of skepticism are often still willing to accept the objective probabilities. Think about the lottery case again. Although you find it hard to say you know the shopper will lose the lottery, you readily agree that it is still very probable that he will lose. What this suggests is that even climate skeptics could budge on their estimated likelihood of climate change without renouncing their initial skepticism. It's easy to say you don't know, but it's harder to commit to an actual low probability estimate in the face of overwhelming contrary evidence.

Socrates was correct that awareness of one's ignorance is virtuous, but philosophers have subsequently uncovered many pitfalls associated with claims of ignorance. An appreciation of these issues can help elevate public discourse on important topics, including the future of our planet.

NOVEMBER 26, 2018

"Transparency" Is the Mother of Fake News

We are now dealing with the problem child of
the techno-utopian worship of data.

Stanley Fish

FOR SOME TIME NOW EVERYONE HAS BEEN WORRYING ABOUT "fake news" or the world of "alternative fact" and wondering just how and why this unhappy phenomenon has flourished. My take on this question is simple, although I hope not simpleminded: Fake news is in large part a product of the enthusiasm—not to say rage—for transparency and absolutely free speech.

I know that this is a counterintuitive proposition. I would like to begin my defense of it with an anecdote.

In November 2016, Scott Titsworth, dean of the Scripps College of Communication at Ohio University, informed the university community of the first meeting of a presidential advisory group charged with recommending free speech policies for the campus. Titsworth reported that the group's first action was to affirm transparency as one of its "core values"; the second action was to decide (unanimously) that its meetings would not be open to the public, but held in private.

As you can imagine, it was easy to make fun of the obvious contradiction, but the contradiction is not so glaring once we understand that two notions of what "free" means are in play here. The group wants (understandably) to be free of the pressures that would be felt if the proceedings were conducted under public scrutiny; at every moment members would be tempted to tailor what they said to the responses and criticisms of an imagined audience. In short, they would not be speaking freely but under a shadow if the meaning of "freely" in force were "entirely without filters, gatekeepers and boundaries."

That sense of "freely" is championed by techno-utopians whose mantra is "Information wants to be free," and who believe that the promised land predicted by the authors of every technological advance—the printing press, newspapers, the telegraph, the railroad, radio, television, the digital computer, the internet—is just around the corner. It is a land in which democracy's potential is finally realized in a communication community where all voices are recognized and none marginalized, with no one hoarding information or controlling access or deciding who speaks and who doesn't.

What Titsworth and his fellow committee members see is that this more ambitious and abstract sense of "freely" is antithetical to the successful completion of their task: Not speaking freely in front of everyone is a condition of speaking freely—without anxiety and mental reservation—on the way to exploring the complexities and difficulties of their charge.

The moral (provisionally, and perhaps prematurely, drawn) is that transparency is not unambiguously a good thing. (I pass over for the moment the prior question of whether it is a possible thing.) And if that is right, then the proliferation of speech may not be a good thing either; silence and the withholding and sequestering of speech may be useful and even necessary in some contexts, like the preparing of a report or maintaining of a marriage. I say this aware that many free speech advocates believe that the more free speech there is, the better the human condition will be, and who believe too that it is the business of our institutions, including our legislatures and courts, to increase the amount of speech available.

At first glance the bias in favor of unlimited speech and information seems perfectly reasonable and even unassailable. What arguments could be brought against it? An answer to that question has been offered in recent years by a small, but growing, number of critics.

In a 2009 essay in the *New Republic* titled "Against Transparency," the law professor Lawrence Lessig (known as an apostle of openness), asked, as I just have, "How could anyone be against transparency?" Lessig responds to his own question by quoting a trio of authors who in their book *Full Disclosure: The Perils and Promise of Transparency* observe that by itself information doesn't do anything; its effects depend on the motives of those who make use of it, and raw information (that is, data) cannot distinguish between benign and malign appropriations of itself. Misunderstanding and manipulation are always more than possible, and there is no way to assure that "new information is used to further public objectives."

Another way to put this is to say that information, data, and the unbounded flow of more and more speech can be politicized—it can, that is, be woven into a narrative that constricts rather than expands the area of free, rational choice. When that happens—and it will happen often—transparency and the unbounded flow of speech become instruments in the production of the very inequalities (economic, political, educational) that the gospel of openness promises to remove. And the more this gospel is preached and believed, the more that the answer to everything is assumed to be data uncorrupted by interests and motives, the easier it will be for interests and motives to operate under transparency's cover.

This is so because speech and data presented as if they were independent of any mechanism of selectivity will float free of the standards of judgment that are always the content of such mechanisms. Removing or denying the existence of gatekeeping procedures will result not in a fair and open field of transparency but in a field where manipulation and deception find no obstacles. Because it is an article of their faith that politics are bad and the unmediated encounter with data is good, internet prophets will fail to see the political implications of what they are trying to do, for in their eyes political implications are what they are doing away with.

Indeed, their deepest claim—so deep that they are largely unaware of it—is that politics can be eliminated. They don't regard politics as an unavoidable feature of mortal life but as an unhappy consequence of the secular equivalent of the Tower of Babel: too many languages, too many points of view. Politics (faction and difference) will just wither away when the defect that generates it (distorted communication) has been eliminated by unmodified data circulated freely among free and equal consumers; everyone will be on the same page, reading from the same script and apprehending the same universal meanings. Back to Eden!

This utopian fantasy rests on a positive, vaguely perfectionist view of human nature: Rather than being doomed by original sin to conflict, prejudice, hatred, and an insatiable will to power, men and women are by nature communitarian, inclined to fellowship and the seeking of common ground. These good instincts, we are told, have been blocked by linguistic differences that can now be transcended by the digital revolution.

A memorable Facebook news release written by Mark Zuckerberg a few years back, cited by Evgeny Morozov in his book *To Save Everything, Click Here*, tells the happy and optimistic story: "By enabling people from diverse backgrounds to easily connect and share their ideas, we can decrease world conflict in the short and long run." The idea, Morozov explains, is that factions and conflict "are simply the unfortunate result of an imperfect communication infrastructure." If we perfect that infrastructure by devising a language of data algorithms and instantaneous electronic interaction that bypasses intervening and distorting institutions like the state, then communication would be perfect and undistorted, and society would be set on the right path without any further political efforts required. Talk about magical thinking!

In the alternative and true story rehearsed by many, human difference is irreducible, and there is no "neutral observation language" (a term of the philosopher Thomas Kuhn's in his 1962 book *The Structure of Scientific Revolutions*) that can bridge, soften, blur, and even erase the differences. When people from opposing constituencies clash there is no common language to which they can refer their differences for mechanical resolution; there are only political negotiations that would involve not truth telling but propaganda, threats, insults, deceptions, exaggerations, insinuations, bluffs, posturings—all the forms of verbal manipulation that will supposedly disappear in the internet nirvana.

They won't. Indeed, they will proliferate because the politically angled speech that is supposedly the source of our problems is in fact the only possible route to their (no doubt temporary) solution. Speech proceeding from a point of view can at least be recognized as such and then countered. You say, "I know where those guys are coming from, and here are my reasons for believing that we should be coming from someplace else"—and dialogue begins. It is dialogue inflected by interests and agendas, but dialogue still. But when speech (or information or data) is just sitting there inert, unattached to any perspective, when there are no guidelines, monitors, gatekeepers, or filters, what you have are innumerable bits (like Lego) available for assimilation into any project a clever verbal engineer might imagine; and what you don't have is any mechanism that can stop or challenge the construction project or even assess it. What you have, in short, are the perfect conditions for the unchecked proliferation of what has come to be called "fake news."

The rise of fake news has been attributed by some to the emergence of postmodern thought. Victor Davis Hanson, a scholar at the Hoover Institution at Stanford University, wrote in 2017 that fake news can be "traced back to the campus," specifically to "academic postmodernism," which, Hanson says, "derides facts and absolutes, and insists that there are only narratives and interpretations."

That's not quite right. The insistence on the primacy of narratives and interpretations does not involve a deriding of facts but an alternative story of their emergence. Postmodernism sets itself against the notion of facts just lying there discrete and independent, and waiting to be described. Instead it argues that fact is the achievement of argument and debate, not a preexisting entity by whose measure argument can be assessed. Arguments come first; when they are successful, facts follow—at least for a while, until a new round of arguments replaces them with a new set of facts.

This is far from the picture of Nietzschean nihilism that Hanson and others paint. Friction, not free invention, is the heart of the process: You commit yourself to the standards of evidence long in place in the conversation you enter, and then you maneuver as best you can within the guidelines of those standards. Thus, for example, a judge who issues a decision cannot simply decide which side he favors and then generate an opinion; he must first pass through and negotiate the authorized routes for getting there. Sometimes the effort at negotiation will fail and he will say that despite his interpretive desires, "This opinion just won't write."

Any opinion will write if there are no routes to be negotiated or no standards to hew to, if nothing but your own interpretive desire prevents you from assembling or reassembling bits of unmoored data lying around in the world into a story that serves your purposes. It is not postmodernism that licenses this irresponsibility; it is the doctrine that freedom of information and transparency are all we need.

Those who proclaim this theology can in good faith ignore or bypass all the usual routes of validation because their religion tells them that those routes are corrupt and that only the nonmethod of having no routes, no boundaries, no categories, no silos can bring us to the River Jordan and beyond.

In many versions of Protestantism, parishioners are urged to reject merely human authority in any form and go directly to the pure word of God. For the technophiles the pure word of God is to be found in data. In fact, what is found in a landscape where data detached from any context abounds is the fracturing of the word into ever-proliferating pieces of discourse, all existing side by side, indifferently approved, and without any way of distinguishing among them, of telling which of them are true or at least have a claim to be true and which are made up out of whole cloth.

That is the world of fake news. It is created by the undermining of trust in the traditional vehicles of authority and legitimation—

major newspapers, professional associations, credentialed academics, standard encyclopedias, government bureaus, federal courts, prime-time nightly news anchors.

When Walter Cronkite was the longtime anchor at CBS, he was known as the most trusted man in America; and when he signed off by saying, "And that's the way it is," everyone believed him. In the brave new world of the internet, where authority is evenly distributed to everyone with a voice or a podcast, no one believes anybody, or (it is the same thing) everyone believes anybody.

This wholesale distrust of authoritative mechanisms leads to the bizarre conclusion that an assertion of fact is more credible if it lacks an institutional source. In this way of thinking, a piece of news originating in a blog maintained by a teenager in a basement in Idaho would be more reliable than a piece of news announced by the anchor of a major network. And, again, what has brought us to this sorry pass is not the writings of Derrida or Foucault or any postmodern guru but the twin mantras of more free speech and absolute transparency.

MAY 7, 2018

What Is the Future of Speculative Journalism?

It is neither true nor false. Perhaps that's what we like about it.

Christy Wampole

W E'VE REALLY GOTTEN AHEAD OF OURSELVES. OUR EAGER-
ness to know what will happen next, particularly in relation to the
Trump saga, manifests itself in a hunger for conjecture in places that
we once relied on to deliver fact—in particular, journalism. Reporters and editors making guesses at what might happen rather than
reporting what did happen results in what is typically called speculative journalism.

While this tendency to speculate has existed in journalism since
its inception, its prevalence in recent months strikes me as peculiar
at a time when all sides seem to be calling for more truth and less
fake news. Because speculation is neither true nor false, it seems to
work as a strange compromise, a third way that shelves for now the
question of what is real and true.

Network news relies on these speculations most frequently, but
newspapers certainly indulge in the practice. A few examples of
speculative headlines from recent days: "Republicans' 2018 Resolution: Bipartisanship. Will It Last?" (the *New York Times*); "A Trump-
Mueller Sitdown: Could the Endless Russia Probe Soon Be Over?"
(Fox News); "How Breitbart Might Change, or Not, Without Steve
Bannon" (the *Washington Post*); "Russia Collusion Inquiry Faces a Big
2018—but Will Trump Let Mueller Finish the Job?" (the *Guardian*);

"Who Is Going to Run for President in 2020?" (the *Wall Street Journal*). All of these articles appear in the news sections of their publication, not in the opinion pages, where speculation might be more fitting.

All this speculation raises a number of new questions in my mind: If this is just clickbait, to what impulse are we responding? Do we simply enjoy the exercise that speculation offers our imaginations? Is the current state of things so unstable, or unbearable, that we now prefer potentiality to actuality? Does speculation provide the same anticipatory thrills as a wrapped gift or the ascent of that first hill on a roller coaster? Is the best journalist now the most clairvoyant one, the one who tells us not how it was but how it will be? These are all speculative questions (as is, you may have noticed, the headline of this piece), but their location here, in an opinion piece, marks them as the open-ended guesswork of a person whose job isn't to report what happened.

One explanation for all this is that the acceleration of information flow has heightened our impatience with not knowing. Until the internet's arrival, the "jour," or day, was the primary unit of time by which journalism functioned. But now that the minute, or better, the second, is the new unit of preference, it might be more fitting to change the profession's name to minutalism or secondalism. In the attempt to capture an event just as it happens, or even before it does, the news becomes less factual and more hypothetical. The absurdity of the word "tomorrowism" might just match the absurdity of the phenomenon.

Another theory is offered by Richard Grusin in his excellent book *Premediation: Affect and Mediality After 9/11*, in which he describes the ways in which the media in all its iterations tries to buffer itself against a repetition of the shock that was September 11. In response to an event that caught everyone off guard and left the nation steeped in residual trauma, premediation allows for the sustainment of a constant, baseline fear by keeping catastrophe always within peripheral view. This is accomplished in part by creating a media apparatus into which any future event might be plugged, offering us the illusion of preparedness. Hurricanes, nuclear wars, stock market plunges, epidemics, terror attacks, earthquakes, and currency collapses: The headlines prepare us for all of these by rehearsing them in advance.

Mr. Grusin writes: "Premediation is not about getting the future right, but about proliferating multiple remediations of the future both to maintain a low level of fear in the present and to prevent a recurrence of the kind of tremendous media shock that the United States and much of the networked world experienced on 9/11." Mediatic readiness—and anticipation—has become necessity.

I believe something similar is going on in response to Trump trauma. Despite efforts to remain poised for all of the world's contingencies through the process of premediation Mr. Grusin describes, many of us were startled by Mr. Trump's victory. The media, which seems to be repenting for having misread or misrepresented polls that showed a sure Hillary Clinton win, now atones by constantly hedging—offering us a tree of all possible outcomes and a range of fairly noncommittal speculations that can be backed away from if their conjectures prove false.

This leads us to a third possible reason speculative journalism thrives today: its mitigation of risk. What the speculative journalist has in common with the gamblers of Las Vegas and Wall Street is the willingness to take risks, but the stakes in this game are relatively low. When the future materializes, there will certainly be winners and losers. Someone will have gotten it right, and this certainty reassures us somehow. But given the superabundance of speculations clouding the mediascape, will anyone remember or care exactly who got it wrong? Those who were right will trumpet their prophetic insight and ascend as soothsayers; those who were wrong will simply keep quiet. One has little to lose but much to gain from this wager.

In the past, a journalist lost integrity when his or her reporting turned out to be incorrect, their sources corrupt, their methods dubious. But in the realm of the hypothetical, these standards vanish. The code of ethics for the journalist who guesses rather than reports has yet to be written. It is less risky, then, to write speculatively than to risk violating, say, the Society of Professional Journalists' Code of Ethics. I find nothing in the code about speculation. Perhaps an amendment is in order?

Finally, of course, there is the role of the president in all this. His utter unpredictability has certainly contributed to the general willingness to speculate about what will happen next under this administration. In fact, there is something eerily Trump-specific about the whole phenomenon. In the chess game between journalists and Mr. Trump, he keeps making off-the-board moves, leaving them at a loss on how to report on him. Speculative journalism offers a solution in that it opens up a little space between what he did and what he'll do, a space in which journalists might average all of his past actions in order to predict his next one. It gives one a sense of control, albeit tenuous, over the situation. It is the only way not to be caught completely unaware.

As in any endeavor, the very best speculative journalism has some beneficial value. There is positive potential in those pieces that aim at exhaustiveness, diagramming all possible outcomes and playing out some of the scenarios as examples, like a Choose Your Own Adventure story whose scaffolding has been revealed. The "if . . . then" logic of such articles does not force the reader to invest too much hope or dread into one particular outcome. They work more like a map than a horoscope, and for this reason serve a navigational purpose for the public. Unfortunately, most speculative pieces do not follow this model and instead poke at those parts of our brains made for wishing or fearing.

The next time you watch network news or read online news, pay attention to the ratio between the reporting of what happened and the speculation about what might happen. Are you pleased with the ratio? If so, what satisfaction do you get from the "would" and "could" and "might" and "maybe"? Is it the same satisfaction derived from reading utopian and dystopian fiction? If so, why not leave speculations to the novelists (or fortune-tellers) and the reporting of facts to the journalists? It is essential, I believe, to keep these tasks separate.

Because the muddling of epistemological categories like truth, fiction, lie, conspiracy, and conjecture changes how we behave politically, it is incumbent on us to revisit these categories with care and to ensure that serious journalists make a concerted effort to maintain strong distinctions among them.

It is easy for me to imagine that most fake news stories or conspiracy theories began as one person's random conjecture that then circulated online or by word of mouth and gained legitimacy by virtue of its repetition and circulation. Could journalists unwittingly be engaged in a similar operation? I could venture a hypothesis, but that would be pure speculation.

JANUARY 22, 2018

IV

SHOULD SPEECH BE FREE?

The End of Satire

The toxic disinformation of social media has rendered
traditional forms of humor quaint and futile.

Justin E. H. Smith

P ARIS—IN JANUARY 2015, NOT LONG AFTER I ARRIVED HERE
to live and teach philosophy, terrorists assassinated twelve people,
including four cartoonists, in an attack on the offices of the French
satirical newspaper *Charlie Hebdo*. This act brought to the surface
and seemingly galvanized a view about censorship I had long held. I
spent considerable energy, in the weeks and months after, defending
the absolute right of satirists to keep doing what I saw as their sacred
work, and criticizing many of my former friends, who found it more
important at that moment to speak out against offending the sensi-
tivities of religious communities, for their moral cowardice in the
face of nihilistic violence.

After the assassinations, with the perpetrators quickly killed in
their turn, the rest of the year seemed to play out as a long public trial
of satire itself. In April, when the writers' organization PEN granted
Charlie Hebdo a freedom of expression award, American progressives roundly condemned the decision, saying that it played into an
American imperialist agenda, and that the death of the cartoonists at
the hands of terrorists did not diminish the implicit Islamophobia of
rewarding a magazine for its offensive caricatures.

In general the most facile and uninterested articulations of what satire is and of how it works satisfied both parties to the controversy. Both sides missed, in particular, that satire is a species of humor that works through impersonation: taking on the voices of others, saying the sort of things they would say, using one's own voice while not speaking in one's own name. It is not surprising that this craft is so often misunderstood, for when satirists do their job convincingly, when they get too close to their target, it is easy to hear them not just as the channelers of the views expressed in the satire, but as defenders of these views as well. It is at such moments that critics like to exclaim that a satirist has "gone too far," while it would be more correct to say that the satirist has only done his job too well.

Today, with the pollution that new technologies have brought to our information ecosystem, this distinction is no longer so easy to make. And this is the real problem, and danger, of satire: not that it mocks and belittles respect-worthy pieties, not that it "punches down," but that it has become impossible to separate it cleanly from the toxic disinformation that defines our era.

To see how things have changed, let's go back even further than the *Charlie Hebdo* attack. In 2002 a satirical article in the *Onion* announced that "Congress Threatens to Leave D.C. Unless New Capitol Is Built." The target here, obviously, were the petulant professional sports teams holding American municipalities at ransom by threatening to leave if they do not get a greater share of local taxes. This was lost, however, on the editors of the *Beijing Evening News*, who took the story as a straightforward sign of the decline of American democracy. I can recall my smirking attitude when the same Chinese newspaper acknowledged soon after that it had been fooled. "Some small American newspapers," the paper chided, "frequently fabricate offbeat news to trick people into noticing them, with the aim of making money."

Today it is no longer publications like the *Onion* that are driving the proliferation of satire. Nor is it the palliative care for liberals offered up by Stephen Colbert and the other late-night talkers, or by *Saturday Night Live*, now into its fifth decade of tedium. It is rather the culture of social media, often coming from obscure or anonymous sources. Here by comparison all other sources of humor, including professional comedians, seem quaint and futile.

In early 2018 the Twitter account known as PixelatedBoat offered what it claimed was an excerpt from Michael Wolff's recently published Trump exposé, *Fire and Fury*. It was related that upon arriving at the White House, the new president complained that the television options there did not include what he called "The Gorilla Channel." So the staff began transmitting gorilla documentaries from a make-shift tower outside his window, until he complained that these were boring, that the gorillas were not fighting enough. So they edited the documentaries down to the fight scenes, at which point the president was appeased, and knelt in front of the TV from morning until night.

This was excellent satire: just believable enough to be entertained as true. I myself believed it for about five minutes, and I was indignant when I realized I had been fooled. I thought of the stiff functionaries in Beijing who had also reacted poorly to getting played. I realized they were right.

The Gorilla Channel was to become one small skirmish in the never-ending American culture war. Some on the right charged that PixelatedBoat had contributed to the overall quantity of disinformation flowing around, and was therefore no less part of the problem of fake news than were the distortions and lies that the right had been condemned for propagating in the lead-up to Trump's election. And those who made this charge were right too.

Throughout the satire trials of 2015 I had resisted the idea that one person's satire is another's propaganda. I insisted that satire was speech in something like a grammatical mood of its own, as different from the declarative as the declarative is from the interrogative, and that it was therefore subject to its own rules. But in this judgment I was mostly considering established print media, venues such as *Charlie Hebdo* that practically announced their own satirical nature as a disclaimer.

By the following year, however, I began to notice the way in which new media blur the line between satire and propaganda. Alt-right personalities were now gleefully acknowledging that their successes in meme warfare relied precisely on the inability of media consumers to distinguish between the sincere and the jocular, between an ironic display of a swastika and a straightforward one.

At the same time, artificial intelligence was increasingly producing texts and images that, whether overtly political or not, contributed to the general sense that we cannot possibly know the ends for which media content is being churned out. There are for example Facebook accounts that do nothing but show images of celebrities with deadpan captions mistaking them for other celebrities: Betty White for Queen Elizabeth, Samuel Jackson for Kofi Annan. Are these satire? No one is called upon to say. They may well be generated by bots, and you cannot possibly discern the intentions of machines that have no intentions. Their cumulative effect, anyhow, is to make media consumers less certain of their grasp on reality.

Lurking in the darker shadows beyond these strange new phenomena, there are porn sites with the faces of celebrities grafted onto the bodies of others; and there are, or will be soon, deepfakes of politicians accepting another sort of graft. There are distortions at a level of intensity and verisimilitude that we could not possibly have imagined in 2002, all being generated, in the end, with the aim of gaining notice and money.

Over the past few years I have been made to see, in sum, that the nature and extent of satire is not nearly as simple a question as I had previously imagined. I am now prepared to agree that some varieties of expression that may have some claim to being satire should indeed be prohibited. I note this not with a plan or proposal for where or how such a prohibition might be enforced, but to acknowledge something I did not fully understand until I experienced it firsthand—that even the most cherished and firmly held values or ideals can change when the world in which those values were first formed changes.

I hate to have to say this, and I feel that while it is an admission necessitated by the changing times, it also could not come at a worse time. The madness of 2015 has not subsided. In an astounding article in the British newspaper the *Independent* in February, Sean O'Grady attempted to stoke the decades-old fatwa against Salman Rushdie for his satirical take on the life of Muhammad in *The Satanic Verses*. "Rushdie's silly, childish book," the columnist writes, "should be banned under today's anti-hate legislation. It's no better than racist graffiti on a bus stop." O'Grady proudly admits that he has never read the book, and in this he is just like the Ayatollah Khomeini before him.

Is my own belated acknowledgment of the need to regulate satire an unwitting discovery of common cause with the likes of O'Grady? I certainly hope not. O'Grady belongs to what seems to be an increasingly common species of moral coward, a dupe of totalitarians, spiritual brother of the *Charlie Hebdo* assassins, whereas I am only trying to respond to the real threats of hitherto unimagined technologies. *The Satanic Verses*, I tell myself, is literature, where free play of the imagination is the rule of the game and the inalienable right of the creator. Twitter is, well, something else.

But the truth is I am not at all sure of this distinction. The truth is that the nature and proper scope of satire remain an enormous problem, one that is not going to get any easier to resolve in the political and technological future we can all, by now, see coming.

APRIL 8, 2019

Should We Cancel Aristotle?

*He defended slavery and opposed the notion of
human equality. But he is not our enemy.*

Agnes Callard

THE GREEK PHILOSOPHER ARISTOTLE DID NOT MERELY CON-
done slavery, he defended it; he did not merely defend it, but defended
it as beneficial to the slave. His view was that some people are, by
nature, unable to pursue their own good, and best suited to be "living tools" for use by other people: "The slave is a part of the master, a
living but separated part of his bodily frame."

Aristotle's anti-liberalism does not stop there. He believed that
women were incapable of authoritative decision making. And he
decreed that manual laborers, despite being neither slaves nor
women, were nonetheless prohibited from citizenship or education
in his ideal city.

Of course Aristotle is not alone: Kant and Hume made racist comments, Frege made anti-Semitic ones, and Wittgenstein
was bracingly up-front about his sexism. Should readers set aside
or ignore such remarks, focusing attention on valuable ideas to be
found elsewhere in their work?

This pick-and-choose strategy may work in the case of Kant,
Hume, Frege, and Wittgenstein, on the grounds that their core philosophical contributions are unrelated to their prejudices, but I do not
think it applies so well to Aristotle: His inegalitarianism runs deep.

Aristotle thought that the value or worth of a human being—his virtue—was something that he acquired in growing up. It follows that people who can't (women, slaves) or simply don't (manual laborers) acquire that virtue have no grounds for demanding equal respect or recognition with those who do.

As I read him, Aristotle not only did not believe in the conception of intrinsic human dignity that grounds our modern commitment to human rights, he has a philosophy that cannot be squared with it. Aristotle's inegalitarianism is less like Kant and Hume's racism and more like Descartes's views on nonhuman animals: The fact that Descartes characterizes nonhuman animals as soulless automata is a direct consequence of his rationalist dualism. His comments on animals cannot be treated as "stray remarks."

If cancellation is removal from a position of prominence on the basis of an ideological crime, it might appear that there is a case to be made for canceling Aristotle. He has much prominence: Thousands of years after his death, his ethical works continue to be taught as part of the basic philosophy curriculum offered in colleges and universities around the world.

And Aristotle's mistake was serious enough that he comes off badly even when compared to the various "bad guys" of history who sought to justify the exclusion of certain groups—women, black people, Jews, gays, atheists—from the sheltering umbrella of human dignity. Because Aristotle went so far as to think there was no umbrella.

Yet I would defend Aristotle, and his place on philosophy syllabi, by pointing to the benefits of engaging with him. He can help us identify the grounds of our own egalitarian commitments; and his ethical system may capture truths—for instance, about the importance of aiming for extraordinary excellence—that we have yet to incorporate into our own.

And I want to go a step further, and make an even stronger claim on behalf of Aristotle. It is not only that the benefits of reading Aristotle counteract the costs, but that there are no costs. In fact we have no reason at all to cancel Aristotle. Aristotle is simply not our enemy.

I, like Aristotle, am a philosopher, and we philosophers must countenance the possibility of radical disagreement on the most fundamental questions. Philosophers hold up as an ideal the aim of never treating our interlocutor as a hostile combatant. But if someone puts forward views that directly contradict your moral sensibilities, how can you avoid hostility? The answer is to take him literally—which is to say, read his words purely as vehicles for the contents of his beliefs.

There is a kind of speech that it would be a mistake to take literally, because its function is some kind of messaging. Advertising and political oratory are examples of messaging, as is much that falls under the rubric of "making a statement," like boycotting, protesting, or publicly apologizing.

Such words exist to perform some extra-communicative task; in messaging speech, some aim other than truth-seeking is always at play. One way to turn literal speech into messaging is to attach a list of names: a petition is an example of nonliteral speech, because more people believing something does not make it more true.

Whereas literal speech employs systematically truth-directed methods of persuasion—argument and evidence—messaging exerts some kind of nonrational pressure on its recipient. For example, a public apology can often exert social pressure on the injured party to forgive, or at any rate to perform a show of forgiveness. Messaging is often situated within some kind of power struggle. In a highly charged political climate, more and more speech becomes magnetically attracted into messaging; one can hardly say anything without arousing suspicion that one is making a move in the game, one that might call for a countermove.

For example, the words "Black lives matter" and "All lives matter" have been implicated in our political power struggle in such a way as to prevent anyone familiar with that struggle from using, or hearing, them literally. But if an alien from outer space, unfamiliar with this context, came to us and said either phrase, it would be hard to imagine that anyone would find it objectionable; the context in which we now use those phrases would be removed.

In fact, I can imagine circumstances under which an alien could say women are inferior to men without arousing offense in me. Suppose this alien had no gender on their planet, and drew the conclusion of female inferiority from time spent observing ours. As long as the alien spoke to me respectfully, I would not only be willing to hear them out but even interested to learn their argument.

I read Aristotle as such an "alien." His approach to ethics was empirical—that is, it was based on observation—and when he looked around him he saw a world of slavery and of the subjugation of women and manual laborers, a situation he then inscribed into his ethical theory.

When I read him, I see that view of the world—and that's all. I do not read an evil intent or ulterior motive behind his words; I do not interpret them as a mark of his bad character, or as attempting to convey a dangerous message that I might need to combat or silence in order to protect the vulnerable. Of course, in one sense it is hard to imagine a more dangerous idea than the one that he articulated and argued for—but dangerousness, I have been arguing, is less a matter of literal content than messaging context.

What makes speech truly free is the possibility of disagreement without enmity, and this is less a matter of what we can say, than how we can say it. "Cancel culture" is merely the logical extension of what we might call "messaging culture," in which every speech act is classified as friend or foe, in which literal content can barely be communicated, and in which very little faith exists as to the rational faculties of those being spoken to. In such a context, even the cry for "free speech" invites a nonliteral interpretation, as being nothing but the most efficient way for its advocates to acquire or consolidate power.

I will admit that Aristotle's vast temporal distance from us makes it artificially easy to treat him as an "alien." One of the reasons I gravitate to the study of ancient ethics is precisely that it is difficult to entangle those authors in contemporary power struggles. When we turn to disagreement on highly charged contemporary ethical questions, such as debates about gender identity, we find suspicion, second-guessing of motives, petitioning—the hallmarks of messaging culture—even among philosophers.

I do not claim that the possibility of friendly disagreement with Aristotle offers any direct guidance on how to improve our much more difficult disagreements with our contemporaries, but I do think considering the case of Aristotle reveals something about what the target of such improvements would be. What we want, when we want free speech, is the freedom to speak literally.

JULY 21, 2020

What "Snowflakes" Get Right About Free Speech

Campus protests against speakers like Richard Spencer are
not censorship. They help secure the basic rights of others.

Ulrich Baer

AT ONE OF THE PREMIERES OF HIS LANDMARK HOLOCAUST
documentary *Shoah* (1985), the filmmaker Claude Lanzmann was
challenged by a member of the audience, a woman who identified
herself as a Holocaust survivor. Lanzmann listened politely as the
woman recounted her harrowing personal account of the Holocaust
to make the point that the film failed to fully represent the recollec-
tions of survivors. When she finished, Lanzmann waited a bit, and
then said, "Madame, you are an experience, but not an argument."

This exchange, conveyed to me by the Russian literature scholar
Victor Erlich some years ago, has stayed with me, and it has taken
on renewed significance as the struggles on American campuses to
negotiate issues of free speech have intensified—most recently in
protests at Auburn University against a visit by the white nationalist
Richard Spencer.

Lanzmann's blunt reply favored reasoned analysis over personal
memory. In light of his painstaking research into the Holocaust, his
comment must have seemed insensitive but necessary at the time.
Ironically, *Shoah* eventually helped usher in an era of testimony that
elevated stories of trauma to a new level of importance, especially in
cultural production and universities.

During the 1980s and '90s, a shift occurred in American culture; personal experience and testimony, especially of suffering and oppression, began to challenge the primacy of argument. Freedom of expression became a flash point in this shift. Then as now, both liberals and conservatives were wary of the privileging of personal experience, with its powerful emotional impact, over reason and argument, which some fear will bring an end to civilization, or at least to freedom of speech.

My view (and, like all the views expressed here, it does not represent the views or policies of my employer, New York University) is that we should resist the temptation to rehash these debates. Doing so would overlook the fact that a thorough generational shift has occurred. Widespread caricatures of students as overly sensitive, vulnerable, and entitled "snowflakes" fail to acknowledge the philosophical work that was carried out, especially in the 1980s and '90s, to legitimate experience—especially traumatic experience—which had been dismissed for decades as unreliable, untrustworthy, and inaccessible to understanding.

The philosopher Jean-François Lyotard, best known for his prescient analysis in *The Postmodern Condition* of how public discourse discards the categories of true/false and just/unjust in favor of valuing the mere fact that something is being communicated, examined the tension between experience and argument in a different way.

Instead of defining freedom of expression as guaranteeing the robust debate from which the truth emerges, Lyotard focused on the asymmetry of different positions when personal experience is challenged by abstract arguments. His extreme example was Holocaust denial, where invidious but often well-publicized cranks confronted survivors with the absurd challenge to produce incontrovertible eyewitness evidence of their experience of the killing machines set up by the Nazis to exterminate the Jews of Europe. Not only was such evidence unavailable, but it also challenged the Jewish survivors to produce evidence of their own legitimacy in a discourse that had systematically denied their humanity.

Lyotard shifted attention away from the content of free speech to the way certain topics restrict speech as a public good. Some things are unmentionable and undebatable, but not because they offend the sensibilities of the sheltered young. Some topics, such as claims that some human beings are by definition inferior to others, or illegal or unworthy of legal standing, are not open to debate because such people cannot debate them on the same terms.

The recent student demonstrations at Auburn against Spencer's visit—as well as protests on other campuses against Charles Murray, Milo Yiannopoulos, and others—should be understood as an attempt to ensure the conditions of free speech for a greater group of people, rather than censorship. Liberal free speech advocates rush to point out that the views of these individuals must be heard first to be rejected. But this is not the case. Universities invite speakers not chiefly to present otherwise unavailable discoveries, but to present to the public views they have presented elsewhere. When those views invalidate the humanity of some people, they restrict speech as a public good.

In such cases there is no inherent value to be gained from debating them in public. In today's age, we also have a simple solution that should appease all those concerned that students are insufficiently exposed to controversial views. It is called the internet, where all kinds of offensive expression flourish unfettered on a vast platform available to nearly all.

The great value and importance of freedom of expression, for higher education and for democracy, is hard to overestimate. But it has been regrettably easy for commentators to create a simple dichotomy between a younger generation's oversensitivity and free speech as an absolute good that leads to the truth. We would do better to focus on a more sophisticated understanding, such as the one provided by Lyotard, of the necessary conditions for speech to be a common, public good. This requires the realization that in politics, the parameters of public speech must be continually redrawn to accommodate those who previously had no standing.

The rights of transgender people for legal equality and protection against discrimination are a current example in a long history of such redefinitions. It is only when trans people are recognized as fully human, rather than as men and women in disguise, as Ben Carson, the current secretary of housing and urban development claims, that their rights can be fully recognized in policy decisions.

The idea of freedom of speech does not mean a blanket permission to say anything anybody thinks. It means balancing the inherent value of a given view with the obligation to ensure that other members of a given community can participate in discourse as fully recognized members of that community. Free speech protections— not only but especially in universities, which aim to educate students in how to belong to various communities—should not mean that someone's humanity, or their right to participate in political speech as political agents, can be freely attacked, demeaned, or questioned.

The student activism that has roiled campuses—at Auburn, Missouri, Yale, Berkeley, Middlebury, and elsewhere—is an opportunity to take stock of free speech issues in a changed world. It is also an opportunity to take into account the past few decades of scholarship that has honed our understanding of the rights to expression in higher education, which maintains particularly high standards of what is worthy of debate.

The recent controversies over the conflict between freedom of expression and granting everyone access to speech hark back to another telling moment. In 1963, Yale University had rescinded an invitation to Alabama's segregationist governor, George C. Wallace. In 1974, after unruly protests prevented William Shockley from debating his recommendation for voluntary sterilization of people with low IQs, and other related incidents, Yale issued a report on how best to uphold the value of free speech on campus that remains the gold standard for many other institutions.

Unlike today's somewhat reflexive defenders of free speech, the Yale report situated the issue of free speech on campus within the context of an increasingly inclusive university and the changing demographics of society at large. While Yale bemoaned the occasional "paranoid intolerance" of student protesters, the university also criticized the "arrogant insensitivity" of free speech advocates who failed to acknowledge that requiring of someone in public debate to defend their human worth conflicts with the community's obligation to assure all of its members equal access to public speech.

It is perhaps telling that in the 1980s and '90s, while I was also a doctoral student there, Yale ultimately became the hotbed of philosophical thinking that acknowledged the claims of people who had not been granted full participation in public discourse. Their accounts, previously dismissed as "unspeakable" or "unimaginable," now gained legitimacy in redefining the rules of what counts as public speech. Lyotard taught at Yale in the early 1990s, and his and others' thoughts on how to resolve the asymmetry in discussions between perpetrators and victims of systemic or personal violence, without curtailing speech too much, seeped into other disciplines.

Lyotard and others were interested in expanding the frames of discourse, as they had been before, when married women were granted full legal status after centuries of having their very being legally suspended upon marriage.

When Yale issued its guidelines about free speech, it did so to account for a new reality, in the early 1970s, when increasing numbers of minority students and women enrolled at elite college campuses. We live in a new reality as well. We should recognize that the current generation of students, roundly ridiculed by an unholy alliance of so-called alt-right demagogues and campus liberals as coddled snowflakes, realized something important about this country before the pundits and professors figured it out.

What is under severe attack, in the name of an absolute notion of free speech, are the rights, both legal and cultural, of minorities to participate in public discourse. The snowflakes sensed, a good year before the election of President Trump, that insults and direct threats could once again become sanctioned by the most powerful office in the land. They grasped that racial and sexual equality is not so deep in the DNA of the American public that even some of its legal safeguards could not be undone.

The issues to which the students are so sensitive might be benign when they occur within the ivory tower. Coming from the campaign trail and now the White House, the threats are not meant to merely offend. Like President Trump's attacks on the liberal media as the "enemies of the American people," his insults are meant to discredit and delegitimize whole groups as less worthy of participation in the public exchange of ideas.

As a college professor and university administrator with over two decades of direct experience of campus politics, I am not overly worried that even the shrillest heckler's vetoes will end free speech in America. As a scholar of literature, history, and politics, I am especially attuned to the next generation's demands to revise existing definitions of free speech to accommodate previously delegitimized experiences. Freedom of expression is not an unchanging absolute. When its proponents forget that it requires the vigilant and continuing examination of its parameters, and instead invoke a pure model of free speech that has never existed, the dangers to our democracy are clear and present.

We should thank the student protesters, the activists in Black Lives Matter, and other "overly sensitive" souls for keeping watch over the soul of our republic.

APRIL 24, 2017

Confronting Philosophy's Anti-Semitism

Should we continue to teach thinkers like Kant,
Voltaire, and Hume without mention of the
harmful prejudices they helped legitimize?

Laurie Shrage

W E COMMONLY ASSUME THAT ANTI-SEMITISM AND RELATED
attitudes are a product of ignorance and fear, or fanatical beliefs, or
some other irrational force. But it is by now well known that some of
the most accomplished thinkers in modern societies have defended
anti-Semitic views. For instance, several of the major Enlightenment philosophers—including Hume, Voltaire, and Kant—developed
elaborate justifications for anti-Semitic views. One common thread
running through the work of these philosophers is an attempt to
diminish the influence of Judaism or the Jewish people on European history.

In "The Philosophical Bases of Modern Racism," the historian
of philosophy Richard H. Popkin wrote: "David Hume apparently
accepted a polygenetic view of man's origin, since in his 'Natural
History of Religion' he made no effort to trace a linear development
of man from the ancient Jews to the modern world, and presented
practically no historical connection between Judaism and Christianity (which he saw more as emerging from pagan polytheism)."
Popkin wrote that Voltaire challenged the biblical account of human
history by asserting that only the Jews were descendants of Adam,

and "everybody else pre-Adamites, though the non-European ones were degenerate or inferior to the European ones. Voltaire saw the Adamites as a major menace to European civilization, since they kept infecting it with what he considered the horrible immorality of the Bible. Voltaire therefore insisted that Europe should separate itself from the Adamites, and seek its roots and heritage and ideals in the best of the pre-Adamite world—for him, the Hellenic world."

Polygenetic racists, such as Hume and Voltaire, regarded the differences between European Christians and others as immutable, because they derived from separate ancestry rather than contingent environmental factors.

Kant too thought that Jews had immutable traits that made them inferior to Christians. According to the scholar Michael Mack, "Though Kant emphasized the common origin of all men, to avoid attacking the biblical account of creation . . . He set out to substantiate his notion of a 'Jewish essence' with recourse to the image of an inseparable tie that bound the Jews immutably to Jehovah."

For Kant, this tie rendered Jews "heteronomous" or incapable of transcending material forces, which a moral order required. In this way, Jews are the opposite of autonomous, rational Christians, and are therefore incapable of being incorporated into an ethical Christian society. Mack, in his 2003 book *German Idealism and the Jew*, wrote that Kant "attempted to remove Christianity's Judaic foundations" by recasting Christian history as a revolutionary or radical parting from Judaism. Mack noted that Kant, in his *Anthropology from a Pragmatic Point of View*, called the Jews "a nation of cheaters" and depicted them as "a group that has followed not the path of transcendental freedom but that of enslavement to the material world."

When the anti-Semitic views of great thinkers such as Kant, Voltaire, or Hume (or Hegel, Schopenhauer, Heidegger, and Wittgenstein, for that matter) are exposed, one typical response is to question whether these prejudices are integral to their important works and ideas. But this may be the wrong question. A better question is: Should those who teach their works and ideas in the twenty-first century share them without mentioning the harmful stereotypes these thinkers helped to legitimize?

For example, the history of Western philosophy is usually presented as a form of inquiry that began with the ancient Greeks and Romans, then jumps to medieval Christian Europe, and picks up again when modern European Christians struggled with religious reform and the rise of secularism and science. When we reiterate this trajectory, are we reinforcing Hume's, Voltaire's, and Kant's purging of Judaism from European history and the history of Western thought and values?

When our curriculum in the history of philosophy excludes Philo of Alexandria or Maimonides (or the schools of thought from outside Europe that have helped shape today's multicultural world), are we circulating an image of the West as racist thinkers have fashioned it? Should we construct Jewish, Islamic, and Buddhist philosophy in our curriculums as "non-Western," or does that reinscribe a fundamental divide between the West and the rest, where the West is portrayed as the major agent of human advancement?

Many of us who teach the works of the European Enlightenment live outside Europe, for example, in North America or Australia. We tend to view our societies as extensions of European or Western or Christian civilization. In the United States before the twentieth century, universities primarily hired Christian theologians to teach philosophy.

Later, when American universities became more secular, philosophy departments were among the last to hire professors of Jewish ancestry. This was not because those who entered the profession were more anti-Semitic than their peers in other fields, but instead because Jews were regarded in the early twentieth century as non-Western and therefore unfit to teach Western philosophy. The Harvard philosopher William Hocking is alleged to have said that "the Jewish mind could not properly interpret and teach the philosophy and history of Western Christian civilization."

After World War II, when European Jews were reimagined as

European, and therefore of the West, social barriers to Jews broke down in most areas of American life, including academic philosophy. Although some of the new arrivals attempted to incorporate Jewish thinkers into the American curriculum, those who did were pushed to the margins of the discipline. This is partly because philosophy itself became more secular, and its practitioners focused more on the epistemology and implications of Western science. Philosophers who engaged with Christian thought or the philosophy of religion were similarly marginalized in this period.

Research and teaching in the history of philosophy has become sidelined too. Those who champion the importance and relevance of philosophy's history to the field mostly defend the traditional Western canon, although there are some new efforts to incorporate the works and ideas of non-European and also women philosophers, and to teach the works of figures like Kant in ways that expose his social biases.

With the resurgence of old hatreds in the twenty-first century, philosophers are challenged to think about the ways we trace the history of our discipline and teach our major figures, and whether our professional habits and pieties have been shaped by religious intolerance and other forms of bigotry. For example, why not emphasize how philosophy emerged from schools of thought around the world? In the fields of history and literature, introductory courses that focus on European studies are being replaced by courses in world history and comparative literature.

There has not been a similar widespread movement to rethink the standard introduction to philosophy in terms of world philosophy. There are philosophers who contend that such projects inappropriately politicize our truth-seeking endeavors, but, as some philosophers of science have shown, objective truth involves the convergence of multiple observations and perspectives. Moreover, the anti-Semitic theories of Hume, Voltaire, and Kant show that philosophy has rarely, if ever, been insulated from politics.

The Ignorant Do Not Have a Right to an Audience

*We could take a big step forward by distinguishing
free speech from just access to the media.*

Bryan W. Van Norden

O N JUNE 17, THE POLITICAL COMMENTATOR ANN COULTER, appearing as a guest on Fox News, asserted that crying migrant children separated from their parents are "child actors." Does this groundless claim deserve as much airtime as, for example, a historically informed argument from Ta-Nehisi Coates that structural racism makes the American dream possible?

Jordan Peterson, a professor of psychology at the University of Toronto, has complained that men can't "control crazy women" because men "have absolutely no respect" for someone they cannot physically fight. Does this adolescent opinion deserve as much of an audience as the nuanced thoughts of Kate Manne, a professor of philosophy at Cornell University, about the role of "himpathy" in supporting misogyny?

We may feel certain that Coulter and Peterson are wrong, but some people feel the same way about Coates and Manne. And everyone once felt certain that the earth was the center of the solar system. Even if Coulter and Peterson are wrong, won't we have a deeper understanding of why racism and sexism are mistaken if we have to think for ourselves about their claims? And "who's to say" that there isn't some small fragment of truth in what they say?

If this specious line of thought seems at all plausible to you, it is because of the influence of *On Liberty*, published in 1859 by the English philosopher John Stuart Mill. Mill's argument for near-absolute freedom of speech is seductively simple. Any given opinion that someone expresses is either wholly true, partly true, or false.

To claim that an unpopular or offensive opinion cannot be true "is to assume our own infallibility." And if an offensive opinion is true, to limit its expression is clearly bad for society. If an opinion is partly true, we should listen to it, because "it is only by the collision of adverse opinions, that the remainder of the truth has any chance of being supplied." And even if an opinion is false, society will benefit by examining the reasons it is false. Unless a true view is challenged, we will hold it merely "in the manner of a prejudice, with little comprehension or feeling of its rational grounds."

The problem with Mill's argument is that he takes for granted a naïve conception of rationality that he inherited from Enlightenment thinkers like René Descartes. For such philosophers, there is one ahistorical rational method for discovering truth, and humans (properly educated) are approximately equal in their capacity for appreciating these truths. We know that "of all things, good sense is the most fairly distributed," Descartes assures us, because "even those who are the hardest to satisfy in every other respect never desire more of it than they already have."

Of course, Mill and Descartes disagreed fundamentally about what the one ahistorical rational method is—which is one of the reasons for doubting the Enlightenment dogma that there is such a method.

If you do have faith in a universal method of reasoning that everyone accepts, then the Millian defense of absolute free speech is sound. What harm is there in people hearing obvious falsehoods and specious argumentation if any sane and minimally educated person can see through them? The problem, though, is that humans are not rational in the way Mill assumes. I wish it were self-evident to everyone that we should not discriminate against people based on their sexual orientation, but the current vice president of the United

States does not agree. I wish everyone knew that it is irrational to deny the evidence that there was a mass shooting in Sandy Hook, but a syndicated radio talk show host can make a career out of arguing for the contrary.

Historically, Millian arguments have had some good practical effects. Mill followed Alexis de Tocqueville in identifying "the tyranny of the majority" as an ever-present danger in democracies. As an advocate of women's rights and an opponent of slavery, Mill knew that many people then regarded even the discussion of these issues as offensive. He hoped that by making freedom of speech a near-absolute right he could guarantee a hearing for opinions that were true but unpopular among most of his contemporaries.

However, our situation is very different from that of Mill. We are seeing the worsening of a trend that the twentieth century German American philosopher Herbert Marcuse warned of back in 1965: "In endlessly dragging debates over the media, the stupid opinion is treated with the same respect as the intelligent one, the misinformed may talk as long as the informed, and propaganda rides along with education, truth with falsehood." This form of "free speech," ironically, supports the tyranny of the majority.

The media are motivated primarily by getting the largest audience possible. This leads to a skewed conception about which controversial perspectives deserve airtime, and what "both sides" of an issue are. How often do you see controversial but well-informed intellectuals like Noam Chomsky and Martha Nussbaum on television? Meanwhile, the former child-star Kirk Cameron appears on television to explain that we should not believe in evolutionary theory unless biologists can produce a "crocoduck" as evidence. No wonder we are experiencing what Marcuse described as "the systematic moronization of children and adults alike by publicity and propaganda."

Marcuse was insightful in diagnosing the problems, but part of the solution he advocated was suppressing right-wing perspectives. I believe that this is immoral (in part because it would be impossible to do without the exercise of terror) and impractical (given that the internet was actually invented to provide an unblockable information network). Instead, I suggest that we could take a big step forward by distinguishing free speech from just access. Access to the general public, granted by institutions like television networks, newspapers, magazines, and university lectures, is a finite resource. Justice requires that, like any finite good, institutional access should be apportioned based on merit and on what benefits the community as a whole.

There is a clear line between censoring someone and refusing to provide them with institutional resources for disseminating their ideas. When Nathaniel Abraham was fired in 2004 from his position at Woods Hole Oceanographic Institute because he admitted to his employer that he did not believe in evolution, it was not a case of censorship of an unpopular opinion. Abraham thinks that he knows better than other scientists (and better than other Christians, like Pope Francis, who reminded the faithful that God is not "a magician, with a magic wand"). Abraham has every right to express his ignorant opinion to any audience that is credulous enough to listen. However, Abraham does not have a right to a share of the intellectual capital that comes from being associated with a prestigious scientific institution like Woods Hole.

Similarly, the top colleges and universities that invite Charles Murray to share his junk science defenses of innate racial differences in intelligence (including Columbia and New York University) are not promoting fair and balanced discourse. For these prestigious institutions to deny Murray an audience would be for them to exercise their fiduciary responsibility as the gatekeepers of rational discourse. We have actually seen a good illustration of what I mean by "just access" in ABC's courageous decision to cancel *Roseanne*, its highest-rated show. Starring on a television show is a privilege, not a right. Roseanne compared a black person to an ape. Allowing a show named after her to remain on the air would not be impartiality; it would be tacitly endorsing the racist fantasy that her views are part of reasonable mainstream debate.

Donald Trump, first as candidate and now as president, is such a significant news story that responsible journalists must report on him. But this does not mean that he should be allowed to set the terms of the debate. Research shows that repeatedly hearing assertions increases the likelihood of belief—even when the assertions are explicitly identified as false. Consequently, when journalists repeat Trump's repeated lies, they are actually increasing the probability that people will believe them.

Even when journalistic responsibility requires reporting Trump's views, this does not entail giving all of his spokespeople an audience. MSNBC's *Morning Joe* set a good precedent for just access by banning from the show Kellyanne Conway for casually spouting "alternative facts."

Marcuse also suggested, ominously, that we should not "renounce a priori violence against violence." Like most Americans, I spontaneously cheered when I saw the white nationalist Richard Spencer punched in the face during an interview. However, as I have noted elsewhere, Mahatma Gandhi and the Reverend Martin Luther King Jr. showed us that nonviolent protest is not only a moral demand (although it is that too); it is the highest strategic cunning. Violence plays into the hands of our opponents, who relish the opportunity to play at being martyrs. Consequently, while it was wrong for Middlebury College to invite Murray to speak, it was even more wrong for students to assault Murray and a professor escorting him across campus. (Ironically, the professor who was injured in this incident is a critic of Murray who gave a Millian defense of allowing him to speak on campus.)

What just access means in terms of positive policy is that institutions that are the gatekeepers to the public have a fiduciary responsibility to award access based on the merit of ideas and thinkers. To award space in a campus lecture hall to someone like Peterson who says that feminists "have an unconscious wish for brutal male domination," or to give time on a television news show to someone like Coulter who asserts that in an ideal world all Americans would convert to Christianity, or to interview a D-list actor like Jenny McCarthy about her view that actual scientists are wrong about the public health benefits of vaccines, is not to display admirable intellectual open-mindedness. It is to take a positive stand that these views are within the realm of defensible rational discourse, and that these people are worth taking seriously as thinkers.

Neither is true: These views are specious, and those who espouse them are, at best, ignorant, at worst, sophists. The invincibly ignorant and the intellectual huckster have every right to express their opinions, but their right to free speech is not the right to an audience.

JUNE 25, 2018

I Am a Dangerous Professor

*My inclusion on a watch list is intended
to shame me into silence.*

George Yancy

T HOSE FAMILIAR WITH GEORGE ORWELL'S *1984* WILL RECALL
that "newspeak was designed not to extend but to diminish the range
of thought." I recently felt the weight of this Orwellian ethos when
many of my students sent emails to inform me, and perhaps warn
me, that my name appears on the Professor Watchlist, a new website
created by a conservative youth group known as Turning Point USA.

I could sense the gravity in those email messages, a sense of relaying what is to come. The Professor Watchlist's mission, among other
things, is to sound an alarm about those of us within academia who
"advance leftist propaganda in the classroom." It names and includes
photographs of some two hundred professors.

The Watchlist appears to be consistent with a nostalgic desire "to
make America great again" and to expose and oppose those voices
in academia that are anti-Republican or express anti-Republican
values. For many black people, making America "great again" is
especially threatening, as it signals a return to a more explicit and
unapologetic racial dystopia. For us, dreaming of yesterday is not a
privilege, not a desire, but a nightmare.

The new "watchlist" is essentially a new species of McCarthyism,
especially in terms of its overtones of "disloyalty" to the American

republic. And it is reminiscent of Cointelpro, the secret FBI program that spied on, infiltrated and discredited American political organizations in the fifties and sixties. Its goal of "outing" professors for their views helps to create the appearance of something secretly subversive. It is a form of exposure designed to mark, shame, and silence.

So when I first confirmed my students' concerns, I was engulfed by a feeling of righteous indignation, even anger. The list maker would rather that we run in shame after having been called out. Yet I was reminded of the novel *The Bluest Eye* in which Toni Morrison wrote that anger was better than shame: "There is a sense of being in anger. A reality and presence. An awareness of worth." The anger I experienced was also—in the words the poet and theorist Audre Lorde used to describe the erotic—"a reminder of my capacity for feeling." It is that feeling that is disruptive of the Orwellian gestures embedded in the Professor Watchlist. Its devotees would rather I become numb, afraid and silent. However, it is the anger that I feel that functions as a saving grace, a place of being.

If we are not careful, a watchlist like this can have the impact of the philosopher Jeremy Bentham's panopticon—a theoretical prison designed to create a form of self-censorship among those imprisoned. The list is not simply designed to get others to spy on us, to out us, but to install forms of psychological self-policing to eliminate thoughts, pedagogical approaches, and theoretical orientations that it defines as subversive.

Honestly, being a black man, I had thought that I had been marked enough—as bestial, as criminal, as inferior. I have always known of the existence of that racialized scarlet letter. It marks me as I enter stores; the white security guard never fails to see it. It follows me around at predominantly white philosophy conferences; I am marked as "different" within that space not because I am different, but because the conference space is filled with whiteness. It follows me as white police officers pull me over for no other reason than because I'm black. As Frantz Fanon writes, "I am overdetermined from without."

But now I feel the multiple markings; I am now "un-American" because of my ideas, my desires and passion to undo injustice where I see it, my engagement in a form of pedagogy that can cause my students to become angry or resistant in their newfound awareness of the magnitude of suffering that exists in the world. Yet I reject this marking. I refuse to be philosophically and pedagogically adjusted.

To be "philosophically adjusted" is to belie what I see as one major aim of philosophy—to speak to the multiple ways in which we suffer, to be a voice through which suffering might speak and be heard, and to offer a gift to my students that will leave them maladjusted and profoundly unhappy with the world as it is. Bringing them to that state is what I call doing "high-stakes philosophy." It is a form of practicing philosophy that refuses to ignore the horrible realities of people who suffer and that rejects ideal theory, which functions to obfuscate such realities. It is a form of philosophizing that refuses to be seduced by what Friedrich Nietzsche called "conceptual mummies." Nietzsche notes that for many philosophers, "nothing actual has escaped from their hands alive."

In my courses, which the watchlist would like to flag as "un-American" and as "leftist propaganda," I refuse to entertain my students with mummified ideas and abstract forms of philosophical self-stimulation. What leaves their hands is always philosophically alive, vibrant and filled with urgency. I want them to engage in the process of freeing ideas, freeing their philosophical imaginations. I want them to lose sleep over the pain and suffering of so many lives that many of us deem disposable. I want them to become conceptually unhinged, to leave my classes discontented and maladjusted.

Bear in mind that it was in 1963 that the Reverend Dr. Martin Luther King Jr. raised his voice and said: "I say very honestly that I never intend to become adjusted to segregation and discrimination. I never intend to become adjusted to religious bigotry. I never intend to adjust myself to economic conditions that will take necessities from the many to give luxuries to the few. I never intend to adjust myself to the madness of militarism, to self-defeating effects of physical violence."

I also recall the words Plato attributed to Socrates during his trial: "As long as I draw breath and am able, I shall not cease to practice philosophy." By that Socrates meant that he would not cease to exhort Athenians to care more for justice than they did for wealth or reputation.

So, in my classrooms, I refuse to remain silent in the face of racism, its subtle and systemic structure. I refuse to remain silent in the face of patriarchal and sexist hegemony and the denigration of women's bodies, or about the ways in which women have internalized male assumptions of how they should look and what they should feel and desire.

I refuse to be silent about forms of militarism in which innocent civilians are murdered in the name of "democracy." I refuse to remain silent when it comes to acknowledging the existential and psychic dread and chaos experienced by those who are targets of xenophobia and homophobia.

I refuse to remain silent when it comes to transgender women and men who are beaten to death by those who refuse to create conditions of hospitality.

I refuse to remain silent in a world where children become targets of sexual violence, and where unarmed black bodies are shot dead by the state and its proxies, where those with disabilities are mocked and still rendered "monstrous," and where the earth suffers because some of us refuse to hear its suffering, where my ideas are marked as "un-American," and apparently "dangerous."

Well, if it is dangerous to teach my students to love their neighbors, to think and rethink constructively and ethically about who their neighbors are, and how they have been taught to see themselves as disconnected and neoliberal subjects, then, yes, I am dangerous, and what I teach is dangerous.

NOVEMBER 30, 2016

Beware of "Snakes," "Invaders," and Other Fighting Words

The power of rhetoric is the ability to convince others
they ought to do what you want them to do.

Jason Stanley and David Beaver

OVER THE PAST FEW YEARS, FAR-RIGHT NATIONALIST POLITI-cal leaders around the world have been using harsh rhetoric against minority groups, particularly immigrants. We know from history that acts of genocide, ethnic cleansing, and terrorism have been pre-ceded by periods in which political and social movements employed such rhetoric. In Nazi Germany, Jews were described as vermin, and Nazi propaganda outlets claimed that Jews spread diseases. The recent ethnic cleansing of the Rohingya people of Myanmar was pre-ceded by propaganda associating Rohingya men with rape.

In the United States, we had the "superpredator" theory. Violent-crime rates in the country started dropping in 1993 and continued dropping throughout the decade. And yet, in 1996, criminologists began spreading an unjustified panic about so-called superpreda-tors—"hardened, remorseless juveniles," according to the political scientist John Dilulio—that led to a wave of new state laws with harsh sentences for minors. Politicians' descriptions of young black men as "thugs" and "gang members" in the 1990s helped transform the United States into the country with the world's highest incarceration rate. Black Americans constitute forty percent of the incarcerated population while representing only thirteen percent of United States residents.

Power over an individual is the ability to change someone else's behavior or thoughts in accord with one's desires. One way to control someone's behavior is through force. A much better way to change others' behavior is by possessing the capacity to change their obligations. If you can convince someone that they ought to do what you want them to do, your power is genuine authority. But do words really have power to change our behavior?

The literature on marketing teaches us that rhetoric can have significant impact on attitudes. Here is one example: Asking people even purely hypothetical questions unconsciously shifts their subsequent preferences and behavior in often dramatic ways. In a 2001 study by the marketing professors Gavan Fitzsimons and Baba Shiv, subjects were told in advance they would be asked purely hypothetical questions. One group was asked, "If strong evidence emerges from scientific studies suggesting that cakes, pastries, etc. are not nearly as bad for your health as they have often been portrayed to be, and may have some major health benefits, what would happen to your consumption of these items?"

Subjects were told that the study "was about the effects of a change in environment on how consumers express opinions about products," and so were directed into another room and offered a choice between snacks placed on a cart between the rooms: chocolate cake or fruit salad. Another group, the control group, was not asked any hypothetical questions.

In the control group, 25.7 percent chose cake. In stark contrast, subjects who were merely presented with the hypothetical question, and no further elaboration, selected the cake 48 percent of the time. Merely urging subjects to "think carefully before you respond to the question" to prepare to justify their answer, later increased cake selection from 48 percent to 66 percent. And subjects were clearly unaware of having been manipulated by the hypothetical question, as without exception they denied that their preferences or their behavior were influenced by the hypothetical question in subsequent in-depth interviews. Every subject maintained that his or her choice was unaffected by being asked the hypothetical question.

The 2000 Republican presidential primaries pitted Governor George W. Bush against Senator John McCain. Before the South Carolina primary, Mr. Bush's campaign polled prospective Republican primary voters with a hypothetical question: "Would you be more likely or less likely to vote for John McCain if you knew he had fathered an illegitimate black child?" Mr. Bush subsequently won South Carolina.

This is a case in which it is the language, the way of phrasing something, that has power; in a hypothetical question, after all, no reason has been given to accept the hypothesis. Another striking example of language manipulation, from the social psychologist Christopher Bryan and colleagues: If we ask you, "How important is it to you to be a voter?" you're much more likely to vote than if we ask you, "How important is it to vote?" Hearing the first makes you reflect on your inherent characteristics regarding voting; the second merely questions your plans. Rhetoric has power; it affects attitudes, behavior, and perceived obligations.

Understanding the mechanisms that give hateful rhetoric its power illuminates the nature of its danger. One way that rhetoric changes perceived obligations is by the recommendation of certain practices. In her 2012 paper "Genocidal Language Games," the philosopher Lynne Tirrell describes how, for some years before the Rwandan genocide, the Hutu majority called their Tutsi neighbors "cockroaches" and "snakes." In Rwanda, snakes are public health threats. Ms. Tirrell writes, "In Rwanda, boys are proud when they are trusted to cut the heads off snakes." Calling a Tutsi a "snake" connected slaughtering Tutsis to the heroic practice of killing snakes.

Calling immigrants "invaders" has the effect of connecting practices one would employ against hostile intruders to immigrant groups. If one simultaneously advances the value system of nationalism, then the kind of practice one is recommending by using "invaders" to describe immigrants is violence. This rhetoric has force because it leads people to view violence against immigrants as obligatory. Denouncing "illegal aliens" in an Oval Office speech in March, President Trump said, "People hate the word 'invasion,' but that's what it is. It's an invasion of drugs and criminals and people." When the rhetorical power associated with describing immigrants as invaders is augmented with the authority of a presidency, it has an especially significant capacity to shift perceived obligations.

Rhetorical power may seem like a magical idea. The fact that the power of words is hard to take as seriously as other varieties of power, however, contributes to its significance as a social force. Rhetorical power changes our attitudes by manipulation. But manipulation is usually something hidden, whereas speech is out in the open. Its openness reinforces the normalcy of the practices it recommends.

MAY 16, 2019

Breaking My Own Silence

The confidence to speak for ourselves is a source of power.

Min Jin Lee

I T MAKES SENSE THAT I'M A WRITER, WHICH ALLOWS ME TO draft, hesitate, then rewrite many times before I say anything that I can live with for good.

In 1976, my mother, father, and two sisters and I immigrated to the United States. I was seven. We moved from Seoul to New York, and Dad enrolled my sisters and me at P.S. 102 in Elmhurst, Queens. None of us girls knew how to speak English.

Even back in Seoul, I was a quiet child who fidgeted and had attention issues. I found school and friendships difficult, and it got worse when I moved to a new country.

The first few weeks in America were tough. There was one other Korean girl in the class. Like me, she had small eyes. Unlike me, she knew English and had friends. She wanted me to stay away.

One day in class, I needed to go to the bathroom, and I didn't know what to do. The Korean girl grimaced when I approached her, but mercifully, she told me to raise my hand and say, "Bassroom."

I said this foreign word, and the kids laughed. The teacher handed me a well-worn, wooden block, which served as a hall pass. I rarely spoke in school again except for when I needed permission to go to the bathroom.

The years that followed were not very different. I did my work and looked forward to being with my sisters, who protected me. I learned to read English and made my way through shelves of borrowed books from the Elmhurst Public Library.

In our first year in America, my father ran a newspaper stand in the lobby of a dingy office building. Then later, my parents had a tiny wholesale jewelry store in Manhattan that sold costume jewelry to peddlers and gift shops. They worked six days a week.

At Junior High School 73 in Maspeth, New York, I had a wonderful teacher named Mr. Sosis, who taught law, and he selected me as a classroom monitor. He allowed his monitors to eat lunch in his classroom, and I don't know if he knew this, but he rescued me from the terror of the middle school lunchroom and from the reality that I did not know how to act around children my age.

I had other fine teachers there, and I started to talk a little more. I did production work for the school play, and when an actor dropped out, I was given her role because I'd already memorized all the lines. For my law class, I did a mock trial, and I was not awful.

I got into the Bronx High School of Science, where my older sister went, and I made up my mind that I had to learn how to talk well.

As a child immigrant, I had read straight through Lois Lenski, Maud Hart Lovelace, Beverly Cleary, Judy Blume, then through Dickens, Hemingway, Austen, Sinclair Lewis, and Dostoyevsky—books recommended by good-hearted librarians and teachers.

In Western books, heroes spoke well and could handle any social situation, not just through action, but also through argument. In Korea, a girl was virtuous if she sacrificed for her family or nation, but in the West, a girl was worthy if she had pluck and if she could speak up even when afraid. As a kid, I'd watched Koreans criticizing a man for being all talk and no work. In America, a man was considered stupid or weak if he couldn't stand up for himself.

Both things were true: I didn't want to talk, and I didn't want anyone to think I was stupid.

My freshman year, I joined the debate team. I could hardly manage group conversations with my peers, but I reasoned it was necessary to learn how to argue. Debate felt almost impossible. I was a terrible debater, but that was better than nothing. I did it for one year before quitting.

One day, I noticed a poster in the hall for summer classes at the Hotchkiss School, which offered electives that Bronx Science didn't have. I sent away for a catalog and found a class on public speaking. I asked my parents for the money so I could take this class, and they gave it to me even though it must have been a lot for them. At Hotchkiss, the teacher gave us assignments like tell a long joke, explain a piece of art, and persuade the listener to an unpopular position. I told a long joke and no one laughed. I was not very good, but I was starting to understand rhetoric. For the following summer, I mailed away for another brochure, this time for Phillips Exeter Academy, and I took another public speaking course.

When I went to Yale for college, I felt outclassed by my peers who had attended the private schools I had visited during the summers. They spoke with ease about music, art, and faraway places and wrote beautiful papers about books I had not read. Some knew Latin and Greek. I stumbled through my classes and ill-advised romantic relationships. I majored in history, and without a clear plan, I went to law school at Georgetown.

Not once did I consider being a litigator because that seemed like professional debating. I thought I'd be better suited as a corporate lawyer. I figured I should try to be financially better off than my parents who worked throughout the year without breaks in an underheated store, scrimping to pay their greedy landlord, who refused to kill the enormous rats that roamed in the basement.

After my first year at Georgetown, I went to the career services office because I needed to learn how to do a job interview. The career counselor, an older white woman, said to me in the gentlest way, "You need to boast about how great you are. You're an Asian girl, and when you boast, you're playing against the stereotype of the meek Oriental. Your interviewer will never think you're bragging. I don't give this advice to pushy white men."

She was telling me how the world might see me. I had to talk, and I had to build myself up, because others might see less than there was. Though I couldn't really do what she said, I never forgot her words.

When I sold my first novel I was no longer a lawyer. I was thirty-eight years old. In preparation for a small book tour, my publisher hired a media trainer to coach me for two hours. The trainer had written a book, so I read it. I learned that each event is about the audience. This idea helped because no matter how insecure I felt, I could forget myself and focus on everyone else.

I write novels, and now and then I give lectures. I come from many tribes—immigrant, introvert, working class, Korean, female, public school, Queens, Presbyterian. Growing up, I never knew that people like me could write books or talk in public. To this day, I worry that if I mess up, others like me might not be asked or allowed. This is how outsiders and newcomers feel. It is neither rational nor fair. I know.

I am fifty years old, and after more than four decades of living in the West, I realize that like writing, talking is painful because we expose our ideas for evaluation; however, like writing, talking is powerful because our ideas may, in fact, have value and require expression.

As a girl, I did not know this power, yet this is my power now.

MAY 20, 2019

V

Happiness and Its Discontents

Are you satisfied with your life? How are you feeling? Does the answer to either question tell us what we really want to know?

Daniel M. Haybron

I.

What does it mean to be happy?

The answer to this question once seemed obvious to me. To be happy is to be satisfied with your life. If you want to find out how happy someone is, you ask him a question like, "Taking all things together, how satisfied are you with your life as a whole?"

Over the past thirty years or so, as the field of happiness studies has emerged from social psychology, economics, and other disciplines, many researchers have had the same thought. Indeed this "life satisfaction" view of happiness lies behind most of the happiness studies you've read about. Happiness embodies your judgment about your life, and what matters for your happiness is something for you to decide.

This is an appealing view. But I have come to believe that it is probably wrong. Or at least, it can't do justice to our everyday concerns about happiness.

One of the most remarkable findings in this area of psychology, for instance, is just how many poor people say they are satisfied with their lives—very often a majority of them, even in harsh environments like the slums of Calcutta. In a recent study of poor Egyptians, researchers asked them to explain why they were satisfied, and their responses often took something like this form: "One day is good and the other one is bad; whoever accepts the least lives." This sounds like resignation, not happiness. Yet these Egyptians were, in terms of life satisfaction, happy.

The problem is that life satisfaction doesn't really mean what we tend to think it means. For you can reasonably be satisfied with your life even if you think your life is going badly for you, and even if you feel bad. To be satisfied is just to regard your life as going well enough—it is satisfactory. You might think even a hard slog through a joyless existence is good enough. It sure beats being dead, and maybe you feel you have no right to complain about what God, or fate, has given you.

Similarly, you might be satisfied with a hard life because you care about things besides avoiding misery. Perhaps you are a dissident in an autocratic state and suffering dearly for it, yet you are satisfied with your life because you believe in what you are doing. But are you happy? Probably not.

I do not mean to suggest that life satisfaction studies can't give us useful information about how people are doing. But I am suggesting that it is misleading to equate satisfaction with happiness, even if it is perfectly ordinary to talk that way at times.

So how else might we define happiness? There is another approach popular among researchers—one that focuses on feelings. If you feel good, and not bad, you're happy. Feeling good may not be all that matters, but it certainly sounds like a more suitable candidate for happiness than a judgment that your life is good enough. Evidently, those Egyptians do not feel good, and that has a lot to do with why it seems unnatural to say that they are happy.

But what exactly is this "feeling good"? The standard view is this: Happiness is pleasure, and unhappiness is pain, or suffering. Philosophers call this view "hedonism" about happiness. If we think of happiness as pleasure, we can see why people value happiness so

highly: Who really prefers misery to enjoyment? Lots of philosophers, like Epicurus, Jeremy Bentham, and John Stuart Mill, have
thought that pleasure and suffering are all that ultimately matters.
Hedonism about happiness has an obvious appeal. It is natural to
think of happiness as a matter of feelings, and what else could this
mean but having pleasant feelings?

But I have come to believe that this approach is also probably
wrong. When you look at the way researchers study this kind of
happiness, you'll notice something peculiar: Their questionnaires
almost always ask about emotions and mood states, and rarely ask
directly about pleasure, pain, or suffering. In fact, you might have
thought that if happiness researchers were really interested in pleasure and pain, among their queries would be questions about pain
("Do you suffer from chronic pain?" and so on). Such pains make a
tremendous difference in how pleasant our lives are, yet happiness
surveys rarely ask about them.

Why not? Because, I would venture, these researchers aren't
really thinking of happiness as pleasure, as they take themselves to
be doing. Rather, they're tacitly thinking of happiness in another,
more interesting way.

II.

I would suggest that when we talk about happiness, we are actually
referring, much of the time, to a complex emotional phenomenon.
Call it emotional well-being. Happiness as emotional well-being
concerns your emotions and moods, more broadly your emotional
condition as a whole. To be happy is to inhabit a favorable emotional state.

On this view, we can think of happiness, loosely, as the opposite
of anxiety and depression. Being in good spirits, quick to laugh and
slow to anger, at peace and untroubled, confident and comfortable
in your own skin, engaged, energetic, and full of life. To measure
happiness, we might use extended versions of existing question-

naires for anxiety and depression from the mental-health literature. Already, such diagnostics often ask questions about positive states like laughter and cheerfulness, or your ability to enjoy things.

The emotional state theory of happiness has significant advantages over the hedonistic view. Consider, for starters, that we don't normally think of pain as an emotion or mood. It seems more natural, for example, to think of back pain as something that causes unhappiness, not as unhappiness itself. A more important point is that we are fundamentally emotional beings. Who we are is in great part defined by our emotional natures, by what ways of living make us happy. Yes, we have animal needs for food, shelter, clothing and the like. But we also have needs as persons, and happiness concerns the fulfillment of those needs.

What sorts of needs are we talking about? Among the most important sources of happiness are: a sense of security; a good outlook; autonomy or control over our lives; good relationships; and skilled and meaningful activity. If you are unhappy, there's a good chance that it's for want of something on this list.

Unhappiness is not just a brute physical or animal response to your life. It is you, as a person, responding to your life as being somehow deficient. Unhappiness, like happiness, says something about your personality. Whereas back pain does not: It is just a sensation, something that happens to you. Accordingly, Buddhists and Stoics do not counsel us not to feel pain; their training aims, instead, at not letting pain and other irritants get to us.

Our language also marks the difference: You merely feel a pain, but you are depressed, anxious, melancholy, or whatever. Similarly, you might have a depressive or anxious or cheerful personality. But we never talk of someone having a "painful" or "pleasureful" personality.

Note also how we don't worry about taking medicine for pain the way we often do about taking "happiness" pills like antidepressants. We worry that by artificially changing our mood we risk not being "us." But no one feels inauthentic because he took ibuprofen to relieve his back pain.

III.

While the emotional-state view of happiness might seem commonsensical, it was barely discussed twenty years ago, and the differences between this approach and hedonism still are not widely acknowledged in the scientific literature on happiness. Why has it been so neglected?

The reason, I suspect, is that we tend to take a superficial view of the emotional realm. In the popular imagination, the rich tapestry of our emotional lives is reduced to nearly a point—or rather, two points for eyes, a "U" for a mouth and a circle enclosing them. But there is much more to happiness than the smiley-face emotion of feeling happy.

Our very language is deficient, and so we sometimes reach for other expressions that better convey the depth and richness of happiness: happiness as a matter of the psyche, spirit, or soul. Researchers rightly tend to avoid such metaphors in their scholarly work, which demands clearly defined terminology. But even those of us who do not believe in immaterial souls often find this sort of language usefully evocative, as our technical vocabulary can be pretty feeble in expressing the complexities of human experience. At times, then, I have found it useful to employ terms like "psychic affirmation" or, for the truly thriving, "psychic flourishing." We are not just talking about "being in a good mood."

So there is something specially human about happiness, something that speaks to our natures and needs as persons. And meeting our needs as persons—our spiritual needs, one might say—seems to have a special importance.

Why should these needs, these aspects of ourselves, be so important? There is a long history of philosophical thought, with roots stretching back at least to Plato and Aristotle in Greece, and the Vedas in India, that conceives of human flourishing in terms of the fulfillment of the self. Human well-being, on this sort of view, means living in accordance with your nature, with who you are. On this way of thinking, we might regard happiness as a central part of self-fulfillment.

Furthermore, our emotional conditions may provide the single best indicator of how, in general, our lives are going. They don't simply track the moment-to-moment flow of events. If you are generally depressed, anxious, or stressed, you will probably not find an answer to your problems by scrutinizing the day's events one by one. It may be wiser, instead, to consider whether the way you are living really makes sense. Often, the signals of the emotional self can set us on the path to better ways of living—and a happiness worthy of the name.

APRIL 13, 2014

The Problem of "Living in the Present"

Taken literally, it's just bad advice. But
philosophy can redeem this self-help cliché.

Kieran Setiya

T HESE DAYS, MANY OF US WOULD RATHER NOT BE LIVING IN
the present, a time of persistent crisis, political uncertainty, and
fear. Not that the future looks better, shadowed by technological
advances that threaten widespread unemployment and by the perils
of catastrophic climate change. No wonder some are tempted by the
comforts of a nostalgically imagined past.

Inspiring as it seems on first inspection, the self-help slogan
"live in the present" slips rapidly out of focus. What would living
in the present mean? To live each day as if it were your last, without a thought for the future, is simply bad advice, a recipe for recklessness. The idea that one can make oneself invulnerable to what
happens by detaching from everything but the present is an irresponsible delusion.

Despite this, there is an interpretation of living in the present,
inspired by Aristotle, that can help us to confront the present crisis
and the perpetual crises of struggle and failure in life. There is an
insight in the self-help slogan that philosophy can redeem.

The beginning of wisdom here is to think about what we are doing.
We engage in all sorts of activities: reading an article in the newspaper, reflecting on life, attending a protest, preparing a report, lis-

tening to music, driving home, making dinner, spending time with family or friends. Though all these activities take time, there is a crucial difference in how they relate to the present moment.

Using terminology from linguistics, we can distinguish activities of two fundamental kinds. Telic activities—from "telos," the Greek word for purpose—aim at terminal states, by which they are completed. Think of reading this article or driving home from work. Once you arrive at the goal, you are finished: The point of the activity has been achieved. You can do it again, but only by way of repetition. Not all activities are like this. Some activities are atelic: They do not aim at terminal states. However much you reflect on life or spend time with your family, you cannot complete these activities. Though you will eventually stop doing them, they do not aim at a point at which there is no more of them to do.

Aristotle made the same distinction, contrasting two kinds of action or praxis: kinesis and energeia. Kinetic actions are telic and therefore incomplete. As Aristotle wrote in his *Metaphysics*: "If you are learning, you have not at the same time learned." When you care about telic activities, projects such as writing a report, getting married, or making dinner, satisfaction is always in the future or the past. It is yet to be achieved and then it is gone. Telic activities are exhaustible; in fact, they aim at their own exhaustion. They thus exhibit a peculiar self-subversion. In valuing and so pursuing these activities, we aim to complete them, and so to expel them from our lives.

Atelic activities, by contrast, do not by nature come to an end and are not incomplete. In defining such activities, we could emphasize their inexhaustibility, the fact that they do not aim at terminal states. But we could also emphasize what Aristotle does: They are fully realized in the present. "At the same time, one is seeing and has seen, is understanding and has understood, is thinking and has thought." There is nothing you need to do in order to perform an atelic activity except what you are doing right now. If what you care about is reflecting on your life or spending time with family or friends, and that is what you are doing, you are not on the way to achieving your end: You are already there.

What would it mean, then, to live in the present, and what do we gain by doing it?

To live in the present is to appreciate the value of atelic activities like going for a walk, listening to music, spending time with family or friends. To engage in these activities is not to extinguish them from your life. Their value is not mortgaged to the future or consigned to the past, but realized here and now. It is to care about the process of what you are doing, not just projects you aim to complete.

The advice is easy to misread. To live in the present is not to deny the value of telic activities, of making a difference in the world. That would be a terrible mistake. Nor can we avoid engaging in such activities. But if projects are all we value, our lives become self-subversive, aimed at extinguishing the sources of meaning within them. To live in the present is to refuse the excessive investment in projects, in achievements and results, that sees no inherent value in the process.

To live in the present is not to avoid hard work or strife. Alongside the projects that occupy you in your profession, or in your political life, the telic activities that matter to you, is the atelic process of protesting injustice or doing your job. To value the process is not to flee from work or political engagement. That is why living in the present is not an abdication of ethical responsibility or a recipe for detachment.

To focus on the telic is to focus, all too often, on the distance and precariousness of our goals: to provide health care for all, to halt the resurgence of white supremacy, to limit global warming to two degrees. Consequences matter, as do activities that aim at them. The point of political protest is to change the world. And yet the process matters too. The value of standing up for what is right, of going on strike or marching in the streets, is not exhausted by the value of its effects. It is not wholly erased by failure. We protest in part because we see no better way to make a difference, in part to make the present count for something, whatever the future holds.

SEPTEMBER 11, 2017

The Happiest Man I've Ever Met

What is it like to be a monk? I spent three days in Greece's revered "Holy Mountain" monastery to find out.

Simon Critchley

ATHENS—IN THE NEARLY THREE MONTHS I SPENT IN THIS fascinating city, I met plenty of rather high-spirited people. But it was not until I visited the monastery at Mount Athos in northeastern Greece that I encountered the happiest person I've ever met.

I'd traveled from Athens with my friend Anthony Papadimitriou, who had very kindly arranged the trip to the Holy Mountain, as it is called here. We share an abiding interest in monasticism, although neither of us is fully monkish in our habits.

We had been on the road since very early in the morning when we left the port of Ouranoupoli, the City of Heaven, in a small white and orange boat with a captain named Yorgos. The only way of approaching the long rocky peninsula of Mount Athos is by water, and it requires a special permit. I had it in my hand, stamped with the seal of the Holy Mountain, with four handwritten signatures. Anthony told me that the monks had checked out my credentials and noticed somewhere online that I was described as an atheist, which is not exactly true. But apparently that was better than being Catholic. On my permit, it read "Anglican," which made me smile.

To understand contemporary Greece, and what connects it (and fails to connect it) with antiquity, you have to consider the Orthodox

Church, which still has considerable ideological power over Greek life, for good or ill. Christianity is the connecting tissue in the body of Hellenism, for it is here that religious traditions and, most important, the Greek language were preserved. Mount Athos, the spiritual epicenter of Orthodoxy, is an entirely self-governing monastic republic, with its own parliament. Legally part of the European Union, Athos is an autonomous state with its own jurisdiction, like the Vatican, although the monks would not appreciate that analogy: The Orthodox Church has still not forgotten the Catholic sacking of Constantinople during the Fourth Crusade in 1204.

The monastic tradition on Athos goes back to the ninth century AD, although the continuous Christian presence is much older. Athonite legend has it that the Virgin Mary traveled to Athos with Saint John the Evangelist and liked it so much that she asked Jesus for it to be her garden. Happy to oblige his mother, Jesus agreed. And since that time, the only female creatures allowed on Mount Athos are cats, who are abundant in the monasteries. The mother of God was apparently the only woman to be allowed in her garden.

We were going to spend three days and two nights in the monastery of Simonopetra, or Simon's Rock, founded in the thirteenth century. The fact that my name is Simon rather amused some of the monks to whom we were introduced.

Simon was a hermit who lived in a cave, a five-minute walk downhill from the monastery. Inside a tiny chapel, a few rocky steps took me up to Simon's cell. It was tiny, cold, and bare. He'd had a vision in a dream of a monastery on the rock in front of his cave and then had the audacity to build it. As one monk said to me, this is the world's first skyscraper. An improbable-looking ten-story building is somehow wrapped around a huge rock with the church at its center. It has been burned down on several occasions, but then rebuilt with great effort. Inside is a bewildering array of staircases, a labyrinth that leads down to the monastic library (there is no elevator).

Today there are sixty-five monks in Simonopetra, mostly Greek; we met French monks and new arrivals from Lebanon and Syria, as well. On Athos itself, there are around two thousand monks, mostly living communally in monasteries, but there are others living in very small communities called sketes, each with three or four monks. Some thirty or so live alone as hermits. I was intrigued.

It was late on our first day there that I met Father Ioanikios. He was a very handsome and physically fit man, probably in his late sixties, with the clearest eyes, olive skin, and a long white beard. He briefly introduced himself to me and said: "Tomorrow you and I will go around Mount Athos. We will see the chestnut forests. You're from New York?" I said yes. "Ah, New York. I used to live there." And with that he shook my hand warmly and disappeared.

The next day, after getting up at four a.m. for church (which lasted for three and a half hours) and a modest lunch around ten-thirty, Father Ioanikios took me for a ride in his Toyota four-wheel drive (pretty much the only model of car I saw on Athos) and told me his story.

He was Greek, but also an American citizen, and had studied mechanical engineering at New York University in the late 1970s before getting a master's degree in economics. He used to live on Thirty-Second Street between Madison and Fifth Avenues. He got a really good job with Mobil Oil in New Jersey and used to commute back and forth. "Back in those days, I used to drink a little and go out," he said. "You know that club that people went to . . ."

"Studio 54?"

"Yeah, I used to go there all the time."

"Did you ever meet Donald Trump?" I asked.

"Trump? That guy? Forget it!"

He was set: living in Manhattan in his mid-twenties, single, and with a good job, and clearly having a ball. But he told me that in his bedroom, he had a small icon of the Virgin Mary, to which he always used to pray before going to sleep, even when he'd had a little too much to drink. Then, in the early 1980s on a trip to see his family in Greece, he visited Simonopetra because his grandmother's brother had been a monk there. He visited the cell of an old and very sick monk who knew his relative well. The monk couldn't speak and could barely move. But Father Ioanikios told me that this wordless encounter stayed with him when he went back to New York. "The old monk had such life in his eyes. Such love," he said. He couldn't get the experience out of his mind.

He returned to the monastery on a second visit and then decided to give up his New York life and become a novice. That was in 1984. He became a monk in 1987 and has been there ever since. When one becomes a monk, there is a second baptism. So Christos became Ioanikios, after a Byzantine saint from the ninth century.

Ioanikios is not an intellectual or a theologian. He is a practical man, in charge of some of the business operations of the monastery, building projects, road repairs, and buying gasoline for the cars, a procedure he explained in some detail while driving. He talked fondly of a JCB mechanical digger that he had bought and about what kind of concrete was required to fix the road after snow and storm damage during the winter. But he is a person of deep and convincing faith. He told me that he frequently prays in the forest because he feels comfortable there. "It's the Garden of Eden," he said. Looking out of the window at the forest, mountains, and blue sea, I sighed in agreement.

When I asked him more closely about his decision to become a monk, he simply said that when he came to Simonopetra he felt called by God and had responded to the call. Not all are called by God and not all who are called respond. But he did.

The first source of disorientation in the monastery is caused by time. Athos follows the old clock of Byzantium, where the day begins at sunset. According to our vulgar, modern time, matins begin at four a.m. and last for three and a half hours. But monks get up much earlier, around one a.m. The father told me that some of the younger, keener monks often get up at eleven p.m. to extend their devotions. There is at least one hour of Bible reading, one hour reciting the Jesus Prayer or the Prayer of the Holy Mountain ("Lord Jesus Christ, have mercy on me," repeated rhythmically over and over again), and one hour of prostrations. The amount of prostrations depends on your age and physical ability, but there should be at least 120; some monks perform up to 2,000. This rather put my Pilates classes into perspective.

After the morning service, monks can nap for two hours. This is followed by a short service of thirty minutes, then lunch, the main meal of the day, at ten-thirty. Meals in the refectory are taken in silence and one can eat only when the head of Simonopetra, Abbot Eliseus, rings the gold bell he has beside him. When a second bell rings, it is permitted to drink either water or a sole glass of sweet red wine from their own vineyards. Mealtimes are fast, about twenty minutes or so, and you have to eat quickly. Throughout the meal, a monk reads aloud from a text; during my stay there was something about Julian the Apostate. Then the bell rings, everyone stops eating and they file silently out.

After lunch, there are four hours of work, which often end with another hour's prayer. After vespers, which lasts for ninety minutes or so, there is a modest dinner, also eaten in silence, and then two hours of free time before sleep, reading or talking with brothers. The whole cycle repeats, with its ritual variations, every day, with no vacations, no breaks, and no Netflix bingeing, until your death. The cassock that the monks wear under their robes has a skull and crossbones at the bottom to remind them of mortality. As the monk Evagrius of Pontus said, the monk should always act as if he were going to die tomorrow.

What struck me during my stay at Simonopetra was the constant emphasis on monasticism as a living experience, as an unbroken continuity of tradition. In the case of Athos, that means at least a thousand years. In this place, every day without exception, the rituals have been followed. Monasticism is not a theology; it is a way of life. Abbot Eliseus told me that there are two foundational monuments in Greece: the Acropolis and Athos. "But one is dead and the other is living," he continued. "One is an idea, the other is a living experience."

Toward the end of our little road trip, Ioanikios looked at me with his clear eyes and spoke quietly: "It is hard being a monk. Man was made for something else, to make a family. And we have chosen a different life. This is only possible when the energy comes from God."

"What is that energy?" I asked.

"It is hard to describe, but you could call it grace." He paused. "When you experience it, it's like you have no enemies. You know what Jesus says in the Sermon on the Mount, 'Love your enemies,' and you think that's a crazy thing to say. How can that be? But when you feel that energy, you feel supported, and it feels like the most obvious thing. You feel only joy and happiness." He repeated the word "joy" three times. "For me, this life is hard, but I feel that joy sometimes when I'm singing."

Let me tell you about the singing. For, truth to tell, I heard Ioanikios sing at vespers before I spoke to him and had remarked on the strength of his voice. I watched him lead his fellow monks for at least eleven hours during my three days in Simonopetra. On either side of the church, there were groups of about ten monks clustered around a lectern chanting, in a constant movement of call-and-response, from one side of the church to the other. With subtle harmonies and occasional deliberate discord, the voices flowed back and forth, complementing and counterpointing each other. Nothing was staccato. Everything was movement and overlapping lines. I have listened to recordings of Byzantine chants, indeed by the choir of Simonopetra itself, but they don't even begin to get close to how it felt in the church.

During the service, some of the monks' faces that I had seen and talked to were transformed and elevated by song. It is impossible to describe what it was like to be there, but the sheer duration and intensity of the services had a powerful effect. I was in church for about thirteen hours during my stay, including a five-hour vigil for the Virgin Mary on Saturday evening. There is an absolute seriousness to the monks during the services, but none of the usual clerical piousness. There was much coming and going during the service and quite a lot of talking among the monks, which seemed like the most natural thing in the world. Once I had got to know Ioanikios, he came over to me a few times during a break in the singing to ask how I was doing or tell me what was happening. ("This is the dance of the angels," he said, as the golden candelabra swung back and forth overhead. "All of heaven is dancing.") Then he would go back to his chanting.

Everything felt loose and completely relaxed. Here were participants in a ritual who knew exactly what they were doing. There was no judgment, hushing, or disapproval of an outsider like me. The scent of myrrh hung heavy in the air from the swinging incense burner that functioned like a percussive accompaniment for the chanting. It was heady. And Anthony and I were only a few feet away from some of the monks as they sang. There were no sermons and no attempts at contemporary relevance. One had the impression that everything was song.

I have never seen a church seem so alive. At certain points in the Divine Liturgy on Sunday, it felt as if the whole church were glowing gold inside as the sunlight began to come up in the morning light. The physical discipline of the monks was hard to comprehend. They stood for hours on end without moving, twitching, fidgeting, or biting their nails. No one drank anything or looked thirsty. At other times, all the candles were extinguished and there was a low droning chant in darkness. Toward the end of the five-hour vigil, around midnight, I noticed one or two stifled yawns, but nothing much. By this time, the monks had been awake for at least twenty-four hours. At the end, Ioanikios looked as fresh as a daisy. I was shattered, hungry, and thirsty (I hadn't eaten since the previous morning and had only a few hours' sleep). But I felt such a lightness.

Before we left Athos, Ioanikios showed me his office in a ramshackle building at their tiny port of Daphne. He has dreams of transforming it into a spiritual center for pilgrims. He gave Anthony and me small, hand-carved wooden crosses and placed them around our necks. He also gave me some prayer beads and told me to repeat the Jesus Prayer. He said it would help dispel any worries I had in my mind: "Lord Jesus Christ, have mercy on me." He repeated the words. "Keep saying the words, and your cares will disappear."

"Don't forget us," he added in leaving. "And come back every year. You are our friend now."

I took off the cross after getting back to Athens late in the evening. I was back in the profane world. And back with my stupid philosophical distance and intellectual arrogance. But my time in Athos was the closest to religious experience that I have ever come. I wonder if I will ever get so close again.

APRIL 3, 2019

A Philosopher on Brain Rest

A mild traumatic brain injury forced me to question
where the "I" in my identity truly lies.

Megan Craig

I N JANUARY 2018, WHILE I WAS CHAPERONING MY DAUGHTER'S
school ice-skating trip, a sturdy third-grade boy lost control and
came sliding into me from behind on his knees. He was just the
right-size projectile to undercut my skates and send me flying backward on the ice, where I landed on my head. Thus began my ignoble
descent into becoming a philosopher on brain rest.

When I got up I was not my usual self. Feeling disoriented and
unable to remember my own address or the date, I was taken to the
emergency room, where I was examined and told I had whiplash and
a concussion. I found the medical terminology for my condition,
"mild traumatic brain injury," confusing and humorous. It was confusing because I'm not sure how anything can be both mild and traumatic at once. It was humorous for the same reason.

The elegant doctor who saw me assured me that I would stop weeping for no apparent reason very soon, and that all I had to do to hasten my recovery was commit to "brain rest"—essentially no reading,
writing, screens, or strenuous thinking until I could sustain focus
without a headache or other symptoms of injury. The predicted time
for recovery was three months. It was at this point that she noncha-

lantly asked me what I do for a living. "I'm a philosopher," I replied. And I'm pretty sure we both thought that was hilarious.

Being a philosopher on brain rest is like being a point guard on hand rest. The major asset for your profession is suddenly not working reliably. I have often lamented the fact that my job as a philosophy professor confines me so much to a chair and a desk. I've wished that philosophy entailed more calisthenics, rugged walking, running outdoors. With my concussion, I found myself suddenly freed from the professional obligation to think. I even had a doctor's note.

Sadly I was in no condition to run, and absent a clear head, walks and daily movement were more difficult and less enjoyable than before. Brain rest itself was elusive, as I seemed incapable of arresting thought. There was no protective cone to keep the wounded place from being itched, no cast to keep the brain still. Perhaps predictably, then, brain rest inspired more thinking about the very nature of thinking.

One of the most disconcerting aspects of the immediate days and weeks following my concussion was the degree to which I found my self missing. I felt bad in so many ways, but the profound gap in my identity had to do with my lack of basic recall and the challenge of carrying out previously simple mental steps. I was moving about with no apparent difficulty, but my head felt like an anvil and my mind felt like slosh. It made me question anew the degree to which I am my brain.

Ever since Descartes insisted upon the separation of mind and body, philosophers (especially feminist philosophers) have tried to impress upon us the necessity of attending to the body. Descartes thought the mind was the divine and indubitable aspect of his own being, that single point of certainty on which to rebuild his crumbling world: "I think therefore I am."

Descartes's theory of mind recalls Plato's theory of the soul as the immortal, essential, and indestructible part of the human being, the body a temporary prison or shell. Mind-body dualism is often ridiculed in contemporary philosophy as a legacy of stubbornly metaphysical, patriarchal, and Western thinking. Dualism oversimplifies both mind and body and leads to a devaluation of the complexly embodied, psychosomatic ways in which beings inhabit the world. No serious philosopher or neuroscientist today thinks that mind and body can be neatly parsed into two distinctly separate objects or systems.

But a concussion has a way of changing one's sense of the balance between mind and body. It's one thing to be hit in the arm or the gut. It is an entirely different thing to be hit in the brain. Dualism is terrifying in part because the separation of mind and body implies the possibility of radical skepticism, brains in vats and other *Matrix*-like specters of disembodied life. Such modern-day versions of Cartesian skepticism ask us to imagine the entirety of the external world as an illusion or the intricate deception of an evil genius. What if we are just brains hooked up to an elaborate virtual reality?

It has been a long time since I took any of these images seriously. They seem easy to dismiss when one's health is good. When things are otherwise, dualism takes on a new dimension. The injury to my brain highlighted the degree to which my identity and my powers of identification have a specific seat in my brain. The concussed condition was an intimation of how terrifying dementia and other brain disorders must feel—the loss of a thread that has so far tied together one's life and tethered it to the lives of those one loves. In my case, the loss was temporary, but it was the first time that I have ever felt so distinctly the efforts of thinking, the brain as a muscle, and the depression that accompanies the feeling of having lost oneself.

Unable to rest my brain, I thought about NFL players and the progressive loss of identity and mental aptitude common to those who experience consecutive concussions and CTE (chronic traumatic encephalopathy). I thought about memory and the loneliness of being unable to recall names and places that are the road marks of a communal life. I thought about the elderly woman with Alzheimer's disease whom I helped to care for when I was in high school. I would arrive each morning at her door only to have her greet me with the same wide-eyed gaze and question: "Who are you?"

Though my condition was transient, it highlighted the degree to which the brain serves as an anchoring center of control. For months, uncertainty accompanied my every move. In the immediate days after the concussion I mustered all of my energy to read my daughter several pages of a Daniel Tiger storybook (against my doctor's orders), only to fail to reach the end. I felt embarrassed and demoralized. I recalled my grandfather, late in his life, describing his own failing mind as a library where all of the books were shelved too high to reach.

Over time my symptoms subsided. I started to read again—not only Daniel Tiger, but Henri Bergson and Toni Morrison—and eventually I began to write. But how does one know when the brain has healed? I'm not sure where my identity resides or even what my identity is or consists of, but I am sure that my brain is crucial in the continuing orchestration of a world that feels inhabitable and a life that feels livable. Brain and body cannot be separated, and yet there are episodes when they fall out of phase, the one wounded and diminished while the other projects a picture of health and ability.

Philosophers tend to make terrible patients. I'm fairly sure that by thinking so much about brain rest I have prolonged my own recovery time. I also suspect that my thinking about my own brain and the specter of dualism is symptomatic of the injury itself. Perhaps when I recover fully, dualism will seem as ridiculous as it once did, receding into the background along with the muscular effort required to read. But I suspect I am altered.

On the bright side, philosophy has been relentless in my life as a thinking person, and a little brain rest was long overdue. Without a doubt, philosophers have to remember and insist upon the dignity and complexity of embodied life. We have to attend to our bodies, to care for our fitness and psychosomatic health. But we also need to care for our brains. I wish someone had told me that long ago, and that my education into philosophy included more commonsense doses of rest for the primary organ of my thinking. It would not have saved me from the injury, but it would have better primed me for the work of recovery.

Now, more than a year since my injury, I am grateful for neural plasticity. I am alert to a difference between the everyday phenomenon of forgetting and blanks that intercede like dark matter in a brain laced with gaps. I remember the date, my address, my children's names, with intention, holding them in place like precious stones in a ring. And I know that rest and recovery are as complex and meandering as thought itself.

JUNE 25, 2019

It's a Terrible Day in the Neighborhood, and That's Okay

Fred Rogers's belief that we should validate emotions,
not suppress them, is wisdom for all ages.

Mariana Alessandri

O N THE FIFTY-FIRST ANNIVERSARY OF THE FIRST TAPING OF
the classic children's show *Mister Rogers' Neighborhood*, Google published an animated "doodle" commemorating him. It depicts Mister Rogers walking through the neighborhood interacting with a variety of people, including a small child with his head hung low. Rogers fashions a paper airplane for the boy, which instantly cheers him up. People commonly caricature Mister Rogers this way—a gentle man intent on making everyone happy—but that may be more a reflection of America's discomfort with dark emotions than of the man himself. The last thing Fred Rogers would do for a sad boy is distract him from his sadness.

Anyone who watched *Mister Rogers' Neighborhood* would know that the host considered all feelings natural—including the dark ones—and believed they don't need fixing. Many of the children raised watching the program are now parents, and a new appreciation for Fred Rogers has blossomed thanks to the 2018 documentary *Won't You Be My Neighbor* and the new feature film *A Beautiful Day in the Neighborhood*, starring Tom Hanks as Fred Rogers. Today, Rogers's philosophy of difficult emotions stands a chance of being heard and heeded.

As a child I preferred the frenetic energy of *Sesame Street* to the dull pace of *Mister Rogers' Neighborhood*, but that changed when I had children of my own and wondered how to raise them thoughtfully without depriving them of television. In my classroom, I regularly teach Neil Postman's book *Amusing Ourselves to Death*, in which he raises a critical eyebrow at attempts to put serious discourse on television, and especially at shows like *Sesame Street* that label themselves as "educational." Mr. Postman implies that slow and even boring shows stand a better chance of teaching children important lessons than fast-paced, loud ones.

My memory of that boring show made me curious to see whether it offered anything valuable. It did, and so began my awakening to Rogers. With (and sometimes without) my children, I've watched hundreds of episodes of *Mister Rogers' Neighborhood* over the last seven years. I've read everything written by and about Fred Rogers and seen all the footage I could find. I saw the 2018 documentary once in the theater and then went back again to take notes. I went into *A Beautiful Day in the Neighborhood* skeptical, since it's much easier to get him wrong than right—and it's critical that we get Fred Rogers right—but I kept my fingers crossed. The film's emotional depth surprised me; in direct contrast to the Google doodle, it thoroughly conveys his philosophy of difficult emotions. It makes sense: the cast and crew had to study Rogers to make the film, which is what's required to accurately represent the man, to animate the caricature.

Despite his sweet pastor's demeanor, Rogers was tuned in to our souls' darkest feelings. He had an uncommon appreciation for anger, fear, stress, sadness, disappointment, and loneliness. He respected the range of emotions and encouraged children to accept all their feelings as natural. This conviction came early: As the only child to proper New England parents (until his sister was adopted when he was eleven years old), Rogers was discouraged from acknowledging sadness. This, along with his childhood experience of getting bullied for being overweight, made "Fat Freddy," as he was called, acutely aware that too often, and usually inadvertently, adults silence children instead of showing them how to deal with troubling feelings.

Rogers believed that variations of the "sticks-and-stones" adages intended to get kids to "shake it off" are stifling; they abandon children to their pain instead of teaching them how to process it. In contrast, Rogers encouraged children to face their dark feelings. Not a trained philosopher, Rogers would likely attribute his education in the emotional landscape of children to the psychologist Margaret McFarland at the University of Pittsburgh, with whom he collaborated for thirty years. And yet there is a foundation for the sort of philosophy of feelings that Fred Rogers practiced that can be traced back more than two thousand years to ancient Greece.

In the *Nicomachean Ethics*, Aristotle described our souls as being made up of feelings, predispositions, and active conditions. Our predispositions name our go-to emotions, those we feel most often in response to certain stimuli. Some people are prone to sadness, others to anger, and the occasional few to genuine cheerfulness. Our feelings, like twigs, catch a spark every time we brush past life's embers, but ignite only when they get stoked by our predispositions. Two individuals responding differently to the same event—getting fired, for example—Aristotle would attribute to their differing predispositions.

I am predisposed to anger, which played better in New York where I grew up than in South Texas where I now live, and yet it humanizes me to students. Those who share my predisposition relax their shoulders when I tell them they're not alone, and they laugh when I say I'm jealous of people who cry easily instead of wanting to punch somebody.

Feelings and predispositions matter, for Aristotle, but more for the sake of self-knowledge than self-improvement. It's helpful to know which feelings I am predisposed to as well as what I am feeling at any given moment, but these two categories are much harder to budge than the third. Aristotle described active conditions as "how we bear ourselves" in the face of our feelings. As a believer in right action, Aristotle suggested that we train our souls to react beautifully to an ugly mess. He was implying that we not fret too much over our troublesome feelings or stubborn predispositions.

Indeed, Aristotle would discourage us from shaming ourselves over feeling sad when we "should" feel happy. He rejected "shoulds" altogether when it came to feelings, since he believed them to be natural and, without accompanying wrong action, harmless. All feelings, for Aristotle, are potentially useful in that they provide an opportunity to practice behaving well. Feelings alone can't jeopardize virtue, he believed, but actions can and often do. Mister Rogers agreed: "Everyone has lots of ways of feeling. And all of those feelings are fine. It's what we do with our feelings that matter in this life."

Rogers believed that all children (and adults) get sad, mad, lonely, anxious, and frustrated—and he used television to model what to do with these difficult and often strong emotions. He wanted to counter the harmful message kids typically receive, some version of the ever-unhelpful, "You shouldn't feel that way."

In one episode, when he couldn't get a flashlight to work, Mister Rogers expressed frustration in front of the camera: He admitted feeling disappointed at the fact that the trick that he had wanted to show his viewers didn't work. In doing so, he validated his disappointment and showed his audience that talking about it helps. One of Rogers's core beliefs was "what's mentionable is manageable," and he considered it an urgent lesson for kids to learn to name their pain. Rogers believed that if children were encouraged to talk about feelings instead of being shamed for them, they could get to work finding appropriate outlets. One of Rogers's recurrent lessons was on anger. Inspired by a child who asked him a question about anger, he wrote a song about it:

> *What do you do with the mad that you feel*
> *When you feel so mad you could bite?*

This song was Rogers's way of teaching kids how to be angry, instead of how not to be angry. The first step is for the child to recognize their anger as well as their temptation to bite, hit, kick. The second step the song suggests is to find appropriate outlets for that anger: punching a bag, pounding some dough, rounding up friends for a game of tag.

Playing the piano as a child, Rogers wrote, taught him to express the whole range of his feelings. He recounts banging on the low keys when he got mad, and I imagine him exploring the minor keys when he felt sad. In multiple episodes, Rogers showed viewers how to tell their feelings through the piano. When he had famous musicians like Yo-Yo Ma or Wynton Marsalis on the program, Rogers would ask whether they played differently when they were sad or angry. They always reported that yes, they did, and that playing their darker emotions helped.

Mister Rogers' Neighborhood was purportedly a show for children. But I think Rogers also meant it for adults. We'd be better off if we'd stop negating children's dark emotions with stifling commands like, "Don't cry," "Calm down," "Be quiet." If we are convinced by Rogers's and Aristotle's claim that feelings are not wrong and that "what's mentionable is manageable," we should begin mentioning our own sad, lonely, and disappointed feelings. In doing so, we would show children—and our grown-up selves—how to appropriately manage them.

NOVEMBER 28, 2019

Nietzsche Made Me Do It

What was I trying to escape by making this dangerous trek?

John Kaag

———————————

FOR A VERY LONG TIME, I CONSIDERED MYSELF A HYPERBOREAN. In Greek mythology, the Hyperboreans are giants who live "beyond the north wind," high in unforgiving mountains, perfectly happy in seemingly unbearable conditions. The Greek poet Pindar said that "neither disease nor bitter old age is mixed in their sacred blood."

I thought of this as I found myself perched on a granite escarpment at eight thousand feet, overlooking the Val Fex on the border between Switzerland and Italy. A Hyperborean wouldn't be scared senseless up here, or worried about getting down. But I was. At the mouth of the valley lay Sils Maria, the onetime summer home of Friedrich Nietzsche. I had spent days trailing the spirit of the philosopher through these mountains. Clearly, he was responsible for this imminent disaster.

I looked down at my beat-up New Balance 990s. "Don't you want to wear something a little more 'technical' on your hike?" my wife had suggested before I'd left. No, of course not. Running shoes would be fine. I would be fine. I was a Hyperborean.

This conviction was surely what led me off the trail four hours earlier, when I went scrambling up the monochromatic green slab that the Swiss call a foothill. Eventually the greenery gave way to granite and led me to the overlook, which was undoubtedly going to be the most beautiful place I'd ever see. I dug around in my day pack and found the précis to Nietzsche's mature philosophy, *The Antichrist*, published in 1898, years after he supposedly went insane.

My family was down there somewhere—maybe five miles away. It felt much farther. This is an advantage of hiking, of walking away more generally: It can create what Nietzsche called the "pathos of distance." This sense of being higher, of looking down, gives rise to the "craving for ever new widening of distances within the soul itself . . . the development of ever higher, rarer, more remote, further stretching, more comprehensive states." This impulse to strive was at the core of Nietzsche's perfectionism. "We are Hyperboreans," he wrote, "we know well enough how remote our place is."

I pitched a small stone over the edge. One. Two. Three. Almost four seconds before it exploded on the rocks below. About three hundred feet. I often tell my six-year-old daughter that having courage doesn't mean that you aren't scared. It means that you do it anyway. What I don't tell her is that courage can eventually get you stuck.

I've hiked the backcountry many times in my thirty-eight years, but I'm still not any good at it. I'm frightened every time I set out. When I was nineteen, on my first trip to the Val Fex, I tried to walk from Splügen to St. Moritz, over the Piz Platta at thirteen thousand feet, in running shoes not unlike these. I thought that if I went in a straight line, skipping all those seemingly unnecessary switchbacks, it would be only twenty-five miles. I could do this. I left the trail in the early morning. Fifteen hours later, I stopped; I had traveled roughly eight miles, quite far enough to be terrified. The next morning, after a frost-nipped night on an unmarked ledge, I turned back. I got lost and it took me two more days to return to Splügen.

The backcountry is an ideal place for Nietzsche's hard questions: What am I trying to escape by making this dangerous trek? What is the point of this risk? Am I really, precisely, this alone? I've found that the disruptions of going "off-road" brings them into sharper focus. Am I going to die? It's only a matter of time. The valley below me lit up with late afternoon light. It began to rain.

I know there are far more treacherous and heroic climbs: Everest, Mont Blanc, Kilimanjaro. I also know there are writers who spend not hours but months or years on the trail of self-realization: Cheryl Strayed's *Wild* and Peter Matthiessen's *The Snow Leopard* spring from such journeys. When I first read these books, I thought the point of arduous walking was to find yourself. And in a certain sense, it is. As Nietzsche says in *The Gay Science*: "What does your conscience say? You should become who you are!"

What I discovered in the mountains, however, is that becoming who you are usually involves getting over who you think you are. In fact the "who"—the idea of oneself—is probably an impediment to growth and honesty. Matthiessen never finds his snow leopard. Nietzsche wants us to be wanderers, "though not as a traveler to a final destination: for this destination does not exist." This is not to say that we can't set goals—quite the opposite. "Set for yourself goals, high and noble goals," a young Nietzsche instructs, "and perish in pursuit of them." If you arrive at a final destination, it's a sign that you've set your sights too low, that your goal isn't high or noble enough. Hyperborea is not a place to come to rest.

I slipped *The Antichrist* back in my bag. I was now entertaining the most forbidden question. One that modern life intentionally obstructs: "Am I dying right now?" Probably. Before I got up, I felt the tread on the bottom of my sneakers. The heels were worn down to the cushion. If I tried to walk down the way I'd come, I'd slip and fall hard. Going on all fours would be safer—I'd crabwalk until I reached softer ground. This was not the way to negotiate the craggy heights of Hyperborea, but I had long since stopped caring.

I'd slither home if I had to, but I wanted to get home. I guess that was it. Maybe that was the whole point of this idiotic trip: I finally knew what I wanted, what I loved. Even the most objectionable parts of life seemed preferable, even lovely, compared with this. Nietzsche's most famous character, Zarathustra, shuttles up and down a mountain, between solitude at the top and companionship at the bottom. Maybe this is what he discovers on the way. Or maybe, in the mountains, he simply confronts what he essentially is—an animal that can be reduced to crawling on all fours, that is in the rapid process of dying.

My daughter often worries about death. I usually give her a version of the story told by the Stoic Epictetus: "I have to die. If it is now, well, then, I die now; if later, then now I will take my lunch, since the hour for lunch has arrived—and dying I will tend to later." So let's eat our lunch and not worry. She thinks that this "Epic Tedious" character is basically right. But after my day on a slippery mountain, I'm not so sure. Maybe the time to die is right now. Maybe that is what I am doing in the process of living. And maybe lunch will taste so much better if I realize that, if I eat it like my last supper.

I got back in one piece. Slightly scraped, but no worse for wear. The next morning, I didn't hurry through breakfast. And I did not make a mad dash for the mountains.

SEPTEMBER 22, 2018

A Revolution in Happiness

The founding fathers weren't talking about personal wellness.

Adriana Cavarero

EVERYBODY WANTS TO BE HAPPY. THIS CLAIM GOES AS FAR back as Socrates, if not further, and in the more than two thousand years since he made it, it has acquired the rare status of something like a universal truth.

Today, evidence of its truth is all around us, in the booming self-help industry, the culture of mood-altering pharmaceutical drugs, and even in higher education. A 2018 *New York Times* article reported that more than a thousand students enrolled in a course at Yale called Psychology and the Good Life aimed at teaching students to lead happier, more satisfying lives. In 2014, an enormous online Science of Happiness course debuted at the University of California, Berkeley. It continues to thrive.

Books, articles, and podcasts dedicated to happiness—especially on how to be happy—abound. Explicitly addressed to individuals rather than groups, they focus on personal happiness, to be enjoyed in the private sphere. Let each and every one be happy!

The topic of what Hannah Arendt called "public happiness" is, by contrast, largely ignored by those who think and write about contemporary culture. Apparently, politics and happiness don't go together anymore. Collective happiness—as Socrates intended it, as a shared political experience—is largely out of the picture.

But I ask this question: Could we be happy together, not simply as the sum of individual happiness but because the very experience of being and acting together makes us happy? Arendt's answer is yes, and she has in mind a historical event that gave birth to the United States: the American Revolution.

Arendt's speculation on the issue is complex. Her main thesis is that the experience of public freedom, discovered by the ancient Greeks but then forgotten by a civilization that came to understand power as domination, had to wait until the eighteenth century and the American Revolution to resurface. Arendt claimed that the founding fathers were compelled to speak of public happiness precisely because they were experiencing public freedom—an experience of acting in concert that makes happiness, as she points out, "not an inner realm into which men escape at will from the pressure of the world," but something inherent in the "public space or marketplace which antiquity had known as the area where freedom appears and becomes visible to all."

This leaves a crucial trace, according to Arendt, in the famous "'pursuit of happiness' which the Declaration of Independence asserted to be one of the inalienable human rights."

Arendt makes it clear, however, that the revolutionary spirit connected with the rediscovery of public happiness goes far beyond the American Revolution. That spirit becomes instead a precious legacy of the modern era, a sort of template for the exercise and pursuit of political freedom that Arendt witnessed and wrote about during her lifetime—in the participatory politics of the Polish Marxist revolutionary Rosa Luxemburg; in the rise of workers' councils; in the Hungarian Revolution, the Prague Spring, and other movements. Arendt argued that the experience of public happiness can be found wherever people participate in the opening of a political space where freedom appears as a worldly reality.

Understanding Arendt's view should allow us to recognize the revolutionary spirit in current movements and political action—examples of radical democracy, which continually seek to extend the reach of freedom and equality in society. These could include the

Women's March in January 2017, when millions of women gathered in Washington and hundreds of cities around the world, in energetic and joyful demonstrations of political resistance; the March for Our Lives in 2018 in Florida and elsewhere, where young people from diverse backgrounds gathered to use their right of free speech to protest gun violence; and in the many movements resisting the authoritarian, exclusionary rhetoric and policies spreading throughout Europe and the United States.

In a recently discovered lecture Arendt composed in the 1960s, included in the collection *Thinking Without a Banister,* she wrote that, for those involved in the American Revolution, the "experience of being free coincided, or rather was intimately interwoven, with beginning something new . . . and obviously, this mysterious human gift, the ability to start something new, has something to do with the fact that every one of us came into the world as a newcomer through birth. In other words, we can begin something because we are beginnings and hence beginners." Because birth "is the ontological condition sine qua non of all politics," Arendt claims, "the meaning of revolution is the actualization of one of the greatest and most elementary human potentialities, the unequaled experience of being free to make a new beginning."

Public happiness is something that happens when we, in public, create something new. Yet we know too well that public happiness is not permanent and definite. In spite of this fragility, acting together gives a tangible experience of happiness unlike any that we can enjoy in private. Public happiness is discovered whenever and wherever people perform for the sake of freedom—and so taste the "birth" of their action.

At the time Thomas Jefferson and John Adams were experiencing public happiness in revolutionary America, Jeremy Bentham, a philosopher in England, was elaborating his famous axiom that "the greatest happiness of the greatest number" is the measure of right and wrong that should guide governments. The idea has been adopted by various utilitarian and liberal thinkers who conceive of happiness as social well-being—the sum of individuals who achieve health, wealth, and security—that the state is called on to produce, increase, and protect.

Today, with too few exceptions, our politicians seem to be fixated on defining and regulating the amount of well-being individual people are supposed to desire. We need to rethink the almost obsessive concern with individual happiness that pervades our culture. As Americans celebrate the revolution that gave birth to their nation, we should turn toward rediscovering the joyful emotions of birth through collective action.

Yes, let us be happy—but publicly, politically, together.

JULY 2, 2019

VI

DOES LIFE HAVE MEANING?

What We Believe About Beliefs

What you think you know is probably
wrong—and that's putting it nicely.

Errol Morris

E VERYBODY HAS HIS OWN CREATION MYTH. HERE'S MINE.
God, in his infinite wisdom, gave man self-deception, figuring that
if he could effectively deceive himself, he would have an easier time
deceiving others.

Years ago I read an anecdote about the nineteenth century utopian community of Zoar. It was mentioned in passing in a book about
forensic psychiatry. And try as I might, I haven't been able to source it
since. The story concerns the last living inhabitant of Zoar, a woman
who on her deathbed said, "Think of all those religions. They can't
all be right. But they can all be wrong."

For me, her words emphasized the insidious nature of belief.
That we can believe whatever we want to believe. And often do. But
in all likelihood, what we believe is wrong. Maybe not just wrong.
Even stupid.

So, here's what I believe. I believe that to believe anything is to
throw yourself down a bottomless pit of error. And the nastiest snake
oil salesman of all is oneself.

Imagine you're in a dark alley. Not Plato's cave—no, no. I have little or no interest in imagining myself in Plato's cave and, anyway, if
Plato is to be believed, we're all in his cave. No, I'm imagining some-

thing quite different. A dark alley where I'm suddenly accosted by a grubby-looking fellow who puts his face a little too close to mine and says, "What's the big idea?"

How should I respond? Let me take a stab at it—although I hesitate to use the word "stab" when talking about an encounter with a grubby-looking fellow in a dark alley. Clearly, he's challenging me. He thinks I'm in possession of some preposterous, ponderous, and possibly pretentious idea. Here are a few examples. Perhaps I could say that there's no such thing as justice, or that truth is inevitably relative, or that foot pain is worse than an earache. Or maybe that all matter is particles, or waves, or, if I'm really trying to be clever, I could say it's both. I could quote the NBC show *ALF* and turn the question back on him: "Why is it called cargo when it comes by ship, and a shipment when it comes by car?"

I'm so glad I didn't go to an Ivy League school. The greasy-looking fellow—did I first say grubby? Okay, he's grubby and greasy—would probably stab me to death.

So what am I supposed to say to this guy? I could say, "There are no really big ideas. Or, if there are, I don't have any." Such an argument might prove ineffective and possibly inflammatory. He could point out that not answering the question is unacceptable.

Hidden in the question "What's the big idea?" is, "What's your big idea?" What's your preposterous assumption, your ridiculous belief that you wish to lay claim to as being a powerful life-changing notion?

We often encounter big ideas in an unpleasant context: someone explaining (mansplaining, womansplaining, it makes no difference) some mystery of the universe to us. The solution to Fermat's last theorem, the precession of the perihelion of Mercury, the origin of species . . . We've all been introduced to popularizers of such ideas offering to help us make sense of them. But what's the point if we're not really capable of understanding these things for ourselves?

I interviewed the mathematician Benoît Mandelbrot in 2010, just before he died. I so much wanted him to tell me the story of his discovery of fractal geometry, which is, arguably, a big idea. But he didn't want to go there. He said that the big idea for him wasn't fractals. He talked about his work on financial markets, a precursor to his work on order amid chaos. But for Mandelbrot, the big idea was that he could have big ideas. Maybe the big idea is that there are such things.

I don't know whether Mandelbrot believed that fractals were a big idea. It's hard to believe otherwise. Perhaps others had to convince him. But he finally said something very, very powerful to me that I will never forget. It was about moments of insight and understanding. He told me they're like heavy curtains that are suddenly drawn up to reveal something profound about the universe.

Maybe the big idea is discovering something that no one had imagined before. Maybe the big idea is something that illuminates the cosmos. Language gives us the ability to lie. But it also gives us the ability to seek the truth. Could the really big idea be the juxtaposition of a sentence with the world around it?

I don't know. I just keep hoping that greasy, grubby-looking fellow in the alley isn't going to kill me.

MAY 28, 2021

The Good-Enough Life

The desire for greatness can be an obstacle to our own potential.

Avram Alpert

IDEALS OF GREATNESS CUT ACROSS THE AMERICAN POLITICAL spectrum. Supporters of Lyndon Johnson's "Great Society" and believers in Ronald Reagan and Donald Trump's "Make America Great Again," for instance, may find themselves at odds, but their differences lie in the vision of what constitutes greatness, not whether greatness itself is a worthy goal. In both cases—and in most any iteration of America's idea of itself—it is.

The desire for greatness also unites the diverse philosophical camps of Western ethics. Aristotle called for practicing the highest virtue. Kant believed in an ethical rule so stringent not even he thought it was achievable by mortals. Bentham's utilitarianism is about maximizing happiness. Marx sought the great world for all. Modern-day libertarians will stop at nothing to increase personal freedom and profit. These differences surely matter, but while the definition of greatness changes, greatness itself is sought by each in his own way.

Swimming against the tide of greatness is a counter-history of ethics embodied by schools of thought as diverse as Buddhism, Romanticism, and psychoanalysis. It is by borrowing from D. W. Winnicott, an important figure in the development of psychoanalysis, that we get perhaps the best name for this other ethics: "the good-enough life." In his book *Playing and Reality*, Winnicott wrote about what he called "the good-enough mother." This mother is good enough not in the sense that she is adequate or average, but that she manages a difficult task: initiating the infant into a world in which he or she will feel both cared for and ready to deal with life's endless frustrations. To fully become good enough is to grow up into a world that is itself good enough, that is as full of care and love as it is suffering and frustration.

From Buddhism and Romanticism we can get a fuller picture of what such a good-enough world could be like. Buddhism offers a criticism of the caste system and the idea that some people have to live lives of servitude in order to ensure the greatness of others. It posits instead the idea of the "middle path," a life that is neither excessively materialistic nor too ascetic. And some Buddhist thinkers, such as the sixth century Persian-Chinese monk Jizang, even insist that this middle life, this good-enough life, is the birthright of not only all humans, but also all of nature as well. In this radical vision of the good-enough life, our task is not to make the perfect human society, but rather a good-enough world in which each of us has sufficient (but never too many) resources to handle our encounters with the inevitable sufferings of a world full of chance and complexity.

The Romantic poets and philosophers extend this vision of good-enoughness to embrace what they would call "the ordinary" or "the everyday." This does not refer to the everyday annoyances or anxieties we experience, but the fact that within what is most ordinary, most basic, and most familiar, we might find a delight unimaginable if we find meaning only in greatness. The antiheroic sentiment is well expressed by George Eliot at the end of her novel *Middlemarch*: "that things are not so ill with you and me as they might have been, is half owing to the number who lived faithfully a hidden life, and rest in unvisited tombs." And its legacy is attested to in the poem "Famous" by Naomi Shihab Nye: "I want to be famous to shuffling men . . . sticky children in grocery lines."

Being good enough is not easy. It takes a tremendous amount of work to smile purely while waiting, exhausted, in a grocery line. Or to be good enough to loved ones to both support them and allow them to experience frustration. And it remains to be seen if we as a society can establish a good-enough relation to one another, where individuals and nations do not strive for their unique greatness, but rather work together to create the conditions of decency necessary for all.

Achieving this will also require us to develop a good-enough relation to our natural world, one in which we recognize both the abundance and the limitations of the planet we share with infinite other life-forms, each seeking its own path toward good-enoughness. If we do manage any of these things, it will not be because we have achieved greatness, but because we have recognized that none of them are achievable until greatness itself is forgotten.

FEBRUARY 20, 2019

Is a Life Without Struggle Worth Living?

A nineteenth century philosopher's nervous breakdown can
teach us something about finding peace in a world in crisis.

Adam Etinson

I N THE AUTUMN OF 1826, THE ENGLISH PHILOSOPHER JOHN STU-
art Mill suffered a nervous breakdown—a "crisis" in his "mental history," as he called it.

Since the age of fifteen, Mill had been caught firmly under the
intellectual spell of his father's close friend Jeremy Bentham. Bentham was a proponent of the principle of utility—the idea that all
human action should aim to promote the greatest happiness of the
greatest number. And Mill devoted much of his youthful energies to
the advancement of this principle: by founding the Utilitarian Society (a fringe group of fewer than ten members), publishing articles
in popular reviews, and editing Bentham's laborious manuscripts.

Utilitarianism, Mill thought, called for various social reforms:
improvements in gender relations, working wages, the greater protection of free speech, and a substantial broadening of the British
electorate (including women's suffrage).

There was much work to be done, but Mill was accustomed to
hard work. As a child, his father placed him on a highly regimented
homeschooling regime. Between the ages of eight and twelve, he
read all of Herodotus, Homer, Xenophon, six Platonic dialogues (in
Greek), Virgil and Ovid (in Latin), and kept on reading with increas-

ing intensity, as well as learning physics, chemistry, astronomy, and mathematics, while tutoring his younger sisters. Holidays were not permitted, "lest the habit of work should be broken, and a taste for idleness acquired."

Not surprisingly, one of the more commonly accepted explanations of Mill's breakdown at the age of twenty is that it was caused by cumulative mental exhaustion. But Mill himself understood it differently. In his autobiography, he wrote:

> I was in a dull state of nerves, such as everybody is occasionally liable to . . . In this frame of mind it occurred to me to put the question directly to myself, 'Suppose that all your objects in life were realized; that all the changes in institutions and opinions which you are looking forward to, could be completely effected at this very instant: would this be a great joy and happiness to you?' And an irrepressible self-consciousness distinctly answered, 'No!' At this my heart sank within me: the whole foundation on which my life was constructed fell down.

In the wake of this episode, Mill slipped into a six-month-long depression.

There is something comical about Mill's self-implosion; it's as if he had spent years looking forward to a sailing trip only to suddenly realize, upon embarkation, that he hated boats.

It is also strangely relatable. We have all lost faith in a deeply held project at one time or another. And, politically, we are in an age of upheaval; faith in old ideals seems to be dying out, creating a vacuum. Perhaps we can learn something about ourselves, and our political moment, by peering into Mill's own crisis of faith.

Why on earth wouldn't Mill want to achieve his life goals?

It wasn't because he thought he had the wrong goals. Mill never did abandon utilitarianism, though he later modified Bentham's doctrine in subtle ways. Instead, Mill tells us that his crisis was born in a concern about whether happiness is really possible in the perfect world he sought to achieve—a world without struggle:

The question was, whether, if the reformers of society and govern-
ment could succeed in their objects, and every person in the com-
munity were free and in a state of physical comfort, the pleasures
of life, being no longer kept up by struggle and privation, would
cease to be pleasures.

Mill is not at all clear about his line of thought here. But we can speculate. One possibility is that he is worried that, if we ever were to achieve an ideal social world, we would quickly take it for granted, or become "spoiled." It's a familiar tale: the child that always gets what he or she wants ends up forever unsatisfied and always wanting more (psychologists call this the hedonic treadmill). And perhaps Mill thought the same is true for adults—that facing a degree of "struggle and privation" in life is essential to happiness, because it provides us with a vivid reminder of how lucky we are when we have it good.

Or was Mill concerned that, in a perfect world, with nothing more to strive for, we might simply grow bored? As the nineteenth century German philosopher Arthur Schopenhauer once upliftingly put it, "Life swings back and forth like a pendulum between pain and boredom." When we are not consumed by the desire to achieve something (food, shelter, companionship, wealth, career, status, social reform, etc.), we are tortured by boredom.

Schopenhauer's vision of life is sensationally pessimistic— indeed, entertainingly so. But there is some evidence that Mill was in a Schopenhaueristic mood in 1826 (though he almost certainly hadn't yet read him). Mill writes that, during his crisis, he was "seriously tormented by the thought of the exhaustibility of musical combinations"—an anxiety he says was highly characteristic of "the general tone" of his mind at the time.

"The octave consists only of five tones and two semitones," he explains. By the laws of mathematics, there is only a finite number of possible tonal combinations. What will happen to music (and, indeed, composers) when there are no more combinations to be dis- covered? And what will life be like when the work of social reform is done? What will consume us then? How will we escape boredom? These are suffocating thoughts.

Somehow new music continues to be written. And, realistically, the work of improving human life and social conditions will never be "done." Still, it is easy to sympathize with Mill's anxiety. Some part of us prefers to struggle or quest after an ideal, rather than attain it. Retirement seems to function in this way for many people: as an orienting goal but a disorienting reality.

Also, there is something disconcertingly alien about a "perfect" world. It is part of the human condition, as that condition is normally understood, that there is some gap between how the world is and how we think it ought to be, what we have and what we want, who we are and who we would like to be. We try to narrow this gap. But its ongoing presence is part of life as we know it. And within certain limits, we even embrace it.

In movies and literature, for instance, our favorite protagonists tend to be flawed or troubled in some way. In *Edward Scissorhands*, it is the monster and the disenchanted teenager that we root for, not the creepily perfect suburbanites. And in music, many prefer the "human"—that is, soulful but imperfect—composition or performance over its technically flawless counterpart. In its early forms, at least, rock music certainly cultivated this kind of ethos.

Did Mill, who admits to being something of a "reasoning machine" throughout his teenage years, suddenly grow weary of mechanistic perfection? Perhaps he was disturbed by the imagined inhumanity of a world without struggle or privation—by the possibility that it might lack the romantic charms of human failure and frailty.

It took Mill two years to find a way out of his crisis. It was only after he began reading, not philosophy, but the poetry of William Wordsworth, that he was fully convinced he had emerged.

What was it about Wordsworth's romantic poetry—intensely emotional (often melancholy), solitary, autobiographical, and infused with bucolic English imagery—that had such a profound healing effect on Mill? He explains:

What made Wordsworth's poems a medicine for my state of mind, was that they expressed, not mere outward beauty, but states of feeling, and of thought coloured by feeling, under the excitement of beauty . . . In them I seemed to draw from a source of inward joy, of sympathetic and imaginative pleasure, which could be shared in by all human beings . . . From them I seemed to learn what would be the perennial sources of happiness, when all the greater evils of life shall have been removed . . . I needed to be made to feel that there was real, permanent happiness in tranquil contemplation.

Mill was searching for a reliable source of joy, one that could survive the unbearable goodness of the world he sought to achieve. He was looking for a happiness that could stave off incursions of dissatisfaction or boredom once the ultimate battle is won, and (at last!) tranquility reigns. The answer, he discovered through reading Wordsworth, is to take refuge in a capacity to be moved by beauty—a capacity to take joy in the quiet contemplation of delicate thoughts, sights, sounds, and feelings, not just titanic struggles.

This discovery is convenient for a philosopher. Mill was trained, from a very young age, to think: to be a quiet contemplator. So, it's no surprise that he was desperate to make sure he could still take joy in his allotted craft, once the hard labor of social reform was done. But, as Mill says, imaginative pleasures are available to "all human beings," not just poets and philosophers.

I hope, and suspect, that Mill is right about this: that we all have the ability to find some durable joy in quietude, normalcy, and contemplation. In our personal lives, and in our political lives too, it would be nice if we could escape Schopenhauer's pendulum: to simply enjoy where we are, at times; to find some peace in the cessation of motion.

If we can do that, then a perfect world might not be so bad after all.

OCTOBER 2, 2017

Waking Up to the Gift of "Aliveness"

My friend and teacher Hubert Dreyfus,
left me a message about life's purpose I am still learning from.

Sean D. Kelly

A FEW WEEKS AGO, I FOUND A SURPRISING LINE IN MY LEC-ture notes. I don't know how long it had been there or how it got in. I don't remember having written it or even having seen it before. It said, "The goal of life, for Pascal, is not happiness, peace, or fulfillment, but aliveness." I believe the line may have been written by my teacher and friend, the philosopher Hubert Dreyfus. Bert died in April at the age of eighty-seven.

It is strange, on the face of it at least, to think that Bert may be speaking to me from the grave. It is stranger still, perhaps, that from that less-than-ideal vantage point he could be telling me about a possible goal of life. But if you knew how my lecture notes work, it might not seem so peculiar.

You see, I've been teaching the seventeenth century French philosopher Blaise Pascal, and the Existentialist tradition he prefigured, since Bert introduced me to them almost thirty years ago. The lecture notes I use started out as notes I took as a student in his courses. Over the years they grew and matured, not only in response to what I learned from my students but also, and especially, in response to many continuing conversations with Bert. The strands of influence in those notes are so many and so various that they have long grown obscure. It is sometimes a surprise, even to me, to discover what they contain.

Surprises like these are wonderful, but sometimes perplexing too. What could it mean, after all, that the goal of life is aliveness? It sounds almost banal, or even tautological. But perhaps, after a bit of thought, it resonates.

Think of the way that life really can become lifeless. You know what it's like: rise, commute, work, lunch, work some more, maybe have a beer or go to the gym, watch TV. For a while the routine is nurturing and stabilizing; it is comfortable in its predictability. But soon the days seem to stretch out in an infinite line behind and before you. And eventually you are withering away inside them. They are not just devoid of meaning but ruthless in their insistence that they are that way. The life you are living announces it is no longer alive.

There are at least two natural, but equally flawed, responses to this announcement: constantly seek out newness or look for a stable, deeper meaning to your existing routine. In the eighteenth century, these responses were centered in Italy and Germany, respectively. Their descendants persevere today.

The Italian—Casanova was the paradigm—decides that what is missing from his life is spontaneity: He has died within his routine because it kills all his natural desires. To become alive again, he commits himself passionately to following his desires, take him where they may. He takes on many lovers—thrilling, consuming affairs!—but eventually he leaves each one for the next; he lives in the moment without a care for his past commitments or his future possibilities. His life moves from one raw excitement to another. Eventually, however, he becomes isolated, inconstant, and unmoored. He hurts those around him. He becomes incapable of genuine connection with anyone and unsure of who he really is. He despairs.

The German takes a different approach. Shall we call him Kant? He decides that what is missing is a reason for his routine. He seeks it out. He tells himself a story, one that delivers a meaningful justification of his daily life. And then he enters into the routine once again, determined this time to live in the knowledge that no matter how deadening it becomes, it is justified and therefore must be pursued. It is his duty to do so. But even though he knows the why of what he is doing, he cannot escape the feeling that he is not living by doing it. The monotony reestablishes itself. He cannot escape the ruthless assertion of its insignificance. He despairs.

We see what these responses are aiming for—the aliveness they hope to achieve—by seeing how they ultimately fall short of their goal. To be alive is to have the passion of Casanova without its isolation, inconstancy, and despair, or the resolute certainty of Kant, without its monotony and insignificance. Indeed, perhaps the best we can hope for is to point to the phenomenon in its absence: Aliveness is whatever is lacking when the monotony of the routine forces itself to the fore. But can we say something positive about what aliveness is?

A complete definition of the phenomenon is no doubt beyond our grasp. But there are two distinctive features of its elusiveness that I believe we can identify. The first is that every apparent source of aliveness disappears upon the inspection of it—the ground of aliveness recedes from view. Consider a simple example: the love you feel gazing at your lover's face. When you are in love, you are alive; the whole world vibrates with significance. It is natural to want to hold on to that aliveness, to make it last forever, to find its source. And where else could it be but in your lover's face? So you look. But beware! Look too closely and something falls apart.

For the greater the love that face evokes, the more transcendent your experience of that person, the less it seems possible that a face, a physical face, could actually be its ground. The phenomenon is filled with the deepest mystery, like the man who is God or the brain that is mind. After all, how could this fleshy, corporeal thing, of skin and veins and muscles and fat, how could this mere physical stuff and substance give rise to the ecstasy and transport of love? Of course it does! But the more you look at what a human face is, the less it seems capable of doing what it does. The object of love, as an object of love, dissolves in looking at it. The ground of aliveness withdraws from view.

The second feature is equally enigmatic. When you really feel alive, your past, your present, and your future somehow make sense together as the unity they have always promised to be. I sometimes feel truly alive, for instance, when I am teaching my students. When it is going well, when we are connected and engaged and the classroom is buzzing, it is not just that we are sharing a special moment together. For me, that moment has the special character that it does because it fulfills the promise implicit in moments like those from my own childhood and youth. It is the validation of what came before just as it is the preparation for what comes after. When you see in your students the sense that what is happening now will stay with them, will remain alive as a future memory that can sustain them in some other moment, far away and very different from the one we are now sharing, then the moment vibrates with an energy it wouldn't otherwise have.

That is at least one sense in which Bert unquestionably did write the line about aliveness in my lecture notes, because he manifested the very phenomenon it was about. For me, Bert's classroom was the most alive place on earth. The line in my lecture notes that three decades later demanded my attention—that line was not an isolated entity. It referred back to and was prepared for by the very phenomenon of aliveness that Bert's classroom introduced me to. The line is the fulfillment of all the aliveness that Bert's teaching held and promised for us.

But recently, I began to wonder whether there isn't a more literal sense in which Bert was the author of that line as well. Don't get me wrong. I don't believe I ever heard him talk about aliveness, and I don't associate the thought with any others I know he had. It doesn't even look like it belongs with the other lines around it there in the notes. But even so I am certain that line somehow emanates from him. For as surprising and unexpected as it is to hear that the goal of life is aliveness, I can see now that it is the view demanded by the life he led. And after all, isn't that the way it is sometimes? There are things that you know must be said, that are necessary, even though you don't know why. And only later, in your later years, will the necessity and the significance of those statements become clear. Because you grow into them, or they grow into you. Or both.

And isn't this, ultimately, another way to be alive? That we overflow with words and actions and ideas, at each moment saying and doing what it seems we must, but rarely understanding in its full depth why it is required? And sometimes we are wrong; we say or do things that mischaracterize or mistake. But sometimes we are right, deeply right—we say what is really and actually true—without knowing that we are right or understanding why. And when that happens our words and actions take on a life of their own—they come from us but extend beyond us, extend beyond even themselves.

So if Bert really was the author of that line, it's not just because he wrote it. It's because moreover, without even knowing it, he somehow buried it there in my lecture notes, long ago, as a secret treasure. And there it lay for years, for decades, waiting for the time when it could sprout up and come to life. A gift. A gift from him.

And now it is announced.

DECEMBER 25, 2017

If You Could Be Someone Else, Would You?

It's normal to wish we could trade lives with people we
admire, but we rarely think about what would be lost.

Todd May

Have you ever looked at someone else's life with
envy, just enough envy that you wish for a moment or two (or longer) that you could be them? Michelle Obama with her combination
of grace and passion; George Clooney with his stylish attractiveness and ironic humor; Usain Bolt or Lionel Messi or some other
icon of sport.

Or maybe somebody not famous, just someone you know who
seems to have a charmed life: a challenging and gratifying job, a
warm and attractive spouse, a spacious apartment with a nice view
(and yes, a habit of getting pre-check when they travel). Are there
moments when, if the opportunity to be them were on offer, you
might be tempted by it?

Would we really want this? And what might we learn about ourselves or how we see our lives if we seriously considered it?

To be sure, there are complications here. If you had someone else's
life, who would raise your children or love your spouse or take care of
your parents in their old age? In fact, if you were someone else your
own children would not have come into existence in the first place.
That's not a happy thought. To address this, perhaps the best way to
cast this is in terms of a trade: If you had their life then they would

have yours, and live it exactly as you would have. Your responsibilities would be covered, so there would be nothing to feel guilty about.

If we think of it this way, then the question of wanting to be someone else is a question of what we might call experience: Is there anybody else whose experience of life you would prefer, assuming everything else would be equal?

One immediate reservation about wanting someone else's experience is that my desire to be someone else (i.e., have his experience) is grounded in values and desires that I have, and so I have to be me in order to want to be him. However, it's not clear that that presents any real hurdle to such a desire. I could say that it is precisely by my own lights that the experience of being them would be better, and that there would be at least enough overlap with them that they are instantiating my values and desires but have a better experience than I do. So I can still prefer to be them.

Alternatively, it might be said that I don't really know anyone else well enough to know whether they really have those values and desires. The idea would be that I don't know enough about others to know whether I would trade experiences with them. But one could still argue that inasmuch as I have a familiarity with another person I would want to be them.

I think that, on reflection, most of us would not want to trade with another person, no matter how successful or enticing their lives seem—or even are in reality. To see why, though, we'll need to switch our angle of vision. We will have to look at our own experiences rather than at theirs, or perhaps look at our experiences first. What would I be willing to give up to be another? My relationships with everyone—children, spouse, friends—and my whole history. I wouldn't have undergone it. My loss would be that of the whole of my own experience.

To be sure, there are people who have had extraordinarily difficult lives. For them a trade of their experience for another's might well be worth it. But how many of us find ourselves there, at that extreme?

I have a particular history with people that I care about. Of course, the person I've traded with would also have cared about them, and in the same way, so what I would have done for their sake will be done. But that history of my own experience is gone. Instead I've had a history with another set of people that I don't know as well as the people I've had relationships with. What would that have been like? I can't really tell. Perhaps the person has a job they enjoy and is comfortable financially and is popular or beautiful. But are those differences from me deep enough for me to want to trade?

At that level it's like asking whether I would trade the experiences of my deepest attachments for some goods that don't seem as important as the relationships. The exact trade would instead be the experience of my attachments for their surface amenities plus the important stuff—stuff I'm not so familiar with in their case.

Looked at this way, such a trade begins to seem a lot less promising.

One objection, though, might be that as long as their relationships are good ones—ones that they have enjoyed experiencing—I don't need to know exactly what they are like. But this objection has a difficulty: Even if those experiences are good ones, would they be the ones I would want to trade for? Here is where my own values and desires, the ones I have developed over the course of my life, really begin to show their force. The experiences that I value in my life stem not simply from the fact of enjoyment but from the fact that those were the experiences I value. And I value them because of who I am.

So the issue is not just that the experiences of the other person are good ones, but above and beyond that, that they are the kind of good experiences that I would want to have, and want to have enough that I would trade in my own for them. The experiences of the other would have to be a lot like my experiences—i.e., the ones that are most important to me—in order to be candidates for a trade.

And that seems not only something I can't know but also something that may not be very likely.

Moreover, we go through many experiences that are difficult with people we care about and do not regret having done so. For instance, when one's child has social difficulties or a friend loses a job, it is not only arduous for them to go through, but we also experience sympathetic pain as we accompany them through their struggles. We would rather they hadn't had to deal with those problems. Given that they did have to, though, we want to have been there to support them. We don't want someone else to have been there. We want to have been there ourselves, even though it was not a joyous experience for us.

Of course we would prefer that they hadn't had those experiences in the first place. But that is more for their sake than for ours. Given that they did have those experiences, we would have chosen to undergo our own unpleasant experiences alongside them. Moreover, to the extent that such experiences were burdensome to us, we might have also preferred for our own sake that they had not occurred, but that is a more trivial issue. It is an issue of how our lives have gone in particular unpleasant moments and not an argument for trading lives. The argument for trading lives would have to be based on a willingness not to have had the relationship at all, with whatever adversities it entailed.

When I ask about trading my life for that of another, I'm looking from my perspective and asking whether I would want to have the particular quality of relationships that the other has. And, whatever that quality is, it is likely to differ from the quality of my own relationships, relationships that are deeply meaningful to me. I'm comparing what I value in my own experience with what I value in an experience the most significant features of which lie outside my grasp. Once we see this, for most of us a trade, even if we could have one, would not likely be in the offing.

We live in world in which the lives of those with more wealth or fame or recognition or influence or beauty are constantly placed before us as though they were something to aspire to. And, of course, there is nothing wrong with aspiration in itself. But to the extent these lives are presented to us as something to be hankered after, as lives we would certainly want if only we could have them, we are presented with an image that asks us to forget what is important to us. In an age of acquisitiveness, and one moreover in which the normative constraints on acquisitiveness have largely fallen away, it is comforting—and perhaps even imperative—to recognize that of all the personal histories that we might choose from, it is our own that would be our likely choice.

JULY 17, 2017

Gratitude: In Sickness and Health

Surviving a painful, near-fatal illness should have made
me intensely grateful for ordinary life. It didn't.

Philip S. Garrity

I REMEMBER STARING UP AT THE CEILING FROM THE DENTIST'S chair as a child and wondering with genuine perplexity, "How am I here again?" It seemed as if I had awakened there, wholly present to the undeniable reality of a cavity filling or tooth pulling. The days that had passed between dental visits were nothing more than a dreamlike filler. Only in the chair did real life flare back into being, the drill keeping me relentlessly awake to the present moment. In the grip of pain, a tinge of anger would arise. How had I let all those carefree days slip past me in what felt like an instant?

I spent a great deal of mental energy in my adolescence trying to capture that dreamlike filler, to perpetually feel what the Buddhist teacher Thich Nhat Hanh calls the "non-toothache" that I unknowingly walked around with most days. It was an exercise in imaginatively conjuring pain in order to appreciate its absence. And not just ordinary pains, but colossal ones. I was looking up the road of my life to see epic losses—of health, of kin, of life itself—and feel the weight of ensuing grief. I wanted to harness that emotional energy, to have it reinfuse my sense of wellness. I wanted to transform future loss into present gratitude.

My efforts proved futile, as loss came too soon. At twenty-four,

I was found to have a rare and aggressive bone cancer. The year of chemotherapy and surgery that followed whittled away even the most basic capacities whose true worth, I learned, was impossible to capture through imaginative effort alone. The ability to walk, to keep food down, to defecate without electric pain were no longer mundane givens, but miraculous gifts. In their absence, the vibrancy of illness burned brightly.

As treatment was nearing its end, my hope of finally being released from its prison was muddled by a subtle despair about life beyond its walls. If a year of backbreaking lows and mind-bending pain would ultimately be erased in the fog of complacency and ingratitude, what did it all amount to? I needed to retain that vibrancy, to resist being lulled into trance by the hum of wellness from which I had struggled to awake since my days in the dentist's chair.

But as my health returned, the vibrancy did fade. Now almost five years in remission, I notice myself falling back into that same pattern of trying to harness the vibrancy of illness, of forcing myself back into the dentist's chair to avoid my failure to feel the non-toothache. I am learning, however slowly, that maintaining that level of mental stamina, that fever pitch of experience, is less a recipe for enlightenment, and more for exhaustion.

The existentialist philosopher Jean-Paul Sartre describes our experience as a perpetual transitioning between unreflective consciousness, "living-in-the-world," and reflective consciousness, "thinking-about-the-world." Gratitude seems to necessitate an act of reflection on experience, which, in turn, requires a certain abstraction away from that direct experience. Paradoxically, our capacity for gratitude is simultaneously enhanced and frustrated as we strive to attain it.

Perhaps, then, there is an important difference between reflecting on wellness and experiencing wellness. My habitual understanding of gratitude had me forcefully lodging myself into the realm of reflective consciousness, pulling me away from living-in-the-world. I was constantly making an inventory of my wellness, too busy counting the coins to ever spend them.

Gratitude, in the experiential sense, requires that we wade back into the current of unreflective consciousness, which, to the egocentric mind, can easily feel like an annihilation of consciousness altogether. Yet, Sartre says that action that is unreflective isn't necessarily unconscious. There is something Zen about this, the actor disappearing into the action. It is the way of the artist in the act of creative expression, the musician in the flow of performance. But, to most of us, it is a loss of self—and the sense of competency that comes with it.

My attempts to harness the vibrancy of illness have largely been to avoid this plunge into the present. Before cancer, I would strain forward to my future self, the one who had already endured loss. He was the older sage that I have always intuited—helplessly, hopelessly—I am on my way to becoming.

After cancer, I've clamored backward to my past self—the one who knew pain, the glaring absence of things. He was the younger, battle-tested soldier whose courage I feel, on most days, has been lost.

Both these selves are removed from me now—not by distance, but by degree. The sage is lost to speculation while the soldier is trapped on the other side of some existential barrier that even memory—no matter how vivid and haunting—cannot penetrate. There is grief in realizing that, in holding one's ear to that wall, exiled to the other side of pain.

I am left with one thing: my ordinary, present self who is as empty-handed as he was the day before diagnosis—no better equipped for the ensuing battles of life, no better shielded from pain he will yet face. And it is not just heroic pain. It is the hurt of parking tickets, the ache of commuting, the grief of deadening routine—small pains to which I was immune while they were eclipsed by cancer. But that moon has since passed.

And yet, that isn't reason for despair. It's strangely consoling to be reminded of my failure, to remember that my efforts to be prepared for epic loss were mostly in vain. I wasn't ready then, and yet, I got through it. I won't be ready next time, but I have reason (and experience) to believe that I will get through it again.

If there is any sage in me, he says I must accept the vulnerability of letting the pain fade, of allowing the wounds to heal. Even in the wake of grave illness—or, more unsettlingly, in anticipation of it—we must risk falling back asleep into wellness.

DECEMBER 18, 2017

Why Do Anything? A Meditation on Procrastination

The procrastinator is both contemplator and man
of action, which is the worst thing to be.

Costica Bradatan

HAVE YOU HEARD THE STORY OF THE ARCHITECT FROM SHIraz who designed the world's most beautiful mosque? No one had ever conjured up such a design. It was breathtakingly daring yet well-proportioned, divinely sophisticated yet radiating a distinctly human warmth. Those who saw the plans were awestruck.

Famous builders begged the architect to allow them to erect the mosque; wealthy people came from afar to buy the plans; thieves devised schemes to steal them; powerful rulers considered taking them by force. Yet the architect locked himself in his study, and after staring at the plans for three days and three nights, burned them all.

The architect couldn't stand the thought that the realized building would have been subject to the forces of degradation and decay, eventual collapse or destruction by barbarian hordes. During those days and nights in his study he saw his creation profaned and reduced to dust, and was terribly unsettled by the sight. Better that it remain perfect. Better that it was never built.

The story is a fable, but its main idea—that a thing's ideal state is before it comes into existence, that it is better to not be born—is equal parts terrifying and uncanny, especially today, when progress and productivity are practically worshipped. And it evokes a philosophical insight with ancient roots that is still worth investigating.

"The world," we read in the Gnostic Gospel of Philip, "came about through a mistake." The demiurge who made it "wanted to create it imperishable and immortal," but eventually he "fell short of attaining his desire, for the world never was imperishable, nor, for that matter, was he who made the world." The Gnostics believed nonexistence to be a mark of perfection, and coming into being a form of degradation.

Basilides, one of the most intriguing figures of early Gnosticism, believed that the highest attribute of divinity is its inexistence. By his own account, Basilides was a theologian of the "nonexistent God"; he referred to God as "he who is not," as opposed to the maker of the world, trapped in existence and time.

Gnostic thinking takes us to a privileged ontological realm: the state of perfection that precedes actualization. That which is yet to be born—be it the world, a person, a piece of furniture, or a piece of writing like this one—may be nothing, but at this stage it is at its utmost. Its nothingness is fuller and richer than any ordinary existence. To fall into existence is to enter time, and with time comes decay, aging, and death.

Modern proponents of this idea are hard to come by, but the Romanian-born French philosopher E. M. Cioran is certainly one. For Cioran, who died in 1995, there was something incomparably worse than death—"the catastrophe of birth," and the "fall in time" that comes with it. In his book *The Trouble with Being Born*, Cioran maps out the vast unfolding of nothingness that preceded coming into existence.

"I am lured only by what precedes me," he writes, by "the numberless moments when I was not: the non-born." From that perspective, he looks at the world with new eyes, and gains a deeper understanding of himself: "I have never taken myself for a being. A noncitizen, a marginal type, a nothing who exists only by the excess, by the superabundance of his nothingness."

Cioran was a man of unusual tastes. He took a liking to the Thracians because they "wept over the newborn," and to the Gnostic sect of Bogomils, who, "in order to justify God, held Satan responsible for the infamy of Creation."

All of this raises an obvious question: Why do anything? Why multiply the cosmic failure, the "infamy of creation"?

Idleness, as we know, has a bad rap in Western culture, but it can be a philosophical experience in its own right. Bertrand Russell wrote a long essay in praise of it, and Oscar Wilde thought that "to do nothing at all is the most difficult thing in the world" as well as the most intellectual. The great, consummate idlers of literature (Ivan Goncharov's Oblomov or Melville's Bartleby) are figures of metaphysical quest: They exemplify ways of being human with unusual complexity.

Idleness, then, reveals an experience of nothingness. While nothingness tends to occupy a central position in Eastern traditions like Buddhism and Taoism, we in the West typically shun it; after all, one of the most characteristic branches of Western philosophy is ontology, the study of that which exists.

Yet, even if we do not choose to embrace nothingness, nothingness itself may choose to embrace us. It may not be that we don't have anything to do, or that we're bored, or that we would rather do it later, but just that we don't see the point of it all. In our idleness we intuit a cosmic meaninglessness, which comes along with the realization that, with every action, we get only more entangled in the universal farce.

Perhaps the most intriguing form of idleness is one nearly all of us are intimately familiar with: procrastination. Idleness is difficult to find in a pure state. Indeed, in a certain sense, it eludes us because, at its most radical, idleness tends to devour its devotees (again, Oblomov and Bartleby). But procrastination is a different business altogether: It is not only more available, but also more dynamic, just as the procrastinator is a more dramatic figure than the idler, who is as ascetic and immobile as a pillar saint.

The drama of procrastination comes from its split nature. Just like the architect from Shiraz, the procrastinator is smitten by the perfect picture of that which is yet to be born; he falls under the spell of all that purity and splendor. What he is beholding is something whole, uncorrupted by time, untainted by the workings of a messed-up world. At the same time, though, the procrastinator is fully aware that all that has to go. No sooner does he get a glimpse of the perfection that precedes actualization than he is doomed to become part of the actualization process himself, to be the one who defaces the ideal and brings into the world a precarious copy, unlike the architect who saves it by burning the plans.

The procrastinator contemplates his deed and realizes all its future imperfection, but—fallen creature, "man of the world," part of the "infamy of Creation" that he is—he must do it. The procrastinator is both contemplator and man of action, which is the worst thing to be, and which is tearing him apart.

What procrastination betrays is above all an anxiety of creation: It pains us unbearably to realize that, for all our good intentions, we are agents of degradation, that instead of creating something that stays whole and incorruptible, we by our very doing make it "perishable and mortal," in the words of the Gnostic author of the Gospel of Philip. Procrastination and mourning are tied tightly together: for to procrastinate is to mourn the precariousness of your creation even before you bring it into the world.

We should perhaps spend more time dwelling on the rich virtuality that precedes the fall into existence. That is, after all, what true contemplation must be about: a commerce with the irreality of things, a learned habit to see them from the privileged perspective of their pre- and nonexistence. Rather than get caught up in the misleading appearance of the material world, we transport ourselves back to a moment when the world, with all its holes and imperfections, hasn't happened yet.

SEPTEMBER 17, 2016

The Universe Doesn't Care About Your "Purpose"

But you do. And you should.

Joseph P. Carter

K EYS IN HAND, I TOOK A DEEP BREATH. I FLIPPED THE IGNI-
tion and the memories of my Papa rushed back, just as the familiar
rumble of his Thunderbird kicked in.

After a series of painful events in late 2016, I struggled to understand how almost everything around me went wrong so suddenly.
If anything, I felt aimless. That is, until the moment I inherited my
grandfather's 1972 Ford Thunderbird. Immediately it reminded me
of the best memories of him—birthday fishing trips, playing with his
model trains, learning to make animal balloons (he was a Shriner
clown), and my brother and I lounging in his hammock by the shore
of Lake Murray, South Carolina. Kitschy as it sounds, restoring his
T-Bird gave me a new sense of purpose.

Purpose is a universal human need. Without it, we feel bereft of
meaning and happiness.

A recent ethnographic study draws a strong correlation between
purposefulness and happiness. Purpose seems beneficial to overcoming substance abuse, healing from tragedy and loss, and achieving economic success. Businesses and organizations champion goals
as ways to unify employees and customers under the banners of brand
strategy, community, and well-being. America, in fact, is founded on
the idea of purpose: life, liberty, and the pursuit of happiness. One

election cycle after another, Americans rally around candidates personifying deeply rooted ideals of what our country is supposed to be.

But, where does purpose come from? What is it? For over two millennia, discerning our purpose in the universe has been a primary task of philosophers.

Aristotle believed that the universe is saturated with it, that everything has an intrinsic drive. Our word purpose comes from the Greek telos, a goal that stipulates what and how something needs to be. For Aristotle, the universe and everything in it has an essential directive. Any deviation from it belies truth and reality. Teleology concerns order, stability, and accomplishment. The goal of my grandfather's T-Bird, for example, is to function successfully as a form of transportation. From cars, trees, animals, all the way to the cosmos itself, Aristotle argued, each thing has an inherent principle that guides the course of its existence.

What about human beings? In his *Nicomachean Ethics*, Aristotle tells us that our purpose is happiness or eudaemonia, "well-spiritedness." Happiness is an ordered and prudent life. Good habits, a sound mind, and a virtuous disposition are some of the steps that lead us there. For Aristotle, nothing is more fundamental for us.

In many ways, we still think like Aristotle. Most everyone strives for happiness. Today, the standing dogma is that purposelessness and disorder are nihilistic. Whether you're mulling a major life change or healing from trauma, being told that there's no purpose in life might be particularly devastating. The chances are better that you're looking for an ultimate explanation. Or you could simply be searching for that something or someone meant for you—God, a soul mate, or a calling of sorts.

I'm certainly no Aristotelian. Not because I reject happiness. Rather, as a materialist, I think there's nothing intrinsic about the goals and purposes we seek to achieve it. Modern science explicitly jettisons this sort of teleological thinking from our knowledge of the universe. From particle physics to cosmology, we see that the universe operates well without purpose.

The second law of thermodynamics, for instance, states that

entropy is always increasing. Entropy is the degree of disorder in a system, for example our universe. Physical disorder is all about equilibrium—everything resting randomly and uniformly. Leave your hot coffee on the desk and it will cool to ambient temperature. Just as the temperature of the coffee and air equalizes, the earth, our solar system, galaxies, and even supermassive black holes will break down to the quantum level, where everything cools to a uniform state. This process is known as the arrow of time. Eventually everything ends in heat death. The universe certainly started with a bang, but it likely ends with a fizzle.

What's the purpose in that, though?

There isn't one. At least not fundamentally. Entropy is antagonistic to intrinsic purpose. It's about disorder. Aristotle's world and pretty much the dominant understanding of the physical universe until the Copernican Revolution is all about inherent order and permanence. But the universe as we understand it tells us nothing about the goal or meaning of existence, let alone our own. In the grand scheme of things, you and I are enormously insignificant.

But not entirely insignificant.

For starters, we are important to each other. Meaning begins and ends with how we talk about our own lives, such as our myths and stories. Sean Carroll, a prominent cosmologist and theoretical physicist at the California Institute of Technology, makes this case in his recent book *The Big Picture*. Fashioning himself the "poetic naturalist," Carroll argues that meaning and purpose "aren't built into the architecture of the universe; they emerge as ways of talking about our human-scale environment." Even materialists can't deny the fact that purposes somehow exist to give us meaning and happiness.

Anthropologists like Dean Falk recently suggested that goal-directed behavior is also evolutionarily advantageous. This doesn't imply that evolution itself has a purpose, of course. (Though some have argued otherwise.) What it does suggest is that as purposeless as human evolution is, we generally benefit as a species from a belief in it.

The twentieth century German philosopher and intellectualist Hans Blumenberg, in *Work on Myth*, provides a way to explain this curious concomitance of teleology and evolution with what he calls the "phantom body" of the development of civilization: "The organic system resulting from the mechanism of evolution becomes 'man' by evading the pressure of that mechanism by setting against it something like a phantom body. This is the sphere of his culture, his institutions—and also his myths."

Purpose springs from our longing for permanence in an ever-changing universe. It is a reaction to the universe's indifference to us. We create stories about the world and ourselves as contours, "phantom bodies," of the inevitability of loss and change. Myths appear timeless; they have what Blumenberg calls an iconic constancy. Stories pass through generations, often becoming traditions, customs, even laws and institutions that order and give meaning to our lives. Purpose grows out of the durability of human lore. Our stories serve as directives for the ways we need the world to exist.

An indifferent universe also offers us a powerful and compelling case for living justly and contentedly because it allows us to anchor our attention here. It teaches us that this life matters and that we alone are responsible for it. Love, friendship, and forgiveness are for our benefit. Oppression, war, and conflict are self-inflicted. When we ask what's the purpose of the recent gassing of Syrian children in the Idlib Province or the torture and killings of Chechnyan homosexual men, we ought not simply look to God or the universe for explanations but to ourselves, to the entrenched mythologies that drive such actions—then reject them when the institutions they inform amount to acts of horror.

The purposes and goals we create are phantom bodies—vestiges of and memorials to the people, places, and things we stand to lose and strive to keep. Purpose indexes the world's impermanence, namely our own. Sure, my grandfather's T-Bird will function well as transportation once I'm finished. But, that goal only makes sense as an enduring reminder of the stories and memories of him. Purpose is about loss, or at least the circumvention of it. And there's nothing wrong with that. We create purposes to establish happy endings in a universe where endings are simply that—endings.

I will never see my Papa again. One day I will die. So will you. The T-Bird will decay along with everything in the universe as the fundamental particles we're made of return to the inert state in which everything began. Entropy demands it.

So, take a moment to think about the mythologies informing your purpose. I'll reflect on mine too. The universe, however, won't. And that might be the most meaningful distinction of all.

JULY 31, 2017

A Life of Meaning (Reason Not Required)

If philosophy is to stay relevant, it must bridge
the gap between feeling and thought.

Robert A. Burton

F EW WOULD DISAGREE WITH TWO AGE-OLD TRUISMS: WE SHOULD strive to shape our lives with reason, and a central prerequisite for the good life is a personal sense of meaning. Ideally, the two should go hand in hand. We study the lessons of history, read philosophy, and seek out wise men with the hope of learning what matters. But this acquired knowledge is not the same as the felt sense that one's life is meaningful.

Though impossible to accurately describe, we readily recognize meaning by its absence. Anyone who has experienced a bout of spontaneous depression knows the despair of feeling that nothing in life is worth pursuing and that no argument, no matter how inspired, can fill the void. Similarly, we are all familiar with the countless narratives of religious figures "losing their way" despite retaining their formal beliefs.

Any philosophical approach to values and purpose must acknowledge this fundamental neurological reality: a visceral sense of meaning in one's life is an involuntary mental state that, like joy or disgust, is independent from and resistant to the best of arguments. If philosophy is to guide us to a better life, it must somehow bridge this gap between feeling and thought.

As neuroscience attempts to pound away at the idea of pure rationality and underscore the primacy of subliminal mental activity, I am increasingly drawn to the metaphor of idiosyncratic mental taste buds. From genetic factors (a single gene determines whether we find brussels sprouts bitter or sweet), to the cultural—considering fried grasshoppers and grilled monkey brains as delicacies—taste isn't a matter of the best set of arguments. Anyone who's tried to get his child to eat something she doesn't like understands the limits of the most cunning of inducements. If thoughts, like foods, come in a dazzling variety of flavors, and personal taste trumps reason, philosophy—which relies most heavily on reason, and aims to foster the acquisition of objective knowledge—is in a bind.

Though we don't know how thoughts are produced by the brain, it is hard to imagine having a thought unaccompanied by some associated mental state. We experience a thought as pleasing, revolting, correct, incorrect, obvious, stupid, brilliant, etc. Though integral to our thoughts, these qualifiers arise out of different brain mechanisms from those that produce the raw thought. As examples, feelings of disgust, empathy, and knowing arise from different areas of brain and can be provoked de novo in volunteer subjects via electrical stimulation even when the subjects are unaware of having any concomitant thought at all. This chicken-and-egg relationship between feelings and thought can readily be seen in how we make moral judgments.

The psychologist Jonathan Haidt and others have shown that our moral stances strongly correlate with the degree of activation of those brain areas that generate a sense of disgust and revulsion. According to Haidt, reason provides an after-the-fact explanation for moral decisions that are preceded by inherently reflexive positive or negative feelings. Think about your stance on pedophilia or denying a kidney transplant to a serial killer. Long before you have a moral position in place, each scenario will have already generated some degree of disgust or empathy.

Nowhere is this overpowering effect of biology on how we think more evident than in the paradox-plagued field of philosophy of mind. Even those cognitive scientists who have been most instrumental in uncovering our myriad innate biases continue to believe in the primacy of reason. Consider the argument by the Yale psychology professor Paul Bloom that we do not have free will, but since we are capable of conscious rational deliberation, we are responsible for our actions.

Though deeply sympathetic to his conclusion, I am puzzled by his argument. The evidence most supportive of Bloom's contention that we do not have free will also is compelling evidence against the notion of conscious rational deliberation. In the 1980s the neurophysiologist Ben Libet of the University of California, San Francisco, showed that the brain generates action-specific electrical activity nearly half a second before the subject consciously "decides" to initiate the action. Though interpretations of the results are the subject of considerable controversy, a number of subsequent studies have confirmed that the conscious sense of willing an action is preceded by subliminal brain activity likely to indicate that the brain is preparing to initiate the action.

An everyday example of this temporal illusion is seen in high-speed sports such as baseball and tennis. Though batters sense that they withhold deciding whether to swing until they see the ball near the plate, their swing actually begins shortly after the ball leaves the pitcher's hand. The same applies to tennis players returning a serve coming at them at 140 miles an hour. Initiation of the action precedes full conscious perception of seeing the approaching ball.

It is unlikely that there is any fundamental difference in how the brain initiates thought and action. We learn the process of thinking incrementally, acquiring knowledge of language, logic, the external world, and cultural norms and expectations just as we learn physical actions like talking, walking, or playing the piano. If we conceptualize thought as a mental motor skill subject to the same temporal reorganization as high-speed sports, it's hard to avoid the conclusion that the experience of free will (agency) and conscious rational deliberation are both biologically generated illusions.

What then are we to do with the concept of rationality? It would be a shame to get rid of a term useful in characterizing the clarity of a line of reasoning. Everyone understands that "being rational" implies trying to strip away biases and innate subjectivity in order to make the best possible decision. But what if the word "rational" leads us to scientifically unsound conclusions?

We describe the decision to jam on the brakes at the sight of a child running into the road as being rational, even when we understand that it is reflexive. However, few of us would say that a self-driving car performing the same maneuver was acting rationally. It's pretty obvious that the difference in how we assign rationality isn't dependent upon how decisions are made, but how we wish to see ourselves in relationship to the rest of the animal kingdom, and indeed even to plants and intelligent machines.

It is hard to imagine what would happen to modern thought if we abandoned the notion of rationality. Scientific method might partly fill the void. With quantum physics, scientists have been able to validate counterintuitive theories. But empirical methods can't help us with abstract, non-measurable, linguistically ambiguous concepts such as purpose and meaning. It's no wonder that preeminent scientists like Stephen Hawking have gleefully declared, "Philosophy is dead."

Going forward, the greatest challenge for philosophy will be to remain relevant while conceding that, like the rest of the animal kingdom, we are decision-making organisms rather than rational agents, and that our most logical conclusions about moral and ethical values can't be scientifically verified nor guaranteed to pass the test of time. (The history of science should serve as a cautionary tale for anyone tempted to believe in the persistent truth of untestable ideas).

Even so, I would hate to discard such truisms such as "know thyself" or "the unexamined life isn't worth living." Reason allows us new ways of seeing, just as close listening to a piece of music can reveal previously unheard melodies and rhythms or observing an anthill can give us an unexpected appreciation of nature's harmonies. These various forms of inquiry aren't dependent upon logic and verification; they are modes of perception.

SEPTEMBER 5, 2016

VII

WHY CAN'T WE ALL JUST GET ALONG?

The Ancient Myth of "Good Fences"

Humans build barriers to define themselves. But cultures
truly flourish when those barriers break down.

Ingrid Rossellini

I N ROBERT FROST'S FAMOUS POEM "MENDING WALL," THE NAR-
rator describes an encounter with his neighbor at the stone wall that
divides their land. They are there to repair the damage inflicted by
winter. Reflecting on nature's apparent dislike of all artificial barriers, the narrator questions the benefits of the task, and gets this
answer: "Good fences make good neighbors."

Do they?

It is clear that Frost's narrator views this bit of folk wisdom with
skepticism, but by refraining from providing a firm answer to our
question, the poem manages to increase our curiosity: Besides the
most obvious, delineating private property, what do "fences" truly
represent?

If one looks at history, the answer seems obvious: What fences
have very often indicated is not simply what is mine and what is
yours, but, more subtly, who I am versus who you are. This tendency
is based on the human inclination to define one's identity in contrast
to someone cast as a different, an untrustworthy Other best kept at
a distance.

The danger that such a separation between the self and the other
can cause is evident throughout history. In ancient Greece, where

a profound appreciation of human reason produced a brilliant civilization, pernicious biases were also established. Women were assumed to be guided by passions rather than rationality, and so they were considered inferior to men and excluded from the cultural and political life of the city-state. As the word "virtue"—from the Latin "vir," meaning "man"—so clearly expresses, the ethos that Greek as well as Roman culture fostered derived from a military and patriarchal mentality. The "fence" of bigotry and prejudice that prevents the flourishing in public life of half the population certainly hobbled the development of Greek and Roman society.

The Greeks held similarly disparaging views toward foreigners, called "barbarians" because they seemed to say "bar-bar-bar" when they spoke. The Greek word "logos," which simultaneously indicated "language" and "rationality," gave further validation to that premise: Those who did not share the Greek idiom were viewed as inferior Others who lacked the intellectual talents that had made possible the free and self-ruled society that the Greek polis represented. (This was in fact a unique achievement; in all other civilizations at that time absolute monarchs reigned uncontested over legions of subjects.)

The sharp division between Greek and non-Greek was vividly represented in the sculptures that were placed on the Parthenon in Athens to celebrate the victory that, against all odds, the small Greek city-states had obtained against the immense Persian Empire. To suggest that the Eastern enemy possessed none of the extraordinary qualities belonging to the Greeks, the Athenian artists used mythological comparisons that described the Persians as monstrous creatures—giants, centaurs, and Amazons, female warriors that the Greeks evoked to ridicule the weak and decadent femininity of all Eastern peoples.

This was also expressed in pottery, especially, by the colorful and whimsical attire the Persians donned for war, which was contrasted with the noble nudity of the brave citizen-soldiers who fought in defense of the Greek polis.

When the Macedonian king Alexander the Great absorbed the Balkan Peninsula as the start of an empire that soon stretched as far as India, the experiment of the polis came to an end. Despite the fear of their Eastern neighbors that the early Greeks had so diligently cultivated, the rapprochement between East and West that the unity of empire made possible proved enormously fruitful for both sides: While the rich culture of Greece reached farther into Asia, the heritage of the East, which besides art and science also included religions such as Judaism, Buddhism, and Hinduism, replenished with all sorts of new perspectives the cultural reservoir of the West.

A new chapter began when Rome established itself as the leader of yet another enormous empire. A major gain for the Romans was the encounter with the Hellenistic heritage that the poet Horace described with these famous words: "When Greece was taken she enslaved her rough conquerors." Despite the enormous cultural debt they owed to the Greeks, the Romans, driven by feelings of envy and competition, promoted a mythical narrative that, echoing old prejudices, portrayed the Greeks as a decadent and effeminate people while the Romans were models of masculine virtue and uprightness.

Thanks to such greatness, the myth suggested, the gods had elected the Romans (rather than the Greeks) to spread civilization over the entire world. Those who failed to swear allegiance to Rome's sacred mission were labeled dangerous Others deserving annihilation.

When the barbarians, emboldened by the many problems that in time began to corrode the empire, finally crossed the borders with which Rome for so long had kept at bay all foreigners, the Eternal City collapsed both in myth and in reality. During the following turbulent centuries different peoples clashed but also mixed and merged, while Christianity became the leading religion of the West. With the rise of Islam, the Other came to be represented by the Muslims, whose rapid territorial expansion (which included cities that had been important centers of Greek and Latin culture) struck fear in the very heart of Europe.

To foster the righteous spirit of the Crusaders, Christian art depicted Muslims with monstrous traits suggesting they were closer to animals than human beings. But the humiliating defeat that the "infidels" dealt to the Crusaders turned out to be an unexpected gift: the Christian world, having come into contact with the Muslim intelligentsia, rediscovered its own cultural roots—the classical heritage that eventually led to the blooming of the Renaissance.

What that seems to prove is that, just as Frost's narrator suggests when he recalls how the winter sabotages walls, the regeneration that culture always needs can occur only when the fences of prejudice are breached to allow encounters between different people, traditions, and ideas.

MAY 14, 2018

The Road to Auschwitz Wasn't Paved with Indifference

We don't have to be "upstanders" to avoid genocides.
We just have to make sure not to help them along.

Rivka Weinberg

T ODAY, EVEN AS THE SEVENTY-FIFTH ANNIVERSARY OF THE
liberation of Auschwitz, on January 27, approaches, our news feeds
are teeming with more and more reports of hate crimes and extreme
ideologies. I am alive because my paternal grandfather's Spidey sense
had him frantically looking for ways out of Germany in 1933. "When
madmen are elected, it's time to leave the country," he said. Now I,
and many others I'm sure, worry that a catastrophe is looming, and
wonder how we can guard against it. Schoolchildren are now taught:
"Be an upstander, not a bystander!" History, we're told, shows that,
as Edmund Burke supposedly said, "The only thing necessary for
the triumph of evil is that good men do nothing." Or, in the words of
historian Ian Kershaw, "The road to Auschwitz was built by hate but
paved with indifference." These aphorisms pithily conjure up images
of wise men stroking their long white beards, but they're wrong.

HOW ATROCITIES HAPPEN

The road to Auschwitz was built by hate but it wasn't paved with
indifference. It was paved with collaboration. Anti-Semitism was
entrenched in Europe for centuries before the Holocaust, supply-

ing the Nazis with many collaborators. During the Holocaust, the local population, the police, and the army often helped the Nazis. Not always, of course. There were resisters (heroes) and bystanders (ordinary people). But one thing is clear: During the Holocaust, where the local population was more anti-Semitic, they tended toward greater collaboration, resulting in a markedly higher murder rate.

To kill people living within a population, you have to be told who and where they are. You don't just march into Poland or France from Germany and magically know who to round up and where they live. It's even more helpful when the local police do the rounding up for you (as some did in Lithuania, France, and Hungary). The correlation between local enthusiasm and the genocidal murder rate of the Holocaust is strong and stark, as Raul Hilberg and Hannah Arendt documented. In Bulgaria and Italy, where the culture wasn't as anti-Semitic, the local populations didn't cooperate with the murder of Jews; most Bulgarian and Italian Jews survived. Romania and Ukraine, on the other hand, had virulently anti-Semitic cultures and many Romanians and Ukrainians actively participated in murdering Jews. Few survived. Poland was also very anti-Semitic, and although there were Poles who sheltered Jews, many instead turned them in and looted their property. Some murdered Jews themselves. Very few Polish Jews survived.

The truth about how massive moral crimes occur is both unsettling and comforting. It's unsettling to accept how many people participated in appalling moral crimes but comforting to realize that we don't have to be heroes to avoid genocides. We just have to make sure not to help them along.

UPSTANDER VS. BYSTANDER REALITIES

Upstander ideology directs us to "stand up" to bullies and hate. Upstanding can be effective and inspiring, but it's dangerous. People who intervene to rescue victims or stop a crime often die in the attempt. It's hard to be a hero, to risk your safety and personal commitments in order to help a stranger. That's a big ask. And by asking people too much, we make being moral too hard—which, paradoxically, can make immorality too easy. "Clearly, being moral is too hard, I'm no hero! Forget it!" we can imagine people thinking.

The incorrect lesson upstander ideology draws from history ignores the fact that perpetrating vast crimes usually requires lots of help. Instead, it implicitly blames moral catastrophes on a failure of heroism. Yet heroism is exceptional, saintly; that's not who most of us are, nor who most of us can be, so we're kind of off the hook. Most of us are ordinary people, neither cruel nor heroic. The fact is that when people can help others avert disaster at negligible cost to themselves, most do. That is, unless they're steeped in hate—in which case being a bystander is a step up from the role of perpetrator they've been primed for.

Bystanding is not the problem. What we need to guard against is hate and collaboration with hate. It's rare for people not motivated by hate to casually witness a serious crime and do nothing about it. (The notorious case of Kitty Genovese, the woman stabbed to death in 1964 in her apartment building vestibule, while supposedly dozens of people within earshot of her screams did nothing, is a case of false reporting.) Of course, we want to encourage resistance to injustice. That's an important part of being human, and when doing so doesn't entail outsized risks, we should do our part. But when helping others is perilous, to help nonetheless is heroic. It's great to be a hero—and encouraging greatness has its place—but it's also important to be realistic and give moral guidance to ordinary people. People of average moral fortitude, if history is our guide, should be educated against collaboration with hate and taught the reality of how widespread, repugnant, and powerful that is. Heroism is aspirational, and worthy of admiration, but it is a pedagogical, moral, and historical error to spend our moral capital insisting on it.

When helping others is risky, the heroes who step forward don't do so because of effective "upstander" education. Research shows that heroic acts are usually done instinctively, without much thought at all. So to whatever extent we want to encourage heroism, moral upstanding training seems unlikely to help. Heroism is not morally obligatory, not teachable, and not what we must demand of citizens in order to avoid catastrophic crimes against humanity. What we must emphasize is the cruelty and destructiveness of hate and the perils of collaborating with it.

THE LESSONS OF HISTORY

Some people unwittingly help atrocities occur by cooperating in an attempt to mitigate a monstrous situation. History demonstrates that this is nearly always a miscalculation. During the Holocaust, Jewish councils organized life in the ghetto and compiled lists of Jews for deportation, often thinking that they were helping Jews manage a nightmare. Ultimately, they helped the Nazis murder Jews by maintaining order and providing the Gestapo with the names of people to be deported and murdered. In his memoir *Legislating the Holocaust*, Bernhard Lösener, a lawyer in the Third Reich's Ministry of the Interior, relays how he hurriedly traveled through the night to get to Nuremberg in time to write the Nuremberg race laws so that the rule of law would be preserved, and how he fought to have the race laws written to count as Jewish those with three Jewish grandparents rather than those with one drop of Jewish blood. He too made the mistake of participating in the atrocity in an attempt to minimize the damages caused by its perpetrators.

Lösener remains the lawyer who wrote the Nuremberg race laws, lending a veneer of legality to a crime. Maybe someone else would have ignored the rule of law or written more draconian laws if he hadn't, but maybe not. What we can decide is whether we will be a participant in terrible things done by terrible people. It never works to participate in the terrible thing in order to try to make it less bad. It's tempting, and can seem like the right thing to do: Lösener's race laws included fewer people than a one-drop rule would (though that had negligible effect). Adolf Eichmann reasoned similarly: "If this thing had to be done at all, it was better that it be done in good order." History shows that when you participate in an atrocity together with the perpetrators, in an attempt to make it somehow a little less horrible, in the end you're still participating in the atrocity—and it is no less horrible.

MORALITY AND MY MOTHER

Like so many other things about me, my perspective on bystanders horrifies my mother. She is appalled that I could think we aren't morally obligated to rescue each other, even at great personal sacrifice. To her, the obligation is obvious. "Do not stand idly by the blood of your neighbor!" she exclaims, channeling Leviticus. Heroic acts of upstanding have shaped my mother's life. She is alive because of someone's heroism, and she lost her job, prematurely ending a treasured career, because of her own. My mother was saved from the Holocaust by Chiune Sugihara, the Japanese consul who ignored orders and issued several thousand transit visas to Lithuanian Jews, allowing them to flee the advancing Gestapo. Many years later, when a colleague was unfairly fired, my mother organized senior employees to speak out against the injustice, even though she knew not only that she would be likely to lose her own job as a result but also that she was unlikely to get another job at her age. She did lose her job, and did not get another one. The loss profoundly affected the trajectory and quality of her life, but she still says she doesn't regret what she did and would do it again.

Listening to my mother, I feel somewhat ashamed. I think I feel the shame of the ordinary person in the face of those who are morally greater than us; my mother is a much better person than I am. But I doubt the average person can be as heroic. Luckily, that is not necessary to avert moral catastrophe.

THE TAKEAWAY

The belief that atrocities happen when people aren't educated against the evils of bystanding has become part of our culture and how we think we're learning from history. "Don't be a bystander!" we're exhorted. "Be an upstander!" we teach our children. But that's all a big mistake. All of it: It's false that doing nothing creates moral catastrophes; it's false that people are generally indifferent to the plight of others; it's false that we can educate people into heroism; and it's false that if we fail to transmit these lessons another Holocaust is around the corner.

Instead, the facts are more quotidian: Terrible things happen when people collaborate with terrible perpetrators; most people are generally helpful to the extent that their circumstances and temperament allow (unless they've been taught to hate); being a bystander is often morally permissible; being a hero is exceptional and instinctual (not taught); and what history teaches us is both easier and harder than the supposed dark dangers of bystanderdom. What history teaches us is: Don't perpetrate; don't collaborate. If you can be heroic, that is laudable. Those lessons are hard to learn, but effective and easy enough to follow to avert most vast moral crimes.

Next time the murderers come, it's understandable if it's too much to ask for us to risk our lives, our children, or even our jobs, to save others. Just don't welcome the murderers, don't help them organize the oppression or make it "less terrible" (that won't work anyway), and don't turn people in. That will usually be enough.

JANUARY 21, 2020

White America Wants Me to Conform. I Won't Do It.

*Even at elite universities, I was exposed to the disease
that has endangered black lives for so long.*

Chris Lebron

I T COULD HAVE BEEN THE DAY I DIED.

It was a fall morning in 2000 and I was on the New York City
subway, heading from the Lower East Side to my not very glamorous stockbroking job in the Financial District. It was casual Friday
and I took that theme to heart, wearing sweats and a leather jacket.
In my car was a large white youth with a backpack who was making it
his business to pace the car banging on the doors and windows. The
conductor had apparently called ahead for the police, and a group of
officers met the train and approached my car from the platform when
we pulled in. I just wanted to get to work, so I stood at the door ready
to leave this scene, but the police swarmed my position. Being a good
citizen, I went to move to another door so that they could apprehend
the culprit.

Instead, I was met by an officer yelling with the kind of authority
that surely got him an A at the academy, "Don't you move!" They also
trained his comrades such that each and every officer put his hand
on his gun, ready to riddle my body with justice. The now-infamous
Amy Cooper has given white women a bad name recently, but that day
it was a white woman's panicked plea that saved me: "No! No! Over

there!" she yelled, pointing to our rambunctious fellow rider. I went to work, alive but also a little dead inside.

As the nation is being rocked by black, brown, and white rage over police killings of George Floyd, Breonna Taylor, and so many other black Americans, I think of that day frequently. The rage is flaring now because it has become entirely too normal for a white man with power to casually, so very casually, apply enough pressure to a vulnerable black neck and cause the soul to vacate in an untimely fashion. America's propensity to dispense with black life is a sickness, a pathology that authorizes public murder for the sake of white supremacy.

Three major medical associations recently declared racism and police brutality public health crises. But I had long ago begun thinking of racism as a kind of social disease. I even gave it a name—Racial Diminishment Syndrome. This disease, like the coronavirus, is hard to detect, highly contagious, and often deadly. Many of the infected exhibit no symptoms, but may be "spreaders." When RDS is active in public spaces (almost always), social distancing will decrease the likelihood of extreme illness or untimely death.

Consider recent cases like Ahmaud Arbery and Atatiana Jefferson: Cause of death—RDS by way of jogging near white people and standing in a window where the police could see you, respectively. George Floyd's alleged offense was passing a fake twenty-dollar bill at a convenience store. Corporate barons rob the American people daily to the tune of millions, but it was Floyd who got a knee to the neck.

However, RDS need not resolve morbidly. For instance, I am still alive. The syndrome more commonly results in discomfort, inconvenience, and the sort of pains that eventually go away but the memories of which do not. Here we are talking about being pulled over for driving while black; a hotel patron assuming I am staff while walking the hall to my own room; professional colleagues failing to consider my point of view; and on and on. Social distancing can help prevent this kind of exposure, but it goes only so far.

In 2007, my wife and I moved to Charlottesville, Virginia. Before arriving I had been heartened by its electoral map—bright blue surrounded by socially menacing red. Once there, I soon learned that a blue town is in some ways worse than a red one because everyone is possessed of the conviction of their own racial virtues, and they're almost all very wrong. My first three years in Charlottesville were spent coldly coming to terms with its radical segregation and the absence of a black middle class. I observed as the police harassed homeless black men on the beloved Downtown Mall while the white frat boys got to shamelessly litter the streets surrounding the University of Virginia with beer kegs. Dionysus surely considered these misfits his chosen ones.

By 2010, nine years after the day I could have died, I was hardly leaving the house. When I did venture out, I kept to myself, avoided small talk, went straight home after doing what I needed to do, grateful when I finally made it back to the safe comfort of my own home. Nothing in particular was happening in the world other than America just being America.

With middle age looming on the horizon, my tolerance for being a social other and possibly in danger just by walking out my front door was atrophying. The equation was becoming clearer in my mind: Me + white spaces = precarity. At the University of Virginia, where I was an assistant professor, I received lessons from senior colleagues who had the power to make or break my career on the need for humility in work I sought to publish. Then there was the time that a colleague, upon learning my wife and I had accepted positions at Yale, saw fit to walk into my office and quip, "If I were angry at you, I would tell you to go [expletive] . . . but I'm not!" He was angry, and he did effectively just tell me that. Social distance was needed; this man was a vector of RDS.

When the Black Lives Matter movement took hold in the wake of Trayvon Martin's murder in 2012, it was almost as if an incantation had been whispered into the ether, because for the next five years America turned into what looked like a sizzle reel for a black snuff film, as images of shot black body after choked black body after broken black body after dragged on the sidewalk black body after violently removed from the public pool black body made their way to our computers and phones. But this was just the most grotesque presentation of RDS. My own experiences on the ground were more mundane, but terrifying in ways one can't quite put into words.

The northwestern edge of Yale's campus is rimmed with expensive shops. The highlight of these is an Apple store. One especially sunny and optimistic-feeling day, as I was walking back to my office from grabbing lunch I witnessed a scene that triggered my subway memory. About ten police officers and six vehicles, some of them vans big enough for several suspects, had converged on the body of a lone weeping young black male, about twenty years old by my guess. The police had him sitting in full display on the curb instead of in a car or wagon, thus a large white audience of Yale students were learning just how dangerous the New Haven natives were.

As I passed, I heard this young man sob: "What you expect me to do? I'm tired, I'm tired!" Maybe his onlookers were confused about his fatigue but I wasn't. He was tired of a mega-rich institution that thrived despite the black poverty that circled the institution like a Trumpian wall. He was tired of things like Yale building two new residential colleges at a cost of hundreds of millions of dollars, yet to look at the construction crews at the building site right next to one of the blackest areas of New Haven, you'd swear someone had said, "Hire anyone except those black people over there."

I didn't care about whatever property he allegedly lifted from the Apple store because I know what had been lifted from him and others on the social edges—a sense of being full and fully respected members of the richest nation on earth. As I walked by this young man I could only wish he had kept his social distance. RDS will get you.

By the time I reached my present job at Johns Hopkins University, I had essentially given up. When the small number of my black colleagues decided to challenge the university's wish to establish an armed police force on campus, one likely to be staffed by former officers from the Baltimore Police Department—one of the deadliest in the nation—I never bothered to join them. Valiant as their attempt was, I know this: When fearful whites and co-opted blacks decide the scariest people on earth are poor blacks, absolutely nothing can stop them from putting the police between them and the black folks they help to keep scary.

The resolution went forward despite opposition and passed, but last week the administration decided to delay the arrival of the armed force by two years. In the face of entire cities defunding or disbanding the police, this can't help but strike me as a hedge for a return of the status quo, rotten as it is. If these black people won't stay in their designated spaces, the police will help remind them. It will be a great surprise if I am not driven to my keyboard within the next few years writing about our campus's very own George Floyd moment. In the meantime, I keep my distance—I don't want to be a candidate for such a moment.

It is not only instances that can result in physical harm I avoid. I almost never attend casual faculty functions. I don't go out for drinks. I don't entertain for dinner parties and I don't seek to ingratiate myself into the lives of my white colleagues. I have a great deal of respect for the many white academics I have worked with. But some of them remain vectors of RDS nonetheless. I know so much about many of these people because I know what it is white America needs me to be for it to allow me inside. What they need is a version of myself that acquiesces and conforms, that is never displeased or contrary—or angry.

I won't do it. I'll social distance. It's already hard enough to breathe in America. Every day you feel like you're living with a knee on your neck. It's a sickness. And I am not immune.

JUNE 16, 2020

Dear White America

If you are white, and you are reading this letter, I ask that
you don't run to seek shelter from your own racism.

George Yancy

*I*N 2015, I CONDUCTED A SERIES OF NINETEEN INTERVIEWS WITH
*philosophers and public intellectuals on the issue of race. My aim was
to engage, in this very public space, with the often-unnamed elephant
in the room.*

*These discussions helped me, and I hope many of our readers, to bet-
ter understand how race continues to function in painful ways within our
country. That was one part of a gift that I wanted to give to readers of The
Stone, the larger philosophical community, and the world.*

*The interviewees themselves—bell hooks, Cornel West, Judith Butler,
Peter Singer, David H. Kim, Molefi Kete Asante among them—came from a
variety of racial backgrounds, and their concerns and positions were even
more diverse. But on the whole I came to see these interviews as linked by a
common thread: They were messages to white America—because they often
directly expressed the experience of those who live and have lived as people
of color in a white-run world, and that is something no white person could
ever truly know firsthand.*

That is how I want to deliver my own message now.

Dear White America,

I have a weighty request. As you read this letter, I want you to listen with love, a sort of love that demands that you look at parts of yourself that might cause pain and terror, as James Baldwin would say. Did you hear that? You may have missed it. I repeat: I want you to listen with love. Well, at least try.

We don't talk much about the urgency of love these days, especially within the public sphere. Much of our discourse these days is about revenge, name calling, hate, and divisiveness. I have yet to hear it from our presidential hopefuls, or our political pundits. I don't mean the Hollywood type of love, but the scary kind, the kind that risks not being reciprocated, the kind that refuses to flee in the face of danger. To make it a bit easier for you, I've decided to model, as best as I can, what I'm asking of you. Let me demonstrate the vulnerability that I wish you to show. As a child of Socrates, James Baldwin, and Audre Lorde, let me speak the truth, refuse to err on the side of caution.

This letter is a gift for you. Bear in mind, though, that some gifts can be heavy to bear. You don't have to accept it; there is no obligation. I give it freely, believing that many of you will throw the gift back in my face, saying that I wrongly accuse you, that I am too sensitive, that I'm a race hustler, and that I blame white people (you) for everything.

I have read many of your comments. I have even received some hate mail. In this letter, I ask you to look deep, to look into your souls with silence, to quiet that voice that will speak to you of your white "innocence." So, as you read this letter, take a deep breath. Make a space for my voice in the deepest part of your psyche. Try to listen, to practice being silent. There are times when you must quiet your own voice to hear from or about those who suffer in ways that you do not.

What if I told you that I'm sexist? Well, I am. Yes. I said it and I mean just that. I have watched my male students squirm in their seats when I've asked them to identify and talk about their sexism. There are few men, I suspect, who would say that they are sexists, and even fewer would admit that their sexism actually oppresses women. Certainly not publicly, as I've just done. No taking it back now.

To make things worse, I'm an academic, a philosopher. I'm supposed to be one of the "enlightened" ones. Surely, we are beyond being sexists. Some, who may genuinely care about my career, will say that I'm being too risky, that I am jeopardizing my academic livelihood. Some might even say that as a black male, who has already been stereotyped as a "crotch-grabbing, sexual fiend," that I'm at risk of reinforcing that stereotype. (Let's be real, that racist stereotype has been around for centuries; it is already part of white America's imaginary landscape.)

Yet, I refuse to remain a prisoner of the lies that we men like to tell ourselves—that we are beyond the messiness of sexism and male patriarchy, that we don't oppress women. Let me clarify. This doesn't mean that I intentionally hate women or that I desire to oppress them. It means that despite my best intentions, I perpetuate sexism every day of my life. Please don't take this as a confession for which I'm seeking forgiveness. Confessions can be easy, especially when we know that forgiveness is immediately forthcoming.

As a sexist, I have failed women. I have failed to speak out when I should have. I have failed to engage critically and extensively their pain and suffering in my writing. I have failed to transcend the rigidity of gender roles in my own life. I have failed to challenge those poisonous assumptions that women are "inferior" to men or to speak out loudly in the company of male philosophers who believe that feminist philosophy is just a nonphilosophical fad. I have been complicit with, and have allowed myself to be seduced by, a country that makes billions of dollars from sexually objectifying women, from pornography, commercials, video games, to Hollywood movies. I am not innocent.

I have been fed a poisonous diet of images that fragment women into mere body parts. I have also been complicit with a dominant male narrative that says that women enjoy being treated like sexual toys. In our collective male imagination, women are "things" to be used for our visual and physical titillation. And even as I know how poisonous and false these sexist assumptions are, I am often ambushed by my own hidden sexism. I continue to see women through the male gaze that belies my best intentions not to sexually objectify them.

Our collective male erotic feelings and fantasies are complicit in the degradation of women. And we must be mindful that not all women endure sexual degradation in the same way.

I recognize how my being a sexist has a differential impact on black women and women of color who are not only victims of racism, but also sexism, my sexism. For example, black women and women of color not only suffer from sexual objectification, but the ways in which they are objectified is linked to how they are racially depicted, some as "exotic" and others as "hyper-sexual." You see, the complicity, the responsibility, the pain that I cause runs deep. And, get this. I refuse to seek shelter; I refuse to live a lie. So, every day of my life I fight against the dominant male narrative, choosing to see women as subjects, not objects. But even as I fight, there are moments of failure. Just because I fight against sexism does not give me clean hands, as it were, at the end of the day; I continue to falter, and I continue to oppress. And even though the ways in which I oppress women is unintentional, this does not free me of being responsible.

If you are white, and you are reading this letter, I ask that you don't run to seek shelter from your own racism. Don't hide from your responsibility. Rather, begin, right now, to practice being vulnerable. Neither being a "good" white person nor a liberal white person will get you off the proverbial hook. I consider myself to be a decent human being. Yet, I'm sexist. Take another deep breath. I ask that you try to be "un-sutured." If that term brings to mind a state of pain, open flesh, it is meant to do so. After all, it is painful to let go of your "white innocence," to use this letter as a mirror, one that refuses to show you what you want to see, one that demands that you look at the lies that you tell yourself so that you don't feel the weight of responsibility for those who live under the yoke of whiteness, your whiteness.

I can see your anger. I can see that this letter is being misunderstood. This letter is not asking you to feel bad about yourself, to wallow in guilt. That is too easy. I'm asking for you to tarry, to linger, with the ways in which you perpetuate a racist society, the ways in which you are racist. I'm now daring you to face a racist history which, paraphrasing Baldwin, has placed you where you are and that has formed your own racism. Again, in the spirit of Baldwin, I am asking you to enter into battle with your white self. I'm asking that you open yourself up; to speak to, to admit to, the racist poison that is inside of you.

Again, take a deep breath. Don't tell me about how many black friends you have. Don't tell me that you are married to someone of color. Don't tell me that you voted for Obama. Don't tell me that I'm the racist. Don't tell me that you don't see color. Don't tell me that I'm blaming whites for everything. To do so is to hide yet again. You may have never used the N-word in your life, you may hate the KKK, but that does not mean that you don't harbor racism and benefit from racism. After all, you are part of a system that allows you to walk into stores where you are not followed, where you get to go for a bank loan and your skin does not count against you, where you don't need to engage in "the talk" that black people and people of color must tell their children when they are confronted by white police officers.

As you reap comfort from being white, we suffer for being black and people of color. But your comfort is linked to our pain and suffering. Just as my comfort in being male is linked to the suffering of women, which makes me sexist, so too you are racist. That is the gift that I want you to accept, to embrace. It is a form of knowledge that is taboo. Imagine the impact that the acceptance of this gift might have on you and the world.

Take another deep breath. I know that there are those who will write to me in the comment section with boiling anger, sarcasm, disbelief, denial. There are those who will say, "Yancy is just an angry black man." There are others who will say, "Why isn't Yancy telling black people to be honest about the violence in their own black neighborhoods?" Or, "How can Yancy say that all white people are racists?" If you are saying these things, then you've already failed to listen. I come with a gift. You're already rejecting the gift that I have to offer. This letter is about you. Don't change the conversation. I assure you that so many black people suffering from poverty and joblessness, which is linked to high levels of crime, are painfully aware of the existential toll that they have had to face because they are black and, as Baldwin adds, "for no other reason."

Some of your white brothers and sisters have made this leap. The legal scholar Stephanie M. Wildman, has written, "I simply believe that no matter how hard I work at not being racist, I still am. Because part of racism is systemic, I benefit from the privilege that I am struggling to see." And the journalism professor Robert Jensen: "I like to think I have changed, even though I routinely trip over the lingering effects of that internalized racism and the institutional racism around me. Every time I walk into a store at the same time as a black man and the security guard follows him and leaves me alone to shop, I am benefiting from white privilege."

What I'm asking is that you first accept the racism within yourself, accept all of the truth about what it means for you to be white in a society that was created for you. I'm asking for you to trace the binds that tie you to forms of domination that you would rather not see. When you walk into the world, you can walk with assurance; you have already signed a contract, so to speak, that guarantees you a certain form of social safety.

Baldwin argues for a form of love that is "a state of being, or state of grace—not in the infantile American sense of being made happy but in the tough and universal sense of quest and daring and growth." Most of my days, I'm engaged in a personal and societal battle against sexism. So many times, I fail. And so many times, I'm complicit. But I refuse to hide behind that mirror that lies to me about my "non-sexist nobility." Baldwin says, "Love takes off the masks that we fear we cannot live without and know we cannot live within." In my heart, I'm done with the mask of sexism, though I'm tempted every day to wear it. And, there are times when it still gets the better of me.

White America, are you prepared to be at war with yourself, your white identity, your white power, your white privilege? Are you prepared to show me a white self that love has unmasked? I'm asking for love in return for a gift; in fact, I'm hoping that this gift might help you to see yourself in ways that you have not seen before. Of course, the history of white supremacy in America belies this gesture of black gift-giving, this gesture of non-sentimental love. Martin Luther King Jr. was murdered even as he loved.

Perhaps the language of this letter will encourage a split—not a split between black and white, but a fissure in your understanding, a space for loving a Trayvon Martin, Eric Garner, Tamir Rice, Aiyana Jones, Sandra Bland, Laquan McDonald, and others. I'm suggesting a form of love that enables you to see the role that you play (even despite your anti-racist actions) in a system that continues to value black lives on the cheap.

Take one more deep breath. I have another gift.

If you have young children, before you fall off to sleep tonight, I want you to hold your child. Touch your child's face. Smell your child's hair. Count the fingers on your child's hand. See the miracle that is your child. And then, with as much vision as you can muster, I want you to imagine that your child is black.

In peace,

George Yancy

DECEMBER 24, 2015

Enough with Crumbs—I Want the Cake

Anarchy can dismantle patriarchy. I do not want
what men have. I want more. I want to be free.

Mona Eltahawy

Like a lot of Black women, I have always had to invent
the power my freedom requires.
—JUNE JORDAN, *ON CALL: POLITICAL ESSAYS* (1985)

I AM A FEMINIST. I AM AN ANARCHIST. TO ME, ANY DISCUSSION
of power is essentially one about freedom, and talk of freedom is
impossible without a reckoning with power.

In *Rethinking Anarchy*, the Spanish social theorist Carlos Taibo
reminds us that "anarchists have frequently defined themselves
first on the basis of what they reject—the state, capitalism, inequality, patriarchal society, war, militarism, repression in all its forms,
authority."

So what is the power that my freedom requires?

As a woman of color, I define power initially by what it is not. To be
powerful is not to be what a man can do or be. Men are not my yard-
stick. If men themselves are not free of the ravages of racism, capitalism, and other forms of oppression, it is not enough to say I want to
be equal to them. As long as patriarchy remains unchallenged, men

will continue to be the default and the standard against which every-thing is measured.

Being powerful must mean more than doing what men do or being what men can be. I do not want what men have. I want much more. I want to be free.

To be free, I must defy, disobey, and disrupt.

"Civil disobedience . . . was not the problem, despite the warn-ings of some that it threatened social stability, that it led to anarchy," the author and activist Howard Zinn wrote in *You Can't Be Neutral on a Moving Train: A Personal History of Our Times*. "The greatest dan-ger . . . was civil obedience, the submission of individual conscience to governmental authority. Such obedience led to the horrors we saw in totalitarian states, and in liberal states it led to the public's acceptance of war whenever the so-called democratic government decided on it."

Power for a few exceptional women is not equality or empower-ment for all, and it is no reason to celebrate. We must define power in a way that liberates us from patriarchy's hierarchies. That is why I am an anarchist—why I defy, disobey, and disrupt. We must imagine the world we want so that we can redefine what power is, what a powerful woman looks like, and how power can be used to subvert rather than uphold patriarchy. We must imagine better. We can imagine better. By imagining that better world, we invent the power required for our freedom.

A shining example of powerful women came to me in 2014, ironi-cally while watching the world's grandest men's sporting event, the soccer World Cup.

My father and I were in a Cairo café to watch the World Cup final, featuring Germany and Argentina playing in Rio de Janeiro's Mara-canã Stadium. Germany won its fourth championship that night, and during the ceremony to hand the cup to the winners, a boy sit-ting with his family at the table next to ours pointed at the televi-sion screen where two women were standing at a podium, awaiting the players.

"Who is that woman, Baba?" the boy asked.

"That is the president of Brazil," his father replied.

"A woman can be president?"

I jumped into action, explaining that the two teams we had just watched had women leaders, as did the country where they had played. Dilma Rousseff, the president of Brazil, and Angela Merkel, the chancellor of Germany, were giving out handshakes and hugs—only Argentine President Cristina Fernández de Kirchner was absent.

I wanted the boy and the two girls sitting with his family to know that women could be presidents and leaders. Much as with ambition, you need to see what you want to become. Egypt once had a queen called Hatshepsut who ruled for more than twenty years during the fifteenth century BC. She was, for a time, the most powerful person in the ancient world. But I wanted someone who was still alive to point to as a reminder that women could be powerful.

Had there been more time, I would have told those children that power is more complicated than presidents and chancellors. That power lives in more places than the presidential office. That there is a difference between power wielded in service of a few and power wielded in service of all.

In the intervening years, two of those countries that were led by women during the 2014 World Cup have served as reminders that when it comes to patriarchy and power, the truth is much more complicated than simply asking, "Can a woman be president?" We must ask equally pertinent questions: Is that woman feminist? Is she invested in dismantling patriarchy? Will she use her power to uphold or diminish patriarchy? Both Brazil and Germany have given us complicated answers.

Brazil might have once elected a female president, but it remains solidly patriarchal. In October 2018, the far-right Jair Bolsonaro became the president of Latin America's largest democracy.

The antithesis of Mr. Bolsonaro was Marielle Franco, a young queer woman who was one of Brazil's few black female politicians. Franco, a member of Rio de Janeiro's City Council and a human rights advocate against the paramilitary gangs that control the city's fave-las, was murdered, possibly by a former police officer with connec-tions to Bolsonaro, seven months before the presidential election.

Queer women of color—marginalized and too often disempow-ered because of their race, gender, and sexuality—are most astute in their definition of what power is.

That Franco—a young, black, queer woman who was outspoken in her condemnation of police brutality—was killed, and Bolsonaro—a misogynist, racist, homophobic white man who champions guns and greater police powers—is president, is a shocking reminder of what Brazil is today.

A 2017 study into right-wing populist voters in Germany, France, Greece, Poland, Sweden, and Hungary by the Friedrich Ebert Foun-dation, which is affiliated with Germany's center-left Social Demo-cratic Party, found that women are increasingly drawn to right-wing populist parties.

Tellingly, the study found that while many right-wing populist parties have prominent female figures among their leadership—such as Marine Le Pen in France, Beata Szydlo in Poland, and Alice Weidel in Germany—women are conspicuous in their absence elsewhere. Most of the right-wing parties' parliamentary representatives are male. In Germany, for example, just ten women are included in the far-right Alternative for Germany's ninety-one seats in Parliament.

"These women are there to give these parties a more open, mod-ern guise and to appeal to female voters," Elisa Gutsche, who edited the study, told Deutsche Welle. "These are not progressive parties; there is no real gender equality."

Those populist women's race matters too. They are almost all white. That gives them a certain proximity to power that shields them and lets them vote against their own interests without fear of too many negative side effects. In the United States, that dynamic explains why the majority of white women voters voted for Donald Trump in 2016 and for Roy Moore, who was accused of sexual abuse and child molestation, in Alabama in 2017. More recently, it explains why a white woman in Alabama sponsored the Human Life Protection Act, the most stringent abortion bill in the United States, and a white woman, Governor Kay Ivey, signed the bill into law. Those are women who uphold, not dismantle, a patriarchy that remains mostly white.

Patriarchy too often throws women crumbs in return for a limited form of power. Women who accept those crumbs are expected in return to uphold patriarchy, internalize its dictates, police other women, and never forget that power bestowed is power that can be retracted. Patriarchy will allow a few women into places they have not been allowed before and call it progress, while at the same time demanding that we not point out that power remains in the hands of those throwing us crumbs.

I don't want crumbs; I want the whole cake, and I want to bake it myself. I want, as June Jordan wrote, "to invent the power my freedom requires."

MAY 28, 2019

Drawing a Line in the "Gay Wedding Cake" Case

Two bakers in Colorado refused to sell cakes to customers.
So why should one refusal be legal and the other not?

John Corvino

AT FIRST GLANCE, THE MASTERPIECE CAKESHOP CASE LOOKS easy. In 2012 Charlie Craig and David Mullins attempted to buy a wedding cake at Masterpiece Cakeshop in Lakewood, Colorado. The owner, an evangelical Christian named Jack Phillips, refused to sell them one. The Colorado Civil Rights Commission found Phillips liable for sexual-orientation discrimination, which is prohibited by the state's public accommodations law. State courts have upheld the commission's decision.

The reason the nation's high court is giving the case a second glance is Phillips's First Amendment claim that he was not, in fact, discriminating on the basis of sexual orientation, but on the basis of a particular message: endorsement of same-sex marriage. Phillips made it clear to the gay couple that he would happily sell them other items: birthday cakes, cookies, and so on. He welcomes LGBT customers; he is simply unwilling to use his artistic talents in the service of a message that he deems immoral.

One might better appreciate Phillips's position by considering a second case. In 2014, not long after the commission announced its Masterpiece decision, William Jack attempted to buy a cake at Azucar Bakery in Denver, Colorado. Specifically, he requested a Bible-shaped cake decorated with an image of two grooms covered by a red X, plus the words "God hates sin. Psalm 45:7" and "Homosexuality is a detestable sin. Leviticus 18:22." The owner, Marjorie Silva, refused to create such an image or message, which conflicts with her moral beliefs. She did, however, offer to sell him a Bible-shaped cake and provide an icing bag so that he could decorate it as he saw fit. The customer filed a complaint alleging religious discrimination, which is also prohibited by Colorado's public accommodations law. But the commission disagreed, arguing that Silva's refusal was based not on the customer's religion, but on the cake's particular message.

Jack Phillips's supporters have been crying foul since. If the First Amendment protects Marjorie Silva's right not to condemn same-sex relationships, they argue, then it protects Jack Phillips's right not to celebrate them. But there is a key difference between the cases, and the difference points to a useful line-drawing principle.

Put aside the plausible objection that treating cakes as speech—especially cakes without writing, as in the Masterpiece case—abuses the First Amendment. And put aside the even more plausible objection that whatever "speech" is involved is clearly that of the customers, not of the baker: As law professors Dale Carpenter and Eugene Volokh explain in a Masterpiece brief, "No one looks at a wedding cake and reflects, 'the baker has blessed this union.' " After all, that objection is arguably just as applicable to the Bible-cake case.

Finally, put aside the objection that "It's just cake!" That could be said to any of the parties in these disputes, and it doesn't alter the deeper rationale for anti-discrimination laws, which are about ensuring equal access in the public sphere—not just for cakes, flowers, and frills, but for a wide range of vital goods and services.

It is tempting to describe Marjorie Silva's Bible-cake refusal as the moral mirror-image of Jack Phillips's wedding-cake refusal: Neither baker was willing to assist in conveying a message to which they were morally opposed.

But that's not quite right. For recall that Silva was willing to sell the customer a Bible-shaped cake and even to provide an icing bag, knowing full well what the customer intended to write. She was willing to sell this customer the very same items that she would sell to any other customer; what he did with them after leaving her store was, quite literally, none of her business.

Therein lies the crucial difference between the cases: Silva's objection was about what she sold; a design-based objection. Phillips's objection was about to whom it was sold; a user-based objection. The gay couple never even had the opportunity to discuss designs with Phillips, because the baker made it immediately clear that he would not sell them any wedding cake at all. Indeed, Masterpiece once even refused a cupcake order to lesbians upon learning that they were for the couple's commitment ceremony.

Business owners generally have wide discretion over what they do and do not sell: A vegan bakery needn't sell real buttercream cakes. A kosher bakery needn't sell cakes topped with candied bacon, or in the shape of crosses. By contrast, business owners generally do not have discretion over how their products are later used: A kosher bakery may not refuse to sell bread to non-Jews, who might use it for ham-and-cheese sandwiches.

(Of course, there are times when the buyer's identity or the intended use is legally relevant. It is permitted—indeed, required—to refuse alcohol to minors, or torches to someone who announces that he is about to commit arson. But that legal concern does not apply here.)

In his defense, Phillips has pointed out that he refuses to sell Halloween cakes or demon-themed cakes; he analogizes these refusals to his unwillingness to sell gay wedding cakes. In other words, he maintains that his turning away the gay couple was about what was requested, not who was requesting it.

The problem with this retort is that "gay wedding cakes" are not a thing. Same-sex couples order their cakes from the same catalogs as everyone else, with the same options for size, shape, icing, filling, and so on. Although Phillips's cakes are undeniably quite artistic, he did not reject a particular design option, such as a topper with two grooms—in which case, his First Amendment argument would be more compelling. Instead, he flatly told Craig and Mullins that he would not sell them a wedding cake.

Imagine a fabric shop owner who makes artistic silk-screened fabrics. It would be one thing if she declined to create a particular pattern, perhaps because she found it obscene. It would be quite another if she offered that pattern to some customers, but wouldn't sell it to Muslims who intend it for hijabs. The Bible-cake case is like the first, design-based refusal; the Masterpiece case is like the second, user-based one.

Or imagine a winemaker. It would be one thing if she declined to produce a special blend. It would be another if she offered that blend, but refused to sell it to Catholic priests who intended it for sacramental use. The latter would run afoul of Colorado's public accommodations law, which prohibits religious discrimination.

But wait: Isn't there a difference between discrimination that's user-based and discrimination that's use-based? The winemaker in our example is not refusing to sell wine to Catholics, or even to priests; she is merely refusing to sell the wine for a particular purpose. Same with the fabric-store owner, who might happily sell to Muslims making curtains. In a similar vein, Jack Phillips is explicitly willing to sell LGBT people a wide range of baked goods, as long as they are not to be used for same-sex weddings.

This kind of sophistry has been rejected by the Court before. As the late Justice Scalia once wrote, "A tax on wearing yarmulkes is a tax on Jews." Some activities are so fundamental to certain identities that discrimination according to one is effectively discrimination according to the other. That's certainly true of wearing hijabs and religion, or celebrating mass and religion; likewise of same-sex weddings and sexual orientation. In such cases, use-based discrimination and user-based discrimination amount to the same thing.

But couldn't one argue in the Bible-cake case that a commitment to a traditional Biblical understanding of sexuality is similarly fundamental to William Jack's identity? Of course. But it doesn't follow that Marjorie Silva, the baker in that case, must alter what she sells in order to help him express that identity. While Jack Phillips, the Masterpiece baker, is akin to the winemaker who won't sell wine for mass, Silva is more like one who sells wine to all customers, but declines to put crosses on the labels. Again, her refusal is design-based, not identity-based or use-based. Unlike Phillips, she is willing to sell this customer the same items she sells to any other customer.

We've seen Jack Phillips's First Amendment argument before. Back in 1964, when Maurice Bessinger of Piggie Park BBQ fought public accommodations laws that required him to serve black customers equally, he invoked his rights to freedom of speech and freedom of religion. Bessinger noted that he was happy to sell black customers take-out food; he simply did not want to be complicit in what he saw as the evil of integrated dining. The Supreme Court unanimously rejected this argument.

The details of the current cases are different, as is the social context. As I've argued before at The Stone, it's a mistake to treat sexual-orientation discrimination as exactly like racial discrimination—just as it's a mistake to treat it as entirely dissimilar. But the underlying principle from Piggie Park holds in the case at hand: Freedom of speech and freedom of religion do not exempt business owners from public accommodations laws, which require them to serve customers equally. The Court should uphold the commission's decision and rule against Phillips.

NOVEMBER 27, 2017

On June 4, 2018, the Supreme Court ruled in favor of Masterpiece Cakeshop, reversing the decision of the Colorado Civil Rights Commission, arguing that the commission's conduct in evaluating Phillips's reasons for declining to make a wedding cake for a same-sex couple violated his right to free exercise.

Education in the Age of Outrage

When pain and suffering are equated with moral authority,
the mission of higher education becomes an impossible one.

Kelly Oliver

A S AN OPENLY BISEXUAL WOMAN WHO DID NOT HAVE A SINGLE female professor throughout my college and postgraduate education in any subject, and who faced harassment and abuse, as well as downright sabotage in graduate school, I am sympathetic to efforts on campuses to give voice and equal power to groups that have been historically excluded and silenced.

Now, as a philosophy professor, I am part of perhaps the most male-dominated (and arguably least feminist-friendly) discipline in the humanities, and have dedicated much of my career to mentoring women and students of color. I understand that injustice and inequality remain firmly in place, and in order to eliminate it, much more work remains to be done.

So it is with some trepidation that I admit that the current political climate in academia confuses me. The more I read about trigger warnings, safe spaces, and petitions to retract scholarly articles, the more my head spins. On top of that confusion, I harbor a fear of expressing views that will offend other progressives, scholars, and teachers who may also be fighting oppression. And I fear being subject to public shaming on social media, and receiving private hate mail. (I still am, after my response in May to the controversy over Rebecca Tuvel's article in the journal *Hypatia*.) In short, I find myself in an educational environment in which outrage, censoring, and public shaming has begun to replace critique, disagreement, and debate.

Public shaming always has a purpose, whether it comes from the left or right, from progressives or conservatives, activists or armchair philosophers. It may be an effective way to close down discussion, or deter others from taking certain unwanted political positions. It may also be a way to circumvent the status quo in the academy and challenge the standards of academic publishing and career advancement.

But the problematic effects of public shaming are many—among them, silencing "allies," blaming individuals rather than examining social context, fostering intolerance and divisiveness, creating a "with-us-or-against-us" ethos, and reducing identity politics to a version of "oppression Olympics." In cases where pain and suffering are equated with moral authority, calling out injustice can operate as a form of signaling virtue.

Let's face it, outrage sells. That's why social media and mainstream news outlets are invested in promoting it; they can both fuel and produce desires by tailoring their content to suit individual tastes. The red and blue news feeds and the "click bait" that proliferate on them produce profits, but they have also helped to make our time one of deep divisions and reactionary hatred, with a radicalization of both sides in a culture war that risks deepening into a civil war, with militarized armies of fascists and anti-fascists fighting in the streets.

In a culture that increasingly values raw emotions uncontaminated by scholarly analysis, the uncritical legitimation of feelings as the basis for moral authority becomes a form of political leveling. If unexamined outrage is the new truth, then we are moving dangerously close to a form of reactionary politics that closes down difficult discussions and prevents us from distinguishing between sexism or racism and critical discussions of them. Certainly, as Pascal said, "the heart has its reasons of which reason knows not," but we have arrived at a point where we need to analyze what they are in order to better understand ourselves and others.

Privileging raw feelings over the cooked analysis of them not only fuels anti-intellectualism, but also conceals the socio-historical context that produces those feelings. In other words, feelings are never completely raw, but always already cooked. So too analysis is never completely devoid of emotion. Pathos and logos aren't polar opposites. Yet to authorize outrage (whether on the left or the right) as foundational and beyond analysis is to deny the ways in which race, class, gender, politics, upbringing, culture, and history shape our emotions.

When outrage becomes an end in itself, it also becomes a form of fundamentalism and part of a dogma of purity that can be potentially aggressive, hostile, and violent. When political activism becomes dogmatic and punishing, it uses the same techniques of exclusion and oppression that it rejects—only now in the name of liberation.

While political purity and fundamentalism are expressions of real distress, they close down self-critical examination of that distress, and our own investments in violence. And, they produce a need for ever more and stronger outrage. Furthermore, if unexamined feelings and outrage always trump arguments and analysis, then the unhappy consequence is that white nationalists and on-campus rapists will be as justified in their claims to victimhood and safe spaces as black men and women abused by police or women who've been raped. We need ways of distinguishing between calling in and calling out to fight oppression-based violence.

Leveling violence and harm, and ignoring socio-historical context, risks undermining the voices of victims of the worst abuse and oppression. Comparing the suffering of perpetrators of racial or sexual violence and hate speech to the suffering of their victims is an unacceptable consequence of accepting outrage as the source of moral authority. Comparing the pain and suffering of being raped to the pain and suffering of being accused of rape not only belittles the experiences of the rape victim, but also coops the discourse of victimhood in ways that demand analysis. So too comparing teachers and scholars criticizing sexism and racism to perpetrators of violence and hate speech closes down discussions necessary to address—and hopefully overcome—those very harms.

Obviously, as teachers and scholars, we make mistakes and need to be open to interminable education. But the conditions for critical teaching and learning are undermined when feelings are equated with reasons in call-out culture.

Certainly, outrage has a place in the academy and in politics. But when emotional pain and suffering are taken as the foundation of moral authority and cannot be analyzed because they are viewed as absolute truths or obvious facts, the mission of higher education—to examine unquestioned assumptions about the world and the self— becomes a mission impossible.

Although social media can be effective for organizing, and for forming communities (on both the left and the right), it is also often fueled by emotional reaction rather than thoughtful response. Life is flattened to fit the screen, and cute cat videos play next to photo- graphs of the latest atrocity. Social media works by leveling and rip- ping bits of life from their contexts as a form of entertainment or news—the more outrageous, the better. As consumers, we engage in the virtual performance of pathos and moral virtue with our likes, crying, or angry emojis, and the circulation of outrage or sympathy through sharing petitions or calls for donations.

In academia, social media has become not just a way to dissemi- nate research, or engage in debate, but also a way to close it down by shaming and cyberbullying. Outrage may be the first word in social transformation, but it shouldn't be the last. In our racist and sexist culture, no one is "pure" when it comes to issues of race and gender, and the moral high ground is always precarious. As teachers, hope- fully we can still agree that education has value, especially when it comes to educating each other and ourselves.

OCTOBER 16, 2017

VIII

WHAT IS THE DIFFERENCE BETWEEN
RIGHT AND WRONG?

What "Justice" Really Means

The word has taken a beating. But what
role does it truly play in our lives?

Paul Bloomfield

I T'S A STAPLE OF COMMON SENSE THAT WE DON'T LET JUDGES
try their own cases. Yet if we are to gain self-knowledge, we all must
do just that: We must judge ourselves to know ourselves. While we
typically think of justice as a virtue of social arrangements or political institutions, the United States has recently borne witness to
this virtue in its first-person aspect—self-regarding justice—while
watching the confirmation hearings of a Supreme Court justice.

The virtue of justice requires not only that we judge others fairly,
but also that we judge ourselves fairly. This is no mean feat. The trouble is that if a person is a poor judge of him- or herself, it is hard to
imagine that person being a good judge of others. Bias toward the self
often leads to bias against others. Justice begins within ourselves.

While justice is important for each of us in our personal lives, it
becomes strikingly important when we think of those in positions of
power. We need leaders motivated by a love of justice and not merely
self-aggrandizement. Leadership without an inner moral compass
reliably pointing toward justice inevitably ends in the abuse of power.

Philosophically, all virtues are ideals that we can only approach
without fully attaining them. So, we can always aspire to do better.

Given this, what role does the virtue of justice play in our personal lives? What role ought it to play?

In fact there are two roles: Justice functions both in our epistemology, or how we form and justify our beliefs, as well as in practical morality, informing our private and public behavior. These ought to be entwined in our lives since we ought not only think in a fair and just manner but also act accordingly.

The apotheosis of justice is the courtroom judge, interpreting the law and ruling on evidence concerning innocence and guilt. Model judges are epistemically just: Their conclusions are not prejudged, their cognitive processes are never biased or unduly swayed, and their verdicts reliably correspond to the facts. Truth is their goal. Not only must there be no thumb on the scale, the evidence must be balanced while wearing a blindfold. The rulings of judges, however, are also undeniably moral, bearing as they do on issues of justice, restitution, and the execution of punishment.

Just people are wise in the ways of fairness, equality, desert, and mercy. They are normally pacific. Just people mind their own business, except when they see and call out injustice, speaking truth to power, which they'll do even at a personal cost. Justice questions authority.

Just people also question themselves. This makes them honest and non-self-deceptive. They vigilantly maintain a clear conscience. Just people are cognizant of their own mistakes and faults, and so they are forgiving of others. They respect who they actually are and not whom they merely wish they were, and their authentic self-respect makes them respectful of others. People who are just do as they say and say as they do: their word is their bond. They are capable of great loyalty and fidelity, but not without limit.

The central epistemic principles of justice require like cases to be treated alike, as captured legally by the concepts of the rule of law and precedent. Weak and strong, rich and poor, all are equal before the law (where this must include the Supreme Court justices and presidents of the United States). While applying general principles alone is sufficient for clear, ordinary cases, a fine sensitivity, experience, and reflection is necessary for reliably judging unusual or exceptional cases. Well-developed justice requires expertise in making hard "judgment calls."

The central moral principles of justice require us to give proper respect to one another: Each of us must recognize the other as a person and not merely as an object. Each of us may testify. The least common denominator among us is that we are all human beings. In addition to that, we each have particular features making us all unique. Justice pays proper attention to what we have in common and to what sets us apart.

In discussing justice as a personal virtue, Aristotle said that being just "is a mean between committing injustice and suffering it, since the one is having more than one's share, while the other is having less." As recklessness and cowardice are opposing vices of courage, arrogance and servility are opposing vices of justice.

From sidewalk sexual harassment to the obstruction of justice, all abuses of power involve an unjust willingness to greedily arrogate more than one's due. Typically, those who abuse their strength or cheat, and then don't get caught or punished, self-deceptively think they've "beaten the system" and "won." But fooling others into thinking you have earned a victory is not the same as genuinely being victorious. Cheaters fool themselves when they elide this difference.

The other way to fail justice is by judging ourselves to be less worthy than we truly are. This is sadly common among oppressed people, but it also arises among the affluent and powerful under the guise of the "impostor syndrome." Humility has its place, but we shouldn't overdo it, nor let it interfere with the intellectual courage required to call out injustice. Those who unfairly put themselves down or are servile, for whatever reason, are doing themselves an injustice by willfully accepting less than their fair share.

Given all this, the virtue of justice plays an important role in families and friendships, between neighbors and citizens, colleagues and clients, acquaintances and strangers. But it is also central to being a good person and living happily, and not merely deceiving oneself into believing that one is a good person and that one is happy.

Bringing justice fully into our lives, thinking in terms of it, will make us more circumspect. We are all too fallible. But it is often the case that we are much better at spotting the faults of others than we are at spotting faults in ourselves. Our blind spots are conveniently located to keep us from seeing our own weaknesses. What a coincidence!

Life is neither just nor fair: Good things happen to bad people, and bad things happen to good people. This, however, only increases our obligation to be as just and fair as we can be, to be honest with ourselves as well as others, to try to correct injustice when we see it, and to do as much right in this unfair world as we can.

OCTOBER 10, 2018

Are We All "Harmless Torturers" Now?

In the age of online shaming, we should push ourselves
to consider the collective consequences of our actions.

Paul Bloom and Matthew Jordan

T HERE IS A DIAL IN FRONT OF YOU, AND IF YOU TURN IT, A stranger who is in mild pain from being shocked will experience a tiny increase in the amount of the shock, so slight that he doesn't even notice it. You turn it and leave. And then hundreds of people go up to the dial and each also turns it, so that eventually the victim is screaming in agony.

Did you do anything wrong? Derek Parfit, the influential British philosopher who died in January 2017, called this the case of the Harmless Torturer. Parfit first considered a simpler scenario in which a thousand torturers each turn the dial a thousand times on their own victim. This is plainly terrible. But then he explores a contrasting case where each of the torturers turns a dial a thousand times—each turn shocking a different one of the thousand victims. The end result is the same; a thousand people in agony. And yet morally it feels different, since in the second case nobody, individually, caused any real harm to any single individual.

This seems like the sort of clever technical example that philosophers love—among other things, it's a challenge to a utilitarian view in which the wrongness of an act is reduced to its consequences—but one with no actual real-world relevance. But the world has changed since Parfit published his scenario in 1986. Today, in 2018, the two authors of this article are Harmless Torturers, and you—regardless of which side of any particular issue you are on—probably are one too.

Parfit's scenario unfolds all the time on social media. Someone writes something ugly about you on Facebook; depending on your relationship with that person, it may or may not be personally hurtful, but nobody notices it, and so it's not a big deal. But if a day later it has a thousand likes and several hundred mocking comments, you might well be crushed. Even though any particular comment on its own may have caused you little or no pain, the aggregate effect is far more severe.

In his 2015 book *So You've Been Publicly Shamed*, Jon Ronson explored the effects of internet mobbing, including the story of a woman whose ironic tweet about white privilege went terribly wrong, generating tens of thousands of angry tweets, leading her to lose her job and go into hiding. Since then, the mob has been busy: its focus has turned to a dentist who killed a lion, a series of white women who without apparent cause called the police on black people, a left-wing professor who asked her friends to expel a journalist from a protest, and many, many others.

When we think of the savagery of social media, we often think of awful individual behavior—death threats and rape threats; the release of personal information, including home addresses and the locations of the victim's children; vicious lies; and the like. Harmless Torturers never go that far; we just like, retweet, and add the occasional clever remark. But there are millions of us, and we're all turning the dial.

Parfit never tells us what motivates the torturers in his thought experiment, but there are a lot of considerations in everyday life. We are moral animals, after all. There is abundant evidence from laboratory studies and from real life that we wish to see immoral agents get their comeuppance. And this is grounded in sound evolutionary logic: If we weren't disposed to punish or exclude bad actors, there would be no cost to being a bad actor, and cooperative societies couldn't get off the ground.

There is also a sort of social credit that comes with being seen as a moralistic punisher; we want to show off our goodness to others, to signal our virtue. We are more likely to punish when others are watching, and there is evidence that third parties think more highly of—and are more likely to later trust—those who punish bad actors versus those who sit back and do nothing.

Moral and social motivations are hard to disentangle in the real world. When a philosopher—Bryan W. Van Norden, writing for The Stone—says, "Like most Americans, I spontaneously cheered when I saw the white nationalist Richard Spencer punched in the face during an interview," it is hard to tell how much of this is a report of genuine pleasure at a racist getting his just deserts and how much of it is the desire to be seen as anti-racist to an approving audience. If the conscious motivation for our condemnation is mostly signaling, the idea of making our victims suffer might never even occur to us. And the ease with which we can express moral outrage online—in most cases without any real-world repercussions—makes this condemnation that much easier. As our Yale colleague Molly Crockett put it in an article recently, "If moral outrage is a fire, is the internet like gasoline?"

There is also a system of reward built into online shaming. In an essay at *Quilette*, "I Was the Mob Until the Mob Came for Me," a self-described former social justice warrior writing under the pseudonym Barrett Wilson described the thrill he felt in his mobbing days: "Every time I would call someone racist or sexist, I would get a rush. That rush would then be reaffirmed and sustained by the stars, hearts, and thumbs-up that constitute the nickels and dimes of social media validation."

But isn't this death by a thousand cuts a good thing? If it were Hitler, wouldn't you be right to let him have it? Yes—but the problem is that when we are infused with moral outrage, acting as part of a crowd, and operating in a virtual world with no fixed system of evaluation, law, or justice, all our enemies are Hitler. There can easily be, as Ronson puts it, a "disconnect between the severity of the crime and the gleeful savagery of the punishment."

Certainly, public shaming can have positive effects; sometimes the angry mob gets it right—punching up and hitting the right target. But Harmless Torturers can just as easily swarm the weak; the mobbing can be based on lies and confusions or ignorantly encouraged by powerful celebrities and politicians, including, notably, the current president.

The Harmless Torturer effect isn't limited to social media; we can also see the effects of aggregation when it comes to more impactful individual actions. Likes and retweets bear a structural similarity to execution by stoning, particularly if the crowd is large: it's hard to see the victim, and nobody has good aim. Social shunning is another case, torture through the accumulation of omissions—individuals avoiding social contact with a certain person—as opposed to actions.

The writer Julian Sanchez, a senior fellow at the libertarian Cato Institute, has used the Parfit example in a discussion of behaviors like whistling at women on the street or jokingly using offensive language. He points out that a typical response to criticism of such behaviors is denial—many feel that there are no bad intentions in these actions and nobody is hurt by them. But even if this is true for certain individual actions, when we consider them in the aggregate, happening over and over and over again, a thousand times from a thousand different people, their impact becomes more clear.

It's difficult to change the sorts of behaviors that Sanchez discusses, and probably even harder to get people to rethink internet mobbing, which, when we feel we have right on our side, can feel so good. Our minds have evolved to think about the effects of our individual actions; it's hard to consider aggregate effects. But the lesson of Parfit's Harmless Torturer is that if we want to be decent people, we should try.

AUGUST 9, 2018

What We Owe to Others: Simone Weil's Radical Reminder

She believed we have obligations to attend to our fellow
humans. How could that spirit change our politics?

Robert Zaretsky

SEVENTY-FIVE YEARS AGO, THE FRENCH PHILOSOPHER AND
mystic Simone Weil joined Charles de Gaulle's Free French movement in London. We do not know if the Catholic and conservative
general, who never met Weil, knew she had left her post as a professor of philosophy in order to work on assembly lines, left her family
to fight alongside anarchists in Spain, and left her country to escape
the anti-Semitic Vichy regime. All we do know is that de Gaulle read
Weil's plan to parachute white-uniformed nurses onto battlefields,
armed only with the obligation to succor the injured and sacrifice
their own lives. Setting down the paper, de Gaulle blurted: "But,
she's crazy!"

De Gaulle was right about the plan, but not the person. In fact,
Weil's reflections on the nature of obligation offer a bracing dose
of sanity in our perplexing and polarizing times. During the final
months of her life—she died in the summer of 1943—Weil wrote of
several of her most subversive and seminal texts. (That they were
essentially position papers for the Free French makes them all the
more extraordinary.) This is particularly true for "Human Personality" and "Draft for a Statement of Human Obligations," both of which

are devoted to distinctions Weil insists upon personal rights and impersonal duties.

When we talk about justice today, we almost always find ourselves talking about rights we believe are entrenched in nature and have been enshrined in our founding documents. This language reflects a liberal conception of human action and interaction, casting us as rational agents who reach agreements with one another through calculation and negotiation. Moreover, as the philosopher Charles Taylor has argued, while each of us "has a conception of the good or worthwhile life," none of us accepts "a socially endorsed conception of the good." In essence, the ideal of right has ceded to the ideal of rights.

The problem, for Weil, with the liberal conception of rights—and the laws that codify them—is that it is rooted in the personal, not the impersonal. Our society, she insists, is one where personal rights are tied at the hip to private property. Taking his cue from Weil, political theorist Edward Andrew suggests that a rights-based society "is the consensual society where everything is vendible at constitutional conventions or the marketplace." This reveals what Weil, like Thomas Hobbes, believes to be the sole universal truth concerning human affairs: certain groups will always wield greater clout than other groups. "Rights talk" deals with the relative and alienable, not absolute and inalienable. For Weil, the old joke about our legal system—"How much justice can you afford?"—takes on a tragic immediacy.

Moreover, the emphasis on "inalienable human rights"—a phrase, Weil declares, history has shown to be meaningless—blinds us to the only true good, one rooted in what Weil calls the "impersonal." This term, paradoxically, describes what is most essential to our flesh-and-blood lives: the needs shared by all human beings and the obligations (and not rights) to one another that they entail. These needs, listed in her "Draft for a Statement of Human Obligations," include nourishment and clothing, medical care and housing, as well as protection against violence. (Though opposed to capital punishment, Weil made an exception for rape.)

With her knack for striking illustrations, Weil confronts us with the limits of rights claims. "If someone tries to browbeat a farmer to sell his eggs at a moderate price, the farmer can say: 'I have the right to keep my eggs if I don't get a good enough price.' But if a young girl is being forced into a brothel she will not talk about her rights. In such a situation, the word would sound ludicrously inadequate."

This is why, when we ask why we have less than others, we are getting personal, but when we ask why we are being hurt, we are getting impersonal. And for Weil, the impersonal is good in every sense of the word. In the case of her illustration, Weil finds the notion of rights ludicrous because the girl is not being cheated of a profit. Instead, she is being cheated of her very humanity. There is no true compensation for such acts. And yet, by confusing personal rights with impersonal (or universally shared) needs, we burden ourselves with a language that deflects us from what is truly at stake. As Weil declares: "There is something sacred in every human being, but it is not their person. It is this human being; no more and no less."

While Weil was responding to the crisis of Western democracies confronting the challenge of fascism, her essays can also help us think about our own crisis of political governance and legitimacy. Take the current debate over the Trump administration's proposal to cut funding for the Supplemental Nutrition Assistance Program, known as SNAP, or food stamps. Rather than receiving cash installments on their electronic benefit-transfer cards, those enrolled in the program will instead receive boxes of tinned and canned food.

Fortunately, the proposal seems fated for the shredding machine, but it still serves as a useful example. Those using rights language would reply that the government hasn't the right to cut their money payments because they have the right to do their own shopping. But we can also frame the criticism in obligation language: "It is unjust to replace financial assistance with box meals, which will punish both our physical and emotional well-being." While the first response would ignite what Weil calls the "spirit of contention," the latter response might "touch and awaken at its source the spirit of attention."

In other words, such a reply asks us to forget about ourselves and instead attend to other lives. Moral situations require, as one of Weil's great fans, Iris Murdoch, wrote, an "unsentimental, detached, unselfish and objective perspective." Such attentiveness allows a moral and political clarity that "rights language" simply cannot. Paying attention, for Weil, is the most fundamental of our obligations. It forces us to recognize that what she calls "le malheur," or suffering, lies in store for all of us. "I may lose at any moment," she wrote, "through the play of circumstances over which I have no control, anything whatsoever I possess, including things that are so intimately mine that I consider them as myself."

This includes my sense of autonomy, reflected in so banal an act as buying groceries, but also in much more dramatic acts. The contemporary philosopher Andrea Nye suggests that Weil also throws a bracing light on the debate over abortion. In effect, the related notions of obligation and attention offer a third way between those who claim the fetus's right to life and those who insist upon a woman's right to choose. Rejecting these rights-based claims, Nye writes, a "Weilian feminist might listen to the women themselves as they attempt to make sense of their lives in order to come to a binding sense of what must be done to restore social balance and create a society in which obligations do not conflict." Such an approach might invite a woman seeking an abortion to fully attend to a situation which does not implicate her alone.

I do not mean to present all this as a panacea to our current political predicament, one that Weil would surely dismiss, as she did France's on the eve of World War II, as an "incredible barrage of lies, of demagogy, of boasting admixed with panic," one of "disarray, in sum a totally intolerable atmosphere." Yet, even if her insights into what she called the "social drama" do not always lead to clarity, they do oblige us to consider how politics would change if we made room for obligation.

In Praise of Lost Causes

Futilely resisting a corrupt world is not a matter
of common sense, but of conscience.

Mariana Alessandri

R IGHT AFTER SPAIN'S SWIFT AND DEVASTATING LOSS TO THE
United States in 1898, the Spanish philosopher Miguel de Unamuno
(1864–1936) resurrected Spain's patron saint of lost causes, Don
Quixote de la Mancha. It is fitting that Unamuno chose as Spain's
hero her crazy uncle, Cervantes's fictional knight-errant who was
himself well acquainted with swift and devastating losses.

While it's technically true that Quixote lost his final battle, which
prompted him to regain his senses just before his death, he is most
beloved for his madness—for "tilting at windmills," for dreaming
impossible dreams. Even Unamuno, who, before the war had celebrated Quixote's deathbed conversion to sanity, afterward repented.
The war triggered in Unamuno the realization that, in hopeless
times, quixotic lunacy could save people from the paralysis that often
accompanies defeatism.

For the rest of his life, Unamuno urged his fellow Spaniards to
practice quixotism, which meant adopting the moral courage necessary to fight for lost causes without caring what the world thinks.
Today, when much of society and politics—both in and outside the
United States—looks like a lost cause to a great number of people, we
might do well to consider Quixote's brand of lunacy.

Abandoning his senses—or rather, his common sense—freed up Quixote to engage in fruitless tasks like charging windmills. In the most famous scene of the book, his squire, Sancho Panza, warns Quixote that the giant he is tempted to charge is just a windmill, and, as such, should be left alone. Sancho's common sense tells him that fights that are sure to be lost are not worth fighting. Yet it is that same common sense that continually keeps Sancho from engaging with the world; likewise, it keeps us from engaging in what are perhaps the worthiest of causes: the lost ones.

Unamuno believed that it was not Quixote but Sancho who was delusional, firm in his belief that windmills are not worth charging, and, more broadly, that unwinnable battles are not worth fighting. The result of this type of thinking will usually be paralysis, since most enemies are windmill-size instead of human-size. Sancho believed that tilting at windmills was dangerous. Today, we might just call it a waste of time, and since common sense also tells us that time is money, we had better steer clear of anything unprofitable.

According to the political theorist Joshua Dienstag in his 2006 book, *Pessimism*, Quixote's loss of common sense offered him a more meaningful metric for deciding which battles are worth fighting. Quixote didn't charge the windmill because he thought he would defeat it, but because he concluded it was the right thing to do. Likewise, if we want to be legitimate actors in the world, Unamuno would say that we must be willing to lose the fight. If we abandon the commonsense belief that deems only winnable fights worth fighting, we can adopt Unamuno's "moral courage" and become quixotic pessimists: pessimists because we recognize our odds of losing are quite high, and quixotic because we fight anyway. Quixotic pessimism is thus marked by a refusal to let the odds of my success determine the value of my fight.

On Unamuno's Marxist interpretation of the windmill scene, Quixote recognized that, though they might look harmless, the "long-armed giants" kept the townspeople sated and distracted enough to forget their oppression at the hands of the modern bread factories. Unamuno complained that instead of asking whether they would ultimately benefit the towns they invade, the townspeople ended up "venerate[ing] and pay[ing] homage to steam and electricity." Contemporary windmills might look like a small town getting a Walmart, or like kindergartners getting free iPads. Common sense fails us in two ways: first and most often, it uncritically believes that technology equals progress, and second, even in cases in which people recognize the potential harm to the community, they generally don't believe that they can resist it. Common sense calls it a waste of time and energy. Quixote rejected this calculus, instead favoring a moral metric to decide who and what to fight. Thus freed, Quixote was left open to fight for lost causes—and lose.

Warning: quixotic pessimism will not go over well in public. If you choose this life, Unamuno says you will face disbelief, judgment, and ridicule. He writes that moral courage "confronts, not bodily injury, or loss of fortune, or the discredit of one's honor but rather ridicule: one's being taken for a madman or a fool." In a real-life context, quixotic pessimism will look like constantly face-planting in public, and we will need moral courage to accept it. People will laugh at us as they do at Quixote. People will mock our decision to fight big machines, but we must do it neither to win nor to impress. We will eventually grow accustomed to ignoring the criticism of our saner colleagues and friends who seem to follow the adage, "If you can't beat 'em, join 'em."

Cultivating moral courage amounts to learning to shift our attention away from those who confuse criticism for action toward our own judgment of what is worthwhile, based on thinking a whole lot about what kind of world we would like to live in and the kinds of people we'd like to be. It is worth noting that Quixote went mad from reading books, and this is precisely the type of crazy that Unamuno supports. We may not be able to improve the world, but we can at least refuse to cooperate with a corrupt one.

Unamuno himself quixotically resisted Primo de Rivera's dictatorship, publicly criticizing him and his supporters. As a result, Unamuno was removed from his position as university rector in 1924 and exiled to the island of Fuerteventura. After six months Unamuno escaped to France, where he declared he would not return to Spain until Rivera fell or died. Rivera fell, and died, six years later in 1930. Unamuno returned to Spain, but soon became a vocal critic of Francisco Franco, who also removed him from his university post and put him under house arrest. There Unamuno died at seventy-two, in 1936—at home like Quixote, but, unlike Quixote, never having regained his senses.

Three centuries before Unamuno, Cervantes detailed a life in praise of futilely resisting a corrupt world. Quixote fought giants because he could not, in good conscience, not fight them. We can similarly transform ourselves into quixotic pessimists—the kind who are called dreamers, idealists, or lunatics—by reading more, rejecting common sense, and reinterpreting what constitutes a waste of time. If we happen to succeed by worldly standards, we will be surprised and perhaps pleasantly so; if we fail, we will have expected it. Praise be to uncertain successes and to certain failures alike.

MAY 29, 2017

The Real Cost of Tweeting About My Kids

When I've told you what my son said,
it's not "his data" anymore.

—————

Agnes Callard

HERE IS AN ANECDOTE I WAS NOT ALLOWED TO POST ON Twitter.

On a recent trip to Costco, the kids were fighting in the back of the car and I asked my husband, "Why do we have such bad children? Is it because we're bad parents?" He said, "Yes, but it's not our fault, we must've had bad parents." I said, "But that's not their fault—" and my six-year-old son interrupted, enraged, yelling from the back of the car, "IT'S ALL GOD'S FAULT!"

Your own reaction to this story can tell you why my son wouldn't let me tweet it: He doesn't want you to think he's cute. (He has consented to have it appear here. No children's rights were violated in the writing of this essay.) When he was saying those words, he was not trying to entertain. He was angry—at me, at my husband, at God, and, after I asked him whether I could tweet it, at you for the way he knew you would react.

My oldest son is fifteen, and he finds my Twitter behavior undignified. ("Why does the world need to know that we are at Costco?") He feels that a teacher, mentor, and role model should cultivate a distance, even a mystique, so as to elicit the kind of respect she needs from her students, advisees, and admirers. If people do not think they know you, then you do not need to worry, as my six-year-old did, that you have left yourself in their interpretive hands. You can restrict their thoughts about you.

To allow others to think about us in whatever way they feel like—perhaps to laugh at us, perhaps to dismiss us—is a huge loss of control. So why do we allow it? What is the attraction of it? I think that it's the increase in control we get in return. Social media has enabled the Great Control Swap. And it is happening right now, beneath our notice.

The first baby step toward the Great Swap was the shift from phone calls to texts. A phone interaction requires participants to be "on the same time," which entails negotiations over entrance into and exit from the conversation. Consider all the time we spend first on, "Is this a bad time to call? Can you talk?" And then later on, "Okay, gotta go, talk to you soon, see you later, good talking to you . . ." (It's only in the movies that you can just hang up on someone.) Everyone has been in a phone conversation that ended much later than they wanted it to; the form subjects us to the will of another.

A text or email interaction, by contrast, liberates the parties so that each may operate on their own time. But the cost comes in another form of control: data. Homer's "winged words" fly from the mouth of one directly to the ear of another, but text-based communication requires stationary words: One person puts them down, so the other can come along and read them at her leisure. And that means they leave a trail.

Imagine a man conducting a romantic affair exclusively by email. He needn't lie to his wife about fake "business trips," since he can pursue his shenanigans right under her nose. Likewise, he avoids undesirable entanglements with his mistress: He doesn't even need to buy her dinner! Email allows him the control to steer the two women out of the way of one another—but the price he pays is a very robust data trail. His affair has a text archive. If his mistress decides to write a book about it, she can be scientific. She needn't rely on memory or vague impressions. She can systematically analyze their interactions and quote his exact words.

Our anger at social media companies resembles this man's anger over his mistress's theft of his "private data." We wanted one kind of control, and didn't reckon with the fact that we'd have to pay for it with another kind. We wanted to be able to interact with other people entirely in our own time, with people who make no demands on us. We wanted entry and exit to be painless. We understood from the start that this form of socializing—like an affair without physical contact—was shallower than the other, more demanding kind. We were prepared to accept that trade-off, but failed to grasp that we were trading away more than depth. We were also trading away a kind of control.

As my children appreciate, the control issue goes well beyond whether Facebook monetizes our data. It is also a matter of making oneself into a thing that others can own. When I've told you what my son said, it's not "his data" anymore. He can't control whether you laugh at it, or what tone you use when you do.

We don't like to acknowledge just how much we are willing to pay for distance from other people. For example, people warn prospective parents that having a baby is expensive, but that isn't exactly true. What's expensive is getting away from your baby. If you don't want to feed them with your body, you buy formula and bottles. If you don't want them looking at you all the time, you buy contraptions to entertain them. A stroller so you don't have to carry them, a crib so you don't have to sleep with them, a house with extra rooms so you don't even have to sleep near them, child care so that you can get farther away yet: These are the costs that add up. You don't pay much for babies, but you pay a lot to escape them.

All of us have a desire to connect, to be seen. But we live in a world that is starting to allow us to satisfy that desire without feeling the commonsense moral strictures that have traditionally governed human relationships. We can engage without obligation, without boredom, and, most importantly, without subjecting our attention to the command of another. On Twitter, I'm never obligated to listen through to the end of someone's story.

The immense appeal of this free-form socializing lies in the way it makes one a master of one's own time—but it cannot happen without a place. All that data has to sit somewhere so that people can freely access it whenever they wish. Data storage is the loss of control by which we secure social control: Facebook is our faithless mistress's leaky in-box.

When we alienate our identities as text data, and put that data "out there" to be read by anyone who wanders by, we are putting ourselves into the interpretive hands of those who have no bonds or obligations or agreements with us, people with whom we are, quite literally, prevented from seeing "eye to eye." People we cannot trust.

The Great Control Swap buys us control over the logistics of our interactions at the cost of interpretive control over the content of those interactions. Our words have lost their wings, and fallen to the ground as data.

NOVEMBER 22, 2019

The Stories We Tell Ourselves

In our echo chambers, we embody the "right"
values, but our real lives are more complicated.

Todd May

H ERE'S A STORY:

I was driving home from work and a car cut me off. The guy was
driving really slowly, and I wound up following him for half a mile.

As it stands, it's not a very interesting story. But suppose we add
another line:

So I laid on my horn the whole time.

Or perhaps a different line:

That's why I'm late.

Each of those two lines add a dimension to the story that wasn't
there before. Now, instead of just a story about me, we have a story
about how I like to see myself, or perhaps how I like myself to be seen.
Either way, I am expressing what might loosely be called a "value."
This value is not necessarily a moral value, but a way of being that I
want to see myself as living, a way of being that I consider valuable for
myself and seek to associate myself with. In the first case, I express
something like, "I am not a person to be messed with." In the second
it is something like, "I am not a tardy person."

Many of our stories about ourselves do this. We tell stories that
make us seem adventurous, or funny, or strong. We tell stories that
make our lives seem interesting. And we tell these stories not only

to others, but also to ourselves. The audience for these stories, of course, affects the stories we tell. If we're trying to impress a date, we might tell a story that makes us seem interesting or witty or caring, whereas if we're trying to justify a dubious act to someone who is judging us (or perhaps ourselves), we might tell a story that makes us out to be without other recourse in the situation. In the latter case, what we are doing is dissociating ourselves from a value we might be associated with and thus implicitly associated ourselves with a different one.

Not all our stories about ourselves express values like these. However, many—perhaps most—of them do. This is so even where a story might seem to express a disvalue. Think, for instance, of people whose stories about themselves are often about things not working out for them. Whatever they try, they fail; the world conspires against them. These stories express values as well, values that often stem from resentment or even despair. They buttress a view of the world that justifies their being who they are and not someone more accomplished or happy or social.

This is not to say that people who tell stories like this are necessarily wrong about their history. There are certainly people whose circumstances do conspire against them. We have seen this recently in the egregious incidents of hate toward traditionally marginalized groups. But when people come to identify themselves with stories about their difficulties, then they are not merely living through difficulties but, in some cases understandably, expressing values about their lives, ways of living that they identify with.

This last point leads to a further one. Some of the values we express are not values we would necessarily want to acknowledge. If someone calls attention to the fact that I am always making myself out to be a victim, I might well deny it. "No, it's not me, it's the circumstances. Everything happened just as I told you." There are ways of being that we might value but not be willing to admit, even to ourselves, that we value. This may seem paradoxical. How could we value something and yet not admit to ourselves that we value it?

However, we know—at least in the abstract—that we do deceive ourselves about certain aspects of who we are and what we are doing. Such self-deception involves, among other things, the expression of values that we are unwilling to acknowledge. When I laid on my horn while following the slow driver—which I confess to you here I did— then I expressed a value that I would really not want to be associated with, and would likely not have admitted to at the time. (Now I try to do better, but as a person raised in New York, I have difficulty. And you will certainly have noticed that even that admission expresses a value associated with being someone from New York.)

If we reflect on the stories we tell about ourselves, both to others and to ourselves, we may well find out things about who we are that complicate the view we would prefer to be identified with.

Why might this matter? Here is one reason. The presidential election has displayed in stark terms a phenomenon that many have commented on in recent years. With the proliferation of various cable news channels, the internet, niche marketing, clustering in communities of like-minded people, most of us live in echo chambers that reflect the righteousness of our lives back to us. We are reinforced to think of ourselves as embodying the right values, as living in ways that are at least justified, if not superior. Reflecting on the stories we tell about ourselves might reveal to us other aspects of who we are and what we value, aspects that would complicate the simple picture provided by our echo chamber.

And that complication, in turn, could lead us to another revelation: that those who live outside our echo chamber might also be more complicated than we have imagined. While the values we take them to be expressing might be mistaken—or even abhorrent—to us, there are perhaps other aspects to their lives as well, other values those lives express, values that would become manifest to us if we listened to some of the stories they tell about themselves. If we are more complicated than we like to think, perhaps others are also more complicated than we would like to think. (And also more complicated than they would like to think.)

None of this is meant to argue for some sort of relativism of values or that everyone is equally justified in the choices they make. The displays of racism, sexism, and xenophobia that this presidential election has brought us—often in the form of stories that express values associated with macho individualism—are to be rejected wholesale. However, in this age of polarization, where it is easy to dismiss others with a righteous wave of our hand, we could perhaps do worse than to reflect on the complications that each of us lives, complications that are often on display in the stories we tell about ourselves.

JANUARY 16, 2017

You Should Not Have Let Your Baby Die

At two days old, Sam could not breathe on his
own. What else could have been done?

Gary Comstock

S AM, YOUR NEWBORN SON, HAS BEEN SUFFOCATING IN YOUR
arms for the past fifteen minutes. You're as certain as you can be
that he is going to die in the next fifteen. He was born two days ago
with "trisomy 18," a disease that proved no obstacle to his cementing
himself immediately and forevermore as the love of your life. Your
wife has already composed his own lullaby, "Sam, Sam, the Little
Man." But she and you and your three other children have spent the
past twenty-four hours learning about the incredible uphill battle
Sam faces.

"Trisomy" means "three chromosomes." Each cell in your son's
body should have a healthy pair of the chromosomes scientists call
No. 18. The unkind twists of the genetic lottery have given him
instead a crippling threesome.

Sam was born breech in an emergency procedure in Mary Gree-
ley Hospital, in Ames, Iowa. You and your wife accepted the attending physician's advice to Life Flight him immediately in a helicopter
to the Infant Intensive Care Unit at the Iowa City Hospitals. You
were told that Sam could not breathe on his own, although no one
ever asked whether you approved his being hooked up to a ventila-
tor. You overheard the emergency personnel relaying in medicalese

the reasons for the flight to Iowa City: microcephaly, low-set ears, flat midface, short stature, proximally placed thumb, and potentially abnormal male genitalia. All signs, you have since learned, of genetic abnormality, and indicators that he will be, as a friend puts it—choking on the words—"mentally retarded."

Not all people with trisomy 18 have problems. The literature reports a dozen cases of individuals living for ten years, and SOFT, a trisomy 18 support group, lists even more living into their twenties and thirties. Those with the conditions known as mosaicism and translocation of the 18 chromosome may live relatively long and happy lives, bring joy to their parents, siblings, and friends, and be relatively free of adverse symptoms. But there is a wide range of disorders associated with trisomy, and for those with Sam's symptoms, life expectancy is brutally short.

Sam's case is classified as one of the worst. His brain cannot regulate his lungs. He grew successfully in your wife's body and came to term because her blood provided him with oxygen. Now that his mother can no longer breathe for him, there is, the genetic counselor gently tells you, little chance that he will ever breathe on his own.

Some eleven hundred infants are born annually in this country with trisomy 18. Many of them die of heart failure or apnea, irregular breathing that stops temporarily. Sam cannot breathe on his own at all. In an era of less technologically sophisticated medicine, your wife suggests, Sam would have died at birth? Yes. Even with today's respirators, cardiac support equipment, and antibiotics, nearly thirty percent will die in the first month; ninety percent will die before their first birthday. Of those who survive, most will have radical cognitive limitations, a condition the most recent revision of the *Diagnostic and Statistical Manual of Mental Disorders* refers to as "profound intellectual disability."

How do you know? You pose the question to Sam's geneticist, a kindly man in his mid-forties. He measures his response. He has an MD and a PhD, and has worked with trisomy infants for fifteen years. You like him. You hear in his voice the ring of years of medical practice, scientific research, and practical wisdom. You see in his eyes the face of a father. Well, he says, as to the diagnosis of the genetic problem, the results of chromosome analysis are accurate 99.9 percent of the time. As for the prognosis? Unfortunately, Sam seems to have a version of trisomy 18 that makes it impossible for his brain to successfully stimulate and coordinate the activities of the respiratory tract.

Are you sure? What would happen if you removed that air hose taped to his face? Have you tried it? Yes, once, for a few seconds. His lungs showed no signs of beginning to operate on their own. It would be inhumane to experiment on him by leaving the tube out for any longer period of time. He cannot breathe.

But couldn't that change? Yes. Some trisomy 18 babies in Sam's condition eventually improve to the point at which they no longer need the respirator. Some leave the hospital and begin to respond to their parents' affection. But a majority never leave the hospital, never respond to the presence of others, and die while still connected to the respirator.

What are the choices? Some parents choose to use all possible means of continuing their child's life in the hope that their child will beat the odds and eventually overcome problems. Others choose to let the children die to spare the babies the pain of the ordeal.

Forget the statistics and what others do or don't do. We would like to know what our Sam's chances are for reaching the point where his life is valuable to him. But there is no answer to that question. No one can tell you whether your son's life is worth living from his perspective, or yours. We cannot say whether your son will ever breathe on his own or look at you. We can say only that the literature suggests the odds are stacked heavily against him.

You and your wife had no warning during the pregnancy that the child might be genetically abnormal. You were offered the services of amniocentesis, a test that may have revealed his condition. You and your wife refused to have genetic testing done on the fetus because your wife opposes abortion on theological and moral grounds. Knowing ahead of time that the child was genetically abnormal would not have provided any useful information. Genetic testing is done to allow parents the choice to abort fetuses with severe problems. But your wife would never abort her baby, so there was no point in having the tests performed.

The two of you have support in deciding to let your baby die: your wife's best friend from church, her mother and sister from two thousand miles away, your own mother and father, your two brothers and sister, and every member of their families, gathered from three hundred miles away. They help you think through the decision to remove the air tube. They squirm with you, hesitating to give their opinions. In the end, they express support for your decision. Your brother calls it "courageous."

There seems to you both a difference between killing your baby and letting him die. You are letting Sam die. Your father gathers the family, nearly twenty adults and children, in the room. You hold hands, collectively sing a psalm, weep through Grandpa's prayer. Everyone leaves. Your wife tries to sing Sam's lullaby to him, one last time, goodbye, Sam, but her voice fails her. She hands him to you. She cannot bear to go through it. Your brother and mother have offered to sit with you, but you decide it is something you must do alone. Just you and Sam.

The nurse comes in, mute. You look at him, sleeping. He seems at peace. You nod your head. She gently pulls the tube. It slides out quickly, as though he were helping to expel it. Without his lifeline, he does not move. A minute later, his eyes open. It is the first time you have seen them. His head jerks slightly forward. He does not cry. He gasps silently for breath. His eyes close. You almost yell for the nurse, to beg her to put it back in. To keep from doing so, you pray, arguing with God that letting him die is best for him. After five minutes, his face pales, then turns a sickly purple. His tiny chest convulses irregularly in an unsuccessful attempt to draw air into the lungs. After twenty minutes, he lies still. His fingers turn gray.

Thirty minutes. There are no visible signs of life. You rock his limp body as tears fall on the blue blanket. You wonder what sort of beast you are. Forty-five minutes. Grandma looks in, ashen-faced, seeing in a glance that it is over. Shortly your wife appears. She immediately takes her son's body in her arms and coddles him. She sits there with him for three hours.

You should not have let your baby die. You should have killed him.

This thought occurs to you years later, thinking about the gruesome struggle of his last twenty minutes. You are not sure whether it makes sense to talk about his life, because he never seemed to have the things that make a life: thoughts, wants, desires, interests, memories, a future. But, supposing that he had thoughts, his strongest thought during those last minutes certainly appeared to be: "This hurts. Can't someone help it stop?" He didn't know your name, but if he had, he would have said: "Daddy? Please. Now."

It seems the medical community has few options to offer parents of newborns likely to die. We can leave our babies on respirators and hope for the best. Or remove the hose and watch the child die a tortured death. Shouldn't we have another choice? Shouldn't we be allowed the swift humane option afforded the owners of dogs, a lethal dose of a painkiller?

For years you repress the thought. Then, early one morning, remembering again those last minutes, you realize that the repugnant has become reasonable. The unthinkable has become the right, the good. Painlessly. Quickly. With the assistance of a trained physician.

You should have killed your baby.

JULY 12, 2017

What Do We Owe the Dead?

The dustup over a *Washington Post* reporter's tweets about
Kobe Bryant raises a moral question and a cultural taboo.

Iskra Fileva

NOT ALL PEOPLE WHO DIE WERE GOOD PEOPLE. YET THERE IS
strong social pressure to pretend they were, at least for a period of
time. Exactly how long a period of time that should be has never been
made clear.

In almost every culture, posthumous praise immediately after a
person's death is the norm. Except in cases of the most obviously evil
figures, it is generally accepted that the hours and days after a death
should be a time of remembrance, grief, and praise.

I believe this is the norm that was violated by the *Washington Post*
reporter Felicia Sonmez, when—shortly after the death of basketball
star Kobe Bryant—she tweeted a 2016 article about the sexual assault
charge brought against Bryant in 2003. Sonmez reportedly received
a swift and intense backlash on social media. Had she written her
tweet a week ago, when Bryant was alive and well, I suspect that she
would have faced little backlash.

This norm is so firmly ingrained that almost everyone, not only
those as widely admired as Bryant, can count on posthumous praise,
and there are both fictional and real cases involving people who faked
their own deaths in part to gain the benefit of reading their own obit-

uaries. For instance, in Isaac Asimov's story "Obituary," a theoretical physicist named Stebbins, frustrated with his own failure to achieve fame, concocts an elaborate plan to fake his own death in an attempt to get publicity and the benefits of an obituary. Stebbins, though not a particularly agreeable character, is right to expect a eulogy.

In general, we pretend that the recently deceased were good or better than they really were. Why? Perhaps we think that we owe it to the deceased person's family to show deference. This makes sense in cases where the deceased person is a public figure who, while reviled by segments of the public, was deeply loved by his or her own immediate relatives. But it does not tell us what is going on in a large number of other cases. Many of those seen as unsavory characters by outsiders are regarded as morally deficient by their families as well. I have personal knowledge of cases in which the adult children of an abusive now-deceased parent were pressured to pretend the deceased was a good mother or father. At least one person I know faced harsh criticism for refusing to comply. This suggests that the norm is so strong, we are willing to force people abused in childhood to hide their pain behind a socially acceptable mask.

One may suppose that we are concerned, rightly, with the deceased person's current inability to defend him- or herself. Decency, it could be argued, requires that we not attack an opponent who happens to be lying defenseless on the ground. And the deceased, it may be thought further, are less capable of fighting back and to that extent, more defenseless than any living person.

I doubt that this is the reason either. We do not have parallel norms, for instance, against gossip behind another's back, even though the harm we can inflict on a living person is much greater than any possible harm to the dead, save the possible damage to their reputation or legacy.

It's possible that we see funerals and memorial services as public affairs and believe we ought not air dirty laundry there, but rather keep up appearances for the sake of family pride. But I suspect that we feel pressure to whitewash the acts of the dead even when only immediate family are present. This stands in stark contrast with the way we behave at family affairs not involving death. Those are not generally known for their high level of decorum. It depends on the family, of course, but it is quite common for people to express mixed feelings (or worse) about family holidays and reunions. We are not, it seems, all that committed to saving face at family gatherings.

I wish to suggest here that there is something about death itself that motivates us to act as we do. Death seems significant and perhaps otherworldly. Think of our tendency to lower our voices when in a cemetery. We see this tendency in both religious and nonreligious people, that is, both people who do and who do not believe that the dead might hear them. What explains that tendency? I am not sure, but my best guess is that it has to do with the perceived otherworldliness of death. If that's right, then perhaps it is not the person who has just died that we want to show respect to—for that person may well have been a terrible human being—but death itself. It's as though death has put a stamp of nobility on the forehead of the one whose heart is no longer beating, and it is that stamp, that halo, that pushes us to act as we do. The deceased belong to death now, not to us. And it may be that we feel that it is not simply other people watching us; we are being watched by death itself. Death has come to visit, and we are all in its presence when we share a room with one of its recent claimees.

I have a good deal of sympathy with this idea, in general. I've often thought that there is something unseemly about celebrating a person's death, even that of a serial killer or a dictator. Dancing on another's grave—even metaphorically—is not the mark of a highly civilized person. What makes this unseemly may not be any quality of the person who's passed away, since there may be no redeeming qualities. (It could be completely appropriate to rejoice in that person's being sentenced to life imprisonment.) It's sometimes death, really—not anything else about the dead person—that rightly gives us pause.

What I wish to suggest here, however, is that there is more than one alternative to posthumously and disingenuously praising deceased bad people. We can engage in, as Sonmez suggested, perhaps a little too quickly, somber and honest reflection on the person's entire legacy—the good, the bad, and the ugly.

There are several reasons to prefer honesty. One is that pretense norms work against the people truly deserving of praise. When we bestow posthumous praise indiscriminately, we are all acting like those professors who give every student an A. As a consequence, the students who earned it get the same grade as the students who didn't. Posthumous evaluation is like a grade of the whole of someone's life. High marks here too ought to be earned.

This is not, of course, to suggest that we should encourage petty vindictiveness against the dead and give a carte blanche to haters whose hatred shows more about them than about the deceased. It is only to say that there is a difference between a norm prohibiting petty vindictiveness and one demanding indiscriminate praise.

In addition, there is no reason somber reflection on the deceased person's legacy should be seen as beyond the pale. While celebrating anyone's death may suggest very bad taste, a serious attempt at a final reckoning should not. In this connection, the French author Voltaire once explained, in a letter to a friend, why some unkind words about a recently deceased abbot appeared in one of Voltaire's books (my translation): "We owe respect to the living; to the dead, we owe only the truth."

I hope that this proposal will be palatable even to those who in following traditional norms aim, perhaps unconsciously, to show an appropriate attitude not so much toward the dead but toward death and its inevitability. Death will claim us all in the end, and every demise that takes place in proximity to us serves as a reminder. But death should not, for this reason, be seen as a universal equalizer. We are all equally mortal and the dead are all equally dead; but neither the living nor the dead are equally good and death need not force us to pretend otherwise.

Finally, while it is true that death will claim us all, it is not necessary to cede ground to it prematurely. The dead are not coming back, and in that sense, they do not belong to us anymore. Yet they lived among us once, and their lives—including both the good and the bad things they may have done—are intimately intertwined with our own stories and identities. The truth about what they did or didn't do, how they treated us or others, may, in a deep sense, be our own—living—truth.

JANUARY 27, 2020

IX

WHAT IS IT LIKE TO BE A WOMAN?

Descartes Is Not Our Father

History tells us he invented modern
philosophy. That history is wrong.

Christia Mercer

R ENÉ DESCARTES HAS LONG BEEN CREDITED WITH THE NEAR-single-handed creation of modern philosophy. Generations of students have read, and continue to read, his famous *Meditations on First Philosophy* as the rejection of medieval ways of thinking and the invention of the modern self. They learned that he doubted all traditional ways of knowing before pivoting to the modern subjective individual. Tumbling into a "deep whirlpool," the doubter of the *Meditations* has no secure footing until he hits upon a single firm and indubitable truth: He is most essentially "a thinking thing." The modern individual is born, with the rejection of the past as its midwife.

It's a dramatic story. But it's false.

Descartes's contemporaries in the seventeenth century would have been stunned to hear these accomplishments credited to him. Although he was rightly famous in his time for some of his scientific and mathematical ideas, many considered his philosophical proposals about the radical difference between mind and body implausible and unoriginal. Even his scientific ideas were often ranked on par with others. For example, the English philosopher Anne Conway considered Hobbes's and Spinoza's account of corporeal nature to be equally influential, and similarly mistaken.

Another contemporary, the German Gottfried Wilhelm Leibniz, agreed, sometimes comparing Descartes's proposals to those of long-forgotten thinkers like Kenelm Digby. Others noted his debt to past thinkers. In his *Dictionnaire Historique et Critique*, Pierre Bayle writes of complaints about Descartes's "pirating" of ideas from earlier sources. Fast forward a century or so to Kant, who does not consider the author of the *Meditations* to be worth much attention.

So if Descartes did not invent modern philosophy, how was this false narrative created and sustained?

The long-standing story about Descartes's creation of a "new philosophy" that broke radically with medieval "ways of thinking" and that marked "the dawn of modern times" was promoted by philosophers who came after Kant and who, oddly enough, turned Descartes into the originator of "Germanic" thought. In his 1820s lectures on the history of philosophy, Hegel asserts that "Germanic, i.e., modern philosophy begins with Descartes." By 1847, Schopenhauer insists "our excellent Descartes" is "the instigator of subjective investigation and in this the father of modern philosophy."

A prominent German professor, Kuno Fischer (1824–1907), published a gripping (and multivolume) story in the 1870s about Descartes's groundbreaking ideas and their impact on subsequent thought. In a revealing passage from his extended discussion of Descartes's life and innovations, Fischer writes: "In the whole range of philosophical literature, there is no work in which the struggle for truth is portrayed in a more animated, personal, captivating manner and, at the same time, more simply and clearly, than in Descartes's essay on method and his first 'Meditation.'"

This nineteenth century invention of the "modern era" excised seventeenth and eighteenth century philosophy of its theological and religious underpinnings—and its women, whether they were overtly theological or not. Even influential Enlightenment figures like the natural philosopher Émilie du Châtelet were ignored, not to mention the contributions of significant seventeenth century radical thinkers like Margaret Cavendish and Anne Conway, a favorite of Leibniz.

The adulation continued into the early twentieth century, when Descartes's heroism was codified by prominent thinkers like the German Ernst Cassirer (1874–1945) and the French Étienne Gilson (1884–1978). In Cassirer's dramatic telling, Descartes single-handedly created the "spiritual essence" of a new epoch, which would "permeate all fields of knowledge," to which eighteenth century philosophers responded, and out of which Kant and other German thinkers would arise as liberating angels.

Based on his interpretation of the seventeenth century as a period of "great metaphysical systems" developed in response to Descartes, Cassirer advised historians to "string its various intellectual formulations along the thread of time and study them chronologically." That is, in order to understand "the sum total" of the period's "philosophical content," it was sufficient to track its systems "lengthwise."

And so people did. One of the most influential treatments of the history of philosophy in the English-speaking world is the hugely ambitious and admirably clear study by Frederick Copleston, an Oxford-trained classicist who converted to Catholicism, became a Jesuit priest, and famously debated his friend A. J. Ayer as well as Bertrand Russell on philosophical and theological matters. In elegant concise prose, Copleston kept to the lengthwise approach, displaying the whole history of philosophy in nine volumes, published between 1946 and 1975 and widely read in the English-speaking world. Although Copleston includes mystics like Meister Eckhart (1260–1328) and prominent Jesuit scholastics like Francisco Suárez (1548–1617), he entirely ignores the richly philosophical spiritual writings of even the most prominent late medieval women, reducing the entirety of philosophy to a series of great men, each responding to the ones who went before.

Analytically trained historians working in the mid–twentieth century were satisfied to rummage through the "great systems" of the canonical great men to find their philosophical gems. And who can blame them? From Bertrand Russell's book on Leibniz (1900) to Peter Strawson's study of Kant (1966), prominent philosophers could grind their own philosophical axes using historical texts. They felt justified in restricting themselves to the standard story about modern philosophy and its limited range of problems, to which they could apply their philosophical tools with the hope of producing innovative ideas and arguments for themselves and their colleagues. One did not need to worry one's head with the social and political complications of early modern Europe, much less dirty one's hands with the messiness of its theology. One could focus on what mattered to properly educated philosophers.

This approach was doomed to fail. The richness and diversity of early modern philosophy were bound to become evident, engendering a growing awareness of the inadequacy of the standard story.

The engendering of that inadequacy was itself gendered. When feminist scholars in the 1980s began to explore early modern women writers, they discovered both the richness of the period's philosophy and the inadequacy of the lengthwise approach. Scholars like Eileen O'Neill dared historians to widen their scope and include long-forgotten figures, foreseeing how women's philosophies would offer significant insights into the period's central debates. This strategy has produced significant results and begun to influence the way historians of philosophy think about the period.

Most relevant to the reconsideration of Descartes and the subjective individual that he was supposed to have invented is the recent recognition that late medieval spiritual meditations—especially those written by women like Julian of Norwich, Hadewijch of Brabant, Catherine of Siena, and Teresa of Ávila—involved the need to focus on the meditator's subjectivity as a means to rethink everything the meditator has previously learned about the world. The point was to learn not to care about the external matters so as to develop new habits and beliefs. For most meditators, the only proper means to do this was through subjective exploration.

Long-standing prejudice against women, their capacities to reason, and their right to teach had left women out of philosophy for centuries. But the twelfth century witnessed the beginning of a shift to meditative practices emphasizing introspection and feelings. Although created by men, the new forms of spiritual practice gave women the right, for the first time in centuries, to write and be read.

Because women were considered naturally predisposed to emotive introspection, their spiritual writings began to be taken seriously. In constant fear of overstepping their bounds, these authors had to find imaginative ways to share their insights while seeming suitably humble. For example, Julian of Norwich writes in late fourteenth century England, "Just because I am a woman, must I . . . not tell you about the goodness of God, when I saw . . . his wish that it should be known?" Women like Julian had to admit their "natural" inferiority and practice their philosophy within the confines of this emotive spiritual genre.

And so they did, brilliantly, writing carefully in their meditations about the subjective individual who doubts everything she was previously taught before progressing to self-knowledge and eventually to truth. It is here in the spiritual writings of late medieval women that we find many of the features that Hegel and Schopenhauer considered new and "Germanic." To be sure, the steps in Descartes's *Meditations* are rendered in more explicitly epistemological terms than those of his predecessors, but his strategy and pivot to self-knowledge were already at the time centuries old. It is no wonder his contemporaries were not very impressed.

Our understanding of history evolves. We can now see Descartes as the benefactor of a long tradition, to which women significantly contributed. The time seems right to rethink the role of women and other noncanonical figures in the history of philosophy and begin to create a more accurate story about philosophy's rich and diverse past.

SEPTEMBER 25, 2017

What Does It Mean to "Speak as a Woman"?

*If I attempt to control a conversation based on the
fact of my gender, I may be a bully, looking for a
way to humiliate you. But I may be justified.*

Agnes Callard

SUPPOSE A MAN AND I ARE HAVING A CONVERSATION ABOUT recent events, and suppose I introduce one of my statements with, "As a woman . . ."

He knew that he was talking to a woman from the beginning of the conversation, but now, all of a sudden, I am speaking to him as a woman. What difference does this make?

It may seem to him that I am attempting to secure an unfair conversational advantage: Instead of asking him to accept my arguments on the grounds of their validity, I am asking him to accept them on the grounds of my status as a woman. To take the most extreme reaction, he may feel that I am bullying him, using him as a scapegoat to exact vengeance on the basis of some grievance I harbor toward some particular man, some group of men, or men in general.

He probably wouldn't react in the same way if he were discussing a topic that touched on physics, and his interlocutor said, "As a physicist . . ." In that case, she has expertise that he is likely to recognize as conversationally relevant. Even if he knew she was a physicist before the conversation began, he might find it reasonable for her to preface some of her assertions with a reminder that she is speaking from a position of special knowledge.

Being a physicist gives a person a certain standing in conversations that have something to do with physics. So why shouldn't being a woman give me a certain standing in conversations that have something to do with gender?

Let's distinguish two ways in which the expertise of a physicist might figure in a discussion of some question. First, it might allow her to introduce facts into the conversation that have bearing on the question. Call this "informational standing." Second, it might put her in a privileged position to manage the conversation: to determine who speaks when, how the question is pursued, when it counts as answered, and so on. Call this "managerial standing."

The idea that being a woman can give me informational standing is relatively unproblematic. For example, perhaps we are talking about the use of alcohol in socializing, and I inform my interlocutor, speaking as a woman, that when you refrain from drinking, people often assume you are pregnant. Perhaps this comes as news to him. Informational standing is a version of expertise. To see this, apply what we might call the "expert replacement test": Could I claim such standing over a male scientist who had extensively studied the relevant domain of the female experience (including first-person reports)? No. And this shows that the demographic fact—in this case, that I am a woman—is not essential to the kind of standing I am claiming. When we get heated over the fact that someone is speaking as an X, it is probably not a claim to informational standing that disturbs us.

It is important to remind ourselves that conversations include, but are not reducible to, exchanges of information. Some of the things we get by talking to people we could get in other ways—this is true of cases in which we take the fact that someone said something as evidence for the truth of what they are saying. We are treating them as a kind of thermostat for reality, in principle replaceable with finding (credible) slips of paper on the ground, or overhearing them talking to someone else, or having them tailed by a private detective.

If conversations were information-extraction exercises, we would be indifferent as to whether our interlocutor was telling the truth, or lying, as long as we knew which "filter" to apply. (Either way, we can extract data from the utterance.) Spies might be satisfied with information extraction, but in normal conversation it is important to us that our interlocutor make an honest effort to speak truthfully. This is because, when we converse, we have the goal of thinking with our interlocutor, and you only invite someone into your mind to the extent that you are willing to lay it open before them; and because you expect them to do the same. The ideas of respect and equality have many applications in civic life, especially in a democracy, but one of the most basic is conversational: mutual recognition as having equal standing to contribute to the discussion of some question.

Conversational equality is inconsistent with managerial standing. If it's my job to decide how the conversation proceeds, then our conversational relationship is hierarchical. I stand over you in the role of a teacher or leader or guide. When the physicist assumes managerial standing over the conversation, she is saying that she cannot sincerely converse as an equal with you. She could have a farce of a conversation in which she nods along while inwardly groaning, or she can give you some instruction. Given the sad state of your education in physics, these are her only options.

This brings us, finally, to the kind of speaking "as a woman" that engenders defensiveness and hostility. When I adopt managerial standing on the grounds of some demographic fact, I am saying that given the difference between us with respect to gender, race, sexual orientation, or socioeconomic status, we cannot converse as equals—moreover, that in order for us to converse, you have to allow me to be in some way in charge of the conversation. You have to hand me the reins.

This demand on my part will sometimes be illegitimate—I may, in fact, be a bully, looking for a way to grab power, humiliate you, or show off in front of others. But is it always illegitimate? If I speak as an X, managerially, I am saying that a certain ideal kind of conversation—conversation among equals—is impossible for us. Could that be, simply, true? Could it be that, as in the case of the physicist, our only option besides putting me in charge is fake conversation?

If the answer is, yes, this won't be because demographic membership constitutes a form of expertise. We can use our expert replacement test: If you are having a conversation about rape with someone who says, "as a rape victim," her claim to managerial standing, unlike any informational claim she might make, will in no way be undermined by the presence of a rape researcher. Unlike informational standing, managerial standing can be demographic "all the way down."

So on what basis might someone claim such standing? Perhaps the most familiar case is one in which systematic and entrenched forms of injustice have ossified group relations into ones of unequal respect. It would not, of course, follow that individual members of those groups were barred from showing one another equal respect—but it would also be plausible that, at times, strangers instantiate these ossified relations, even unknowingly. In such a case, speaking as a member of the disrespected group could be a way of both drawing attention to this fact, and attempting to redress it. Such a speaker is saying, given the presence of structural inequality, an unequal conversation is the only sincere, honest way forward. Anything else would require her to nod along, inwardly groaning.

These issues of structural injustice can be very tricky. Consider the summer of 2018 controversy that arose around the work of Kathleen Stock, a philosophy professor who argues against redefining the category of woman and lesbian to include trans women. Why does the terminology matter so much here? Among other things, what is at stake is the question of whether trans women have managerial standing to speak as women.

It is also important to note that not every case of demographic managerial standing will be predicated on injustice. Someone with personal experience of a natural disaster might not be able to speak on that topic without getting emotional. Allowing that person to manage the conversation may make it possible for him to be as rational as he can be, under the circumstances.

One could avoid demographically managed conversations by restricting one's interlocutors. You might think that a philosopher would be inclined to do this. Philosophers place special value on a specific kind of conversation—those in which strict equality between participants makes possible the no-holds-barred argumentative warfare that is our bread and butter. We think that when people refute us, they are doing us a favor. And refutation does not fit comfortably in demographically managed conversation: If you are the manager, my refuting you undermines my acceptance of your managerial standing, and if I am the manager, refuting you might well constitute an abuse of it.

But philosophers are also teachers of philosophy, charged with producing the next generation of philosophers. We not only conduct but also induct people into such conversations, and this means that we are interested in the porousness of the boundary that surrounds them. We don't choose our students, we don't choose our society, and we can't always choose our conversations.

For this reason, I think all of us—even philosophers—should be prepared, at times, to accept demographic claims of managerial standing; but I also think we should aspire to navigate each of those conversations with the kind of intellectual excellence, respect, and sensitivity that would allow them to become the full-fledged, unmanaged conversations they aspire to be.

DECEMBER 3, 2018

Who Counts as a Woman?

The attempt to exclude trans women from the
ranks of women reinforces the dangerous idea
that there is a right way to be female.

Carol Hay

WHO COUNTS AS A WOMAN? IS THERE SOME SET OF CORE EXPE-
riences distinctive of womanhood, some shared set of adventures
and exploits that every woman will encounter on her journey from
diapers to the grave? The recent debates over the experiences of
trans women gives us new reason to return to a question feminists
have been grappling with for decades.

Ever since Simone de Beauvoir quipped in 1949 that one is not
born a woman, but becomes one, feminists have been discussing
the implications of understanding gender as a cultural construct.
But more recently, this approach to gender has come under scrutiny. After all, it's all well and good to say that gender is a cultural
construct, but it's a mistake to then pretend that cultures construct
gender the same way for all people. Let's just say that the sisterhood
hasn't always been great about attending equally to the experiences
of all sisters.

But thanks to the past forty years of work from intersectionalist
feminists, we're finally paying attention to what women of color have
been saying since at least the days when Sojourner Truth had to ask
if she, too, got to count as a woman: that what it's like to be a woman

varies drastically across social lines of race, socioeconomic class, disability, and so on, and that if we try to pretend otherwise, we usually just end up pretending that the experiences of the wealthy, white, straight, able-bodied women who already have more than their fair share of social privilege are the experiences of all women.

You might think we just need to get over the thought that there's anything like the female experience, that the search for a shared female experience is dicey at best, fraught with way too many historical examples of feminists getting it wrong and making things worse for less-privileged women along the way. At the limit, these concerns result in the view that the category of "womanhood" itself is fundamentally confused and thus better abandoned entirely. This is the route taken by feminists like Judith Butler in her iconic 1990 book *Gender Trouble*.

There's a reason that after describing gender as fundamentally a performance, Butler counsels people to revel in messing with its scripts, to treat gender as nothing more than an ironic parody. Gender categories need to be taken down a notch, she thinks, but not only because they harm people in all the ways feminism spends so much time criticizing. Butler charges that in their focus on spelling out the harms of gendered socialization, feminists unwittingly entrenched the very things they claimed to be criticizing. By demarcating feminism's subject matter—by articulating a concrete category of harms that deserved feminist attention—feminists inadvertently defined womanhood in a manner that implies that there are right and wrong ways to be a woman. "Identity categories are never merely descriptive," she insists in *Gender Trouble*, "but always normative, and as such, exclusionary."

Any attempt to catalog the commonalities among women, in other words, has the inescapable result that there is some correct way to be a woman. This will inevitably encourage and legitimize certain experiences of gender and discourage and delegitimize others, subtly reinforcing and entrenching precisely those forces of socialization of which feminists claim to be critical. And what's worse, it will inevitably leave some people out. It will mean that there are "real" women whom feminism should be concerned about and that there are impostors who do not qualify for feminist political representation.

The women who are accused of being impostors these days are often trans women. You might think that a shared suspicion of conventional understandings of sex and gender would make feminists and trans activists natural bedfellows. You'd be wrong. It all started with Janice Raymond's controversial book *The Transsexual Empire: The Making of the She-Male*, published in 1979. Reissued in 1994, the book continues to inspire "gender-critical" or "trans-exclusionary" radical feminists—TERFs, for short. (For the record, while some consider the acronym derogatory, it is a widely accepted shorthand for a literal description of the views these feminists hold; also for the record, many of us who are critics of TERFs consider Raymond's book to be hate speech.)

Feminists who deny "real woman" status to trans women seem to rely on a false assumption—that all trans women have lived in the world unproblematically as men at some point—and claim the importance of affirming the identity and experiences of those who've spent entire lives in women's shoes. Even the feminist icon Chimamanda Ngozi Adichie has echoed this, claiming in a 2017 interview, "It's about the way the world treats us, and I think if you've lived in the world as a man with the privileges that the world accords to men and then sort of change gender, it's difficult for me to accept that then we can equate your experience with the experience of a woman who has lived from the beginning as a woman and who has not been accorded those privileges that men are."

TERFs also sometimes complain that the performances of femininity enacted by trans women are chiefly retrograde stereotypes, caricatures of a femininity designed primarily for the pleasure of men. When Caitlyn Jenner says that she has always felt like a woman, for example, what she seems to mean by this is that she wants to be an airheaded piece of arm candy all dolled up for delights of the male gaze. "The hardest part of being a woman," she infamously quipped, "is figuring out what to wear."

It's nonsense like this that motivated Germaine Greer to call

Glamour magazine "misogynist" for honoring Jenner at its Women of the Year ceremony, claiming that the move was tantamount to affirming that with enough plastic surgery someone who is assigned male at birth can "be a better woman" than someone "who is just born a woman."

While the rhetoric used by those in the trans-exclusionary camp is frequently inexcusable, you might think that some of their frustration is understandable. Feminists who've spent the better part of their lives fighting against a status quo that uncritically affirms gender stereotypes might be forgiven for getting a little resentful when women like Jenner seem to suggest that these stereotypes tell us what it's "really like" to be a woman. On the other hand, it's worth asking why the full brunt of the most extreme TERFs' ire is so often directed at individual trans women who are just trying to get by like the rest of us, rather than on the fact that the media insists on focusing so single-mindedly on trans performances of gender that endorse a regressive, man-pleasing version of femininity to the exclusion of the many diverse others.

For the most part, Greer and Raymond and others who share their view are outliers in contemporary feminism, particularly in North America. Adichie, for instance, could not accurately be called a TERF: She thinks trans women's oppression is not the same as the oppression experienced by women who are assigned female at birth, yet recognizes that trans women are undoubtedly oppressed and should be "part of feminism." Most feminists these days go even further, however, fully rejecting trans-exclusionary rhetoric and agreeing that trans women are women, full stop.

Thankfully, feminists have finally started to realize that the varied experiences of trans women have a thing or two to teach us, if only we're willing to actually listen. All the way back in 1974, Andrea Dworkin launched an early salvo in what would become the "TERF wars," remarking, "It is commonly and wrongly said that male transvestites through the use of makeup and costuming caricature the women they would become, but any real knowledge of the romantic ethos makes clear that these men have penetrated to the core experience of being a woman, a romanticized construct." (There are some important objections that should be made about her terminology here—"transvestite" is no longer the preferred nomenclature, and she doesn't distinguish between male drag queens and trans women—but it would be anachronistic to get too fussed about it.)

Instead of complaining that trans women like Jenner are cartoons of reality, Dworkin would have us be honest with ourselves about the absurd amount of time and energy cis women are expected to invest in our performances of femininity. If cis women were honest about this, we'd admit that if some trans women occasionally camp up their femininity a little more than TERFs might like, they're not doing anything we're not just as guilty of. If we don't like what we see when trans women turn the mirror of femininity toward us, we have only ourselves to blame.

Further driving home the importance of not throwing stones when you live in glass houses, Lori Watson, a professor of philosophy at the University of San Diego, points out that when cis women live as cis, they too are affirming a world of binary gender identifications, a world of gender stereotypes, a world with a limited number of acceptable ways to be a woman, just as much as any trans woman does.

When I, a cis woman, perform my not terribly original rendition of conventional femininity, I am in part saying that this is what women should be like. "In fashioning myself, I fashion Man," Jean-Paul Sartre said. I might not always like it, but when I present myself in ways that I know that others around me will read as female, I'm not only going along with but actually affirming their conventional beliefs about what women are like. (This, in part, is the power of Butler's advice to mess with our performances of gender: doing so unsettles people's unthinking preconceptions.)

But if I'm as guilty of entrenching regressive gender stereotypes as anyone else, why do TERFs think it's trans women who are specially culpable for shoring up gender essentialism? Why aren't they going after cis women like me too? We might all agree that the goal is to get to a world free of the shackles of conventional gender ascriptions, but that is not the world we currently live in. "The criticism of trans women as failing to act in ways that are consistent with an ideal of liberation from sex and gender," Watson cracks, "is a little like criticizing any of us for making a decent living under capitalism, or investing our retirement funds in the stock market, if the aim of liberation is the destruction of capitalism as a social, political, and economic system. Even Karl Marx had to eat in the here and now."

Talia Mae Bettcher, a professor of philosophy at California State University, Los Angeles, demonstrates how trans people are caught in a double bind. If a trans person successfully passes as cis and is later discovered to be trans, they're seen as an "evil deceiver" who has lied about who they really are. Trans people who are open about being trans, on the other hand, are seen as "make-believers"—cheap counterfeits, pathetically attempting to be something they couldn't possibly actually be. The problem with this view of trans people as either deceptive or pathetic frauds is that it presupposes that there's a real thing that trans women are failing to be. And this sounds an awful lot like the biological essentialism that almost all feminists reject.

The current debates over trans women bring us back to the question of what set of core experiences supposedly make someone who was assigned female at birth a "real" woman. Is it menstruation or childbirth? Nope—lots of women don't experience those, either by fate or by choice. What about being subject to sexual violence and harassment? Trans women face as much if not more sexual violence than cis women. How about simply a lifetime of unwanted objectifying male sexual attention? There are plenty of women who don't meet the standards of superficial sexual attractiveness who do not get such attention, and some of them even long for it. And surely we don't want to go back to the days of defining women by their hormones or even their chromosomes—if for no other reason than we'd leave out the estimated 1.7 percent of women who are intersex.

When a cis woman complains that trans women haven't had the same experiences as "real" women-born-women, then what she's really saying is, "Trans women haven't had the same experiences as women like me." If thirty-plus years of intersectional feminism has taught us anything, it's that this is precisely the move that feminists need to stop making.

APRIL 1, 2019

A Power of Our Own

For centuries, men have colonized storytelling.
That era is over.

Elena Ferrante

POWER, ALTHOUGH HARD TO HANDLE, IS GREATLY DESIRED. There is no person or group or sect or party or mob that doesn't want power, convinced that it would know how to use it as no one ever has before.

I'm no different. And yet I've always been afraid of having authority assigned to me. Whether it was at school or at work, men were in the majority in any governing body and the women adopted male ways. I never felt at ease, so I stayed on the sidelines. I was sure that I didn't have the strength to sustain conflicts with men, and that I would betray myself by adapting my views to theirs. For millennia, every expression of power has been conditioned by male attitudes toward the world. To women, then, it seems that power can be used only in the ways that men have traditionally used it.

There is one form of power that has fascinated me ever since I was a girl, even though it has been widely colonized by men: the power of storytelling. Telling stories really is a kind of power, and not an insignificant one. Stories give shape to experience, sometimes by accommodating traditional literary forms, sometimes by turning them upside down, sometimes by reorganizing them. Stories draw readers into their web, and engage them by putting them to work, body and soul, so that they can transform the black thread of writing into people, ideas, feelings, actions, cities, worlds, humanity, life. Storytelling, in other words, gives us the power to bring order to the chaos of the real under our own sign, and in this it isn't very far from political power.

In the beginning I didn't know that storytelling was a kind of power. I became aware of this only slowly, and felt an often paralyzing responsibility. I still do. Power is neither good nor bad—it depends on what we intend to do with it. The older I get, the more afraid I am of using the power of storytelling badly. My intentions in general are good, but sometimes telling a story succeeds in the right way and sometimes in the wrong way. The only consolation I have is that however badly conceived and badly written—and therefore harmful—a story may be, the harm will always be less than that caused by terrible political and economic mismanagement, with its accouterments of wars, guillotines, mass exterminations, ghettos, concentration camps, and gulags.

What to say, then? I suppose that I chose to write out of a fear of handling more concrete and dangerous forms of power. And also perhaps out of a strong feeling of alienation from the techniques of domination, so that at times writing seemed to be the most congenial way for me to react to abuses of power.

However, I chose to write mainly because, as a girl, I mistakenly thought that literature was particularly welcoming to women. The *Decameron*, by Giovanni Boccaccio (1313–1375), made a great impression on me. In this work, which is at the origin of the grand Italian and European narrative traditions, ten youths—seven women and three men—take turns telling stories for ten days. At around the age of sixteen, I found it reassuring that Boccaccio, in conceiving his narrators, had made most of them women. Here was a great writer, the father of the modern story, presenting seven great female narrators. There was something to hope for.

Only later did I discover that even though in the fiction of the *Decameron* Boccaccio had been generous toward women, in the real world things were very different—and continue to be. We women have been pushed to the margins, toward subservience, even when it comes to our literary work. It's a fact: Libraries and archives of every sort preserve the thought and actions of a disproportionate number of prominent men. To construct instead a potent genealogy of our own, a female genealogy, would be a delicate and arduous task.

If things had turned out differently, would we have done any better than men? Are we, ultimately, better than they are? As a young woman I thought so, but today I don't know.

I tend to avoid any idealization. It's not good for our cause, in my view, to imagine that all women are honorable, good-natured, extremely smart, fearless and blameless, and, above all, no longer the accomplices of men.

Our widespread complicity is in fact a serious problem. Power is still firmly in male hands, and if, in societies with solid democratic traditions, we are more frequently given access to positions of command, it is only on condition that we show that we have internalized the male method of confronting and resolving problems. As a result, we too often end up demonstrating that we are acquiescent, obedient, and equal to male expectations.

Suppose a woman pushes her way into the structures of power using an unconventional political intelligence that bends the rules, both written and unwritten. The fact is that she can succeed only if her unconventionality remains consistent with the traditional male culture of command. Why win, then? Merely for the pleasure of winning?

I've never been particularly swayed by the rhetorical formula, "At last, a woman president!"—or prime minister, or Nobel winner, or any other position atop our current political or cultural hierarchies. The question is, rather: Within what culture, within what system of power, are women rising to the top?

Pressing changes are under way. Everything is becoming something else, unpredictably. A completely new outlook is required. The challenge for now and the foreseeable future is to extract ourselves from what men have engineered: a planet long on the edge of catastrophe.

But how? Maybe now is the moment to bet on a female vision of power—one constructed and imposed with the force of our achievements in every field. For now our exceptionalism is the exceptionalism of minorities. Men can afford to grant us some recognition with good-humored condescension because there are still too few truly autonomous women who can't be made subservient, who can't be dismissed by the expression, "You're so good, you seem like a man."

But things are shifting rapidly. Women's achievements are multiplying. We don't always have to prove that we're acquiescent or complicit to enjoy the crumbs dispensed by the system of male power. The power that we require must be so solid and active that we can do without the sanction of men altogether.

The seven female narrators of the *Decameron* should never again need to rely on the great Giovanni Boccaccio to express themselves. Along with their innumerable female readers (even Boccaccio back then knew that men had other things to do and read little), they know how to describe the world in unexpected ways. The female story, told with increasing skill, increasingly widespread and unapologetic, is what must now assume power.

This essay was translated from the Italian by Ann Goldstein.

MAY 17, 2019

#IAmSexist

It's time that we men take responsibility for our
role in the problem of violence against women.

George Yancy

M EN, LISTEN UP.

In light of a year of disturbing revelations from the #MeToo movement and from last month's profoundly troubling Brett Kavanaugh hearings and his eventual confirmation to the Supreme Court, it is time that we, men, act.

Certainly, some of us men have spoken out on behalf of women. But many more of us have remained silent. Some have kept silent out of fear of being judged, fear of criticism or censure, others out of genuine respect. In fact, silence has become the default stance of many men who consider themselves "allies" of women. But given all that has transpired, staying out of it is no longer enough.

I've decided not to cut corners. So, join me, with due diligence and civic duty, and publicly claim: I am sexist!

In fact, perhaps it is time that we lay claim to a movement—#IamSexist. Think about its national and international implications as we take responsibility for our sexism, our misogyny, our patriarchy.

It is hard to admit we are sexist. I, for instance, would like to think that I possess genuine feminist bona fides, but who am I kidding? I am a failed and broken feminist. More pointedly, I am sexist. There are times when I fear for the "loss" of my own "entitlement" as a male. Toxic masculinity takes many forms. All forms continue to hurt and to violate women.

For example, before I got married, I insisted that my wife take my last name. After all, she was to become my wife. So, why not take my name, and become part of me? She refused. She wanted to keep her own last name, arguing that a woman taking her husband's name was a patriarchal practice. I was not happy, especially as she had her father's last name, which I argued contradicted her position against patriarchy. But as she argued, "This is my name and it is part of my identity." I became stubborn and interpreted her decision as evidence of a lack of full commitment to me. Well, she brilliantly proposed that we both change our last names and take on a new name together showing our commitment to each other.

Despite the charity, challenge, and reasonableness of the offer, I dropped the ball. That day I learned something about me. I didn't respect her autonomy, her legal standing and personhood. As pathetic as this may sound, I saw her as my property, to be defined by my name and according to my legal standing. (She kept her name.) While this was not sexual assault, my insistence was a violation of her independence. I had inherited a subtle, yet still violent, form of toxic masculinity. It still raises its ugly head—I should be thanked when I clean the house, cook, sacrifice my time. These are deep and troubling expectations that are shaped by male privilege, male power, and toxic masculinity.

If you are a woman reading this, I have failed you. Through my silence and an uninterrogated collective misogyny, I have failed you. I have helped and continue to help perpetuate sexism. I know about how we hold on to forms of power that dehumanize you only to elevate our sense of masculinity. I recognize my silence as an act of violence. For this, I sincerely apologize.

I speak as an insider. I know about what so many of us men think about women—the language we use, the sense of power that we garner through our sexual exploits, our catcalling and threatening, our sexually objectifying gazes, our dehumanizing and despicable sexual gestures, and our pornographic imaginations. This is not simply locker room banter but a public display of unchecked bravado for which we often feel no shame.

We have heard many accounts from women of what it is like to live under the yoke of our self-serving construction of a violent, pathetic, and problematic masculinity. It is time that we stop gaslighting their reality.

By now, many of you are probably saying, "This doesn't apply to me—I'm innocent."

It's true that many of us, including me, have not committed vile acts of rape, sexual assault, and sexual abuse the likes of which Harvey Weinstein has been accused of. We have not, like Charlie Rose, been accused of sexual harassment by dozens of women who worked for us; and we are not, like Bill Cosby, being sent to prison for drugging and sexually assaulting a woman, in this case Andrea Constand. Yet I argue that we are collectively complicit with a sexist mindset and a poisonous masculinity rooted in the same toxic male culture from which these men emerged.

I'm issuing a clarion call against our claims of sexist "innocence." I'm calling our "innocence" what it is—bullshit. As bell hooks writes in *The Will to Change: Men, Masculinity, and Love*, men unconsciously "engage in patriarchal thinking, which condones rape even though they may never enact it. This is a patriarchal truism that most people in our society want to deny." When women speak out about male violence, hooks writes, "folks are eager to stand up and make the point that most men are not violent. They refuse to acknowledge that masses of boys and men have been programmed from birth on to believe that at some point they must be violent, whether psychologically or physically, to prove that they are men." We have learned it. In the language of Simone de Beauvoir, "One is not born, but rather becomes" masculine.

We have hidden behind a myth that "boys will be boys"—a myth that distorts our moral compass, that stunts our growth, maturity, and self-respect, and smothers our capacity to love and experience the genuine ecstasy of Eros. Audre Lorde writes in *Uses of the Erotic: The Erotic as Power* (1978), "The erotic has often been misnamed by men and used against women." She adds, "Pornography is a direct denial of the power of the erotic, for it represents the suppression of true feeling." Not only are we as men taught to deny our feelings, but we also are taught that sexual vulnerability is weakness, not the province of "real men."

We mask that vulnerability. I find hooks's description powerful and true to my own experience as a boy: "Learning to wear a mask (that word already embedded in the term 'masculinity')," as hooks writes, "is the first lesson in patriarchal masculinity that a boy learns. He learns that his core feelings cannot be expressed if they do not conform to the acceptable behaviors sexism defines as male. Asked to give up the true self in order to realize the patriarchal ideal, boys learn self-betrayal early and are rewarded for these acts of soul murder."

What does hooks mean by "soul murder"?

When I was about fifteen years old, I said to a friend of mine, "Why must you always look at a girl's butt?" He promptly responded: "Are you gay or something? What else should I look at, a guy's butt?" He was already wearing the mask. He had already learned the lessons of patriarchal masculinity. I was in an unfortunate bind. Either I should without question objectify girls' behinds or I was gay. There was no wiggle room for me to be both antisexist and antimisogynistic and yet a heterosexual young boy. You see, other males had rewarded his gaze by joining in the objectifying practice: "Look at that butt!" It was a collective act of devaluation. The acts of soul murder had already begun.

Yet I too participated in acts of soul murder. As early as elementary school, the young boys would play this "game" of pushing one another into girls. The idea was to get your friend to push you into a girl that you found attractive in order to grind up against her. I was guilty: "Hurry up! Push me into her." He pushed, and the physical grind was obvious. She would turn around, disgusted, and yell, "Stop!" Youthful? Yes. Was it sexist and wrong? Yes. This was our youthful collective education; this is what it meant for us to gain "masculine credibility" at the expense of girls.

Later, I was also made to believe that girls were "targets," objects to be chased down and owned. That is the contradiction. For example, at about sixteen, we used to play a game called "Catch a girl, get a girl." There was no equivalent called "Catch a boy, get a boy." After all, as boys, we named the game. We would count to give the girls a head start. We would then run after them. If you caught a girl, you could steal a kiss. Some of the boys attempted to grope the girls.

The logic governing the game, unseen by both the boys and the girls, was predicated upon sexist assumptions that relegated the girls to positions of prey. This is what American male culture taught us early on: Women were like "meat" and we must always nurture a voracious appetite. This fact alone should challenge how we construe "mutual consent." The game was orchestrated around what the philosopher Luce Irigaray would call a "dominant phallic economy." We chased; they ran. We were the pursuers; they were the pursued. Our objective was to "get them." We gazed upon the prey and then we would strike. Though the girls played, they were not to blame. We were the "winners," possessors of conquered territory. That is part of the early training that I received when it came to my toxic masculinity.

Looking back, I wish that I could speak face-to-face to that younger self and undo the soul murder. Yet, I am not beyond redemption. That young boy is still learning from the older me. I have tremendous love to give him, a demanding love that he learn to undo the toxicity of male masculinity.

This is why Donald Trump Jr. got it all wrong when he was asked which of his children he is most concerned for and he answered, "Right now, I'd say my sons." This is pure obfuscation, a substitution of fictions for facts, and a form of dangerous denial regarding the reality that his daughters may one day face. With that statement, he lied to his daughters.

Trump Jr. should get his priorities straight. In a male-dominated and sexist toxic world, a world where his own father grabs women's genitalia and kisses them without their permission, it is our daughters who should concern us as targets of sexual violence. Trump Jr.

should be concerned about raising his sons not in the image of his own father but in the image of those of us men who are prepared to recognize our soul murder, our toxic masculinity, and to do something about it.

What are we afraid of?

We all recently lived through the public spectacle of the Brett Kavanaugh hearings. What is at stake transcends but also includes Christine Blasey Ford's allegations that Kavanaugh sexually assaulted her when they were both in high school during the 1980s. The history of toxic and violent masculinity should have been enough for us to give full weight to the reasonableness and believability of Ford's testimony. But we did not.

Donald Trump's cruel public mocking of Ford in Southaven, Mississippi, days after her testimony was despicable and must be seen as another violation of Ford's character. And as the crowd laughed and applauded, including women present, Ford's words, her emotional testimony, were denounced as the ramblings of someone without any claim on the veracity of her experiences. To add insult to injury, Sarah Huckabee Sanders's defense that Trump was just "stating the facts" is both a blatant lie and a further act of cruelty, a denial of Ford's pain and denial of the collective suffering of women more generally from acts of sexual violence.

I can imagine being passionate about defending myself if put in Kavanaugh's position. Kavanaugh, however, unabashedly reinforced white male machismo and aggressiveness such that even if one thinks that he is innocent of what Ford accused him of, he put on full display the performance of a cantankerous white male who is recklessly determined to seek revenge against those he claimed were out to get him.

The history of male violence against women speaks to Ford's pain and suffering. The statistics regarding sexual assault are telling: One in five women are raped at some point in their lives; ninety percent of rape victims are female; in the United States one in three women experience some form of contact sexual violence in their lifetime; roughly half of female victims of rape reported being raped by an intimate partner and forty percent by an acquaintance; in eight out of ten cases of rape, the victim knew the perpetrator. We can no longer deny this reality.

I know that if you are a woman, you don't really need me as a man saying to you that you are not paranoid when it comes to male violence, sexual and otherwise. I speak not for you but with you. In my view, and in the view of many others, Kavanaugh failed himself, and you. And we have all played our part in that failure. I don't want to fail women anymore.

Since the world is watching, we, as men, need to join in the dialogue in ways that we have failed to in the past. We need to admit our roles in the larger problem of male violence against women. We need to tell the truth about ourselves.

OCTOBER 24, 2018

In July 2021, the Pennsylvania Supreme Court reversed Cosby's conviction on the grounds that prosecutors had violated his rights by reneging on an apparent promise not to charge him.

The Gender Politics of Fasting

Both Cesar Chavez and Simone Weil starved their
bodies for spiritual and political reasons. Why is
only one of them remembered as anorexic?

Mariana Alessandri

L AST SUMMER I TOOK PART IN A TWENTY-FOUR-HOUR FAST, AS
part of a "Break Bread Not Families" prayer and fasting chain. I spent
a day not eating, in spiritual solidarity with the twenty-four hundred
children who had been separated from a parent at the border. Many
of these children were being detained a few miles from my house in
McAllen, Texas, where their parents were signing deportation papers
on the promise of reunification—and where President Trump visited
last Thursday. The hosting organization was LUPE (La Unión del
Pueblo Entero), a nonprofit organization that works on local issues
in South Texas and was founded by the labor activists Dolores Huerta
and Cesar Chavez in 1989.

Chavez—who died in 1993 and is considered a hero by many for
founding, along with Huerta and other labor organizers, the United
Farm Workers of America—was a deliberate undereater. He under-
took three major fasts in his life—the first public fast lasted for
twenty-five days in 1968, the second for twenty-seven days in 1972,
and the last for thirty-six days in 1988—with frequent shorter ones in
between. Chavez claimed that he didn't fast primarily to nudge political action, much less to change his body shape. As a Roman Catho-

lic, he described fasting as a means of purifying his body, mind, and soul, and he saw it as an opportunity to do penance, join in solidarity with others, and draw attention to the maltreatment of farmworkers.

Chavez called fasting "probably the most powerful communicative tool that we have," emphasizing the spiritual nature of the medium. In fasting, he believed that one soul could speak directly to another one, bypassing political and religious differences. Chavez described fasting as a "sacrifice for justice" and a "reminder of suffering." Each fast was deeply personal, but Chavez knew that he was tapping into the history of not eating as a way of speaking truth to political power.

Chavez also knew that he was risking his life and worrying loved ones by undereating, but he insisted that he didn't fast "out of a desire to destroy myself." Yet despite knowing that some fasters die around the fifteen-day mark, Chavez persisted ten days longer than that in his first public fast. He died at sixty-six, his body certainly weakened by his fasting.

Most people would not be surprised to know that Chavez was not—either during his life or posthumously—generally considered to have an eating disorder. His fasting was believed to have served a higher purpose. That was not the case with another well-known Catholic, who, decades before Chavez, was drawn to the idea of refusing food for a social good and to connect with God.

The French philosopher and mystic Simone Weil (1909–1943)—not a traditional Catholic but a Catholic nonetheless—was a faster too. She systematically denied herself food three times in her life. At five, Weil gave up sugar upon learning that French soldiers didn't have access to it. The second time, she ate only what factory workers could afford to eat. The third time she died, at thirty-four, after having for too long eaten only the quantity of food that her compatriots in occupied France would have access to.

Weil stated that her fasts were motivated by a sense of solidarity with France's emaciated outcasts, and her empathy found a home in her empty stomach. But she confessed that her fasting had as much to do with what she called the "void" where God lived as it did with solidarity. She wrote a considerable amount about the spiritual relationship between God and emptiness.

"We have to fasten onto the hunger," she wrote, since hunger reminds us that we are not self-sustaining, that God is spiritual bread. She believed that loving God was akin to renouncing food even when one is hungry. Food can't fill the void inside of us, she thought, since that's where God belongs. For Weil, hunger was a sign that there was room enough for God.

Weil claimed that her fasting was spiritual and social, as Chavez did. Both systematically underfed themselves and claimed religious grounds for doing so. In both cases, loved ones worried about them, and in both cases, these periods of undernourishment hastened their deaths. They each provided religious reasons for not eating, but only one of them was believed.

In many of the subsequent accounts of her life, Weil has been labeled an anorexic, like Saint Catherine of Siena, the fourteenth century nun who was also convinced that she could reach God through her empty stomach. This was not the fate of Chavez, who is today still admired for carrying out a centuries-old ascetic practice, nor of Mohandas Gandhi—nor, for that matter, Jesus Christ, who in the Bible is said to have fasted for forty days and nights in the desert.

Today, even though one-third of diagnosed eating disorders are found in men, we overwhelmingly associate the medical diagnosis of anorexia nervosa with women (a more obscure term, anorexia mirabilis, denotes undereating as a form of religious asceticism, and is not listed as a medical condition in the *Diagnostic and Statistical Manual of Mental Disorders*). All this suggests that in society when a woman intentionally fasts, we are more likely to see her as sick; and when a man does it, we consider him spiritual. It's certainly possible that Weil hid a case of anorexia nervosa behind a mask of spirituality. By that logic, though, Chavez might have done the same thing.

The same double standard applies outside of a religious context. Just like yoga, meditation, and other spiritual practices that get popular when they jettison their religious trappings, fasting has become a health practice in recent years, often in male circles. Some research now supports the idea that the body does well when it gets deprived of food for certain lengths of time, from twelve hours to three days, a concept known as Intermittent Fasting. Like the Paleo movement (a diet often marketed to men), IF remembers us as Paleolithic humans in the wild, with days of plenty sandwiched by days of nothing. Today, magazines and podcasts aimed at men promote the idea that IF is good for a man's physique. Notably absent is public worry that these men will develop eating disorders. In contrast, when a female student in my class announced that she was going to start practicing IF, other students quickly warned her to "be careful."

To point out this gender disparity around fasting is not to ignore the very real problem of eating disorders. In an age where anorexia nervosa and bulimia are prevalent among both men and women, there is sufficient reason to be cautious in branding any fast as "spiritual"—doing so might give cover by offering a religious justification in cases that may very well be psychological and physical in nature. The American cultural obsession with thinness and the demonization of body fat that magnify critical self-image and the psychological aspects of eating disorders should not be taken lightly. But that does not negate the misunderstanding and gender stereotyping that often surrounds intentional fasting for spiritual or political purposes.

My own one-day fast confirmed that I love food, but also that I am capable of systematically denying it to myself for a higher cause. Like Weil, I had hoped the pain in my stomach would serve as a reminder of the emotional pain of the children who lacked not food but mothers. It did: Every time my stomach groaned I imagined temporarily orphaned children. Privation joined me to them, even if mine was self-imposed and temporary. Like Chavez I felt repentant, as in, turned back toward the good, toward justice, toward God. Fasting made me feel utterly connected to these children, and thoroughly Catholic. By fasting I was tapping into my own religious, ascetic history, and I had triumphantly joined Weil and Chavez in their quest to share in the suffering of others.

Something telling also happened that day. I kept wondering if my desire to not eat was indicative of a latent eating disorder. In eating (and other areas), women are taught to doubt themselves. Perhaps the power radiating from the sickly bodies of Gandhi and Chavez contrasts too sharply with the medical diagnoses of bodies like Weil's, leading women to believe that deep inside, our souls are sick. I doubt that the men I fasted with that day in Texas heard a critical voice in their head, incessantly pressing them to examine their motives.

As a philosopher, I am in no position to make diagnoses for either of these historical figures, but I can insist that their actions—and ours—be viewed in the same light, with the same kind of scrutiny.

JANUARY 14, 2019

Is There a "Rational" Punishment for My Rapist?

*I would like the man who raped and abused me to be put
to death or imprisoned for life. That is not irrational.*

Amber Rose Carlson

"IMAGINE YOUR RAPIST HAD BEEN FOUND GUILTY AND SEN-
tenced in court. What would you want his sentence to be?"

This was the question asked to me in January 2016 by my therapist
during a session of eye movement desensitization and reprocessing
therapy (EMDR)—a treatment that researchers tout as one of the best
remedies for severe trauma and post-traumatic stress disorder.

I was raped repeatedly during a three-year span from age thirteen to sixteen. I was also subject to physical and emotional abuse
during that time. I've since undergone years of traditional talk and
group therapy with trauma specialists, and I am more healed today
than I ever thought possible. Still, recovering from trauma is a serious endeavor, and I hoped for more healing.

I had never thought filing a police report was a viable option. I was
now in my thirties; the statute of limitations had long since passed.
My therapist's thought experiment, then, was truly an exercise in
pure imagination. Unsure how to proceed, I took a methodological
approach; I would first imagine the harshest sentence possible, then
a sentence slightly less severe, moving backward until I found a sentence that seemed fitting.

Supposing I brought my rapist to trial, that he was convicted by a judge and sentenced to death, it was surprising to me that I deemed this punishment wholly appropriate.

I'm not a proponent of the death penalty primarily because the flaws in our criminal justice system are egregious and increasingly well documented. The thought experiment's framing, however, circumvented my usual concerns about unjust sanctions. I know what my rapist did to me, so I know he is guilty. Worries about the inhumanity of capital punishment were also blunted in part because this was purely hypothetical and in part because of the inhumanity he exhibited those long years with his penchant for violence.

Although the death sentence seemed wholly appropriate, I still considered how I would feel if a judge gave my rapist a less severe punishment: a natural life sentence—a life sentence with no chance for parole without a successful appeal. In this scenario, my feelings were just as clear: I would be slightly disappointed, but I would still feel mostly satisfied. Anything less than a death or natural life sentence, I knew, would seem inadequate.

After reporting back to my therapist, she offered another thought experiment. "What if," she said, "your rapist had been sentenced to death, but then had been pardoned?" I did not have to mull this question over. I knew I would feel exactly as I do now, exactly as I have felt for the past two decades: that the world is a terribly unjust place. It is a place where my life can be irrevocably transformed because a man could exert control, manipulation, and violence over me for years without repercussion. It is a place where my rapist and others like him are enabled at both societal and local levels. His mother, for example, simply told us to quiet down whenever she heard my screams—a response as horrifying as it is understandable given the many ways society tolerates violence against women.

A hypothetical pardon would allow him to escape repercussions just as he has escaped them in reality. Nearly twenty years later as I began trauma therapy again, he has a secure job, an accomplished and beautiful wife, and a healthy daughter. He is living a life many dream of, while my life is disrupted as I continue to heal from the wounds he inflicted when I was a child. EMDR begins with the choice of reliving either the earliest traumatic memory or the most painful, rendering it as harrowing as it is effective; EMDR is not for the faint of heart.

In February 2016—only weeks after the thought experiments with my therapist—the philosopher Jennifer Lackey published an opinion piece in The Stone. In the article, she uses her experience teaching philosophy to inmates to argue for the irrationality of natural life sentences. Lackey bases her argument against natural life sentences on two reasonable claims: (1) people (criminals, specifically) can and do change in profoundly transformative ways, and (2) we cannot know the future.

For Lackey, the fact that we have good statistical evidence that criminals can and do change is especially problematic given our vast epistemic limitations regarding the future. "Natural life sentences," she wrote, "say to all involved that there is no possible piece of information that could be learned between sentencing and death that could bear in any way on the punishment the convicted is said to deserve, short of what might ground an appeal." Citing the possibility of prisoner transformation, Lackey then puts her question about rationality directly: "How is it rational," she asks, "to screen off the relevance of this information? How, that is, is it rational to say today that there can be no possible evidence in the future that could bear on the punishment that a decades-from-now prisoner deserves?"

Natural life sentences, Lackey notices, are a "glaring exception" to the way we think about rational decision making in other contexts. Natural life sentences "permit binding, life-altering decisions to be made in a state of radical epistemic impoverishment."

Lackey's argument strongly suggests that transformation is an exceedingly important consideration for sentencing. This is not an alien notion; the criminal justice system often takes good behavior and contrition as evidence of transformation that is relevant to one's sentence. This occurs not just under the direction of theories that value rehabilitation, but in all but the "crudest forms of retributive justice." Rehabilitation, then, is one aspect that many believe separates crude justice theories from other, presumably better, justice theories.

I read Lackey's article very soon after the thought experiments with my therapist. I noticed that Lackey's argument easily applied to the death penalty, and I realized that the sentences I desired for my rapist were precisely the ones Lackey condemns as irrational. Since nothing in her argument prevented me from applying her logic to my own desires, I had to wonder if her argument also concluded that I was irrational for desiring permanent punishments. If it is irrational for the state to prescribe a permanent punishment given our epistemic limitations and prisoners' likelihood for change, wouldn't it be similarly irrational for victims to ignore these considerations?

There are, of course, crucial differences between victim's desires and punishments carried out by the state. While sometimes the criminal justice system considers the wishes of victims and their families, the criminal justice system's central aim is to protect the interests of the state and the community. This aim does not always coincide with the interests or wishes of the victim. Admittedly, there are often very good reasons for the state to ignore the wishes of victims. But my concern is less about what the state should do in practice and more about what arguments that prioritize transformation say about victims who desire permanent punishments.

Here I will be blunt: it matters very little to me whether my rapist is transformed at some point in his life. It matters to me only to the extent that I will readily agree that it would be better if he became the sort of person who did not inflict violence upon others. I would be very happy hearing that no other women would be harmed by him. But in terms of the punishment that he deserves? Transformation does not matter to me. And this is not irrational: There are many carefully considered reasons one might want a natural life sentence for perpetrators of egregious and irrevocable harm.

Desiring death or a natural life sentence for those who inflict traumatic violence is a rational response because whether or not my particular rapist transforms is irrelevant to whether or not I will ever have the chance to be the sort of person I might have been. His transformation is irrelevant to whether or not I will be able to live the sort of life I could have were it not for the injustice done to me. I desire a death or natural life sentence for my rapist because that is what seems appropriate given the amount of damage he wrought in my life.

Rape is itself a transformative experience. I will never be the same, and I have no idea how my life might have been different without the experience. My rapist expertly dismantled my sense of self as he isolated me from friends and family. He manipulated me so that he could more effectively inflict violence and exert power and control over me. I know that I have suffered, that I have struggled, and that I might not have survived. I've read about the neurological effects of prolonged trauma, and I know that I am now—and perhaps always will be—affected in some capacity by the things he did to me. After plenty of rational consideration, I cannot imagine any personal transformation that would make me think he deserves anything less than a permanent punishment.

In response, one might call my stance a crude form of retributive justice. Perhaps it is. I know that expressing desire for retribution is a risky move in its unpopularity. Social narratives have long praised forgiveness and love especially for those who have wronged us. Theories of justice have also moved beyond ones that emphasize retribution—and for good reason in many cases. I understand this perspective: For many years it was abhorrent for me to think of responding to the violence I suffered with more violence. But calling the desire for permanent punishment crude does not render it irrational however unpopular it might be.

One might, in the end, respond by saying that arguments like Lackey's are proposing only policy change. These arguments, we might say, are not meant to prescribe the appropriate feelings for victims. If so, we might think that my worries about what arguments can say to individual victims is off the mark. While it's clear that policy change can be a central aim, audiences of such arguments include victims of traumatic crimes. Yet it is not clear that such arguments always take victims into account.

Although my attitude is in no way representative of all victims, epistemic arguments that prioritize criminal transformation must contend with the implication that they can be used to paint trauma victims irrational when they desire retribution.

It's certainly important to advocate for prisoners who are wrongly incarcerated and for those who were victims of the overzealous war-on-crime era. The injustices in our criminal justice system are too numerous and too serious to ignore. But criminal justice reform should not be so myopic that it compounds trauma survivors' victimization. Those who manage to survive traumatic crimes have enough to battle without arguments that undermine their rational considerations. Advocates for criminal justice reform can, and should, do better.

OCTOBER 23, 2017

Feminism and the Future of Philosophy

Viewing it only as a political cause that benefits
women ignores its full potential.

Gary Gutting

"THERE IS A DEEP WELL OF RAGE INSIDE OF ME. RAGE ABOUT
how I as an individual have been treated in philosophy; rage about
how others I know have been treated; and rage about the conditions
that I'm sure affect many women and minorities in philosophy, and
have caused many others to leave." Those words, written a decade ago
by Sally Haslanger, a distinguished professor of philosophy at MIT,
well express the moral energy behind the feminist ferment currently
shaking American philosophy.

This ferment has overturned the male dominance of our primary
professional organization, the American Philosophical Association,
with women (who make up about one-fourth of the members) holding over half of the seats on its governing board. This change cor-
relates with the recent vigorous efforts of the APA to increase the
proportion of women (and minorities) in philosophy and to root out
all forms of bias and discrimination. The organization's website lists
a dozen projects and resources devoted to diversity, and its Committee on the Status of Women has established a site-visit program
open to any department that wants advice on improving its climate
for women.

This organizational shift, combined with supportive actions from many major philosophy departments, has decisively furthered philosophical feminism as a political cause. The discipline now seems committed in principle to gender equality, despite considerable disagreement about just what that means and how best to achieve it. We can still expect many intense and even rancorous disputes over these questions. Here, however, I want to put aside these unavoidable disputes and reflect on the importance of feminist philosophy for the future of philosophical thinking.

It's easy to conclude that feminist philosophy is little more than the vehicle of a political movement. The editors of the recent *Routledge Companion to Feminist Philosophy* note that feminist philosophy "originated in feminist politics" and "included from the start discussion of feminist political issues and positions."

Nowadays, major feminist philosophers often define their work in explicitly political terms. Elizabeth Anderson, for example, says that feminist epistemology and philosophy of science "identifies ways in which dominant conceptions and practices of knowledge attribution, acquisition, and justification systematically disadvantage women and other subordinated groups, and strives to reform these conceptions and practices so that they serve the interests of these groups." And Sally Haslanger, in her seminal analysis of gender and race, says, "At the most general level, the task is to develop accounts of gender and race that will be effective tools in the fight against injustice." She goes on to offer the following definition of "woman": "S is a woman [if and only if] S is systematically subordinated along some dimension—economic, political, legal, social—and S is 'marked' as a target for this treatment by observed or imagined bodily features presumed to be evidence of a female's biological role in reproduction."

Philosophers uneasy with strong feminist claims about the current poor treatment of women—or who just think it's wrong to presuppose such claims in philosophical discussions—may feel that feminist philosophy has nothing to offer them. Even sympathetic male philosophers may see such philosophy as the province of women, particularly since most writing on feminist topics is by

women and feminists sometimes seem not to welcome male contributions. (The fifty-six essays in the *Routledge Companion* are all
by women.)

In fact, however, feminist philosophy should be an essential
resource for all philosophers, whatever their views about its political agenda. To see why, it will help to reflect on an earlier disruption
to the philosophical establishment: the "pluralist revolt" against the
dominant analytic philosophy of the 1970s and '80s. The pluralists
were a disparate group of philosophers: pragmatists in the tradition of Peirce, James, and Dewey; metaphysicians following classical thinkers such as Aristotle and Aquinas or the process philosophy
of Whitehead; and, most prominently, "continental philosophers"
working out of recent European movements such as phenomenology
(Husserl, Heidegger, Sartre); post-structuralism (Foucault, Derrida); and critical theory (Habermas and the Frankfurt School).

Pluralists challenged the dominance of the APA by the analytic
philosophy that they saw as modeling itself on mathematics and natural science. This mode of thought, they said, imposed standards
of conceptual clarity and logical rigor that restricted philosophical thinking to a narrow range of abstract and artificial questions.
These restrictions, they argued, marginalized pluralist philosophers and, more important, excluded the great perennial questions
that had defined philosophy from Plato to Hegel.

The pluralists gained a good deal of power within the APA, made
room for alternative voices, and no doubt played a role in the broadening of analytic interests. Their efforts supported an increased
interest in traditional questions, particularly in metaphysics and
ethics, and a turn to pragmatic positions in epistemology. But the
pluralists did not overcome the analytic hegemony, with analytic
philosophers remaining a large majority in the most highly regarded
departments.

Further, the pluralists did little to blunt the sharp division
between analytic philosophy and so-called continental philosophy,
which maintained its own (relatively marginalized) departments,
national organization, and journals. Indeed, we are now seeing a

good deal of work on "continental" philosophers move from philosophy to other humanistic disciplines (for example, in language, communication, and film studies departments) and to the softer social sciences.

Today, feminist philosophy has produced an awakening far beyond that of the pluralist revolt. It has already further broadened and deepened analytic philosophy and shows promise of promoting serious engagement with continental thinkers.

It's interesting that the new feminist directions sometimes derive from the stereotypical roles that society has imposed on women. In ethics, as Rosemarie Tong and Nancy Williams note in their *Stanford Encyclopedia of Philosophy* article on feminist ethics, "proponents of feminist care ethics . . . stress that traditional moral theories . . . are deficient to the degree they lack, ignore, trivialize, or demean values and virtues culturally associated with women."

So, for example, societies have often directed women toward subordinating their interests to others (husbands or children, for example). As a result, women tend to be particularly sensitive to "care" as an ethical value, and feminist philosophers (like Nel Nodding and Virginia Held) have developed various "ethics of care" that supplement or displace "masculine" ethical values such as autonomy and self-fulfillment. Even an other-directed principle such as "Act for the greatest happiness of all" takes on a deeper meaning when understood not as a duty toward generic humanity but as a call to personal engagement with those in need.

In a different vein, women live in a society that presents as "natural" what they experience as arbitrary constraints. This can provide them with a particular sensitivity to injustices that are due less to individual ill will than to the structures of established practices and institutions. Feminist social philosophers like Nancy Fraser have developed this line of thought in dialogue with the work of Marx, Foucault, Habermas, and other continental thinkers.

Feminist epistemologists have developed the notion of situated knowledge to counter standard analytic approaches that treat knowledge as the goal of an isolated mind (à la Descartes), abstracted from concrete life situations such as the knower's body, emotions, values, and social roles. Continental traditions like Marxism and existential phenomenology have long emphasized such situated knowledge. But feminist philosophers like Louise Antony and Helen Longino have offered strong analytic arguments for enriching the "masculinist" view of knowledge with elements previously ignored, perhaps as signs of "feminine" cognitive weakness.

Similarly, feminist metaphysicians have argued that metaphysical distinctions between superior and inferior categories (mind/matter, essential/contingent, self/other) were often used to express male superiority. This has led to the suggestion that such dichotomies did not express eternal necessities but rather historically constructed social categories—a suggestion feminists found supported by the work of continental philosophers like Simone de Beauvoir and Michel Foucault.

Feminists' personal and political rage against injustice (and parallel emotional reactions against their claims) could, of course, create an atmosphere inimical to fruitful philosophical reflection. But looking at the significant achievements of feminist philosophers, feminism promises to improve not only the climate for women but also philosophical thinking itself.

SEPTEMBER 18, 2017

X

WHY DOES ART MATTER?

Five Theses on Creativity

It permeates life, and, like love, it can break your heart.

Eric Kaplan

THE WORD "ART" CAN SEEM PRETENTIOUS: WHEN PEOPLE HEAR it, they worry someone will force them to read a novel, or go to a museum, or see a movie without any explosions in it.

To me, art simply refers to those aspects of our lives that can be suffused and transformed by creativity. And having creativity in our lives is important. Without it we're just going through the motions, stuck in the past. With it we feel alive, even joyous.

But if I say that art is simply life imbued with creativity, isn't that just a case of obscurum per obscurius—of explaining the murky with the even murkier? After all, what exactly is creativity?

To help unravel this puzzle, here are five theses on creativity:

Thesis No. 1: Creativity makes something new. A different way of talking can suddenly make our world seem new. Here's an example: In the Middle Ages, a road was something people walked on, the ocean a terrifying expanse of blue. But when the anonymous author of the Old English epic poem *Beowulf* called the ocean a "whale-road," he made his readers experience the ocean afresh. The ocean may be an obstacle for us land-bound humans, but for whales it's a road.

Thesis No. 2: Creativity hides itself. Creativity is shy. It's easy to miss that creativity is about making something new, because, as soon as we succeed, the new thing we've created appears obvious, as if it had always been there. "Whale" and "road" were just there hanging around when someone said "whale-road." And then people said, "Of course! The ocean may be a barrier for us, but it's not for whales. They swim in it." All that one person did was say what there was to be said—except it wasn't there to be said, until he or she said it.

Creativity can seem like a tool for solving problems: We need a new word for the ocean! But creativity doesn't just solve problems; it also makes or discovers new problems to solve. Hundreds of years ago, nobody knew the old words for ocean weren't cutting it, until someone said "whale-road." And everyone was like, "Wow! It is a whale-road!" Creativity always hides itself—it makes itself disappear.

That's a helpful point to keep in mind when thinking about science, because creativity is fundamental there, too. We tend to think of science as a series of nonoptional statements about how the world works—as a collection of things we must believe. But if that's true, how can scientists be creative? They can't really say anything new; they just have to passively express things as they are.

But, of course, that isn't how science works at all. We actually have to create it. When Newton came up with his second law of motion (force equals mass times acceleration) he was being just as creative as the person who came up with "whale-road." And as with "whale-road," Newton's creativity was concealed by the success of his creative act: His formulation pointed toward something that already existed, but also didn't. The more successful we are, the more it will seem like the things we created didn't need to be created. Creativity hides.

Thesis No. 3: Creativity permeates life. Creativity fills our lives like ocean water fills the grains of a sandcastle—saturating the spaces between this moment and the next, this action and the next, this word and the next. As a consequence, you can be creative when you're doing pretty much anything: You can be creative in the way you walk to work, respond to grief, make a friend, move your body when you wake up in the morning, or hum a tune on a sunny day.

We are constantly remaking our lives through acts of creativity. In fact, creativity makes life possible—just like water makes a sandcastle possible. Without water a sandcastle falls apart, and a life that is completely routinized and uncreative is no life at all.

Thesis No. 4: Creativity can break your heart. It's inherently risky. You might say, "Creativity seems so joyous and fun—why isn't everybody creative all the time? Why do people steal and plagiarize instead? Why do they follow rules when they're trying to be creative? Why do they always make the hero a handsome man, or always make song lyrics rhyme? Why do they copy what's worked before?"

Because creativity can fail. If you knew ahead of time that the thing you were making would work, you wouldn't be engaged in creativity. And when it doesn't work, it breaks your heart. You look like a fool; what's worse, you feel like a fool. It's very embarrassing. But you can't get the joy of creativity without risking pain and failure—which is also true of love.

Thesis No. 5: Creativity is a kind of love. That's why it can break your heart, and why, at the same time, it can make the world come alive. When you're creative, you make things fresh and new; when you love someone or something, you do the same.

That's also why creativity is shy, why it hides. We don't want the way we love to be captured by someone else's loveless formulation. We don't want someone to say, "Oh, he loves everybody with blond hair," or "He loves everybody who reminds him of his mother." We don't like it when people think they can manipulate us by figuring out whom or what we love—it's an insult to those we love, to us, to love itself. So we're a bit guarded when we talk about love; we don't want people using the way we love to take advantage of us.

Corruptio optimi pessima—the corruption of the best is the worst: Love is the best part of our lives and can permeate our entire being, but it's the most terrible thing when it's misused or misunderstood. It's the same with creativity.

MAY 29, 2020

Art Is a Different Kind of Cosmic Order

Its patterns help us access the inner truths
that science can't articulate.

Brian Greene

T HE TORRENTIAL RAINS AT THE SUMMER RESORT IN THE Catskills, where my dad was a weekend bass player, entitling us to the use of a free if leaky bungalow, drove all us campers into the cavernous dance hall for an impromptu game of trivia. I was five years old, and the first up. "Where are you from?" the head counselor asked when I had climbed onto the stage.

I was so intently focused on my private, newfound passion that I hardly registered the question. "Math!" I answered, only to be baffled when everyone around me erupted in laughter.

Mathematics is a universal language of pattern. Equations articulate relationships. They speak to unassailable truths that stand beyond the vagaries of perception and interpretation. Every flat, right-angled triangle drawn before Pythagoras, and every one after, until eternity, satisfies the famous theorem that bears the ancient Greek philosopher's name. There are no exceptions. That's the nature of mathematical insight. And through its terse, pristine delineation of inflexible truth, mathematics offers us the comfort of reliability and the beauty of precision. Since my earliest introduction, I have felt the deep allure of these unchanging patterns. Patterns that are impervious to authority. Patterns that transcend all things personal.

It is a perspective I have found to be widely shared among those who practice mathematics or physics as a profession.

All the same, many more of us are drawn to patterns of a different sort, patterns conveyed through particular combinations of sounds and colors and shapes and textures and movements, yielding works of music or dance or film or painting or sculpture—patterns, that is, which emerge as creative human expression. These are patterns we value because of, not in spite of, their capacity to reflect thoroughly personal, deeply subjective responses to the infinite spectrum of human experience. As cave paintings, ancient figurines, and archaic musical instruments attest, since the earliest glimmers of thought our species has intensely pursued and consumed such expression.

And that presents a puzzle.

I have little doubt that should we ever make contact with an extraterrestrial intelligence, they will understand our mathematics, especially the equations we have developed to explain the regularities of reality. After all, recognizing the patterns inherent in physical phenomena is central to survival. We have prevailed because we can sense and respond to the rhythms of the world. Every tomorrow will be different from today, but beneath the myriad comings and goings we rely on enduring qualities.

The sun will rise, rocks will fall, water will flow. The vast collection of allied patterns we encounter from one moment to the next profoundly influence our behavior. Instincts are essential, and memory matters, because patterns persist. While the specific environment of a distant intelligence may differ significantly from our own, it is likely that it too prevailed by developing a refined sense of pattern described with precision through some version of mathematics.

Yet when it comes to our artistic yearnings, there's a chance that the extraterrestrials will be thoroughly perplexed. Why would any species spend time and energy on creative works that seemingly have no survival value? In a precarious world with limited resources, the puzzle is thus to understand why we are drawn to activities that relate so obliquely to the goals of securing food, or a mate, or shelter.

Charles Darwin himself took up this question, and wondered

if the goals might not be as oblique as they seem. Perhaps, he suggested, the art impulse originated as a type of mating call, drawing various of our forebears together and thus steering the propagation of the species. Other researchers have suggested that the creation and consumption of artistic works may provide an intellectual playground, where ingenuity and imaginative problem-solving skills are brought forth and refined in a safe environment. According to this view, the sorts of minds that can summon forth everything from *The Starry Night* to *Guernica*, from the *David* to *The Burghers of Calais*, from the *Goldberg Variations* to the *Ode to Joy* finale, are minds that have creatively imagined their way out of one potentially devastating challenge after another. Perhaps, then, art matters because it primed our very capacity to survive.

Among those who think carefully about the relationship between art and evolutionary selection, there is as much controversy as there is consensus. Establishing an irrefutable Darwinian basis for art is no small challenge. Moreover, in considering why art matters today, not just in our ancestral past, the adaptive role may give us insight but at best would provide only a partial accounting. To fill in that account, we must focus on the many nuances of truth.

Mathematics and science seek objective truth. Physicists approach it through their analyses of fundamental particles and the mathematical laws that govern them. Chemists illuminate it by invoking collections of these particles, organized into atoms and molecules. Biologists consider higher levels of organization, amalgamating atoms and molecules into the fantastic complexity evident to us within cells and life-forms. Psychologists, neuroscientists, and philosophers add further layers still, examining the workings of the mind and the questions minds can pose about themselves and their experiences. No single story tells it all. Only by blending insights from each of these accounts can we gain the fullest understanding.

Art is a critical component of this project, a pathway toward a yet broader variety of truths that encompasses subjective experience and celebrates our distinctly human response to the world. This is vital. There are truths that stand beyond articulation, whether in the language of mathematics or that of human discourse. There are truths we can sense, truths we can feel, that would be diminished by translation from inner expression. Art is our most refined means for accessing such truths. There is no universal summary of art, no definition that unambiguously delineates it. Our reactions to art are uniquely our own. But it is this very flexibility, this dependence on the individual, this reliance on the subjective, that makes art essential for grasping our all-too-human place in the cosmic order.

Whereas the patterns of math and science matter because they speak to qualities of reality that exist beyond us, the patterns of art matter because they speak to qualities of reality that exist within us.

MAY 20, 2020

What We Believe About Storytelling

In the rarefied world of art and luxury design, our stories help us negotiate a complex dynamic between personal beliefs and public expectations.

Ini Archibong

A T SOME POINT MOST PEOPLE WANT TO KNOW MORE ABOUT THE objects I design. Whether it's a watch, a vibrant crystal chandelier, or a monolithic calendar made of black granite, it's as though my work points to something important that I have chosen to leave unspoken, yet is fully present.

It's true that my work is vested with very personal content; sometimes with feelings that reach to my core so deeply that I have never found a way to express them except through the things I create.

Within that core reside unchallenged fears and difficult questions that I'm still waiting for the universe to answer. And there are also beliefs, beliefs that have been growing and evolving my entire life, yet remain tethered to beliefs passed down to me by my forebears. The best way to summarize my beliefs about human existence is as follows: We are all born heroes.

But as the academic and mythologist Joseph Campbell taught us, the universe's biggest truths and secrets are too random and nebulous to communicate and understand empirically, so mankind has applied one of its greatest gifts to the task: storytelling, often in the form of folktales and legends.

Within the luxury goods industry, story is everything. You would be hard-pressed to find a successful luxury object or brand that has no story surrounding its concept or its origins. If we're being honest, the story is actually more important than the object's usefulness or value, let alone the superiority of its function.

The transition from everyday object to luxury item doesn't occur until you speak to people's hearts and souls. Effective storytelling helps buyers identify the signifiers that convey a brand's virtues and values, which they feel resonate with their own beliefs. And in grasping those signifiers they share in a tribal identity.

As a design student, I struggled with the need to express myself in terms of who I am, as opposed to designing for a specific audience or group of consumers. At my core is a belief in the ultimate potential of all humans to play a significant role in the sustenance of the universal system. To share a unified vision of reality, yet respect our inner, more spiritual selves and recognize that we are all infinitely powerful in our own particular way, destined for greatness.

How does one design an object that speaks to a world of diverse and divergent souls, while still maintaining the identity of both oneself and the brand one is associated with?

I don't pretend to have the answer to that question, but I have gotten far enough to know that empathy is part of the equation. Do our stories leave us enough room for sympathy and compassion?

Consider a red rose, and all it can suggest and symbolize. Its color is a mere consequence of the wavelength of light it reflects back at us; all others in the spectrum are absorbed by the flower as it offers up its redness to the universe. What if our beliefs were to operate in a similar fashion? What if our identities became most poignant when we allowed ourselves to empathize with and internalize the stories and beliefs of others without losing sight of the vibrancy of our own?

In terms of my own narrative, I was born and raised in Pasadena, California, the son of Nigerian immigrants. By the time I was about twenty years old I had reached a breaking point. As a rambunctious, inquisitive, strong-willed, impulsive, and hyperactive black boy, I was burdened with all the requisite labels: Troublemaker. Criminal.

Class clown. Underachiever. And, of course: Threat. Alongside these there was the burdensome weight of my own promise; what I knew was my enormous potential.

One day I realized that, despite my extreme efforts, there was simply no light at the end of this particular tunnel. In fact, there was no tunnel. I would never be all the things that others believed me to be.

This simple realization allowed me to accept and appreciate the things I had rejected. It allowed me to have a fuller understanding of who I was; to tell myself my own story, again and again, in whatever voice I chose. I realized that in a sense, everything that I am not makes me everything I am. From that moment on, all of my sufferings were reduced to chapters in the origin story of the hero I knew I was destined to become.

My vulnerabilities became superpowers, blessings bestowed upon me for the benefit of others. I dedicated myself to a life of service, as a hero here to serve the world in my own particular way.

Two years ago, I started to create immersive environments such as the Pavilion of the African Diaspora for the 2021 London Design Biennale at Somerset House. I saw the project, a platform for reflection on the past, present, and future of the historical dispersion of Africans, as an opportunity to continue my storytelling in a potentially more powerful way: by asking questions.

What if all of us, all the children of the diaspora, remained connected today by a forgotten yet timeless mythology? Could such a story guide us on our journey to liberation and harmony?

Approaching things in this manner has a twofold effect: sparking my imagination first and foremost, but also freeing my audience from the kind of fear that could prevent them from hearing my message in the first place.

My design for the pavilion consists of a trio of twisting sculptural structures I call the Shell, the Wave Gate, and the Sail. I envision the Shell reverberating with the many voices of the unified African diaspora, which will gain form in the Wave Gate and send sonic reverberations forth into the world by filling the Sail, carrying us all to a brighter future.

In a world that has been in a near-constant state of social, political, racial, and ideological strife, could it be possible that the majority of our problems stem from our fear of accepting the validity of differing beliefs and empathizing? Storytelling allows me to see that everything I am not is actually essential to discovering who I truly am: a single, irreplaceable piece seeking to find my place in an intricate and complex puzzle.

JUNE I, 2021

A Cog in the Machine of Creation

The many roles involved in producing a film rule
out the notion of a single, indispensable artist.

Wes Studi

A
S AN ARTIST, I AM A CREATOR, THOUGH REFERRING TO
myself that way makes me somewhat uncomfortable. For most of my
life, the word "creator" has meant the Creator of all things, especially
in the native tradition, and I would not by any means compare my
meager efforts at creation to Creation.

But art is truly an act of creation. And creation is an act of art.

When we create art, it's a product of three components: the mind,
the heart, and our past experiences. As an actor, sculptor, and author,
I have found that this interconnectedness is a large part of why
art matters.

The mind, of course, is where initial ideas are conceived, whether
through whimsy, inspiration, or suggestion. What matters at the
inception of creation is deciding whether an idea is worth pursuing.
The heart then reveals to us how we feel about the idea, and we again
ponder the worthiness of the pursuit. Past experiences help us weigh
the personal significance of the creation we are considering. As artists, we ask ourselves: Will it serve a purpose beyond our own need to
create? Does it need to?

As an actor, I have at times wondered whether acting is a true art
form. Is an actor merely an interpreter of an idea created in a screen-

play, script, or play? Is performance in this context merely a craft, or is it an act of creation itself?

In this context, the answer might seem simple: The writer is the artist, the creator. The actor is the journeyman who interprets the plan, the story to be told.

But the actor must also rely on many other people to do his work: makeup artists, hairstylists, costume designers, directors. Photography and set design are also prime considerations. The many roles involved in producing a film rule out the notion of a sole creator or artist. The actor becomes a cog in a larger machine of creation. And each cog is an absolute necessity.

As for the question of whether an actor is a creator or an interpreter, I lean toward considering myself an indispensable craftsman tasked with a particular act of creation: a performance worthy of the story being told.

While the original idea may have been created by another, it falls to the performer to fit the situation.

Filmmaking is an especially collaborative function, and acting encompasses a bit of craftsmanship. *Dances with Wolves*, for instance, the 1990 film in which I played a Pawnee warrior, required the coordination of thousands of bison for a hunting scene, and battle scenes featured dozens of riders on horseback, along with actors doing their part to bring to life a unique story. I had to learn some of the Pawnee language to better portray my character. In fact, in my career I have spoken some twenty languages for various roles, including one that did not exist: I was asked to work with linguists crafting the language of the Na'vi, the Indigenous culture in *Avatar*, because I spoke Cherokee and had studied phonetic languages, a valuable part of my past that I brought to that film.

As a Native American actor, I've remained keenly aware that the wars and invasions that ravaged native populations throughout the Americas have never really ended. That knowledge, along with my own past experience, enabled me to empathetically portray characters like the Apache warrior Geronimo on-screen, and to better convey the deep sense of injustice that the real Geronimo faced.

While as an actor I'm either an arty craftsman or a crafty artist, adding and building on another's idea, as a sculptor carving stone I find things a bit different. I remove rather than build, shaping and carving, transforming a stone from its original organic form into something familiar and pleasing to the eye. These carvings satisfy my need both to create and control the process as much as the stone allows; an added factor is the journey of creating something unique. That these pieces of art are appreciated is, of course, additionally gratifying.

I can say the same for book writing: *The Adventures of Billy Bean*, a children's book I wrote in Cherokee and English many years ago, was also an act of creating characters in my mind and heart, and rooted in past experiences. I hope that the stories in the book provided entertainment and an uplifting message about life for young people becoming acquainted with the world around them.

If sculpting makes me a sculptor, then so be it. If writing makes me an author, then so be it. With minds, hearts, and pasts, we all commit acts of creation.

MAY 31, 2020

Naming the Disappeared, Raising the Dead

Art can give witness to those whom governments
have tried to erase from history.

Doris Salcedo

I AM A POLITICAL ARTIST WHO WORKS IN THE MIDST OF CRISIS. I have produced most of my work in Colombia, a country trying to end a fifty-year war. In 2016, the government and the FARC guerrillas signed a peace accord. But we have yet to put an end to the brutal armed conflict, which has claimed more than nine million victims through death, disappearances, sexual violence, and forceful displacement. Colombia continues to be one of many epicenters of catastrophe today—one of many places where tragedy seems to be a single continuous event.

I believe it is precisely in times of crisis that art achieves its most profound meaning.

Zealously and stubbornly, I have remained in Bogotá for more than thirty years, driven by the obsessive need to render visible the experience of the most vulnerable and anonymous victims of political violence, not only in Colombia but around the world. Victims who, through senseless acts, have been expelled from the story of humanity.

This is the single issue I have chosen to address in my work. It is not simply because I am Colombian—although that, in a way, gives me a deeper understanding of the effects of political violence. It is also because I strongly believe that violence defines the ethos of our society.

Since the final days of the nineteenth century, updates to the tools people use to kill and the appearance of concentration camps in various forms have made death more efficient, while also reducing it to an insignificance trivialized and inscribed into our everyday life. Death has become what the philosopher Martin Heidegger called the "manufacture of corpses."

That is why the testimonies of victims are not only at the center of my work, but are actually a requirement for the very existence of each and every one of my pieces.

The silencing of victims of political violence—the reduction of those who have suffered to lamentation and weeping—demonstrates its worst consequence: its paralyzing power. Political violence can destroy our capacity to represent and narrate what has happened to us. Art matters because it articulates and materializes painful experiences into images that are capable of breaking that hold.

In my sculptures I address the experiences of those who dwell on the borders, on the periphery of life, and in the depths of catastrophe. I have devoted my work to those who, as the philosopher Emmanuel Levinas wrote, have nothing but the vulnerability of their own skin. Or, as the poet Paul Celan said, those who are "unsheltered even by the traditional tent of the heavens."

Naming is art's immemorial task. In naming, art addresses aspects of reality that the establishment has chosen to ignore. It names in order to bring to light what those in power believe should remain invisible, unnamed, and faceless.

Art matters because its ability to name exceeds the type of administrative thinking that is so often applied to marginalized communities, who are perceived as worthless unless they produce economic gain. In the face of this, art reinvents itself anew and expands society's viciously narrow definition of who qualifies as human. Celan believed that in every work of art, "even in the least ambitious one, there is this ineluctable question, this exorbitant claim" demanding that we reconsider who belongs to mankind. Art, he says, tries to wake us up by bringing into our own lives the existence of the stranger.

In doing so, art requires a radical break with indifference. It demands that we immerse ourselves in specific traumatic events that have a distinct political immediacy.

In Colombia we are currently witnessing the daily, unstoppable killings of hundreds of social and community leaders and human rights advocates. Each murder imposes on our society a devastating feeling of impotence and sadness.

My response to those crimes was *Quebrantos*, a monumental, ephemeral act of mourning realized last year in collaboration with Colombia's Truth Commission. It was meant to be both a forceful gesture and a tool that could be used by the community to communicate the painful experiences it has been forced to endure.

I invited 103 community leaders who have received death threats and, in some cases, have survived attacks, to come to Bogotá to write in broken glass the names of 165 of their slain fellow activists.

Helped by hundreds of volunteers, those who came slowly but continuously shattered twenty-one tons of glass. We worked for twelve hours, sometimes in the rain, until we had completely covered Bogotá's main square.

The act of breaking what should be whole is a painful one, but when it is done in a compulsive manner, it becomes excruciating. The act of breaking glass while naming victims reminds us that glass, like life, is fragile, and once it is broken, it can never be mended.

Taken in that context, art allows us to recall our recent history not as a means to preserve intact the memory of violent events, but rather to reenact the past through images capable of renewing what otherwise would lie forgotten.

The making of political art is like a solitary liturgy in which the unbearable, the unknowable, and the painful are accepted and forged into images that bear witness to life. In the images art offers us there is not only the memory of oppressed existence, but also the light of an immemorial ethos. That is why art matters.

MAY 25, 2020

I'm Not "Mrs. America." That's the Point.

Art allows us to investigate, illuminate, and hopefully
understand the apparent gap between us.

———————————

Cate Blanchett

I WAS HOMESCHOOLING MY FIVE-YEAR-OLD DAUGHTER ALMOST
two weeks into our Covid-19-induced lockdown when our pug, Doug,
suddenly began chasing his tail. "He's bonkers," I said.

"What does 'bonkers' mean?" my daughter asked without looking
up from her coloring. "Mad," I said. "Mad," she repeated to the half-
finished mermaid in front of her.

Then she asked: "What does 'mad' mean?" " 'Mad' means you
don't make sense to anyone but yourself," I replied. I had hurried
past the word's countless implications in the grown-up world, but
she seemed to understand how it applied to our pug, locked in his
own paranoid tail-chasing.

In coming to that simple, but very complicated, understanding
with my daughter, I realized just how important a shared sense of
meaning is in our brave new world of social distancing and self-iso-
lation. Communication and comprehension are as critical to the delicate social fabric that holds us together as facts and research are to
scientific investigation and advancement. And art, in turn, is a social
investigation, with the results contributing to the advancement of
society. It is one of the key ways we work out, as a group, what makes
sense to us and how best to communicate that awareness.

That act of building a shared understanding is what attracts me to a particular role or story, or the work of one director over another. Work with themes and stories beyond my ken is vital to my developing any deeper understanding, appreciation, or acceptance of the interwoven global culture that all art comes from.

Recently, for example, I played the conservative icon and staunch anti-feminist Phyllis Schlafly in the FX series *Mrs. America*. On first encounter, Schlafly and I are, let's say, two guests you wouldn't invite to the same dinner party. But that was precisely why I was attracted to the role. I was drawn to investigate, illuminate, make sense of, and hopefully understand the apparent gap between us.

Simply put, there seems to exist a deep divide between Schlafly and me, between "staying at home" and "making your way in the world." Between, from one perspective, obedience and adventure. Or, seen differently, between the demands of faith and the indulgence of the self.

But that divide is an illusion. A rhetorical tool. A simplified antagonism that shattered a generation. What I found in the show is that its women—Schlafly, Gloria Steinem, Betty Friedan—although sometimes on opposing sides, are bound together in a complex battle charged with conflicting emotions and desires. Those emotions drive them in similar ways, and subsequently tear them all to pieces. At first, the challenges they have embraced are oversimplified by others. The charged feelings born of that oversimplification are then exaggerated and politicized along partisan lines, separating the women initially from each other, and eventually from their husbands, sons, lovers, and friends. When expediently embraced and cynically championed, such exaggerated divisions can quickly fracture society, splinter communities, and ultimately disintegrate relationships.

The world today is similarly split, but we have more opportunities to create a unified social understanding rather than segregating ourselves based on misinterpretations and political disagreements. Informed by science and attention to the facts, the coronavirus emergency has forced us to make sacrifices as a group, for the common good. Inside those sacrifices are real pain, real loss, and real loneliness. When we venture into a social or public space, we have to imagine new ways of being together that incorporate the silence and the stillness that has been imposed on us.

The virus is here to stay; we will have to learn to live with a mutating, evolving, shifting threat. We are being asked to live with doubt, uncertainty, and the unknown. But when life begins to return to normal, certain spaces will help us overcome that fear. They are art galleries, theaters, cinemas, places of worship—those hybrid public/private spaces housing millions of potential connections among strangers, millions of ways to communicate.

Seemingly vast divides—whether political or viral—can leave us frightened and paranoid, more likely to draw back than to try to bridge them. But art, in its ability to cross social, partisan, and even temporal gaps, can help foster a shared sense of understanding. It can bring us together physically and emotionally. And it can teach us about one another, inspiring empathy rather than anger. Art matters because it lets us engage with our complex social fabric, allowing us to cross divides and work toward a safer and more meaningful existence together.

MAY 21, 2020

What We Believe About Culture

Art helps reverse stereotypes and creates a path for better
representation in a complex and dynamic world.

_____

Shahzia Sikander

BEING ASIAN AMERICAN—OR ASIAN ANYTHING—IN THE
West often means living the paradox of being invisible while standing out. It's a broad racial category in which many different nations,
ethnicities, classes, cultures, histories, communities, and languages
have to vie to be recognized. The construct of a single person's identity may vary based on personal experience, but it is always tied to
society's deep racial hierarchies, which are based on unfounded
beliefs and irrational fears perpetuated by stereotypes.

Confoundingly, the opposite experience—living in the majority
while still being erased—is just as commonplace elsewhere in the
world. Growing up in the 1980s in Lahore, Pakistan, I saw the legacy of a singular, colonial interloper as it whitewashed the nuances
and history of local and national identities. I attended an English-
medium school, which at the time was seen as culturally advantageous. No one questioned the dated English curriculum, a residue
of the British colonial era, or why examination papers were sent to
Cambridge to be graded. Textbooks did not reflect local realities or
languages. To this day, I need help reading Urdu poetry, and I never
became fluent in Punjabi.

When I went to the National College of Arts in Lahore, traditional miniature painting was stigmatized as kitsch and derivative. "Miniature," a colonial term, encompassed premodern Central and South Asian manuscript painting. There were barely any students studying it, although interestingly, the subject was initially taught as part of an English colonial project meant to revive Indian crafts. The school's first principal was the British colonial official and artist John Lockwood Kipling, the father of the author Rudyard Kipling.

My interest in premodern manuscripts was sparked in response to that largely dismissive attitude, as well as by a collective lack of deep cultural knowledge in both Pakistan and the United States. Because artifacts and historical paintings from South Asia existed mostly in collections in the West, my peers and I had no real connections to our own region's historical art traditions.

Our understanding of art history has long been Eurocentric, so we come into the world primed to belittle or dismiss anything outside the Western canon. Beliefs in binaries such as East-West, Islamic-Western, Asian-white, or oppressive-free are deeply entrenched in how we view the world. When we inherit those one-sided, polarizing constructions from the past, we unconsciously keep marching down the same paths.

History itself is effectively just an account of the movement of objects and bodies. Trade, slavery, migration, colonial occupation—these are underlying currents, the root axes of modernity. How history is told, and who gets to tell it, exposes the hierarchies of power in our world.

During the European colonial era in the Indian subcontinent, for example, many South Asian manuscripts were dismembered, scattered, and sold for profit, stunting the canon of Central and South Asian pictorial traditions for good. The most significant manuscripts can be found in the collections of Western museums like the Metropolitan Museum of Art, the British Museum, and the Royal Library. And it's no secret that one of the most significant manuscripts, the *Shahnama* of Shah Tahmasp from 1524—the region's equivalent to the *Mona Lisa*—was cut up and sold piecemeal in secondary auctions.

The Tehran Museum of Contemporary Art traded a de Kooning for some of its pages.

As I studied and taught miniature painting in Lahore, I became attuned to the art form's complicated provenance and how it could be made to yield to new narratives. Transforming its status from a traditional and nostalgic form into a contemporary idiom became my personal goal. I carried that burden to MFA programs in the United States in the early 1990s, when most people weren't familiar with the style. Because my work engaged with traditions that did not sit at the center of Western art history, it would often be glossed over and interpreted very narrowly in terms of my biography. One of the first questions I was asked in graduate school was, "Are you here to make East meet West?"

Thus began a decades-long experience of daily indignities. I, like many other Asians, am routinely spoken to in loud, slow English. People ask me where I'm really from, or if I'm the new nanny or a practicing Muslim. I am subjected to hours of interrogation by Homeland Security officers almost every time I travel to or from the United States.

To counter that, I use my work to deconstruct exclusionary racial representations and stereotypes, rejecting the colonial and male gazes and reimagining archetypal characters to tell richer stories. When I create contemporary miniatures in which women resist simplistic categorizations, I am responding to the difficulty of finding feminist representations of brown South Asians in contemporary culture.

My art also reflects the back-and-forth of being both invisible and hyper-visible in the United States by illuminating the mercurial nature of identity—it's only partially in our control; the rest comes from other people's perceptions of us. For some projects, I've tapped into my own experience of being in America and how I've been mistaken for Mexican, Hawaiian, Bengali, Nepalese, Native American, Chinese, Guatemalan, Puerto Rican, or Malaysian, depending on what I wore and where I was in the country. I try to uncover what social forces entitle people to speculate about my origins, and how these forces (mis)inform their guesses.

The female avatars in my art have thoughts, emotions, feelings, and iconographies born out of the intellectual and virtuosic manuscript traditions of Central, South, and East Asia. They come from vast, heterogenous, syncretic, layered visual histories with many different roots: Jain, Buddhist, Zoroastrian, Jewish, Christian, Hindu, Islamic, Sikh. Women in my paintings are multidimensional—at times androgynous, and always complex, proactive, confident, intelligent, and, in their playful stances, connected to the past in imaginative ways without being tied to a heteronormative lineage or conventional representations of diaspora and nation.

By decolonizing and reimagining miniature paintings through feminist critique, I recontextualize those stories. It's a reminder that cultures are dynamic, not static, and histories are multidimensional.

Language changes, and today, scholars and artists of manuscripts have begun to move away from the term "miniature" as they decolonize their fields. Finally, I am not alone. There are many contemporary artists engaging the premodern manuscript art form in different ways. Our voices tell stories from many perspectives, helping to give a more complete view of both history and the present.

What we believe shifts and evolves based on how we approximate, reproduce, and reenact certain aspects of our own culture and history. If we use art, media, and culture to reverse stereotypes about gender, race, immigrants, and the unfamiliar, the beliefs we pass on to future generations will reflect the complex and dynamic world we live in.

MAY 25, 2021

Art Never Dies

It outlives the contentious political veneer
that we cast over everything.

———

Sonny Rollins

W HEN PEOPLE TALK ABOUT ART, THEY TEND TOWARD A SPE-
cific type of question. Who was the first to play a tune? Who owns
a specific style? Who can judge when borrowing crosses the line?
Those are questions for a political, technological world. In my mind,
debates about black versus white—whether a guy can make a hundred
dollars a year or a million a year from his art—are just dead ends. And
technology, as Aldous Huxley said, is just a faster way of doing ignorant things.

Technology is no savior. We can eat, sleep, look at screens, make
money—all aspects of our physical existence—but that doesn't mean
anything. Art is the exact opposite. It's infinite, and without it, the
world wouldn't exist as it does. It represents the immaterial soul:
intuition, that which we feel in our hearts. Art matters today more
than ever because it outlives the contentious political veneer that is
cast over everything.

In art, we can find a humbling sort of wisdom. We see themes and
ideas repeat over many lifetimes. Those ideas don't belong to any one
person, and as they evolve, disappear, and reappear, they remind us
that regardless of what's happening now, our lives on this earth will
always be part of something bigger. Any astronomer can tell you that

what we know about the universe makes up a fraction of what there is to be discovered. Art, in the same way, both inspires us to go out and find something new and highlights what we don't know.

Music is slightly removed from this, but it's similar. There's an axiom that says there is no such thing as "original" music. After what we could consider to be the first sound, from a spiritual perspective— "om" to some, "amen" to others—it's all the same. Musicians borrow different parts and make them their own, but there's nothing really new, nothing that hasn't been done before. Claude Debussy and Johann Sebastian Bach may sound different, but what they did was all there already, in a sense.

When I was young, growing up in Harlem, I heard Fats Waller perform. His playing struck me, and I realized that jazz would be my path in this life. Jazz being the great interpretive music that it is, of course, I didn't have to sound like Waller. But regardless of who I sounded like, the difference between us would never be more than surface-level, because behind one guy's personal style is something else.

In jazz, we don't consciously borrow in the same way that other artists might. The beauty of improvisation is that it lets you do anything. I don't know what I'm going to play—that's where intuition, and art, comes in.

If I want to improvise during "Mary Had a Little Lamb," for example, first I memorize it. That's because when I'm performing onstage, I want to let my mind be completely free. "Mary Had a Little Lamb" is there, and I can come back to it if I want, but what I'm creating is greater than the sum of the parts—technical ability, notes, themes— I've collected along the way. The song is in the back of my brain where many other things are stored, and in that way, it becomes just another item that I can call upon when I'm playing. The spirit of art shines through in a performance when I stop thinking—when I let the music play itself, not just the one song that I've memorized, but all of the songs and experiences I have in my mind. And as things come to me, unplanned, I surprise even myself.

I believe in reincarnation, which means that a person playing music has got a lot of things in his mind that he's heard already. He puts them together and that comes out in his style. So you might recognize Louis Armstrong's style, but it's still derivative of every kind of music that exists. Any experiences that he's had, or things that he's played, he takes and folds into himself, and they become something new. Charlie Parker, Dizzy Gillespie, John Coltrane—their styles are ultimately made up of many lives, spanning back to that first sound. And that material is there for all musicians and artists to access. It's an accumulation of wisdom, the context art gives us that puts life into perspective.

When I go to the museum and I look at a piece of art, I'm transported. I don't know how, or where, but I know that it's not a part of the material world. It's beyond modern culture's political, technological soul. We're not here to live forever. Humans and materialism die. But there's no dying in art.

As told to Ian Carlino.

MAY 18, 2020

XI

IS THIS THE END OF THE WORLD
AS WE KNOW IT?

How to Be a Prophet of Doom

We could use a new graphic reminder of what
nuclear war would mean for humanity.

Alison McQueen

———————

I N SEPTEMBER 1961, HANS J. MORGENTHAU DECIDED TO TER-
rify the world. Morgenthau, a German Jewish émigré professor at the
University of Chicago, had already written *Politics Among Nations*, a
work that would help define the study of international relations for a
generation. Now he had become convinced that the threat of a nuclear
apocalypse was real and that people needed to be afraid. Very afraid.

His response was "Death in the Nuclear Age," an essay in *Commentary* magazine that detailed in stark terms the cost a nuclear war
would exact on humanity. It was both a warning and an attempt to
spread existential fear.

One might think that Americans in the 1960s were already afraid.
This was, after all, the era of the doomsday clock, duck-and-cover
drills, and home fallout shelters.

But we tend to forget how strong the culture of nuclear denial was
at the time. In 1956, two years after the United States' largest thermonuclear detonation, at Bikini Atoll in the Marshall Islands, President
Dwight Eisenhower's National Security Council ordered a classified
study of the effects of the threat of nuclear annihilation on American
attitudes. The report concluded with an extraordinary statement of
optimism. An all-out nuclear war might provide an opportunity "to

make the very best of the very worst" and to "raise hope for a new dynamics of the human race. It is a vision, indeed, but where visions flourish nations endure."

In a series of works published in the early 1960s, Herman Kahn, a RAND strategist, was arguing that the United States could survive an all-out nuclear war and even resume something like a normal life. Magazines like *Life* and *Time* were running features on civil defense that showed happy families emerging from their fallout shelters ready to build the world anew. Within a few days of a nuclear attack, a *Time* article predicted, people might begin to emerge: "With trousers tucked into sock tops and sleeves tied around wrists, with hats, mufflers, gloves and boots, the shelter dweller could venture forth to start ensuring his today and building for his tomorrow."

No wonder Morgenthau thought Americans were in need of a healthy dose of nuclear terror. Like Kahn, he had become convinced that we must be willing to "think about the unthinkable." But the optimism of Kahn and others seemed to make the unthinkable even more likely. Hopeful visions that we could survive or even prosper after a nuclear war gave cover to wage one. Morgenthau needed to find a way to make the unthinkable less likely.

Have we lost the ability to think about the unthinkable?

President Trump's decision on Tuesday to pull the United States from the Iran nuclear agreement—not to mention the careless and unpredictable war of words he has waged with Kim Jong-un of North Korea over the past year—and the anxiety it has caused in countries across the globe suggest that we should listen again to the alarm that Morgenthau sounded.

"Death in the Nuclear Age" begins by invoking that most basic human fear—of death. It is "the great scandal in the experience of man." It negates everything that "man experiences as specifically human in his existence: the consciousness of himself and of his world, the remembrance of things past and the anticipation of things to come, a creativeness in thought and action which aspires to, and approximates, the eternal."

Human societies, Morgenthau wrote, have tried to transcend death. For much of history, we denied the reality of death through faith in the immortality of the body or the soul. In a secular age, this strategy is no longer available.

This leaves us with two options, both of which nuclear annihilation renders absurd. First, we can master death by choosing to end our lives through suicide or sacrifice. The latter gives us the best chance of being remembered by posterity. The hero who sacrifices himself for a cause gives his death and his life a larger meaning. However, this meaning depends on there being a culture or civilization that will live on to interpret and remember this courageous act.

Without this expectation, he could not make sense of his sacrifice. Thermonuclear war destroys the possibility of heroism.

Like other Jewish émigrés writing in the postwar era, Morgenthau found in the Holocaust the closest parallel to the prospect of nuclear annihilation.

"There is meaning," he wrote, "in Leonidas falling at Thermopylae, in Socrates drinking the cup of hemlock, in Jesus nailed to the cross. There can be no meaning in the slaughter of the innocent, the murder of six million Jews, the prospective nuclear destruction of, say, 50 million Americans and an equal number of Russians."

With all reduced to ashes, human remains will be unsalvageable, eliminating our most meaningful practices of mourning and commemoration. There will be no posterity.

The second way that secular individuals transcend death is by leaving behind evidence of their existence. We live on through our children. Our monuments pass on "an inheritance of visible things not to be consumed but to be preserved as tangible mementos of past generations." Some of these monuments are ambitious—world orders and lasting empires. But most are the ordinary stuff of life. The trees we plant, the houses we build, whose lives outlast our own.

Perhaps most important, we produce works of the imagination—books, poetry, art—which are lasting testaments to a distinctly human capacity for creativity. When an individual creates, he participates in "an unbroken chain emerging from the past and reaching into the future, which is made of the same stuff his mind is made of and, hence, is capable of participating in, and perpetuating, his mind's creation."

A nuclear catastrophe would destroy this world we have built together. It would evaporate the artifacts, institutions, and communities that bind us together and reach across the generations.

In the essay's most remarkable passage, Morgenthau envisioned the apocalyptic annihilation whose enormity his contemporaries seemed unable to grasp:

> *Nuclear destruction is mass destruction, both of persons and of things. It signifies the simultaneous destruction of tens of millions of people, of whole families, generations, and societies, of all things that they have inherited and created. It signifies total destruction of whole societies by killing their members, destroying their visible achievements, and therefore reducing the survivors to barbarism. Thus nuclear destruction destroys the meaning of death by depriving it of its individuality. It destroys the meaning of immortality by making both society and history impossible. It destroys the meaning of life by throwing life back upon itself.*

It is easy to ridicule or dismiss Morgenthau's warnings now. After all, we avoided an all-out nuclear war. If Morgenthau was a "prophet of doom," his prophecy failed. But this was surely his intention. He was a self-defeating prophet of doom. He foretold a nuclear apocalypse to help us imagine—and so to avoid—what had been unthinkable.

Today, there are about ninety-two hundred stockpiled nuclear warheads in the world. About forty-three hundred of these are controlled by Vladimir Putin's Russia, which has been investing heavily in modernizing its forces and ominously flaunting a new range of destructive weapons. North Korea's Kim Jong-un, contrary to President Trump's triumphalist Twitter announcement, has not promised "denuclearization" in any commonsense understanding of the term.

About four thousand of the world's nuclear warheads are in the hands of a United States president whose nuclear "policy" oscillates between antagonizing and inexplicably praising the ruthless leaders of nuclear states. Trump is now supported by a secretary of state and a national security adviser who hold even more alarming views. And yet most of America seems to be in denial.

What would Morgenthau say to us now? And would we listen?

MAY 11, 2018

Mary Shelley Created *Frankenstein*, and Then a Pandemic

Her novel *The Last Man* predicted the political causes
of and collective solutions for global plague.

Eileen M. Hunt

THE WORLD TEETERS IN COLLECTIVE ANXIETY IN THE MIDST
of a pandemic. A novel and lethal plague spreads its tentacles around
the earth. It ravages human populations and simultaneously undermines their interconnected economic and political systems. An elite
group of political leaders gathers to ask, What should be done in the
face of a worldwide public health crisis?

This story line should sound familiar. But I am not summarizing
the news headlines about Covid-19. I am recalling the plot of a great
work of literature. It is Mary Shelley's futuristic novel about a global
plague, *The Last Man* (1826).

Shelley saw that the disaster of a pandemic would be driven by
politics. This politics would be deeply personal yet international in
scope. The spiraling health crisis would be caused by what people and
their leaders had done and failed to do on the international stage—in
trade, war, and the interpersonal bargains, pacts, and conflicts that
precede them.

As we heed scientists' warnings that we are entering "the age of
pandemics," we can benefit from reading *The Last Man* as the first
major postapocalyptic novel. In her second great work of science

fiction after *Frankenstein* (1818), Shelley—the child of two philoso-phers—gave her readers an existential mindset for collectively deal-ing with the threat of a global man-made disaster.

The Last Man is set in the year 2100. The novel's driving conflict is a highly contagious disease. Like the coronavirus, the novel's plague spreads by a combination of airborne particles and contact with car-riers. In both cases, it has been incubated, exacerbated, and left unchecked by destructive human behavior.

The Last Man has been so influential that you are already famil-iar with its basic plot even if you have not read it yet. It presents the history of the ostensible sole survivor of a global plague. Much like *Frankenstein*, *The Last Man* has repeatedly been remade in the sci-ence fiction and horror genres—from the works of Edgar Allan Poe to countless zombie apocalypse movies inspired by the 1964 film *The Last Man on Earth*. The latter starred none other than the king of hor-ror, Vincent Price. He played the last human left alive on the globe after a virulent contagion turned other people into vampires.

In Shelley's novel, it is a man named Lionel Verney who finds himself in this extreme and precarious position. In her allegorical reworking of biblical narratives of the fall and rebirth of human-kind, Verney is a humble shepherd boy who marries into the royal family at Windsor Castle. He quickly ascends to the top of the lead-ership ranks. He serves as a trusted adviser to lords, ministers, and legislators as the plague breaks out in Constantinople, then creeps toward London.

After Verney leads a failed expedition of plague survivors from the crumbled republic of England to the vacant coast of Italy, he is left alone in Rome to contemplate the future. He climbs to the top of the dome of St. Peter's Basilica and carves the year—2100—in the stone. From that sublime vantage, he surveys the remains of human civilization. He summons the hope that there must be other survi-vors somewhere on the planet. In the final frame, Verney departs on an epic sea journey to discover them. For companions, he brings some signs of his humanity: his mutt, and the works of Homer and

Shakespeare. Although Verney is not certain that he will find fellow humans, he discerns a deeper obligation to himself and the whole planet to act upon that hope.

In other words, Verney realizes that even if he is the last man on earth, he must live as though he is not. He must sustain humanity by acting upon his profound sense of the interconnectedness of his fate with other forms of life—human or not.

Shelley completed *The Last Man* when she was a twenty-eight-year-old widow. She was grieving the loss of her husband, the poet Percy Bysshe Shelley, and three of their children. Her first baby girl was born prematurely and survived less than two weeks, the next daughter died of a fever, and her firstborn son died of malaria. Then her young husband drowned in a sailing accident at the peak of his career. Writing *The Last Man* was her attempt to reconcile herself to the tragedies of life without losing hope in humanity itself.

Shelley located the human roots of her fictional plague in a centuries-long war between Greece and Turkey. Scientists think that the spread of the new coronavirus grew from a toxic mix of economic, political, and environmental factors surrounding the largely unregulated market for wild animal meat in China and beyond. It has since percolated into an irresponsible game of blame among nations, whose leaders spread rumors that the coronavirus is a foreign bioweapon or even deny the seriousness of the public health crisis within their own borders. As with the coronavirus outbreak, travelers in *The Last Man* disperse the deadly disease across continents, infecting their own families and communities.

Much like Shelley's first novel, *Frankenstein*, *The Last Man* proves to be a work of political science fiction. *Frankenstein* shows how a scientist's abandonment of his artificially made creature brings ripple effects of suffering to them and the community. The teenage Shelley may have identified with Victor Frankenstein's so-called monster, for her birth had killed her own mother, Mary Wollstonecraft, via a surgically transmitted infection.

Similarly, *The Last Man* originates in the author's experience of devastating personal loss. After Shelley suffered a mental crisis about whether she could live after the loss of almost everyone she loved, she wrote a cosmopolitan answer to this existential question. The unexpectedly hopeful ending of *The Last Man* suggests that all disasters—however threatening to particular individuals or countries—are ultimately about humanity's responsibility to the world as a whole.

Wise beyond her years, Shelley reminds us through the heroic voice of Verney that we should always act upon hope for retaining what makes us loving, humane, and connected to others, even in the face of total catastrophe.

Reading the story lines about the escalating coronavirus outbreaks around the world, we feel worry—even fear—especially for ourselves and our loved ones. But like Shelley and her avatar Verney, we should summon the strength to look beyond that fear with an attitude of hope and collective problem-solving. Only then might we humanely work together to fight the spread of Covid-19, instead of contributing to yet another international epidemiological disaster.

MARCH 13, 2020

To Philosophize Is to Learn How to Die

Facing death can be a key to our liberation and survival.

Simon Critchley

W E'RE SCARED. WE'RE ON EDGE, UNABLE TO CONCENTRATE. We can't find focus. Our minds flit and float around flealike from one update to the next. We follow the news, because we feel we should. And then we wish we hadn't, because it's terrifying and sad. Daytime naps seem involuntary and fitful. Sleep will often not descend. But when it does, we sometimes wake, in a mortal panic, with hypochondriac symptoms we feel to be real but we know are not; and then we feel selfishly stupid for having them in the first place. We take our temperature. We wait. We take it again. It goes on. Feelings of powerlessness and ennui slide into impotent rage at what is being done and, most of all, what is not being done, or is being done poorly, irresponsibly, dishonestly.

The thought of dying alone with a respiratory sickness is horrifying. The knowledge that this is what is happening to thousands of people right here, right now, is unbearable. Lives are being lost and livelihoods ravaged. Metaphors of war feel worn out and fraudulent. The social structures, habits, and ways of life we took for granted are dissolving. Other people are possible sources of contagion, and so are we. We advance masked and keep our distance.

Each of us is adrift on our own ghost ships. And it is so eerily quiet here in New York City. Comical memes circulate. We feel a moment's mirth, share it with our friends, and then slide back into separateness, teeth slightly clenched. A few weeks into this new situation, the initial fever of communication and the novelty of long phone calls with close or distant friends has subsided into something more somber, more sullen, and altogether more serious. We know we're in it for the long haul. But we don't know what that might mean.

How can we, or how should we, cope?

Philosophers have had a long, tortured love affair with social distancing, beginning with Socrates confined to his cell; René Descartes withdrawn from the horrors of the Thirty Years' War (in which he was a participant) into a room with an oven in the Netherlands to ponder the nature of certainty; others like Boethius, Thomas More, and Antonio Gramsci, all part of this long tradition of isolation and thought.

But what of philosophy itself? It has long been derided for its practical uselessness, its three-thousand-year track record of failing to solve humankind's most profound problems. So how might it help us through this immensely difficult moment? Can philosophy offer some form of illumination, even consolation, in this devastated new reality marked by anxiety, grief, and the terrifying specter of death?

Perhaps this: To philosophize is to learn how to die. This is how Michel de Montaigne, the sixteenth century French essayist—the inventor of the genre of the essay—puts it, quoting Cicero, who is himself thinking of Socrates condemned to death. Montaigne says that he developed the habit of having death not just in his imagination but constantly in his mouth—in the food he ate and the drink he imbibed. For those of you who have taken up cooking and are perhaps drinking a little too much in your isolation, this might sound morbid. But it is not at all. Montaigne completes this thought with the astonishing sentence, "He who has learned how to die has unlearned how to be a slave." This is an amazing idea: Slavery consists in bondage to the fear of death. It is the terror of our annihilation that keeps us enslaved.

Liberty, by contrast, consists in accepting our mortality, that we are bound to die. Freedom is only felt truly in the knowledge that our lives are shaped by death's inevitable and ineluctable approach, day by day, hour by hour. In this view, a life lived well, a philosophical life, is one that welcomes death's approach. Existence is finite. Death is certain. This is hardly news. But a philosophical life has to begin from an impassioned affirmation of our finitude. As T. S. Eliot said of the Jacobean playwright John Webster, we have to see the skull beneath the skin.

Yet we're still scared. We're still on edge. Let's try and think about this in terms of a distinction between fear and anxiety. We've known at least since Aristotle that fear is our reaction to an actual threat in the world. Imagine that I have a peculiar fear of bears. If a huge bear showed up at the door of my apartment, I would feel terror (and quite possibly surprise). And if the bear suddenly retreated into the street, my fear would evaporate.

Anxiety, by contrast, has no particular object, no bear. It is instead a state in which the particular facts of the world recede from view. Everything suddenly feels uncanny and strange. It is a feeling of being in the world as a whole, of everything and nothing in particular. I would argue that what many of us are feeling right now is this profound anxiety.

The peculiar nature of the pandemic is that the virus is, while all too real, invisible to the naked eye and all-pervasive. Covid-19 has formed itself into the structure of reality: a disease everywhere and nowhere, imprecisely known and, as yet, untreatable. And most of us have the feeling of having been swimming in a sea of virus for many weeks now, possibly months. But perhaps beneath the trembling of fear lies a deeper anxiety, the anxiety of our mortality, our being pulled toward death. And this is what we might try to seize hold of, as a condition of our freedom.

It is vitally important, I think, to accept and affirm anxiety and not hide away, flee, or evade it, or seek to explain anxiety in relation to some object or cause. Such anxiety is not just a disorder that needs to be treated, let alone medicated into numbness. It needs to be acknowledged, shaped, and honed into a vehicle of liberation. I'm not saying this is easy. But we can try to transform the basic mood of anxiety from something crippling into something enabling and capable of courage.

Most of us, most of the time, are encouraged by what passes as normality to live in a counterfeit eternity. We imagine that life will go on and death is something that happens to others. Death is reduced to what Heidegger calls a social inconvenience or downright tactlessness. The consolation of philosophy in this instance consists in pulling away from the death-denying habits of normal life and facing the anxiety of the situation with a clear-eyed courage and sober realism. It is a question of passionately enacting that fact as a basis for a shared response, because finitude is relational: It is not just a question of my death, but the deaths of others, those we care about, near and far, friends and strangers.

A few weeks ago I found myself talking blithely about plague literature: Boccaccio's *Decameron*, Defoe's *A Journal of the Plague Year*, Camus's *The Plague*. I thought I was clever until I realized a lot of other people were saying the exact same things. In truth, the thinker I have been most deeply drawn back to is the brilliant seventeenth century French mathematician and theologian Blaise Pascal, in particular his *Pensées*.

Pascal writes of the inability to sit quietly alone in a room as the source of all humanity's problems; of inconstancy, boredom, and anxiety as defining traits of the human condition; of the machinelike power of habit and the gnawing noise of human pride. But most of all, it is Pascal's thought that the human being is a reed, "the weakest of nature," that can be wiped away by a vapor—or an airborne droplet—that grips me.

Human beings are wretched, Pascal reminds us. We are weak, fragile, vulnerable, dependent creatures. But—and this is the vital twist—our wretchedness is our greatness. The universe can crush us, a little virus can destroy us. But the universe knows none of this, and the virus does not care. We, by contrast, know that we are mortal. And our dignity consists in this thought. "Let us strive," Pascal says, "to think well. That is the principle of morality." I see this emphasis on human fragility, weakness, vulnerability, dependence, and wretchedness as the opposite of morbidity and any fatuous pessimism. It is the key to our greatness. Our weakness is our strength.

APRIL II, 2020

Montaigne Fled the Plague, and Found Himself

As disease and war ravaged the nation, he
left town and invented the essay.

Robert Zaretsky

I N THE SUMMER OF 1585, THE MAYOR OF BORDEAUX LEARNED, from the comfort of his nearby chateau, that the bubonic plague had burst upon his city. Those who could were fleeing, he was told, while those who could not were "dying like flies." What to do? His term in office, on the one hand, was nearly over and his last official duty was to attend the transition ceremony. On the other hand, perhaps his duty was with those still inside the city walls.

Both hands on the reins of his horse, the mayor rode to the city's edge and wrote to the municipal council to ask whether his life was worth a transition ceremony. He did not seem to receive a reply and returned to his chateau. By the time the plague subsided, more than fourteen thousand people—about a third of the city's population—had died horrible deaths. As for the former mayor, he returned to a far more pressing task: the writing of essays.

The mayor was Michel de Montaigne. Known today as the author of the *Essays*, the classic of self-reflection and self-knowing, Montaigne was better perhaps known in his own lifetime as a man of politics. Yet his efforts—quite literally, his essais—at politics and his essais at portraying himself are not unrelated. In both cases, Montaigne probed the limits of what he could do in the world and what he could know about himself.

Bordeaux was a hot spot for both bacteriological and theological plagues in the late 1500s. The wars of religion, a series of eight distinct conflicts between Catholics and Protestants—replete with massacres on both sides—had ravaged France between 1562 and 1598. As both mayor and diplomat, Montaigne tried several times to broker accords between the two sides. He was known (and despised) by both sides as a politique: someone who, for the sake of all, tried to find common ground in a land savaged by zealotry.

In this, Montaigne never succeeded, yet he was not one to waste a plague. In his essay "On Physiognomy," written in 1585, he described the wars as "profitable disasters." The mutual butcheries, in effect, prepared him for the next plague. The cruelty and fury, ambition and avarice that consumed both sides taught him "to rely on myself in distress."

The trick, though, was to first find that self. Or, more accurately, to found that self. In effect, as he wrote and rewrote his essays until his death in 1592, Montaigne wrote and rewrote his own self. In "On Giving the Lie," he observed the strange alchemy between paper and person, between writing one's life and becoming that life: "I have no more made my book than my book has made me—a book consubstantial with its author."

More than a millennium earlier, thinkers like Epicurus and Seneca had already mapped out this path. Inscribing their words on the pages of his essays—as well as in the roof beams of his library—Montaigne grasped that, unlike philosophers in his day (or our own), these teachers sought not to inform their students, but instead to form them. As the classical scholar Pierre Hadot has argued, Stoicism and Epicureanism offered not airy abstractions but real-world "spiritual exercises." Though the methods of these schools varied, their mission was the same: to teach students how to master physics and ethics not as an end, but as the means to master their own selves and so better deal with life's daily challenges, no less than its sudden catastrophes.

Yet self-mastery was itself a means to a greater end: the aligning of the self with the world. The recognition of reality—of what can and cannot be changed—teaches the need for self-control. This "plague of the utmost severity" in 1585 challenged Montaigne's self-mastery even more than the wars did. When the pestilence reached his estate, he fled with his family in order to protect them. From the road, he recalled, he saw peasants digging their own graves.

We will never know what these men and women thought when they saw Montaigne and his household pass them on their horses and carriages. But what should we think? For many critics, Montaigne was, if not clearly a coward, less than a hero: Imagine if Mayor Bill De Blasio, learning that New York City had been struck by the coronavirus while he was vacationing in the Berkshires, had emailed the City Council to wish them good luck. Yet we need to remember that Montaigne never pretended or sought to be a hero. Instead, he sought to do what could be done—in this case, save his family—and sought to find what could be found in this experience.

In the end, what he found was the essay—less the masterpiece he had written, though, than the life he had lived. In the many essays of his life he discovered the importance of the moderate life. In his final essay, "On Experience," Montaigne reveals that "greatness of soul is not so much pressing upward and forward as knowing how to circumscribe and set oneself in order." What he finds, quite simply, is the importance of the moderate life. We must then, he writes, "compose our character, not compose books." There is nothing paradoxical about this because his literary essays helped him better essay his life. The lesson he takes from this trial might be relevant for our own trial: "Our great and glorious masterpiece is to live properly."

JUNE 28, 2020

Does the Pandemic Have a Purpose?

Only if we give it one. The coronavirus is neither
good nor bad. It wants only to reproduce.

Stephen T. Asma

NATURE DOESN'T CARE ABOUT YOU. THAT MAY SEEM HARSH,
but strictly speaking, nature doesn't care about anyone or anything,
except passing genes into the next generation. We know this if we've
studied evolution. It was Darwin's great achievement to explain the
adaptation of organisms without appeal to God's design or mystical
idealism. Darwinian evolution is true (corroborated by mountains
of evidence), but it's also a cold metaphysics. The biologist Stephen
Jay Gould described it as a "cold bath view" of nature—not warm and
fuzzy in the way religion characterizes nature.

Reflect for a moment on the Rhizocephala, or "root-headed" bar-
nacle, which lives its life feeding inside crabs and other crustaceans.
It gets inside the crab as a seed and begins to spread throughout
the host in a series of complex root systems, often infiltrating, like
a creeping vine, every limb of the crab. This root system castrates
its host (preventing the crab's continuation of gene line), stops the
crab's molting cycle, and keeps it alive (all the while feeding off it)
for years. Or consider the tarantula hawk, a giant wasp that hunts
tarantulas as a food supply for its larvae. The wasp paralyzes a tarantula with its powerful sting and lays an egg on the spider's paralyzed
body. When the wasp larva hatches out, it feeds slowly on the still-

living tarantula—even carefully avoiding at first the consumption of working vital organs, to guarantee extended freshness. Not even the most inventive Hollywood writers can spin tales this fantastic, yet it is the bread and butter of everyday biology.

Should we thank the *E. coli* in our guts that help us to digest? Should we alternatively fault the virus that is breaking down our immune systems and spreading through the host population? These organisms are not evil or noble, intentionally wreaking havoc on our health—they are simply doing what comes naturally, surviving and reproducing. This is not meant to sound callous or insensitive. It's obvious that our struggle with other organisms matters a great deal to us—causing real despair and tragedy. But from the more general evolutionary perspective, this drama is value-neutral. Strictly speaking, it isn't even a drama because there is no plot in nature.

Many religious people see something benevolent in nature, or at least see purpose dimly grasped in the interworking of biology. But there's something even deeper than religious optimism. There is a broader conception of nature—shared by monotheists, polytheists, Indigenous animists, and now politicians and policymakers. It is the mythopoetic view of nature. It is the universal instinct to find (or project) a plot in nature. A mythopoetic paradigm or perspective sees the world primarily as a dramatic story of competing personal intentions, rather than a system of objective, impersonal laws. It's a prescientific worldview, but it is also alive and well in the contemporary mind.

President Trump, for example, has described the coronavirus as our great enemy in an "all-out war," saying, "The virus will not have a chance against us," and a few weeks later, "We will win this war!" But strictly speaking, wars are fought against malicious agents—people who mean you harm. The coronavirus is like every other virus or pathogen—it does not mean us harm. It wants only to reproduce. After Darwin we see that nature can be horrifying, but not evil (nor good). When Mr. Trump puts a moral frame on the spreading virus, he interprets it in a mythopoetic manner, and we clearly understand him because we too apply the mythopoetic frame easily and naturally.

If we must frame this in terms of politics, the left is just as mytho-poetic as the right. I have heard many liberal commentators lately moralize on the grounds that our encroachment on pristine nature and our environmental sins have brought the zoonotic spillover as nature's retribution. The left, proposing a mythopoetic tragedy of hubris, suggests that we brought this upon ourselves. Pope Francis suggested that pandemics may be nature's retaliation for human abuse of the environment. "I don't know if these are the revenge of nature," he said, "but they are certainly nature's responses."

In reality, zoonotic spillover, parasitism, predation, extinction, are not punishments at all, but business as usual. They have always been here and always will be. Most of the known pathogens that infect humans have zoonotic origins, and human abuse of the environment is not their principal cause. Most spillover and transmission result from our domestication of animals, the adaptation of animals (e.g., rodents) to our urban environments, and the unprecedented human mixing of urbanization.

Disease and death are not bugs in the system, but features. In fact, the cold-bath truth is that natural selection works only because many more organisms are born than can survive to procreate. Natural selection is not malevolent, but it's clearly not benevolent either.

Against the frightening neutrality of nature, we humans marshal the powerful imagination. Imagining that we are in a species-wide war with a biblical-style evil enemy may be factually absurd, but I recommend we embrace this powerful fiction anyway. We evolved to capture and clarify our experience in mythic stories—plots with good guys and bad guys: We draw upon "The Force," we pray for divine intercession, we try to get in harmony with the Dao, enlist the Dharma, forge good karma, make sacrifices to purify ourselves (Ramadan, Lent, Yom Kippur), and generally try to turn nature and destiny to our benefit. How could we do otherwise? The stakes are the survival of our very kin. The more vulnerable we are, the more our mythopoetic imagination comes to the fore. Medicine and science will hopefully find a vaccine, but for those of us who don't have research labs, imagination can aid in the battle.

Imagining that we are at war with an enemy will help us make the difficult personal sacrifices (like social distancing and sheltering in place) that go beyond our own egoistic hedonism. Imagining that the sins of our failed environmentalism have brought nature's vengeance will help us prepare better for the future and course-correct our environmental policies. Personifying nature can be adaptive and beneficial.

Imagining our lives as a dramatic struggle with occasional enemies (microscopic and macroscopic) can help us change hearts and minds, embolden convictions, inspire sacrifice, and thereby change the actual outcome of epidemics and other trials and tribulations. But mythopoetic views of disasters like this one are easily influenced by charismatic leaders (formerly shamans and priests, now presidents and politicians). The "enemy" we war against gets personified into an ethnic group for scapegoating. So let us put our faith in science and give our gratitude to health care workers, but let us also use our imaginations carefully and responsibly, so that the denouement of this story is eventually a human victory, not just a national or political one.

Some might argue that a human victory is not what's needed here, that the neutrality of nature free of concepts of good and evil obviates a winner or loser. That may be true, if we view it from a distance, but in the thick of it, the imperative of our genetic survival remains. It is our unique Darwinian legacy.

As a naturalist, I resist the theological version of human exceptionalism, but as a philosopher, I'm inclined to recognize that nothing has intrinsic value until we humans imagine it so. Since we cannot find our species' value objectively by looking at the neutral laws of nature, then we must just assert it. And simply affirm that the universe is more remarkable with us in it.

APRIL 16, 2020

Our Cruel Treatment of Animals Led to the Coronavirus

The conditions that lead to the emergence of new infectious
diseases are the same ones that inflict horrific harms on animals.

David Benatar

———————

THERE IS THE OBVIOUS AND THEN THERE IS WHAT SHOULD BE
obvious. The obvious is that the coronavirus pandemic has brought
much of the human world to a standstill. Many countries are in lockdown. So far, more than 1.7 million have been infected, more than
100,000 have died, and billions live in fear that the numbers of sick
and dead will rise exponentially. Economies are in recession, with
all the hardship that entails for human well-being.

What should be obvious, but may not be to many, is that none of
this should come as a surprise. That there would be another pandemic was entirely predictable, even though the precise timing of
its emergence and the shape of its trajectory were not. And there is
an important sense in which the pandemic is of our own making as
humans. A pandemic may seem like an entirely natural disaster, but
it is often—perhaps even usually—not.

The coronavirus arose in animals and jumped the species barrier
to humans and then spread with human-to-human transmission.
This is a common phenomenon. Most—and some believe all—infectious diseases are of this type (zoonotic). That in itself does not put
them within the realm of human responsibility. However, many zoonotic diseases arise because of the ways in which humans treat ani-

mals. The "wet" markets of China are a prime example. They are the likely source not only of Covid-19 but also of Severe Acute Respiratory Syndrome (SARS) and some outbreaks of avian influenza, for example. (Another possible source of the coronavirus that causes Covid-19 may be one of the many mixed wildlife-livestock farms in China, but humans are responsible for those too.)

The "wet" markets, which are found not only in China but also in some other East Asian countries, have a number of features that make them especially conducive to spawning infectious zoonotic diseases. Live animals are housed in extremely cramped conditions until they are slaughtered in the market for those who have purchased them. In these conditions, infections are easily transmitted from one animal to another. Because new animals are regularly being brought to market, a disease can be spread through a chain of infection from one animal to others that arrive in the market much later. The proximity to humans, coupled with the flood of blood, excrement, and other bodily fluids and parts, all facilitate the infection of humans. Once transmission from human to human occurs, an epidemic is the expected outcome, unless the problem is quickly contained. Global air travel can convert epidemic to pandemic within weeks or months—exactly as it did with the coronavirus.

It is these very conditions that facilitate the emergence of new infectious diseases and that also inflict horrific harms on animals— being kept in confined conditions and then butchered. Simply put, the coronavirus pandemic is a result of our gross maltreatment of animals.

Those who think that this is a Chinese problem rather than a human one should think again. There is no shortage of zoonoses that have emerged from human maltreatment of animals. The most likely origin of HIV (human immunodeficiency virus), for example, is SIV (simian immunodeficiency virus), and the most likely way in which it crossed the species barrier is through blood of a nonhuman primate butchered for human consumption. Similarly, variant Creutzfeldt-Jakob disease probably had its origins in its bovine analogue—bovine spongiform encephalopathy (BSE), or "mad cow disease." The most probable mechanism of transmission is through human consumption of infected cattle.

In the future, we should fully expect our maltreatment of animals to wreak havoc on our own species. In addition to future pandemics, we face the very real risk of breeding antibiotic resistance. The major contributor to this is the use of antibiotics in the animal agriculture industry, as a growth promoter (to bring animals to slaughter weight as quickly as possible) and to curb the spread of infections among animals reared in cruel intensive "factory farmed" conditions.

It is entirely possible that the human future will involve a return to the pre-antibiotics era, in which people died in droves from infections that have been effectively treated since the discovery of penicillin and other early antibacterial agents. If so, it may turn out that the antibiotics era was a brief interlude between two much longer periods in human history in which we succumbed in large numbers to bacterial infections. That prospect, which is even more awful than the current crisis, is no less real for that. We, as a species, know about this problem, but we have not yet done what needs to be done to avert it (or at least minimize the chances of its happening).

What these and many other examples show is that harming animals can lead to considerable harm to humans. This provides a self-interested reason—in addition to the even stronger moral reasons—for humans to treat animals better. The problem is that even self-interest is an imperfect motivator. For all the puffery in calling ourselves *Homo sapiens*, the "wise human," we display remarkably little wisdom, even of a prudential kind.

This is not to deny the many intellectual achievements of humankind. However, they are combined with many cognitive and moral shortcomings, including undue confidence in our ability to solve problems. In general, humans respond to pandemics rather than act to prevent them—we attempt to prevent their spread after they emerge and to develop treatments for those infected. The current crisis demonstrates the folly of this approach. The closest we come to prevention is the effort to develop vaccines. But even this sort of prevention is a kind of reaction. Vaccines are developed in response to viruses that have already emerged. As the coronavirus experience shows, there can be a significant lag between that emergence and the development of a safe and effective vaccine, during which time great damage can be done both by the virus and by attempts to prevent its spread.

Real prevention requires taking steps to minimize the chances of the virus or other infectious agents emerging in the first place. One of a number of crucial measures would be a more intelligent—and more compassionate—appraisal of our treatment of nonhuman animals, and concomitant action.

Some might say that it is insensitive to highlight human responsibility for the current pandemic while we are in the midst of it. Isn't it unseemly to rub our collective nose in this mess of our own making? Such concerns are misplaced. Earlier warnings of the dangers of our behavior, offered in less panicked times, went unheeded. Of course, it is entirely possible that even if we are now momentarily awakened, we will soon forget the lessons. There is plenty of precedent for that. However, given the importance of what lies in the balance, it is better to risk a little purported insensitivity than to pass up an opportunity to encourage some positive change. Millions of lives and the avoidance of much suffering are at stake.

APRIL 13, 2020

Our "Pursuit of Happiness" Is Killing the Planet

We need to strike a new balance between our
private pleasures and our collective survival.

James Traub

As THE CORONAVIRUS CONTINUES TO SPREAD, THE CHANCES
that any one of us will be placed in quarantine goes up considerably.
I know that being locked away like that would drive me nuts. Two
weeks subtracted from my life! Still, I'd accept the justice of my confinement because I would recognize that my liberty had come to pose
a real danger to my fellow humans.

Now, let's ratchet up the sacrifice: Suppose you were required by
law to turn the thermostat up to seventy-five in the summer, and
down to sixty-six in the winter, in order to reduce your carbon foot-
print. The principle is the same: Your freedom to live as you wish
turns out to jeopardize public well-being. I, for one, would bristle; I
can't stand being hot in summer. Maybe you wouldn't mind. But what
if you were also told that you had to eliminate most or all of the red
meat from your diet? What if Greta Thunberg persuades President
Sanders that we need to ration jet travel? At some point you'll begin
to think that the increasing globalization of bad things like climate
change and infectious diseases is threatening liberal society.

You'd have a point. At the foundation of classical liberalism is
John Stuart Mill's principle that every individual must be free to

speak and act as he wishes "so long as he refrains from molesting others in what concerns them, and merely acts according to his own inclination and judgment in things which concern himself." For instance, drinking to excess, Mill said, deserves reprobation, but not prohibition; it's a self-regarding act. But there's a problem with this formulation: Even in his own time Mill was criticized for drawing a largely artificial distinction between behavior which does and does not impinge on others. The filaments that bind people to one another are incomparably stronger today than they were in Victorian England. What would Mill have said if England had had then, as it does now, a public health system in which everyone shared the cost of treatment for alcoholism? What would he have said about smoking if he knew about the effects of secondhand smoke? Indeed, second-hand smoke is rapidly becoming a metaphor for our time.

I first started fretting over this question a few weeks ago, when I went to a Manhattan high school where I serve as a volunteer writing tutor. I was working with a young woman who had written an essay weighing the evidence that we could reduce global warming by switching to a vegetarian or vegan diet. She had learned that, thanks to the methane and nitrous oxide released by cows and manure, livestock is responsible for as large a fraction of CO_2 emissions as the entire transportation sector (including air travel)—about a seventh. (In fact, the figure for livestock includes, among other things, the emissions caused by transporting meat and dairy products, which properly belongs under transportation.)

In order to take account of human frailty, including her own, the student advocated something called "the two-thirds vegan diet," in which you get to eat meat and dairy one meal per day. I asked which meal she'd indulge her vices in.

"Breakfast."

"Really? What about lunch and dinner?"

"I guess I'd have salads."

"I would never have the strength to do that." I wasn't kidding. I haven't sworn off meat, even after reading the horror stories about the raising of poultry and livestock, and learning that an animal-protein diet is bad for the planet. But maybe I should; maybe, in fact, I will be compelled to.

Am I being too alarmist? Possibly. Sweeping legislative proposals like the Green New Deal place virtually all of the burden on utilities and industry, rather than end-users like us, by imposing a price on carbon so high that these businesses will be forced to switch to renewable energy by 2050. The recently passed Dutch climate change law proposes to reduce emissions by half within a decade through a large increase in offshore wind production, a swift transition to electric cars, and technical upgrades to electricity grids. But it's unlikely the world will be able to get to net-zero without serious changes in personal behavior. The Green New Deal also mandates "sustainable farming," which usually includes reductions in methane emissions from livestock, while the Dutch law takes aim at ham through limits to pork production.

The other obvious objection to my scenario would be, in effect, so what? The First Amendment doesn't protect your right to eat steak; nothing in the Bill of Rights prohibits a quarantine. Whatever discomfort or vexation arises from these restrictions should hardly be classed as a violation of liberty. Yet that's not quite right. Very few of us care so much about our rights of speech or conscience to test their constitutional boundaries. There's a reason people got so angry when Mayor Michael Bloomberg tried to ban the sale of large-size soft drinks; they were defending a right they actually cared about.

Another great nineteenth century liberal, Benjamin Constant, put the matter squarely. As a young man, Constant had watched the French Revolution, and then the Terror, unfold from the safety of Switzerland, and concluded that the most dangerous people are fanatics who tell the rest of us how to live; totalitarians, as we would learn to call them in the twentieth century. In a brilliant, now largely forgotten, lecture delivered in 1819, Constant wrote that the democrats of Greece and Rome, like the revolutionaries of his own day, "admitted as compatible with this collective freedom the complete subjection of the individual to the authority of the community." By contrast, Constant wrote, "the aim of the moderns is the enjoyment of security in private pleasures, and they call liberty the guarantees accorded by institutions to those pleasures."

Constant wasn't thinking of Marie Antoinette's right to play at shepherdess while her subjects starved, but the right to open a shop and build yourself a home rather than be drafted into Napoleon's army spreading republicanism across the face of Europe. We moderns build institutions, and establish tacit norms, to guarantee the security of such private pleasures. That's liberal individualism. But what do we do once we see that some of those choices threaten the health and lives of others? We will have to strike a new equilibrium between what society has the right to demand of us and what we have a right to retain for ourselves.

But we've done that before. To take the most obvious example, President Franklin D. Roosevelt curbed the excesses of the marketplace in order to nurse a devastated economy back to health, thereby incurring the wrath of much of the business community. FDR was a liberal—that was the word he used to describe himself—but he was willing to restrict some liberties in order to advance larger ones. A liberal, as he once put it, was prepared to use government to ensure the ordinary citizen "the right to his own economic and political life, liberty, and the pursuit of happiness."

Liberal societies, in short, have always faced the problem of secondhand smoke, but what once was exceptional has now become endemic. One man's meat is another man's poison, as FDR put it, more prescient than he knew. In the cataclysm of the Depression, the president was able to summon up the sense of collective purpose needed to embark on large-scale change. Our own crisis, of course, still appears to many far too remote for any such call to sacrifice. To make matters worse, we've elected as president a libertine devoted not to fostering a spirit of collective purpose, but to his right to do anything he pleases. Indeed, Donald Trump is illiberal in every respect save for his single-minded commitment to private pleasures.

Can we forge a new equilibrium before Miami is underwater? I would like to think we'll do so as part of a larger process of democratic deliberation. The Green New Deal envisions a ten-year phase of "transparent and inclusive consultation," which sounds just about right. I note, however, that the authors seem more committed to consulting with "vulnerable communities" and "worker cooperatives" (I didn't know we had that many) than with recalcitrant carnivores, or for that matter with energy companies. That does not put one in mind of FDR.

The Dutch can reach consensus on painful social questions because they've spent the last thousand years working cooperatively to build dikes; the climate accord adopted last year came after a full year of discussion among representatives of all interest groups. That's not how American democracy works, and especially so in recent years. We allow those interest groups to wage a pitched battle using all the money and influence they can muster against one another. Legislation emerges only after a war of attrition. That's a very self-defeating way of doing business when all parties must be called on to sacrifice. At some point, presumably, things will get so bad that President Ocasio-Cortez manages to ram a green-enough new deal through Congress. Then we'll adjust our thermostats and go two-thirds vegan the same way we got used to the chaos and tedium of airport security check-ins: We'll have no choice.

Or just maybe we'll rise to the occasion: With the flood upon us, we too will learn how to build dikes together.

MARCH 6, 2020

Would Human Extinction Be a Tragedy?

Our species possesses inherent value, but we are devastating the earth and causing unimaginable animal suffering.

Todd May

HERE ARE STIRRINGS OF DISCUSSION THESE DAYS IN PHILO-sophical circles about the prospect of human extinction. This should not be surprising, given the increasingly threatening predations of climate change. In reflecting on this question, I want to suggest an answer to a single question, one that hardly covers the whole philosophical territory but is an important aspect of it. Would human extinction be a tragedy?

To get a bead on this question, let me distinguish it from a couple of other related questions. I'm not asking whether the experience of humans coming to an end would be a bad thing (though Samuel Scheffler has given us an important reason to think that it would be). I am also not asking whether human beings as a species deserve to die out. That is an important question, but would involve different considerations. Those questions, and others like them, need to be addressed if we are to come to a full moral assessment of the prospect of our demise. Yet what I am asking here is simply whether it would be a tragedy if the planet no longer contained human beings. And the answer I am going to give might seem puzzling at first. I want to suggest, at least tentatively, both that it would be a tragedy and that it might just be a good thing.

To make that claim less puzzling, let me say a word about trag- edy. In theater, the tragic character is often someone who commits a wrong, usually a significant one, but with whom we feel sympathy in their descent. Here Sophocles's Oedipus, Shakespeare's Lear, and Arthur Miller's Willy Loman might stand as examples. In this case, the tragic character is humanity. It is humanity that is committing a wrong, a wrong whose elimination would likely require the elimina- tion of the species, but with whom we might be sympathetic none- theless for reasons I discuss in a moment.

To make that case, let me start with a claim that I think will be at once depressing and, upon reflection, uncontroversial. Human beings are destroying large parts of the inhabitable earth and caus- ing unimaginable suffering to many of the animals that inhabit it. This is happening through at least three means. First, human contribution to climate change is devastating ecosystems, as the recent article on Yellowstone Park in the *Times* exemplifies. Second, increasing human population is encroaching on ecosystems that would otherwise be intact. Third, factory farming fosters the cre- ation of millions upon millions of animals for whom it offers nothing but suffering and misery before slaughtering them in often barbaric ways. There is no reason to think that those practices are going to diminish anytime soon. Quite the opposite.

Humanity, then, is the source of devastation of the lives of con- scious animals on a scale that is difficult to comprehend.

To be sure, nature itself is hardly a Valhalla of peace and har- mony. Animals kill other animals regularly, often in ways that we (although not they) would consider cruel. But there is no other crea- ture in nature whose predatory behavior is remotely as deep or as widespread as the behavior we display toward what the philosopher Christine Korsgaard aptly calls "our fellow creatures" in a sensitive book of the same name.

If this were all to the story there would be no tragedy. The elim- ination of the human species would be a good thing, full stop. But there is more to the story. Human beings bring things to the planet that other animals cannot. For example, we bring an advanced level of reason that can experience wonder at the world in a way that is foreign to most if not all other animals. We create art of various kinds: literature, music, and painting among them. We engage in sciences that seek to understand the universe and our place in it. Were our species to go extinct, all of that would be lost.

Now, there might be those on the more jaded side who would argue that if we went extinct there would be no loss, because there would be no one for whom it would be a loss not to have access to those things. I think this objection misunderstands our relation to these practices. We appreciate and often participate in such practices because we believe they are good to be involved in, because we find them to be worthwhile. It is the goodness of the practices and the experiences that draw us. Therefore, it would be a loss to the world if those practices and experiences ceased to exist.

One could press the objection here by saying that it would only be a loss from a human viewpoint, and that that viewpoint would no longer exist if we went extinct. This is true. But this entire set of reflections is taking place from a human viewpoint. We cannot ask the questions we are asking here without situating them within the human practice of philosophy. Even to ask the question of whether it would be a tragedy if humans were to disappear from the face of the planet requires a normative framework that is restricted to human beings.

Let's turn, then, and take the question from the other side, the side of those who think that human extinction would be both a tragedy and overall a bad thing. Doesn't the existence of those practices outweigh the harm we bring to the environment and the animals within it? Don't they justify the continued existence of our species, even granting the suffering we bring to so many nonhuman lives?

To address that question, let us ask another one. How many human lives would it be worth sacrificing to preserve the existence of Shakespeare's works? If we were required to engage in human sacrifice in order to save his works from eradication, how many humans would be too many? For my own part, I think the answer is one. One human life would be too many (or, to prevent quibbling, one innocent human life), at least to my mind. Whatever the number, though, it is going to be quite low.

Or suppose a terrorist planted a bomb in the Louvre and the first responders had to choose between saving several people in the museum and saving the art. How many of us would seriously consider saving the art?

So, then, how much suffering and death of nonhuman life would we be willing to countenance to save Shakespeare, our sciences, and so forth? Unless we believe there is such a profound moral gap between the status of human and nonhuman animals, whatever reasonable answer we come up with will be well surpassed by the harm and suffering we inflict upon animals. There is just too much torment wreaked upon too many animals and too certain a prospect that this is going to continue and probably increase; it would overwhelm anything we might place on the other side of the ledger. Moreover, those among us who believe that there is such a gap should perhaps become more familiar with the richness of lives of many of our conscious fellow creatures. Our own science is revealing that richness to us, ironically giving us a reason to eliminate it along with our own continued existence.

One might ask here whether, given this view, it would also be a good thing for those of us who are currently here to end our lives in order to prevent further animal suffering. Although I do not have a final answer to this question, we should recognize that the case of future humans is very different from the case of currently existing humans. To demand of currently existing humans that they should end their lives would introduce significant suffering among those who have much to lose by dying. In contrast, preventing future humans from existing does not introduce such suffering, since those human beings will not exist and therefore not have lives to sacrifice. The two situations, then, are not analogous.

It may well be, then, that the extinction of humanity would make the world better off and yet would be a tragedy. I don't want to say this for sure, since the issue is quite complex. But it certainly seems a live possibility, and that by itself disturbs me.

There is one more tragic aspect to all of this. In many dramatic tragedies, the suffering of the protagonist is brought about through his or her own actions. It is Oedipus's killing of his father that starts the train of events that leads to his tragic realization; and it is Lear's high-handedness toward his daughter Cordelia that leads to his demise. It may also turn out that it is through our own actions that we human beings bring about our extinction, or at least something near it, contributing through our practices to our own tragic end.

DECEMBER 17, 2018

XII

DO WE NEED GOD?

Dear God, Are You There?

We are in a deep spiritual crisis that can't be
relieved by politics, or philosophy.

George Yancy

D EAR GOD,

This letter was prompted by the twenty-two precious lives taken in El Paso on August 3, 2019, by a twenty-one-year-old white supremacist gunman. He told investigators that he wanted to kill as many Mexicans as possible—people who Donald Trump, in his campaign for the office of president, described as criminals "bringing drugs" and "bringing crime," and as "rapists."

Just hours after I sat down to write, I heard about the horrible killings of nine more people, this time in Dayton, Ohio, carried out by a twenty-two-year-old white male gunman. How much can any of us take? We are failing ourselves. We are not asking the right questions; we are failing to use truthful and courageous discourse to describe the suffering from human violence, the sort that is nationally and globally predicated upon forms of white nationalism.

Regarding those killed in El Paso, President Trump said, "God be with you all." Personally, I've had enough of empty rhetoric and religious hypocrisy when it comes to naming white supremacy.

I have no idea what Trump means when he utters those words, or what they amount to, other than an effort at mass distraction and obfuscation. To sow seeds of white racist divisiveness, hatred, and xenophobia, and then cynically use the words of a healing spiritual message stinks of religious duplicity; it is discourse steeped in denial.

As You know, God, Trump recently tried to smear four congresswomen of color (Alexandria Ocasio-Cortez, Ilhan Omar, Ayanna Pressley and Rashida Tlaib) with remarks that included, "Why don't they go back and help fix the totally broken and crime infested places from which they came." The language is both divisive and violent.

This is the same Trump who, after Representative Greg Gianforte's violent assault on a reporter in 2017, said, "Any guy that can do a body slam, he's my type." This is not just about tone; it is about character; it is about what Trump believes. A racist mass shooting, which is clear in the case of El Paso, is what "go back" looks like when it materializes in physical violence. Trump's words are weaponizable. He makes it easy.

I'm tempted to say that for Trump and his vast evangelical following enough is never enough. And if this is so, something has gone theologically awry. We have not become more loving as a nation. As James Baldwin writes, "If the concept of God has any validity or any use, it can only be to make us larger, freer and more loving. If God cannot do this, then it is time we got rid of Him." Baldwin doesn't mean to offend; he is, I'm certain, a prophet of love.

So, why write this letter? Ralph Waldo Emerson argues: "Our age is retrospective. It builds the sepulchers of the fathers. It writes biographies, histories, and criticisms. The foregoing generations beheld God face to face; we through their eyes. Why should not we also have an original relation to the universe?" Emerson emboldens a legitimate question, though one with a theological inflection: Why can't I have an original relation to You, God? There is nothing about our universe that proves a priori that this letter will not be heard by You. So, I'll just take the leap.

I realize that the act of writing such a letter is itself hasty as it assumes that You exist. Of course, if You don't, and there is no absolute, faultless proof that You do, then this letter speaks to nothing at all. The salutation is perhaps a bit silly. Yet, that is the risk that I take. In fact, it is a risk worth taking.

Karl Marx would be quick to remind me that I have been seduced by religion, the opium of the people. Sigmund Freud would tell me that I'm infantile, needing a "God-figure" that functions as an illusion to restrain certain human impulses. Bertrand Russell would tell me that many arguments for Your existence (cosmological, ontological, teleological) are simply false and that science, in terms of its access to genuine knowledge, eclipses religion. The atheists Richard Dawkins, Sam Harris, Daniel Dennett, and, before his death, Christopher Hitchens, have no place for You in their thinking unless it is to show that You have been created by human religious superstition, whose history, they might add, has proved to be morally abysmal. Yet, the astrophysicist Neil deGrasse Tyson at least calls himself an agnostic; he is on the proverbial fence until there is verifiable evidence to the contrary.

I'm often possessed by a visceral angst, at times unbearable, a sense of suffering that I feel isn't satisfied by atheism, agnosticism, or, paradoxically, theism. Theists, after all, are too certain; for me this certainty can too quickly satisfy that profound sense of searching, of really wanting to know, of painfully screaming in the night for Your existence to be revealed, a face-to-face moment. You, of course, remain hidden (Deus Absconditus). Why? Is it too much to ask, as a philosopher in the twenty-first century, to reveal yourself to me, to the world, to have an original relation to You, like Moses?

I'm not even sure of your name. I hope that confession speaks to a loving posture, an openness to know Your name and be touched by that truth, and not a failure of will on my part. So, I will call you by various names—Yahweh, Allah, Jehovah, Adonai, Brahma, Shiva, Vishnu, Ahura Mazda, Kami, Obatala, and Oshun. To be fair to Judaism, Islam, Christianity, Hinduism, Zoroastrianism, Shintoism, and Yoruba deities, these names I speak with respect. Of course, there are so many more names. Some, especially religious believers of various persuasions, might consider this act of naming to be an instance of idolatry. I see it as an act of humility, a longing. I stand by that humility because I long to know if You exist, where even that desire to know might itself be filled with pride.

This letter is not meant to proselytize, to convert. Rather, the letter is meant to entreat that which is perhaps beyond all of the major religions and yet inclusive of all of them, hoping that perhaps each one has something to say partially about You. I say all of this even as I define myself as a hopeful Christian theist, the kind who hopes, without any certainty, that You exist and that the strength of agape, Christian love, is possible and liberating in a world filled with so much existential, social, and political catastrophe, where anguished parents cry long into the night because their children have been taken too soon by acts of mass violence.

This letter is a lamentation; it speaks to our human pain and suffering, but it also speaks to this philosopher's dread in the face of apparent silence. Rabbi Abraham Joshua Heschel said, "It is not just that we are in search of God, but that God is in search of us, in need of us." That is not a philosophical argument, but I eagerly respond: I am here!

This is not a private prayer, but an entreaty shared publicly. It is intended to be inclusive, to speak on behalf of human suffering that is hard for any of us to bear alone. As a philosopher, I realize that I'm supposed to be "philosophical," objective, calm under pressure. As You already know, I'm not that kind of philosopher. I weep too much. I feel too deeply. I'm impatient when it comes to human suffering, especially forms of suffering that I helped to create. My anger and my frustration overflow, the existential devastations that I witness are too great to remain philosophically poised.

I am not like René Descartes sitting in his stove-heated room delineating "proofs" for Your existence. I am facing a non-ideal world where I witness haunting images of unspeakable tragedy. I'm thinking here, as You know, of the Salvadoran father Óscar Alberto Martinez Ramirez and his two-year-old daughter, Valeria, who were found floating facedown in the Rio Grande; they drowned as they attempted a border crossing. In what world do I live such that it continues after their deaths? We should stop in our tracks, refuse to go on living as normal, and bring an end to this level of suffering—today. And what about the lifeless body of three-year-old Alan Kurdi, who lay face-down on a Turkish beach after his family tried to flee violence from Syria? When I look at those photos, or think about the tragic deaths in El Paso and Dayton, or about the three killed at the Gilroy Garlic Festival in Gilroy, California, on July 28, it is my death that I see. John Donne had it right. All human death "diminishes me." And Donne continues, "Therefore never send to know for whom the bell tolls; it tolls for thee."

Yahweh, I die just a little when Palestinian children are killed by Israeli forces. Allah, I die just a little when Israeli children are killed by the hands of Palestinians. According to one report, 2,175 Palestinian children and 134 Israeli children have been killed since September 29, 2000. There is a deep feeling of personal moral failure when I read about such deaths. Shiva, Vishnu, Ahura Mazda, Oshun, Kami—we need your help. Allah, if you are there, please hear the cries of those Israeli children. Yahweh, if you are there, please hear the cries of those Palestinian children. Even as billions of religious believers across religious traditions prostrate themselves in ritualistic prayer, we continue to suffer from horrible acts of violence.

The weight of myopic fanaticism and dreams of white national purity takes its toll. I'm thinking of the nine who were killed at Emanuel African Methodist Episcopal Church in Charleston, South Carolina, on June 17, 2015; the eleven who were killed at the Tree of Life synagogue in Pittsburgh on October 27, 2018; the fifty-one who were killed at the mosque in Christchurch, New Zealand, on March 15, 2019.

So, it is with this letter that I seek You, that I ask for something more than we seem to be capable of, more than the routine prayers that are said in response to tragedy and sorrow. I don't want to simply repeat clichés and recall platitudes. I am a philosopher who weeps; I am a human being who suffers.

This letter is not for me alone. It can't be. The suffering of others is too great not to be moved by it, not to feel somehow partially responsible for it. So, it is with this letter that I seek an original relation, one that seeks our collective liberation, one that desires to speak especially on behalf of children and to free them from our miserable failure as adults to honor their lives more than we honor flags, rhetorical mass distraction, political myopia, party line politics, white nationalistic fanaticism, and religious vacuity.

AUGUST 7, 2019

What Religion Gives Us (That Science Can't)

No amount of scientific explanation or sociopolitical
theorizing is going to console a grieving mother.

Stephen T. Asma

I T'S A TOUGH TIME TO DEFEND RELIGION. RESPECT FOR IT HAS
diminished in almost every corner of modern life—not just among
atheists and intellectuals, but among the wider public too. And the
next generation of young people looks likely to be the most reli-
giously unaffiliated demographic in recent memory.

There are good reasons for this discontent: continued revelations
of abuse by priests and clerics, jihad campaigns against "infidels,"
and homegrown Christian hostility toward diversity and secular culture. This convergence of bad behavior and bad press has led many to
echo the evolutionary biologist E. O. Wilson's claim that "for the sake
of human progress, the best thing we could possibly do would be to
diminish, to the point of eliminating, religious faiths."

Despite the very real problems with religion—and my own historical skepticism toward it—I don't subscribe to that view. I would
like to argue here, in fact, that we still need religion. Perhaps a story
is a good way to begin.

One day, after pompously lecturing a class of undergraduates
about the incoherence of monotheism, I was approached by a shy
student. He nervously stuttered through a heartbreaking story,

one that slowly unraveled my own convictions and assumptions about religion.

Five years ago, he explained, his older teenage brother had been brutally stabbed to death, viciously attacked and mutilated by a perpetrator who was never caught. My student, his mother, and his sister were shattered. His mother suffered a mental breakdown soon afterward and would have been institutionalized if not for the fact that she expected to see her slain son again, to be reunited with him in the afterlife where she was certain his body would be made whole. These bolstering beliefs, along with the church rituals she engaged in after her son's murder, dragged her back from the brink of debilitating sorrow, and gave her the strength to continue raising her other two children—my student and his sister.

To the typical atheist, all this looks irrational, and therefore unacceptable. Beliefs, we are told, must be aligned with evidence, not mere yearning. Without rational standards, like those entrenched in science, we will all slouch toward chaos and end up in pre-Enlightenment darkness.

I do not intend to try to rescue religion as reasonable. It isn't terribly reasonable. But I do want to argue that its irrationality does not render it unacceptable, valueless, or cowardly. Its irrationality may even be the source of its power.

The human brain is a kludge of different operating systems: the ancient reptilian brain (motor functions, fight-or-flight instincts), the limbic or mammalian brain (emotions), and the more recently evolved neocortex (rationality). Religion irritates the rational brain because it trades in magical thinking and no proof, but it nourishes the emotional brain because it calms fears, answers to yearnings, and strengthens feelings of loyalty.

According to prominent neuroscientists like Jaak Panksepp, Antonio Damasio, and Kent Berridge, as well as neuropsychoanalysts like Mark Solms, our minds are motivated primarily by ancient emotional systems, like fear, rage, lust, love, and grief. These forces are adaptive and help us survive if they are managed properly—that is if they are made strong enough to accomplish goals of survival, but not so strong as to overpower us and lead to neuroses and maladaptive behavior.

My claim is that religion can provide direct access to this emotional life in ways that science does not. Yes, science can give us emotional feelings of wonder at the majesty of nature, but there are many forms of human suffering that are beyond the reach of any scientific alleviation. Different emotional stresses require different kinds of rescue. Unlike previous secular tributes to religion that praise its ethical and civilizing function, I think we need religion because it is a road-tested form of emotional management.

Of course, there is a well-documented dark side to spiritual emotions. Religious emotional life tilts toward the melodramatic. Religion still trades readily in good-and-evil narratives, and it gives purchase to testosterone-fueled revenge fantasies and aggression. While this sort of zealotry is undeniably dangerous, most religion is actually helpful to the average family struggling to eke out a living in trying times.

Religious rituals, for example, surround the bereaved person with our most important resource—other people. Even more than other mammals, humans are extremely dependent on others—not just for acquiring resources and skills, but for feeling well. And feeling well is more important than thinking well for my survival.

Religious practice is a form of social interaction that can improve psychological health. When you've lost a loved one, religion provides a therapeutic framework of rituals and beliefs that produce the oxytocin, internal opioids, dopamine, and other positive affects that can help with coping and surviving. Beliefs play a role, but they are not the primary mechanisms for delivering such therapeutic power. Instead, religious practice (rituals, devotional activities, songs, prayer, and story) manage our emotions, giving us opportunities to express care for each other in grief, providing us with the alleviation of stress and anxiety, or giving us direction and an outlet for rage.

Atheists like Richard Dawkins, E. O. Wilson, and Sam Harris are evaluating religion at the neocortical level—their criteria for assessing it is the rational scientific method. I agree with them that religion fails miserably at the bar of rational validity, but we're at the wrong bar. The older reptilian brain, built by natural selection for solving survival challenges, was not built for rationality. Emotions like fear, love, rage—even hope or anticipation—were selected for because they helped early mammals flourish. In many cases, emotions offer quicker ways to solve problems than deliberative cognition.

For us humans, the interesting issue is how the old animal operating system interacts with the new operating system of cognition. How do our feelings and our thoughts blend together to compose our mental lives and our behaviors? The neuroscientist Antonio Damasio has shown that emotions saturate even the seemingly pure information-processing aspects of rational deliberation. So something complicated is happening when my student's mother remembers and projects her deceased son, and embeds him in a religious narrative that helps her soldier on.

No amount of scientific explanation or sociopolitical theorizing is going to console the mother of the stabbed boy. Bill Nye the Science Guy and Neil deGrasse Tyson will not be much help, should they decide to drop over and explain the physiology of suffering and the sociology of crime. But the magical thinking that she is going to see her murdered son again, along with the hugs from and songs with fellow parishioners, can sustain her. If this emotionally grounded hope gives her the energy and vitality to continue caring for her other children, it can do the same for others. And we can see why religion persists.

Those of us in the secular world who critique such emotional responses and strategies with the refrain, "But is it true?" are missing the point. Most religious beliefs are not true. But here's the crux. The emotional brain doesn't care. It doesn't operate on the grounds of true and false. Emotions are not true or false. Even a terrible fear inside a dream is still a terrible fear. This means that the criteria for measuring a healthy theory are not the criteria for measuring a healthy emotion. Unlike a healthy theory, which must correspond with empirical facts, a healthy emotion is one that contributes to neurochemical homeostasis or other affective states that promote biological flourishing.

Finally, we need a word or two about opiates. The modern condemnation of religion has followed the Marxian rebuke that religion is an opiate administered indirectly by state power in order to secure a docile populace—one that accepts poverty and political powerlessness, in hopes of posthumous supernatural rewards. "Religion is the sigh of the oppressed creature," Marx claimed, "the heart of a heartless world, and the soul of soulless conditions. It is the opium of the people."

Marx, Mao, and even Malcolm X leveled this critique against traditional religion, and the critique lives on as a disdainful last insult to be hurled at the believer. I hurled it myself many times, thinking that it was a decisive weapon. In recent years, however, I've changed my mind about this criticism.

First, religion is energizing as often as it is anesthetizing. As often as it numbs or sedates, religion also riles up and invigorates the believer. This animating quality of religion can make it more hazardous to the state than it is tranquilizing, and it also inspires a lot of altruistic philanthropy.

Second, what's so bad about pain relief anyway? If my view of religion is primarily therapeutic, I can hardly despair when some of that therapy takes the form of palliative pain management. If atheists think it's enough to dismiss the believer on the grounds that he should never buffer the pains of life, then I'll assume the atheist has no recourse to any pain management in his own life. In which case, I envy his remarkably good fortune.

For the rest of us, there is aspirin, alcohol, religion, hobbies, work, love, friendship. After all, opioids—like endorphins—are innate chemical ingredients in the human brain and body, and they evolved, in part, to occasionally relieve the organism from misery. To quote the well-known phrase by the German humorist Wilhelm Busch, "He who has cares has brandy, too."

We need a more clear-eyed appreciation of the role of cultural

426 STEPHEN T. ASMA

analgesics. It is not enough to dismiss religion on the grounds of some puritanical moral judgment about the weakness of the devotee. Religion is the most powerful cultural response to the universal emotional life that connects us all.

Teaching Calvin in California

Some think theology has no place in a secular
classroom. I've learned otherwise.

Jonathan Sheehan

B ERKELEY, CALIF.—WE SPEND A GREAT DEAL OF TIME WOR-
rying about theology these days. From extremist violence to the
American culture wars, the theological imagination can feel like an
existential threat to liberal democracy. Or more simply, just to common decency. No surprise that many believe that theology has no
place in the secular college classroom.

Over the years, I have decided that this is wrong. I learned to
think otherwise teaching Calvin in California.

Given my profession, I am naturally curious about theology. But
it takes collaborative work in the classroom to persuade students
that they should be too. To persuade them that theology is more than
its bad press; that it is a rich subject as likely to provoke disbelief as
belief; that it is more likely to open than to close interesting conversations about religion and public life. To persuade them, in short,
that theology matters to a liberal education.

In my history of Christianity course, we read a number of challenging writers. Each one I ask students to read with as much sympathy, charity, and critical perspective as they can muster. But nothing
outrages them—not the writings of Augustine or Erasmus or Luther—
more than two or three pages of John Calvin.

Calvin was the most influential religious reformer of the sixteenth century. His theological imagination and organizational genius prepared the way for almost all forms of American Protestantism, from the Presbyterians to the Methodists to the Baptists. He was also a severe and uncompromising thinker. The Ayatollah of Geneva, some have called him.

Late in the third book of his 1536 *Institutes of the Christian Religion*—when he seeks to describe the utter power of God over man, and our utter dependence on him—is usually where my students revolt. These young people come from all walks of life. They are atheists, agnostics, Christians, Jews, Muslims, and more besides. They are the face of California diversity, young people with wildly different social, religious, ethnic, and racial experiences.

Diverse as they may be, their reaction is the same when they read a sentence like this: "Some are born destined for certain death from the womb, who glorify God's name by their own destruction." This is the heart of Calvin's teaching of predestination, his insistence that God determined each human destiny before the creation of the world. The elect are bound for heaven, the reprobate to hell, and there is absolutely nothing to be done about it, ever. "Jacob is chosen and distinguished from the rejected Esau, by God's predestination, while not differing from him in merits," is how Calvin put it. Your merits, your goodwill, your moral action: None of these make a difference. The chosen Jacob is no better than the rejected Esau. The damned glorify God's name. And God is pleased by the whole business.

The classroom erupts in protest. Nothing has prepared my students for an idea like this. Secular students object: How can so much arrogant misanthropy pass itself off as piety? Non-Christian students are agitated too. What kind of God is this, they ask, that took pleasure in creating man so that he might be condemned to everlasting damnation? And the various types of Christian students are no less outraged. "Follow me," Christ said, and doesn't that mean that we are asked to choose, that the choice between death and salvation is a free one? All different concerns, but the outcome is the same: rejection, usually disgust.

I ask the students to read on. After all, Calvin anticipated these objections, since they were raised in his day too. He dedicated a whole chapter to dismissing the "insolence" of the human understanding when it "hears these things." He knew that our first reactions would be anger and denial, that we would be baffled by predestination. So he demanded that his readers, then and now, think alongside him. His argument goes like this: If God alone created all things, doesn't that mean that he did so freely? If he is free in his choices, how can it be otherwise than that God himself determines our fates, right to the edges of hell? Once you grant the first premise—that there is no God besides God and that he made the universe—reason itself apparently requires we assent to this terrible thought.

None of the students are persuaded by Calvin's logic. But again, Calvin probably knew that they wouldn't be, since many of his own readers weren't either. For this saying, "No," the rejection of this terrible idea, is a natural, even reasonable reaction. "Monstrous indeed is the madness of men, who desire to subject the immeasurable to the puny measure of their own reason," Calvin exclaimed.

Human reason seeks to subject God to itself, but predestination tells us that we cannot. Reasoning itself needs to come to an end before humans can experience the proper relationship to God.

Here we can see something special about the theological reasoning that Calvin practiced. This is not philosophy, after all. His work is not aimed at an abstract audience. Instead it is a direct address to you. Confronting the doctrine of predestination is a kind of psychological experiment. Nothing else can "suffice to make us as humble as we ought to be" as "a taste of this doctrine" of predestination, as Calvin put it. Exactly here, in this rejection and anger, Calvin insists, you finally feel in your gut the greatness of God. You finally feel the difference between his Majesty and your limitation.

Believers in the classroom feel the bite of this argument in their own ways, often struggling to keep the first premise but to deny what seems to follow from it. Even the students who don't believe any of this, though, can feel the power of the argument, if only in the disgust that it fosters in them. Of course you feel disgusted, Calvin would say, that's exactly how an atheist should react!

The experience of reading Calvin has unexpected lessons, then, for religious and secular students alike. The first lesson that Calvin teaches us is about the power of an idea, uncompromisingly expressed and shrewdly argued. I tell the students that their reactions were shared by generations of European theologians and philosophers. In the late seventeenth century, for example, the German philosopher and co-inventor of the calculus Gottfried Leibniz coined the word "theodicy" and wrote the first comprehensive philosophical defense of God's justice to manage the "horror" all good people feel at the thought that God by choice saves so few "and abandons all others to the devil his enemy, who torments them eternally and makes them curse their Creator."

And so students learn that they are not alone in feeling the terribleness of Calvin's challenge. Indeed, that they find it terrible at all (and not just irrelevant or bizarre) already puts them into the very conversation with the past that a history classroom hopes to forge. In their reactions, they are already participating in the intellectual revolutions of the modern world.

The second lesson Calvin teaches us, secular and religious, is this: Be careful what you believe in. Consider the consequences of your commitments. Investigate what your own views demand. These are lessons neither of secular reason nor of Christian reason. They are lessons about reasoning itself. Once we begin to talk at this level, what results are powerful conversations about powerful questions that cut across religious and secular life. Do we think that the world has a purpose and an order? If it does, where do they come from? If it doesn't, what does a meaningful life look like? If we believe in a God, where does that belief drive us? If we don't, what kinds of commitments do we actually have?

Calvin was certainly no liberal, but these are questions that the liberal arts classroom was designed to nurture. His theology spurs secular and religious students to discuss issues of common concern, to delineate differences and similarities, to build a community of inquiry.

The third lesson is this: that we don't need to take Calvin's bait. Religious and secular students both come to this on their own, examining Calvin's text more deeply than perhaps even he did. Look at this sentence, one says: "All those who do not know that they are God's own will be miserable through constant fear." But how is anyone supposed to know that she is God's own? she asks. If we feel humiliated and bereft of reason, how are we supposed to feel certain? And what kind of society would this produce, this lack of certainty, this humiliation?

At this point, then, they learn how theology does what it always does, how it shades into politics, history, social life. The German sociologist Max Weber's view—that it was precisely the uncertainty generated by Calvin's doctrine of election that helped spur the rise of capitalism—is one canonical analysis that I can now share with them. The historian Perry Miller's view—that the inability to hew to election was crucial to the formation of colonial American Protestantism—is another.

Whether they buy these or not—and both models are easy to critique—my students have now experienced for themselves how Calvin's thought demands a way of life that would support it. They have wrestled with this thought together, religious and secular. Perhaps they have come to different conclusions about the theology or the history but, when all goes well, they have done so with integrity, reason, creativity, and charity.

If these are not intellectual virtues that we need in our modern world, then I don't know what are.

SEPTEMBER 12, 2016

What's So Good About Original Sin?

Perhaps it's time for a new Puritanism. With fewer witch trials
this time around, it could make the world a better place.

Crispin Sartwell

THE DOCTRINE OF ORIGINAL SIN HAS OFTEN BEEN HELD TO BE intolerably dark, a counsel of despair. It says we are by nature morally flawed, that we are born in error and live in it irremediably, that each of us deserves punishment and will receive it, unless redeemed by God's arbitrary grace. It insists that we cannot cure ourselves by our own efforts, and it has led some people to make extraordinarily disturbing claims, such as that children who die in infancy could burn in eternal hellfire.

It's hard to argue with the fact that inherent depravity is a profoundly pessimistic idea, and one with potentially bad effects. A rejection of the idea of original sin might argue that if we believe we can be good and do good by our own efforts, we are likelier to strive to do so. If we believe we are intrinsically evil, it follows, we will cease trying to make ourselves or the world better. Why not, then, think more positively about ourselves and believe in the possibility of human goodness and our potential for improvement right here in this world?

It would take a book or a shelf of them to examine original sin as a theological doctrine, going back to Augustine's interpretation of Adam and Eve. Even so, it is not clear that the preachers of original sin have managed to explain why a benevolent God would create such profoundly flawed creatures as they believe us to be. And if you don't believe in God at all, or not in that sort of God, the whole line of argument is moot.

Despite all of that, I would like to entertain the notion that a secularized conception of original sin is plausible, and that believing it might have good effects. In short, perhaps it's time for a new Puritanism, though with fewer witch trials this time around.

When I look within, I see certain extreme failings. I have not been able to get rid of most of them, and I have accumulated others as I've gone along. Perhaps you've done better, but most of us certainly come up short of our own ideals, ones I hope most people, religious or not, generally share—to be generous, peaceful, energetic in helping others and hesitant to help ourselves at their expense; to take care of the world we inhabit; to not only not kill one another (or even think about it), but to love one another. Even by our own mortal standards, we are profoundly flawed.

To complicate matters further, action undertaken for apparently good motives can often yield unintended harmful consequences, outweighing any possible good effects. We can intend, at best, only a tiny proportion of the effects of any of our actions. In trying to make the world an excellent place for human beings to live by developing and applying ingenious technologies, for example, we may wind up rendering it uninhabitable. Or in trying to keep ourselves safe and secure by stockpiling defensive weaponry, we may annihilate life on earth. There's really no need for God's punishment when you're making your own hellfire. As Paul told the Romans (according to David Bentley Hart's excellent recent translation of the New Testament), "I do not know what it is that I accomplish" and "what I wish, this I do not do; instead, what I hate, this I do."

Even the sheer fact that we are finite in our knowledge and in our power leads us to make terrible moral mistakes. But many of us commit those sort of transgressions knowingly, because we have malicious or violent impulses and motivations. We may even justify or defend them.

There is some level of self-scrutiny too merciless for most of us, some inner corridor too dark. We are mystified, or purport to be, by mass shooters, for example. What could possibly motivate a person to want to kill—everyone? What could turn them so against their own species? I suggest that to answer a question like that we must look within ourselves—at our own violent fantasies, the ways we hate or negate the world, our moments of imagined annihilation of people we fancy to be our enemies, our feeling at times that we are being arbitrarily persecuted or misunderstood. Perhaps, if we were witheringly honest, we might see a school shooter within us, or a bully or abuser of the sort that helped create people like that.

This insight is not the exclusive province of Christian theology. Ralph Waldo Emerson once wrote, "I have within me the capacity for every crime." Not long after, the American feminist Voltairine de Cleyre amplified this sentiment. Few readers of Emerson, she wrote, believed that he truly meant those words, but rather they took it as an attempt by Emerson to "say something large and leveling." She went on:

> *But I think he meant exactly what he said. I think with all his purity Emerson had within him the turbid stream of passion and desire; for all his hard-cut granite features he knew the instincts of the weakling and the slave; and for all his sweetness, he had the tiger and the jackal in his soul. I think that within every bit of human flesh and spirit that has ever crossed the enigma bridge of life, from the prehistoric racial morning until now, all crime and all virtue were germinal.*

We may regard a shooter—or a racist, a sexual predator, an addict, or someone who commits suicide (as de Cleyre herself tried to do at least once)—as alien. This reinforces, to ourselves and others, our sense of our own sanity and goodness; it is a way to keep us safe not only from those who would commit such crimes, but from the parts of ourselves who are like them, or who could have gone down that road.

But what if we put aside such defenses? What if, by connecting with the criminal, with the deranged or patently evil—and I believe this is what Emerson was striving to do—we gain some deeper understanding?

The doctrine of original sin—in religious or secular versions—is an expression of humility, an expression of a resolution to face our own imperfections. In undertaking any such act there is risk. To allow the self-scrutiny required in this act to turn to self-loathing would be debilitating. But a secularized doctrine of original sin, a chastened self-regard, doesn't entail consigning ourselves to the flames. There is much to affirm in our damaged selves and in our damaged lives, even a sort of dignity and beauty we share in our imperfect awareness of our own imperfection, and our halting attempts to face it, and ourselves.

MAY 21, 2018

Abandon (Nearly) All Hope

*Faith and optimism can be forms of denial
that only prolong our suffering.*

─────────

Simon Critchley

WITH EASTER UPON US, POWERFUL NARRATIVES OF REBIRTH and resurrection are in the air and on the breeze. However, winter's stubborn reluctance to leave to make way for the pleasing and hopeful season leads me to think not of cherry blossoms and Easter Bunnies but of Prometheus, Nietzsche, Barack Obama, and the very roots of hope. Is hope always such a wonderful thing? Is it not rather a form of moral cowardice that allows us to escape from reality and prolong human suffering?

Prometheus the Titan was punished by the Olympian Zeus by being chained to a rock in the Caucasus, quite possibly not that far from Crimea. Each day for eternity, an eagle pecked out his liver. Every night, the liver grew back. An unpleasant situation, I'm sure you would agree. His transgression was to have given human beings the gift of fire and, with that, the capacity for craft, technological inventiveness, and what we are fond of calling civilization.

This is well known. Less well known is Prometheus's second gift. In Aeschylus's *Prometheus Bound*, the chained Titan is pitilessly interrogated by the chorus. They ask him whether he gave human beings anything else. Yes, he says, "I stopped mortals from foreseeing doom." How did you do that? they ask. His response is revealing: "I sowed in them blind hopes."

This is a very Greek thought. It stands resolutely opposed to Christianity, with its trinity of faith, love, and hope. For Saint Paul— Christianity's true founder, it must be recalled—hope is both a moral attitude of steadfastness and a hope for what is laid up in heaven for us, namely salvation. This is why faith in the resurrection of Jesus Christ is so absolutely fundamental to Christians. Christ died on the cross, but he was resurrected and lives eternally. Jesus is our hope, as Paul writes in the First Letter to Timothy, namely he is the basis for the faith that we too might live eternally. Heaven, as they say, is real.

In his Letter to the Romans, Paul inadvertently confirms Prometheus's gift of blind hope. He asserts that hope in what is seen is not hope at all, "For who hopes for what he sees?" On the contrary, we should "hope for what we do not see" and "wait for it with patience."

Now, fast-forward to us. When Barack Obama describes how he came to write his keynote speech to the 2004 Democratic National Convention, the speech that instantly shot him to fame and laid the basis for his presidential campaign and indeed his presidency, he recalls a phrase that his pastor, the Reverend Jeremiah A. Wright Jr., used in a sermon: the audacity of hope. Obama says that this audacity is what "was the best of the American spirit," namely "the audacity to believe despite all the evidence to the contrary."

It is precisely this kind of hope that I think we should try to give up. It is not audacious, but mendacious. As the wise Napoleon said, "a leader is a dealer in hope" who governs by insisting on a bright outlook despite all evidence to the contrary. But what if we looked at matters differently? What if we expected more from political life than a four-yearly trade-in of our moral intelligence to one or other of the various hope dealers that appear on the political market to sell us some shiny new vehicle of salvation?

The problem here is with the way in which this audacious Promethean theological idea of hope has migrated into our national psyche to such an extent that it blinds us to the reality of the world that we inhabit and causes a sort of sentimental complacency that actually prevents us from seeing things aright and protesting against this administration's moral and political lapses and those of other administrations.

Against the inflated and finally hypocritical rhetoric of contemporary politics, I think it is instructive to look at things from another standpoint, an ancient and very Greek standpoint. Just as our stories shape us as citizens, their stories shaped them and might shape us too. So, let me tell you a little story, perhaps the most terrifying from antiquity.

In *The History of the Peloponnesian War*, Thucydides, the sober and unsentimental historian, describes a dialogue between the representatives of the island of Melos in the Aegean Sea, which was allied with Sparta, and some ambassadors from invading Athenian military forces. The ambassadors present the Melians with a very simple choice: Submit to us or be destroyed.

Rather than simply submit, the Melians wriggle. They express hope that the Spartans will come to rescue them. The Athenians calmly point out that it would be an extremely dangerous mission for the Spartans to undertake and highly unlikely to happen. Also, they add, rightly, "We are masters of the sea." The Spartans had formidable land forces, but were no match for the Athenian navy.

The Melians plead that if they yield to the Athenians, then all hope will be lost. If they continue to hold out, then "we can still hope to stand tall." The Athenians reply that it is indeed true that hope is a great comfort, but often a delusive one. They add that the Melians will learn what hope is when it fails them, "for hope is prodigal by nature."

With consummate clarity and no small cruelty, the Athenians urge the Melians not to turn to Promethean blind hopes when they are forced to give up their sensible ones. Reasonable hopes can soon become unreasonable. "Do not be like ordinary people," they add, "who could use human means to save themselves but turn to blind hopes when they are forced to give up their sensible ones—to divination, oracles and other such things that destroy men by giving them hope."

At this point, the Athenians withdraw and leave the Melians to consider their position. As usually happens in political negotiations, the Melians decide to stick to exactly the same position that they had adopted before the debate. They explain that "we will trust in the fortune of the Gods." In a final statement, the Athenians conclude: "You have staked everything on your trust in hope . . . and you will be ruined in everything."

After laying siege to the Melian city and some military skirmishes back and forth, the Athenians lose patience with the Melians and Thucydides reports with breathtaking understatement, "They killed all the men of military age and made slaves of the women and children."

*   *   *

Thucydides offers no moral commentary on the Melian Dialogue. He does not tell us how to react, but instead impartially presents us with a real situation. The dialogue is an argument from power about the nature of power. This is why Nietzsche, in his polemics against Christianity and liberalism, loved Thucydides. This is also why I love Nietzsche. Should one reproach Thucydides for describing the negotiations between the Athenians and the Melians without immediately moralizing the story and telling us how we should think? Not at all, Nietzsche insists. What we witness in the Melian Dialogue is the true character of Greek realism.

Elected regimes can become authoritarian, democracies can become corrupted, and invading armies usually behave abominably. What we need in the face of what Nietzsche calls "a strict, hard factuality" is not hope, but "courage in the face of reality."

For Nietzsche, the alternative to Thucydides is Plato. With his usual lack of moderation, Nietzsche declares that Platonism is cowardice in the face of reality because it constructs fictional metaphysical ideals like justice, virtue, and the good. Nietzsche sees Platonism as a flight from the difficulty of reality into a vapid moralistic idealism. Furthermore, he adds, we have been stuck with versions of moral idealism ever since Plato, notably in Christianity, with its hope in salvation, and modern liberalism, with its trust in God and its insistence on hope's audacity contrary to all evidence.

Where does this leave us? Rather than see Thucydides as an apologist for authoritarianism, I see him as a deep but disappointed democrat with a clear-eyed view of democracy's limitations, particularly when Athens voted to engage in misplaced military adventures like the disastrous expedition to Sicily that led to Sparta's final victory over Athens in the Peloponnesian Wars. Thucydides would have doubtless had a similar view of the United States's military expeditions to countries like Afghanistan and Iraq on the basis of metaphysical abstractions like enduring freedom or infinite justice. But he would have thought it was even worse for democracies to speak out of both sides of their mouths, offering vigorous verbal support for invaded or embattled peoples and talking endlessly of freedom and hope while doing precisely nothing.

When democracy goes astray, as it always will, the remedy should not be some idealistic belief in hope's audacity, which ends up sounding either cynical or dogmatic or both. The remedy, in my view, is a skeptical realism, deeply informed by history. Such realism has an abiding commitment to reason and the need for negotiation and persuasion, but also an acute awareness of reason's limitations in the face of violence and belligerence. As Thucydides realized long before the 2004 Democratic National Convention, it is not difficult to make beautiful speeches in politics, but they very often do little to change people's minds and effect palpable improvement in social arrangements.

Thinking without hope might sound rather bleak, but it needn't be so. I see it rather as embracing an affirmative, even cheerful, realism. Nietzsche admired Epictetus, the former slave turned philosophy teacher, for living without hope. "Yes," Nietzsche said, "he can smile." We can too.

You can have all kinds of reasonable hopes, it seems to me, the kind of modest, pragmatic, and indeed deliberately fuzzy conception of social hope expressed by an anti-Platonist philosopher like Richard Rorty. But unless those hopes are realistic we will end up in a blindly hopeful (and therefore hopeless) idealism. Prodigal hope invites despair only when we see it fail. In giving up the former, we might also avoid the latter. This is not an easy task, I know. But we should try. Nietzsche writes, "Hope is the evil of evils because it prolongs man's torment." Often, by clinging to hope, we make the suffering worse.

APRIL 19, 2014

What We Believe About Prophecies

Letting go of fantasies—political, spiritual, or both—is much harder than you might think.

T. M. Luhrmann

THE NEW EVANGELICAL CHRISTIANITY THAT EMERGED OUT OF the cultural tumult of the 1960s and 1970s was vividly supernatural. It was born out of the fear that Americans were turning away from Christianity, and it promised a God who was intensely present, always loving, and almost magically invincible.

Preachers promised that ordinary people could heal and prophesy in Jesus's name. (Here they might quote John 14:12: "Whoever believes in me will do the works I have been doing.") Churches like Bethel Redding, in California, founded schools of Supernatural Ministry. Throughout the country, Christians went on prayer walks to cleanse their cities. They began to sniff out demons and exorcise people.

In 2006, the Pew Research Center found that about a quarter of the country belonged to "renewalist" churches like these. For reasons still poorly understood, most of these churches were politically conservative. As the 2020 election approached, many within them prophesied that President Donald J. Trump would be reelected. When President Biden was sworn in on January 20, 2021, it was a massive disconfirmation of their beliefs.

Many are waiting for those who believed in the fantasies to come back to their senses. There are two reasons to think that this might take some time.

First, the intensity of belief commitment can actually increase in the face of refutation before declining. Decades ago, the psychologist Leon Festinger found that when people recognize that their beliefs conflict with facts in the world (he called this "cognitive dissonance"), they will work to reduce the tension—but not always by changing their original commitments. The more strongly they have invested in the original belief, the more they will work to change the world instead.

Dr. Festinger explored a famous example of this phenomenon in *When Prophecy Fails*, a book he wrote with Henry Riecken and Stanley Schachter about a Midwestern doomsday cult that predicted the world would end on December 21, 1954. When that date passed and nothing happened, group leaders picked up the phone, called the press, and began to proselytize. They now interpreted their beliefs differently. The global calamity, from which this group would be saved by flying saucers and in which everyone else would die, had been postponed by God. They found proof of a partial calamity (an earthquake here and there) and insisted that the spaceships were here to stay (the aliens were examining the faults in the earth's surface). "A man with a conviction," the book opens, "is a hard man to change."

Second, the arcane knowledge found in this new evangelical Christianity (often called charismatic) can be intensely satisfying. Effective religions create a kind of paracosm for the faithful. By that I mean that gripping faith offers a shared imagined world that is accessible only to insiders, who follow the clues, read the texts, and spin theories. This kind of Christianity—and even more QAnon, its political kin—built a paracosm with obscure symbols, rare words with uncommon meanings, and elaborate historical genealogies, a set of particulars to interpret as brain-bending as the hardest puzzle. Knowing these texts and solving these puzzles turns ordinary desk clerks into esoteric grandmasters. It's hard to give that up.

After the election, many of those who prophesied that Mr. Trump would be victorious and who listened to those prophecies remained committed to the cause. To be sure, some of the believers have peeled off. Kris Vallotton, a pastor at Bethel Redding and a towering figure in charismatic evangelical Christianity, in November gave a heart-felt and moving apology for having misheard the "word" God gave him about who would win the election. Some of the Proud Boys (a political organization, although many members are evangelical) declared Mr. Trump a failure.

Others grew more fervent. J. Derrick Lemons, an associate pro-fessor of religion at the University of Georgia, found himself startled as he participated (for fifty hours) as an anthropological observer in the Zoom prayer sessions held after the election by some of the evangelical leaders Mr. Trump frequently consulted with during his presidency. They were clear that Mr. Trump had won and that his victory would be recognized. As the weeks went by and Mr. Trump's lawsuits attempting to overturn the election's results continued to fail, the prayers became more heated and more public, expand-ing to Facebook Live and YouTube. The stakes went up. The leaders prayed not against malevolent Democrats, but against a deep-state Republican and Democratic cabal that controlled all government, and from which they needed Mr. Trump to free them. Mr. Lemons said they spoke of Mr. Trump as a modern-day Cyrus to lead them out of captivity and into the apocalyptic battle that would end with Christ's return.

There is a deep lesson here about religious commitment. Faith is always about living with the contradictions between the world as it should be (as understood by the person of faith) and the world as it is. God is good, but injustice abounds. You pray to an omnipotent king that your mother will recover, but she does not. Faith is always, to some extent, about cognitive dissonance.

Most people live with a cognitive flexibility around the relation-ship of their faith to the everyday. They believe that God can do any-thing, but they never rely on God to feed the dog. They do not expect God to write their term paper. They do not allow their faith commit-ment to the world as it should be to violate the reality constraints of the world as it is. One can find this sentiment in many faiths. A famous Islamic hadith asks whether one should tie up one's camel, or leave the camel untied and trust in Allah. Trust in Allah, the hadith says, but do not forget to tie up your camel.

Yet some people of faith deliberately disregard the real world. They march on with an outsize commitment to the world as their faith wants it, and not to the world as it is. The more someone becomes emotionally invested in such a group, the more it takes to wrest that person free.

Many years ago in San Diego I spoke with a woman who had joined the movement of the spiritual leader known as Bhagwan Shree Rajneesh back in the 1970s when it was fun and free, when he was known as the "sex guru" and when her days were full of dancing meditations. She followed him when he left his ashram in Pune, India, in 1981 to build an enormous new commune in Oregon. She remained as activities shifted from dynamic yoga to hard labor, with devotees constructing buildings on the property. She stayed with him through the period in 1984 when group leaders hatched assassination plots and deliberately poisoned hundreds of Oregonians with salmonella.

She left him, she said, only in 1985, when FBI helicopters landed in the commune and the Bhagwan was charged with immigration fraud and deported. She had come to talk to me, the new anthropologist of religion in town, to ask why she had stayed for so long.

People stay longer in reality-challenging faiths when their news is tightly controlled. They stay longer when it is hard to find people outside the group. And they stay yet longer when they feel that they will be ridiculed by those in the society to which they will return.

For those who cannot accept the results of an election, this will take some time.

MAY 20, 2021

Why Mortality Makes Us Free

The heart of spiritual life cannot be found in
nirvana or heaven, but in the mutual recognition
that this life is our ultimate purpose.

Martin Hägglund

O F ALL THE WORLD RELIGIONS, BUDDHISM ENJOYS THE GREAT-
est respect and popularity among those who seek a model for "spiritual life" beyond traditional religion. Even the prominent atheist
Sam Harris turns to the meditational exercises of Buddhism in his
best-selling book *Waking Up: A Guide to Spirituality Without Religion*.
This is understandable, since Buddhist meditation practices can be
employed to great effect for secular ends. In particular, there has
been success in adapting various forms of meditation techniques for
cognitive therapy as well as for practical forms of compassion training. If you learn Buddhist meditation techniques for such therapeutic purposes—or simply for the sake of having more strength and
energy—then you are adapting the techniques for a secular project.
You engage in meditational practices as a means for the end of deepening your ability to care for others and improving the quality of
your life.

The aim of salvation in Buddhism, however, is to be released from
finite life itself. Such an idea of salvation recurs across the world
religions, but in many strands of Buddhism there is a remarkable
honesty regarding the implications of salvation. Rather than prom-

ising that your life will continue, or that you will see your loved ones again, the salvation of nirvana entails your extinction. The aim is not to lead a free life, with the pain and suffering that such a life entails, but to reach the "insight" that personal agency is an illusion and dissolve in the timelessness of nirvana. What ultimately matters is to attain a state of consciousness where everything ceases to matter, so that one can rest in peace.

The Buddhist conclusion may seem extreme when stated in this way, but in fact it makes explicit what is implicit in all ideas of eternal salvation. Far from making our lives meaningful, eternity would make them meaningless, since our actions would have no purpose. This problem can be traced even within religious traditions that espouse faith in eternal life. An article in U.S. Catholic asks: "Heaven: Will it be Boring?" The article answers no, for in heaven souls are called "not to eternal rest but to eternal activity—eternal social concern." Yet this answer only underlines the problem, since there is nothing to be concerned about in heaven.

Concern presupposes that something can go wrong or can be lost; otherwise we would not care. An eternal activity—just as much as an eternal rest—is of concern to no one, since it cannot be stopped and does not have to be maintained by anyone. The problem is not that an eternal activity would be "boring" but that it would not be intelligible as my activity. Any activity of mine (including a boring activity) requires that I sustain it. In an eternal activity, there cannot be a person who is bored—or involved in any other way—since an eternal activity does not depend on being sustained by anyone.

An eternal salvation is therefore not only unattainable but also undesirable, since it would eliminate the care and passion that animates our lives. What we do and what we love can matter to us only because we understand ourselves as mortal. That self-understanding is implicit in all our practical commitments and priorities. The question of what we ought to do with our time—a question that is at issue in everything we do—presupposes that we understand our time to be finite.

Hence, mortality is the condition of agency and freedom. To be free is not to be sovereign or liberated from all constraints. Rather, we are free because we are able to ask ourselves what we ought to do with our time. All forms of freedom—the freedom to act, to speak, to love—are intelligible as freedom only insofar as we are free to engage the question of what we should do with our time. If it were given what we should do, what we should say, and whom we should love—in short: if it were given what we should do with our time—we would not be free.

The ability to ask the question of what we ought to do with our time is the basic condition for what I call spiritual freedom. To lead a free, spiritual life (rather than a life determined merely by natural instincts), I must be responsible for what I do. This is not to say that I am free from natural and social constraints. I did not choose to be born with the limitations and abilities I happen to have. Moreover, I had no control over who took care of me; what they did to me and for me. My family—and the larger historical context into which I was born—shaped me before I could do anything about it.

Likewise, social norms continue to inform who I can take myself to be and what I can do with my life. Without social norms, which I did not invent and that shape the world in which I find myself, I can have no understanding of who to be or what to do. Nevertheless, I am responsible for upholding, challenging, or transforming these norms. I am not merely causally determined by nature or norms but act in light of norms that I can challenge and transform. Even at the price of my biological survival, my material well-being, or my social standing, I can give my life for a principle to which I hold myself or for a cause in which I believe. This is what it means to lead a spiritual life. I must always live in relation to my irrevocable death—otherwise there would be nothing at stake in dedicating my life to anything.

Any form of spiritual life must therefore be animated by the anxiety of being mortal, even in the most profound fulfillment of our aspirations. Our anxiety before death is not reducible to a psychological condition that can or should be overcome. Rather, anxiety is a condition of intelligibility for leading a free life and being passionately committed. As long as our lives matter to us, we must be animated by the anxiety that our time is finite, since otherwise there would be no urgency in doing anything and being anyone.

Even if your project is to lead your life without psychological anxiety before death—for example by devoting yourself to Buddhist meditation—that project is intelligible only because you are anxious not to waste your life on being anxious before death. Only in light of the apprehension that we will die—that our lifetime is indefinite but finite—can we ask ourselves what we ought to do with our lives and put ourselves at stake in our activities. This is why all religious visions of eternity ultimately are visions of unfreedom. In the consummation of eternity, there would be no question of what we should do with our lives. We would be absorbed in bliss forever and thereby deprived of any possible agency. Rather than having a free relation to what we do and what we love, we would be compelled by necessity to enjoy it.

In contrast, we should recognize that we must be vulnerable— we must be marked by the suffering of pain, the mourning of loss, the anxiety before death—in order to lead our lives and care about one another. We can thereby acknowledge that our life together is our ultimate purpose. What we are missing is not eternal bliss but social and institutional forms that would enable us to lead flourishing lives. This is why the critique of religion must be accompanied by a critique of the existing forms of our life together. If we merely criticized religious notions of salvation—without seeking to overcome the forms of social injustice to which religions respond—the critique would be empty and patronizing. The task is to transform our social conditions in such a way that we can let go of the promise of salvation and recognize that everything depends on what we do with our finite time together. The heart of spiritual life is not the empty tranquility of eternal peace but the mutual recognition of our fragility and our freedom.

MARCH II, 2019

Can We Learn to Believe in God?

And what does *The Breakfast Club* have to do with it?

———————

Agnes Callard

*L*ET US WEIGH THE GAIN AND THE LOSS IN WAGERING THAT *God is. Let us estimate these two chances. If you gain, you gain all; if you lose, you lose nothing. Wager, then, without hesitation that He is.*

So runs Blaise Pascal's famous wager. His thought is simple: If there is a God, believing in him ensures an eternity of happiness, while denying him secures an eternity of suffering. If there is no God and you believe in him, the downside is relatively minimal. Even if the chance he exists is tiny, believing is the right bet.

This argument has produced few converts, as Pascal would not have been surprised to learn. He knew that people cannot change their beliefs at will. We can't muscle our mind into believing something we take to be false, not even when the upside is an eternity of happiness. Pascal's solution is that you start by pretending to believe: attend church, speak the prayers, adopt religious habits. If you walk and talk like a believer, eventually you'll come to think as one. He says, "This will naturally make you believe, and deaden your acuteness."

But many of us recoil at this suggestion. We don't want to lie to ourselves. Say there were a pill that would do the trick: Pop it in your mouth and you'll be a religious believer. Someone convinced by Pascal's argument—at least to the extent of thinking that believing is the best bet—might nonetheless refuse to take this pill. She might be repulsed by the thought of going behind her own back to acquire this belief.

Pascal seems to concede that trying to believe is a matter of wishful thinking, self-deception, or self-manipulation. He thinks we should do it anyway. But I think our hope of becoming better people—whether in respect of religion, friendship, or justice, or in any number of different ways—rests on the possibility that there is a more straightforward and less self-abasing way to try to believe.

Consider a thought experiment. Suppose you have a friend who doesn't get why people listen to music, read novels, or eat fine food. He watches (what you consider) trashy TV and has no ambitions as regards career or romance. Since the person I have described is someone you consider a Philistine, I'll call him Phil. He is not depressed or irresponsible: Phil takes his job seriously (though he has deliberately chosen an undemanding one). He loves his friends and family. You don't doubt that he is happy with what he has, but you think he could be much happier, overall, than he is.

So you attempt to broaden his horizons. You take him to national parks and fancy restaurants; you introduce him to potential romantic partners. Phil views your efforts with amusement and affection rather than with irritation. Nonetheless, he is unmoved. He finds prestige TV boring and camping uncomfortable; he has no interest in marriage or child-raising; he doesn't see why one wouldn't just eat rice and beans. You get frustrated with him, and you say, "You are not even trying!"

What do you want from Phil? You are not proposing that he pretend to like these things, nor that he trick himself into thinking that hiking or romance is better than he takes it to be. Rather, you want him to try to believe them to be more valuable than he currently has reason to, in order to learn their true value. When we try to believe in this sense—with a view to learning what we aim to believe—it is a rational, transparent means of belief acquisition. I call it aspirational faith.

Like many protagonists of thought experiments, Phil is idiosyncratic. What is strange about Phil is that he seems to have transitioned from childhood to adulthood without a radical change in his tastes, hobbies, or goals. For many of us, the teenage period sees the beginning of some of our lifelong passions: We start reading big novels, performing music, seeking romance, caring about our appearance, looking toward the prospect of a career. Lacking a complete grasp of the identity toward which she guides herself, the teenager must have faith in the person she's trying to become, and in what that person cares about. Otherwise she'll become trapped in childhood.

John Hughes's movie *The Breakfast Club* (1985) is a classic movie of its genre precisely because it captures this feature of the teenage experience. Five teenagers from different cliques ("a brain, an athlete, a basket case, a princess and a criminal") bond during enforced Saturday detention. Over the hours together, they discover a common humanity that transcends the social roles into which each had been slotted.

Having made themselves vulnerable to one another, they ask themselves, in the movie's climactic scene, whether they will acknowledge one another in school on Monday. Claire ("the princess") answers in the negative and is consequently accused by Bender ("the criminal") of being nothing more than what she initially seemed: "You just stick to the things that you know: shopping, nail polish, your father's BMW . . ." Claire in turn, accuses Bender of being unwilling to face the facts. She says, "I'm telling the truth." The eventual romantic resolution of this dispute—the two characters kiss—is a cinematic way of signaling that the correct attitude to their future lies somewhere in the middle.

Claire is wrong to be so cynical: If she believes that their association was merely temporary or convenient, then what has happened between them is insignificant and each character is truly trapped in his or her pigeonhole. Consider this line from the *New Yorker* critic Pauline Kael's correspondingly cynical review: "The movie is about a bunch of stereotypes who complain that other people see them as stereotypes." Kael is not wrong that the characters are stereotypes.

But the point of the movie is to give us a glimpse of them trying to be more than that.

Notice, however, that the antidote to cynicism cannot be Bender's naïve conviction that everything is different now. A person cannot, in a day, do the work needed to transcend years of internalized stereotyping. At the end of the movie, detention ends and the five teenagers part ways with a fragile, doubt-filled faith in the connections they have forged. They have tasted enough of the value of true friendship to know that they have not plumbed its depths and are therefore liable to ignore one another in the halls on Monday morning; their attitude toward the goods of friendship is not one of possession but one of aspiration.

Lacking the grounds to conclude that they will greet one another, they can nonetheless have aspirational faith—try to believe—that they will do so. The movie suggests that it is possible to see something in the prospect of stereotype-transcending friendship without taking oneself to have seen all that there is to see. What keeps aspirational faith honest is its provisional character, the aspirant's recognition that she still has a long way to go.

The problem with Pascal's wager is that it is a wager, and so the stakes are fixed in advance. Betting is about winning some value you are already aware of, not learning that there is something new out there to be valued. If you set out to acquire beliefs without learning, you are cheating: gaining epistemic ground without doing epistemic work. By contrast, in the cases of aspirational faith, coming to believe that, e.g., we will still be friends on Monday, is part and parcel of a bigger project of learning to become a different kind of person. The project is intellectual, involving a change in beliefs, but it is not only intellectual—and its intellectual character is inseparable from its affective and motivational character.

Pascal may have been making a related point, to the effect that the mind does not have a monopoly on wisdom, when he famously proclaimed that "the heart has its reasons, which reason does not know." But that sentiment, however beautifully expressed, leaves the crucial questions unanswered. Because suppose that Pascal is right, and someone's heart has reasons that her reason does not know. Do things have to stay that way? Couldn't her reason learn those reasons? And wouldn't that, in turn, be her heart's opportunity to grow?

JANUARY 8, 2018

XIII

NOW WHAT?

We're Doomed. Now What?

*Our human drive to make meaning is powerful
enough to turn nihilism against itself.*

Roy Scranton

T HE TIME WE'VE BEEN THROWN INTO IS ONE OF ALARMING AND bewildering change—the breakup of the post-1945 global order, a multispecies mass extinction, and the beginning of the end of civilization as we know it. Not one of us is innocent, not one of us is safe. The world groans under the weight of seven billion humans; every new birth adds another mouth hungry for food, another life greedy for energy.

We all see what's happening, we read it in the headlines every day, but seeing isn't believing, and believing isn't accepting. We respond according to our prejudices, acting out of instinct, reflex, and training. Right-wing denialists insist that climate change isn't happening, or that it's not caused by humans, or that the real problem is terrorism or refugees, while left-wing denialists insist that the problems are fixable, under our control, merely a matter of political will. Accelerationists argue that more technology is the answer. Incrementalists tell us to keep trusting the same institutions and leaders that have been failing us for decades. Activists say we have to fight, even if we're sure to lose.

Meanwhile, as the gap between the future we're entering and the future we once imagined grows ever wider, nihilism takes root in the shadow of our fear: If all is already lost, nothing matters anyway.

You can feel this nihilism in TV shows like *True Detective*, *The Leftovers*, *The Walking Dead*, and *Game of Thrones*, and you can see it in the rush to war, sectarianism, and racial hatred. It defines our current moment, though in truth it's nothing new. The Western world has been grappling with radical nihilism since at least the seventeenth century, when scientific insights into human behavior began to undermine religious belief. Philosophers have struggled since to fill the gap between fact and meaning: Kant tried to reconcile empiricist determinism with God and Reason; Bergson and Peirce worked to merge Darwinian evolution and human creativity; more recent thinkers glean the stripped furrows neuroscience has left to logic and language.

Scientific materialism, taken to its extreme, threatens us with meaninglessness; if consciousness is reducible to the brain and our actions are determined not by will but by causes, then our values and beliefs are merely rationalizations for the things we were going to do anyway. Most people find this view of human life repugnant, if not incomprehensible.

In her recent book of essays *The Givenness of Things*, Marilynne Robinson rejects the materialist view of consciousness, arguing for the existence of the human soul by insisting that the soul's metaphysical character makes it impervious to materialist arguments. The soul, writes Robinson, is an intuition that "cannot be dispelled by proving the soul's physicality, from which it is aloof by definition. And on these same grounds, its nonphysicality is no proof of its nonexistence."

The biologist E. O. Wilson spins the problem differently: "Does free will exist?" he asks in *The Meaning of Human Existence*. "Yes, if not in ultimate reality, then at least in the operational sense necessary for sanity and thereby for the perpetuation of the human species." Robinson offers an appeal to ignorance, Wilson an appeal to consequences; both arguments are fallacious.

Yet, as Wilson suggests, our dogged insistence on free agency makes a kind of evolutionary sense. Indeed, humanity's keenest evolutionary advantage has been its drive to create collective meaning. That drive is as ingenious as it is relentless, and it can find a way to make sense of despair, depression, catastrophe, genocide, war, disaster, plagues, and even the humiliations of science.

Our drive to make meaning is powerful enough even to turn nihilism against itself. As Friedrich Nietzsche, one of Western philosophy's most incisive diagnosticians of nihilism, wrote near the end of the nineteenth century: "Man will sooner will nothingness than not will." This dense aphorism builds on one of the thoughts at the core of Nietzsche's philosophy, today so widely accepted as to be almost unrecognizable, that human beings make their own meaning out of life.

In this view, there is no ultimate, transcendent moral truth—or, as Nietzsche put it in an early essay, "On Truth and Lies in a Nonmoral Sense," truth is no more than a "mobile army of metaphors, metonyms, and anthropomorphisms." If we can stomach the moral vertigo this idea might induce, we can also see how it's not necessarily nihilistic, but in the right light a testament, rather, to human resilience.

The human ability to make meaning is so versatile, so powerful, that it can make almost any existence tolerable, even a life of unending suffering, so long as that life is woven into a bigger story that makes it meaningful. Humans have survived and thrived in some of the most inhospitable environments on earth, from the deserts of Arabia to the ice fields of the Arctic, because of this ability to organize collective life around symbolic constellations of meaning: anirniq, capital, jihad. "If we have our own why in life," Nietzsche wrote, "we shall get along with almost any how."

When he wrote, "Man will sooner will nothingness than not will," Nietzsche was exposing the destructive side of humanity's meaning-making drive. That drive is so powerful, Nietzsche's saying, that when forced to the precipice of nihilism, we would choose meaningful self-annihilation over meaningless bare life. This insight was horrifically borne out in the Götterdämmerung of Nazi Germany, just as it's being borne out today in every new suicide attack by jihadi terrorists—even as it's being borne out here at home in our willfully destructive politics of rage. We risk it as we stumble toward another thoughtless war, asking young men and women to throw their lives away so we might continue believing America means something. As a character in Don DeLillo's novel *White Noise* put it: "War is the form nostalgia takes when men are hard-pressed to say something good about their country"—which is to see war as an active nihilism supplanting a passive one.

Nietzsche wasn't himself a nihilist. He developed his idea of truth as a "mobile army of metaphors" into a more complex philosophy of perspectivism, which conceived of subjective truth as a variety of constructions arising out of particular perspectives on objective reality. The more perspectives we learn to see from, the more truth we have access to. This is different from relativism, with which it's often confused, which says that all truth is relative and there is no objective reality. Fundamentally, Nietzsche was an empiricist who believed that beyond all of our interpretations there was, at last, something we can call the world—even if we can never quite apprehend it objectively. "Even great spirits have only their five fingers' breadth of experience," he writes. "Just beyond it their thinking ceases and their endless empty space and stupidity begins."

Nietzsche's positive philosophical project, what he called his "gay science," was to create the conditions for the possibility of a human being who could comprehend the meaninglessness of our drive to make meaning, yet nonetheless affirm human existence, a human being who could learn "amor fati," the love of one's fate: this was his much-misunderstood idea of the "overman." Nietzsche labored mightily to create this new human ideal for philosophy because he needed it so badly himself. A gloomy, sensitive pessimist and self-declared decadent who eventually went mad, he struggled all his life to convince himself that his life was worth living.

Today, as every hour brings new alarms of war and climate disaster, we might wish we could take Nietzsche's place. He had to cope only with the death of God, after all, while we must come to terms with the death of our world. Peril lurks on every side, from the delusions of hope to the fury of reaction, from the despondency of hopelessness to the promise of destruction.

We stand today on a precipice of annihilation that Nietzsche could not have even imagined. There is little reason to hope that we'll be able to slow down global warming before we pass a tipping point. We're already one degree Celsius above preindustrial temperatures and there's another half a degree baked in. The West Antarctic ice sheet is collapsing, Greenland is melting, permafrost across the world is liquefying, and methane has been detected leaking from seafloors and Siberian craters: it's probably already too late to stop these feedbacks, which means it's probably already too late to stop apocalyptic planetary warming. Meanwhile the world slides into hate-filled, bloody havoc, like the last act of a particularly ugly Shakespearean tragedy.

Accepting our situation could easily be confused with nihilism. In a nation founded on hope, built with "can do" Yankee grit, and bedazzled by its own technological wizardry, the very idea that something might be beyond our power or that humans have intrinsic limits verges on blasphemy. Right and left, millions of Americans believe that every problem has a solution; suggesting otherwise stirs a deep and often hostile resistance. It's not so much that accepting the truth of our situation means thinking the wrong thought, but rather thinking the unthinkable.

Yet it's at just this moment of crisis that our human drive to make meaning reappears as our only salvation . . . if we're willing to reflect consciously on the ways we make life meaningful—on how we decide what is good, what our goals are, what's worth living or dying for, and what we do every day, day-to-day, and how we do it. Because if it's true that we make our lives meaningful ourselves and not through revealed wisdom handed down by God or the Market or History, then it's also true that we hold within ourselves the power to change our lives—wholly, utterly—by changing what our lives mean. Our drive to make meaning is more powerful than oil, the atom, and the market, and it's up to us to harness that power to secure the future of the human species.

We can't do it by clinging to the progressivist, profit-seeking, technology-can-fix-it ideology of fossil-fueled capitalism. We can't do it by trying to control the future. We need to learn to let our current civilization die, to accept our mortality, and practice humility. We need to work together to transform a global order of meaning focused on accumulation into a new order of meaning that knows the value of limits, transience, and restraint.

Most important, we need to give up defending and protecting our truth, our perspective, our Western values, and understand that truth is found not in one perspective but in their multiplication, not in one point of view but in the aggregate, not in opposition but in the whole. We need to learn to see not just with Western eyes but with Islamic eyes and Inuit eyes, not just with human eyes but with golden-cheeked warbler eyes, coho salmon eyes, and polar bear eyes, and not even just with eyes at all but with the wild, barely articulate being of clouds and seas and rocks and trees and stars.

We were born on the eve of what may be the human world's greatest catastrophe. None of us chose this, not deliberately. None of us can choose to avoid it either. Some of us will even live through it. What meaning we pass on to the future will depend on how well we remember those who have come before us, how wisely and how gently we're able to shed the ruinous way of life that's destroying us today, and how consciously we're able to affirm our role as creators of our fated future.

Accepting the fatality of our situation isn't nihilism, but rather the necessary first step in forging a new way of life. Between self-destruction and giving up, between willing nothingness and not willing, there is another choice: Willing our fate. Conscious self-creation. We owe it to the generations whose futures we've burned and wasted to build a bridge, to be a bridge, to connect the diverse human traditions of meaning-making in our past to those survivors, children of the Anthropocene, who will build a new world among our ruins.

Are We the Cows of the Future?

The pastures of digital dictatorship—crowded conditions,
mass surveillance, virtual reality—are already here.

Esther Leslie

T HERE WAS A MOMENT, IN THE EARLY DAYS OF THE PANDEMIC, when reports surfaced here and there of improvements in air and water quality across the world, as production and traffic abruptly diminished. Images circulated of herds of mountain goats and wild boars exploring deserted city streets and schools of dolphins exuberant in the Bosporus. Some were hoaxes, but all spoke momentarily to the idea that the disruption that had come from some sort of imbalance in human-animal relations could result in a rerighting in favor of nature.

In these hopes, nature was made to play a familiar role: as a haven to guarantee human well-being. Utopian thinking is full of this fantasy. The Hyperboreans of Greek legend, for example, led a perfect existence beyond the north winds in a permanent spring, and the denizens of Thomas More's *Utopia* "cultivate their gardens with great care so that they have both vines, fruits, herbs, and flowers in them." Later, William Morris drew nature—made almost palpable on the walls on well-furnished parlors—into his utopian counterimagining of the factories of industrial society. Today's utopians, dreaming of shopping malls turned into wetlands, are similar in spirit.

In this view, nature guarantees cyclicality, reproduction, and predictability, unlike history, with its contingency, its sudden twists and turns. But this is an illusion. Nature, of course, is very much subject to history; what seemed more or less eternal is now undergoing extinction, unstoppable melting. Nature is not settled and permanent, but always in flux. It is not something separate from humans, reliably ready to soothe our woes and restore our spirits. It is rather entangled in the web and substance of humanity, its helter-skelter activity, its ceaseless pursuits.

Human intervention in plant and animal life, for example, is legion. Take cattle. Cows' bodies have historically served as test subjects—laboratories of future bio-intervention and all sorts of reproductive technologies. Today cows crowd together in megafarms, overseen by digital systems, including facial- and hide-recognition systems. These new factories are air-conditioned sheds where digital machinery monitors and logs the herd's every move, emission, and production. Every mouthful of milk can be traced to its source.

And it goes beyond monitoring. In 2019 on the RusMoloko research farm near Moscow, virtual reality headsets were strapped onto cattle. The cows were led, through the digital animation that played before their eyes, to imagine they were wandering in bright summer fields, not bleak wintry ones. The innovation, which was apparently successful, is designed to ward off stress: The calmer the cow, the higher the milk yield.

A cow sporting VR goggles is comedic as much as it is tragic. There's horror too in that it may foretell our own alienated futures. After all, how different is our experience? We submit to emotion trackers. We log in to biofeedback machines. We sign up for tracking and tracing. We let advertisers' eyes watch us constantly and mappers store our coordinates.

Could we, like cows, be played by the machinery, our emotions swayed under ever-sunny skies, without us even knowing that we are inside the matrix? Will the rejected, unemployed, and redundant be deluded into thinking that the world is beautiful, a land of milk and honey, as they interact minimally in stripped-back care homes? We may soon graze in the new pastures of digital dictatorship, frolicking while bound.

The notion of nature as something external, benevolent, and consolatory might be part of the problem. Theodor Adorno, the great German philosopher and cultural critic of the mid–twentieth century, observes in *Aesthetic Theory* how nature that has evaded human cultivation—alpine moraines or moonscapes—resembles the unnatural forms of industrial waste mountains and is just as terrifying.

For Adorno, idyllic nature, pristine, pretty, has more to do with oppressive sexual morality than with what nature is or can be. Against the insistence that nature should not be ravished by technology, he argues that perhaps technology could enable nature to get what "it wants" on this sad earth. And we are included in that "it."

Nature, in truth, is not just something external on which we work, but also within us. We too are nature. "My tears well up," wrote the German Romantic poet Johann Wolfgang von Goethe. "Earth, I am returning to you." Adorno took our overawed sensations when confronted with the magnitude of untamed nature as a signal of an awareness of our natural essence. The sublime—whether encountered in the world or in art—provokes in us tears, shudders, and overwhelming feeling. Our ego is reminded of its affinities with the natural realm. In our collapses into blubbering wrecks, eyes wide and wet, we become simultaneously most human and most natural.

For someone associated with the abstruseness of avant-garde music and critical theory, Adorno was surprisingly sentimental when it came to animals—for which he felt a powerful affinity. It is with them that he finds something worthy of the name Utopia. He imagines a properly human existence of doing nothing, like a beast, resting, cloud gazing, mindlessly and placidly chewing cud.

To dream, as so many Utopians do, of boundless production of goods, of busy activity in the ideal society, reflects, Adorno claimed, an ingrained mentality of production as an end in itself. To detach from our historical form adapted solely to production, to work against work itself, to do nothing in a true society in which we embrace nature and ourselves as natural, might deliver us to freedom.

Rejecting the notion of nature as something that would protect us, give us solace, reveals us to be inextricably within and of nature. From there, we might begin to save ourselves—along with everything else.

JANUARY 5, 2021

A Utopia for a Dystopian Age

Our impulse to imagine better worlds has nearly
been extinguished. But we desperately need
a new vision of inhabiting the planet.

Espen Hammer

THE TERM "UTOPIA" WAS COINED FIVE HUNDRED YEARS AGO.
By conjoining the Greek adverb "ou" ("not") and the noun "topos"
("place") the English humanist and politician Thomas More conceived of a place that is not—literally a "nowhere" or "noplace." More's
learned readers would also have recognized another pun. The pro-
nunciation of "utopia" can just as well be associated with "eu-topos,"
which in Greek means "happy place." Happiness, More might have
suggested, is something we can only imagine. And yet imagining it,
as philosophers, artists, and politicians have done ever since, is far
from pointless.

More was no doubt a joker. *Utopia*, his fictional travelogue about
an island of plenty and equality, is told by a character whose name,
Hythloday, yet another playful conjoining of Greek words, signifies
something like "nonsense peddler." Although More comes across as
being quite fond of his noplace, he occasionally interrupts the narrative by warning against the islanders' rejection of private property. Living under the reign of the autocratic Henry VIII, and being
a prominent social figure, More might not have wanted to rock the
boat too much.

Precisely that—rocking the boat—has, however, been the underlying aim of the great utopias that have shaped Western culture. It has animated and informed progressive thinking, providing direction and a sense of purpose to struggles for social change and emancipation. From the vantage point of the utopian imagination, history—that gushing river of seemingly contingent micro-events—has taken on meaning, becoming a steadfast movement toward the sought-for condition supposedly able to justify all previous striving and suffering.

Utopianism can be dreamy in a John Lennon "Imagine"-esque way. Yet it has also been ready to intervene and bring about concrete transformation.

Utopias come in different forms. Utopias of desire, as in Hieronymus Bosch's painting *The Garden of Earthly Delights*, focus on happiness, tying it to the satisfaction of needs. Such utopias, demanding the complete alleviation of pain and sometimes glorious spaces of enjoyment and pleasure, tend, at least in modern times, to rely on technology. The utopias of technology see social, bodily, and environmental ills as requiring technological solutions. We know such solutions all too well: ambitious city-planning schemes and robotics as well as dreams of cosmic expansion and immortality.

The utopias of justice are perhaps even more familiar. Asking, typically, for great personal sacrifice, these utopias call for the abolition of all social injustice. While the French Revolution had its fair share of such visions, they reached an apotheosis in twentieth century Marxist politics. Despite his own personal rejection of utopianism, Lenin, high on his pedestal addressing workers in October 1917, came to be the embodiment of all three forms of utopia. At the heart of the Soviet vision there were always those burning eyes gazing intently, and with total confidence, toward the promised land.

Today, the utopian impulse seems almost extinguished. The utopias of desire make little sense in a world overrun by cheap entertainment, unbridled consumerism, and narcissistic behavior. The utopias of technology are less impressive than ever now that—after Hiroshima and Chernobyl—we are fully aware of the destructive potential of technology. Even the internet, perhaps the most recent candidate for technological optimism, turns out to have a number of potentially disastrous consequences, among them a widespread disregard for truth and objectivity, as well as an immense increase in the capacity for surveillance. The utopias of justice seem largely to have been eviscerated by twentieth century totalitarianism. After the Gulag Archipelago, the Khmer Rouge's killing fields, and the Cultural Revolution, these utopias seem both philosophically and politically dead.

The great irony of all forms of utopianism can hardly escape us. They say one thing, but when we attempt to realize them they seem to imply something entirely different. Their demand for perfection in all things human is often pitched at such a high level that they come across as aggressive and ultimately destructive. Their rejection of the past, and of established practice, is subject to its own logic of brutality.

And not only has the utopian imagination been stung by its own failures, it has also had to face up to the two fundamental dystopias of our time: those of ecological collapse and thermonuclear warfare. The utopian imagination thrives on challenges. Yet these are not challenges but chillingly realistic scenarios of utter destruction and the eventual elimination of the human species. Add to that the profoundly anti-utopian nature of the right-wing movements that have sprung up in the United States and Europe and the prospects for any kind of meaningful utopianism may seem bleak indeed. In matters social and political, we seem doomed if not to cynicism, then at least to a certain coolheadedness.

Anti-utopianism may, as in much recent liberalism, call for controlled, incremental change. The main task of government, Barack Obama ended up saying, is to avoid doing stupid stuff. However, anti-utopianism may also become atavistic and beckon us to return, regardless of any cost, to an idealized past. In such cases, the utopian narrative gets replaced by myth. And while the utopian narrative is universalistic and future-oriented, myth is particularistic and backward-looking. Myths purport to tell the story of us, our origin and of what it is that truly matters for us. Exclusion is part of their nature.

Can utopianism be rescued? Should it be? To many people the answer to both questions is a resounding no.

There are reasons, however, to think that a fully modern society cannot do without a utopian consciousness. To be modern is to be oriented toward the future. It is to be open to change, even radical change, when called for. With its willingness to ride roughshod over all established certainties and ways of life, classical utopianism was too grandiose, too rationalist, and ultimately too cold. We need the ability to look beyond the present. But we also need More's insistence on playfulness. Once utopias are embodied in ideologies, they become dangerous and even deadly. So why not think of them as thought experiments? They point us in a certain direction. They may even provide some kind of purpose to our strivings as citizens and political beings.

We also need to be more careful about what it is that might preoccupy our utopian imagination. In my view, only one candidate is today left standing. That candidate is nature and the relation we have to it. More's island was an earthly paradise of plenty. No amount of human intervention would ever exhaust its resources. We know better. As the climate is rapidly changing and the species extinction rate reaches unprecedented levels, we desperately need to conceive of alternative ways of inhabiting the planet.

Are our industrial, capitalist societies able to make the requisite changes? If not, where should we be headed? This is a utopian question as good as any. It is deep and universalistic. Yet it calls for neither a break with the past nor a headfirst dive into the future. The German thinker Ernst Bloch argued that all utopias ultimately express yearning for a reconciliation with that from which one has been estranged. They tell us how to get back home. A twenty-first century utopia of nature would do that. It would remind us that we belong to nature, that we are dependent on it, and that further alienation from it will be at our own peril.

JUNE 26, 2017

The Courage to Be Alone

On our daily walks together, my young daughter
and I begin to navigate a new reality.

Megan Craig

MY YOUNGEST DAUGHTER HAS TOLD ME THAT ANNABELLE, her baby doll, might have the coronavirus. We talk about it as we take a daily walk up the road. She's not sure yet whether it is diabetes or the virus. Annabelle's symptoms vary, but she has not left the small cradle by the side of my daughter's bed in days. I have been told I can babysit for Annabelle, but only if I promise to hold her gently and not give her candy. My daughter holds my hand as we walk. She wants to talk about her doll's sickness every day. Not surprisingly, she's not sure when or if Annabelle will get a test.

I ask whether she's anxious about Annabelle. She says not really. She thinks she will recover and maybe just needs a shot. We walk on in the sloppy spring snow. The days are getting longer and the walks are getting longer, our conversation looping like piles of old garden hose.

In addition to Annabelle, we have talked about rocks and crystals and a pretend set of sisters (of which she, my youngest, is the oldest). One of the sisters is pregnant and one is traveling in Europe. My daughter tells me that she is married and her husband is a "good guy" but has left that morning by plane for Florida. He is apparently a reporter in Sanibel. We pick up some rocks and put them in our pockets. Later I will have to give her my hat to hold all her treasures, and later still, I will put my cold hands in my pockets and find dirt.

I have told her that her grandpa has cancer, a surprise to her. It's not serious, I say, and that sounds insane. I clarify that it's the best form of cancer one could possibly hope for—a highly inactive form of leukemia. She is now nodding at me in the same way I nodded at her before.

We are walking along a path made of wood chips. It cuts through the forest along lines created by fallen oaks in a tornado that ripped through Connecticut in May of 2018. That spring I came to this same place and sat among the shattered trees. Many of the trunks exploded eight or ten feet up from the ground in the shape of splattered palms. Others lay prone in piles. Several split in the middle, leaving gaping shapes that framed the disaster like keyholes into a broken world. Now the area is clear and open and flooded with sun.

While we walk, I have to remind my daughter to keep moving. The faster she talks, the slower she goes. I am trying to listen to her, but half of my mind is thinking about other things. If I am quiet for too long, she tugs at my hand, pulling me back into conversation. It is hard to keep in focus the reality of her mittened fingers and the reality of the world at once, both of them vying for my attention.

Suddenly I am reminded of William James's essay "On a Certain Blindness in Human Beings," in which he writes about the difficulty of being present to another person's life. James uses a Robert Louis Stevenson story of young boys who form a secret club of "lantern bearers," hiding small tin lanterns under their heavy coats as a secret emblem of participation. From the outside they look just like anyone else hurrying by in the cold night. But when they meet one another, they lift the edge of their coats to reveal a hot burning light hanging from a belt loop. I have always loved the image of these kids hiding fire, their faces momentarily illuminated to one another in lamplight, triumphant in their allegiance to the game.

James was writing about how hard it is to see someone else's inner light—the thing that keeps them illuminated in dark times—especially when we are fixated on our own lives. We pass one another, intent on ourselves and our own problems, never imagining the burning fire under the dark coat.

I am thinking about James and remembering being in Italy last summer, watching the lights across the valley in Assisi coming on in a dotted dance as the sun went down, a smatter of earthly stars. And then I try to recall something the philosopher Emmanuel Levinas wrote in an essay after the Holocaust, something about how difficult it would be to teach children born after the war the lessons they would need, and especially, the strength required to survive in isolation. I would like to hold that text and read it again. It was written in French but called "Nameless" in the English translation.

We are cresting a small hill and my daughter suddenly sits down. She is hungry and tired and doesn't want to walk anymore. I sit beside her, still wondering about what Levinas said. It was something about the courage required to be alone, about a fragile consciousness, and the importance of the inner life. Yes, that was it. The lanterns shining under the coats of those young boys, the rocks in our pockets, the inner life that cannot be seen or guessed or known from the outside and that therefore cannot be so easily extinguished or taken away. The inner life that kept Levinas alive after being captured by the Nazis and sent to a prison camp in France in 1940, separated from his wife and daughter, apart from the world. Something secret to hold on to that cannot perish or crack or fall, something private and still at the core of a life.

As we sit at the edge of the trail, the snow glints and I think of those across the globe who are dying alone in rooms closed off to the outside, left with their inner lives, tending their own fires. Snow is falling slowly in fat flakes. The ground is cold, even as daffodils have pushed up early this year. We may look for a Jack-in-the-Pulpit later today, hoping to find the purple and green leaf curled around the tiny white spadix, nestled there like a prayer.

All is quiet in the woods except for the clatter of a woodpecker somewhere nearby. As if answering the rhythm, bits of songs begin replaying in my head, linking together the inner life and the weak lights—the duo September 67: "you once called me a lantern . . .";

Nick Drake: "The sun went down and the crowd went home, I was left by the roadside all alone, I turned to speak as they went by, but this was the time of no reply"; Leonard Cohen: "Hold on, hold on my brother, my sister hold on tight. I've finally got my orders, and I'll be marching through the morning, marching through the night, moving through the borders of my secret life." I am inadvertently humming the tune when I hear her say, "Mom, stop it."

We are walking again, a little stiff and grumpy, ready to be home. I am listening to something about another baby doll. This one is named Zoe. She is having a birthday party later and I am invited. Annabelle is too sick to attend. We talk about the decorations and the cake. Now we are picking up speed, discussing the guest list and games, coming down the hill in the sharp wind. To simply reply as if this is what matters is the best I can do. It is her world and these are her tiny lights, her babies tucked in their beds, the rocks and crystals in her fists, all of it fiercely real and important as the world seems to fall apart around us.

Someday, if she finds herself in isolation and I am not there, she will have her own songs and some courage based in these walks and this circuitous make-believe (as good as any philosophy), a rhythm of talking and walking etched in her memory to repeat on her own, an inner life rich with voices and creatures and the remembered pressure of our hands. I hope so. Her grip suddenly drops mine as she begins to run toward home. We are learning together how to be alone.

MAY I, 2020

In Dark Times, "Dirty Hands" Can Still Do Good

To transcend our complicity in the world's worst
crises, we need self-knowledge and humility.

John Kaag and Clancy Martin

MEET HELEN, A MIDDLE-AGED WOMAN NEWLY DEVOTED TO Tibetan Buddhism, living in the American Midwest. She has recently taken a vow to limit and alleviate suffering in the world. She thinks one way to do this is to make a pilgrimage to Taktsang Monastery, or the Tiger Nest, in the mountains of Bhutan, to receive rare and precious teachings that will spiritually prepare her for her life of compassionate action. According to legend, the eighth century Buddhist master Guru Rinpoche flew to this location from Tibet on the back of a tigress, but Helen takes a 737 from Kansas City, Missouri.

The fossil fuels burned on this trip damage the natural environment; the food that Helen eats on the plane is prepared by underpaid workers and supports industrial agriculture; the clothes she wears and the seats she sits on were made in sweatshops; the airline itself is part of an enormous multinational conglomerate.

You get the point: Even what we see as our most high-minded and noble journeys can perpetuate the destructive forces that we hope to escape. In the words of the American Transcendentalist Ralph Waldo Emerson, "My giant goes with me wherever I go." Helen's actions, though well-intentioned, hover between hypocrisy and self-defeat.

But perhaps we shouldn't be so quick to judge Helen. We live in an age of deep complicity—and not just the political sort. The world's most pressing problems are global—poverty, hunger, environmental decimation, and warming—and implicate us all. To a greater or lesser extent, and often with the best intentions, we have done our part in contributing to the mess.

Seen this way, then, Helen's complicity is not necessarily her fault. Helen did not create the circumstances in which she finds herself: it is impractical, next to impossible, and probably undesirable, for Helen to find another way to Bhutan and her Buddhist goals. If she is to be a Buddhist in any sense, however, she must find a way to work through the complicity that remains the fact of the matter.

This is not unlike what Western ethicists call the "problem of dirty hands": the difficulty of tidying up the world's atrocities with hands that can never be washed clean, and may get dirtier in the process. "You can't fix the system from the outside . . ." is how this kind of complicity is normally sold to someone who is being drawn into what C. S. Lewis derided as "The Inner Ring," the place of morally inappropriate compromise.

What should we make, then, of this situation that many of us find ourselves in today, perhaps especially we Americans? What is a person to do when she is at least partly responsible for the evils she would like to escape, reduce, or remedy? What if our desire to do good in the world is tainted by our own harmful actions? Is it possible to act morally or maintain spiritual traditions in a broken world?

These are not, of course, new questions. And certainly not new to Buddhist practitioners. They were of great concern in particular to the thirteenth century Japanese master Shinran, the founder of the Jodo Shinshu sect. Master Shinran believed he lived in what is known in Buddhist cosmology as the Age of Dharma Decline, a period, not unlike our own, when traditional forms of spiritual cultivation were on the brink of collapse. Shinran is famous for suggesting that the way to respond to "dirty" times—of social and spiritual dissolution and decay—is to cultivate a path to the Pure Land, a simple pristine faith in Amitabha Buddha.

While the object of faith may be pristine, however, Shinran taught that the way to the Pure Land wasn't, and still isn't, pure at all. On his account, we can both be complicit and hold ourselves responsible for trying to make a difference. This is a lesson particularly suited to degenerate times. Pure Land Buddhism does not want us to give up our moral lives, but to give up the pretensions that often accompany them. It believes in very modest forms of moral improvement, eked out over the life of individuals and their communities, especially when they are largely flawed.

Shin Buddhism responded very directly to the problem of inevitable and thoroughgoing complicity. Unlike the more traditional Buddhists Dogen and Honen—two closely related teachers—Shinran was never able to shake the sense that he was, from the start, unable to fulfill the duties and ideals of monastic life; he was simply too botched. In the past, salvation might have been achieved by good works or karmic progress, but, according to the Buddhist cosmology to which Shinran adhered, this time was long gone. It is precisely where he failed, however, that he succeeded as a teacher. The pain of self-understanding (that he wasn't suited for the priesthood) passed seamlessly into self-critique, and, ultimately, into a form of confession that remains unique in Buddhist teaching today. His suggestion is clear: Salvation may turn on pure faith, but sincere faith turns on the constant acknowledgment of unavoidable imperfection.

Shinran writes: "Each of us in outward bearing makes a show of being wise, good, and dedicated. But so great are our greed, anger, perversity and conceit that we are filled with all forms of malice and cunning." This is the sort of admission that many spiritual seekers (and, for that matter, angry, self-righteous moralists or politicians) don't want to hear. It suggests that there is no transcendent escape, that, in Shinran's words "hell is my permanent abode, my house." To be clear, this admission is not spoken from a place of despair or a certain type of quietism; it is, instead, a brave realism about the human condition that is clear-eyed about the realities of moral and spiritual development.

Alexis Shotwell, a Canadian sociologist and philosopher whose recent book *Against Purity* resonates with strains of Jodo Shinshu, writes that "what's needed, instead of a pretense to purity that is impossible in the actually existing world, is something else. We need to shape better practices of responsibility and memory for our placement in relation to the past, our implication in the present and our potential creation of different futures." Aiming for individual purity, Shotwell says, echoing the ancient sage, is counterproductive. When we do, she argues, we become solipsistic, narcissistic, and self-focused.

When one bathes, or meditates, or hikes, or works out, or eats—one typically does so, at least in the West, by oneself. It is my naturally harvested luffa sponge, my thoughts to control and my mind to clear, my three-hundred-dollar alpine boots, my home gym, my cucumber-on-sprouted-bread sandwich, my quest for perfection. And decidedly not yours. Part of the problem, Shinran believes, is that each of us actually thinks we know the way to purity and enlightenment. Each of us thinks we can get there by ourselves. He is quite clear on this point: We don't have a clue how to achieve salvation. "I know nothing at all of good and evil," Shinran admits, ". . . with a foolish being full of blind passions—in this burning house—all matters without exception are empty and false."

This is what Western philosophers term "epistemic humility"—a deep Socratic sense that one knows that he or she doesn't know. For Shinran, this is a pivotal form of spiritual prostration—a laying low of the last vestiges of selfhood. Everything in human existence is equally meaningful or meaningless, take your pick.

In being "against purity"—in knowing "nothing at all about good and evil"—Shinran also stood against the standard way that most Buddhists of his day understood themselves and enlightenment. He was neither a monk nor a layperson, and didn't fit in anywhere. Traditional teachers called him a fool or a heretic, and upon being exiled to the remote province of Echigo, Shinran embraced his outsider status, assuming the name Gutoku—"the stubble-faced idiot." There are stubble-faced idiots who don't know they are stubble-faced idiots, and there are those who do. These idiots—the ones with self-knowledge, like Shinran—might be better equipped to mitigate the effects of their idiocy.

Some Buddhists worry that Pure Land Buddhism takes the dharma too far in the direction of resignation away from the world in favor of faith. But resignation has its virtues. It means that you might have the chance to get over yourself and consider the power and vulnerability of something else. Resignation is not regarded as a virtue in our society, but perhaps it should be. Perhaps knowing when to let go, when to relinquish control, when to free ourselves from the habits of thought that so often constrain us—maybe this is true prudence, what many ancient sages regarded as the virtue of virtues.

There is no habit of thought that is as pervasive as the aspiration to purity and perfection, but we suspect, along with Shotwell and Shinran, that it is almost always self-defeating. It comes as no surprise that the greatest champions of purity and perfection among us are revealed as the most flagrant hypocrites. Until we confront our complicity, we can never improve ourselves or the moral and spiritual circumstances we inhabit and help to create. It is high time to make our home in the "impure land." After all, it is where most of us already live.

DECEMBER 4, 2017

What Would David Bowie Do?

Five years after his death, the dystopian world
that his music describes seems closer than ever.
But maybe he can show us a way out of it.

Simon Critchley

E VERYTHING WENT TO PIECES AFTER DAVID BOWIE DIED.
It's been five years since his death was announced. I won't catalog
the catastrophes that have befallen us since that blank, cold January
in 2016. You know them all too well. Brexit, it turns out, was just a
minor warm-up act from out of town playing its first gig.

It does feel as though things began to fall apart with Bowie's
death. World events slid from bad to worse, and from there it has all
been one long downhill slalom that has exceeded the bounds of sense
(and even satire) and avalanched into this: hateful violence, political chaos, insurrection, and the grinding gruesomeness of the pandemic present. One million poor souls dead.

But before we get into that, let's cast our minds back five years.

It is unclear what counts as a good death, but at least Bowie left
us on his own terms. All that was made public of his death was the
barest of facts on Facebook. And rightly. It was a death in absolute
privacy with dignity intact, unsullied by tawdry details and gossip.

This is rarely the fate of our cultural heroes. Just think of Prince,
who was to the 1980s what Bowie was to the 1970s (cosmic twins channeling the spirit of Little Richard from the 1950s). With most great art-

ists, there is a falling off or a falling apart, a tailing off in the quality of their work, and often their death feels beneath them: a final indignity.

Bowie's death was something else. It came just after his final album of new material, *Blackstar*, released on January 8, 2016, his sixty-ninth birthday. A birth and death separated by forty-eight hours. Like Christ, in reverse.

I had been listening to *Blackstar* obsessively in the two days after its release and talking about it with friends. But with the news of his death we heard *Blackstar* differently, closer to its true intention: It was a farewell message to his fans. Bowie's was a death in the form of art, which was exactly what he wanted. "Ain't that just like me?" he sings at the end of "Lazarus," a song I still find very painful to listen to.

At its best, music is able to summon a feeling, which can be a joy, but it can also be the expression of an inchoate background fear, sadness, or yearning desire, which is deeper than cognition, concepts, or consciousness. With Bowie, it is often all these feelings at once. Music can somehow hold that emotion and hold us there for that moment. And we are the music for as long as it lasts.

Looking now at the video for "Lazarus," with its Button Eyes character, head wrapped in gauze, that Bowie concocted with the artist Johan Renck, it seems clear what Bowie is trying to show us: his true self, dying but addressing us with exhilarating, indeed breathless passion.

My mother, Sheila, died in England a month before Bowie, on December 5, 2015. Five years. I was holding her hand tightly when she died. In the minutes, hours, days, and weeks that followed, I felt that time had stopped. Stopped its flow, its movement, its diurnal and nocturnal round. Time was somehow sticking to me and would not budge. I had lost the knack of making time move.

Her death made no sense to me, other than as a brute datum. I could speak of it only in platitudes and banalities. But Bowie's death some five weeks later somehow enabled me think about my mother through speaking about Bowie. This was fitting, as she had bought "Starman" as a seven-inch single in 1972 and fostered my early fandom. My grief for him and the release of talking with friends and strangers, some strangers who became friends, opened up the possibility of giving some meaning to my mother's death. Time began to move again. But it still sticks and clings when I think of her and listen to him. I don't think I am alone in having such experiences.

I recall how perfectly New York City played itself those dolorous dollar days after Bowie's death. There were vigils and flower shrines near his apartment building on Lafayette Street. There were Ziggy and Aladdin Sane murals and graffiti. People somehow knew what to do without being told to do it.

I mostly remember walking around in the East Village and closer to home, in Brooklyn. It was beautiful. Every bar seemed to have its doors open and Bowie's music poured into the streets. It seems bizarre to think now of bars full of people, listening to music and having a good time, sad but happy to grieve together.

I had written a little fan book on Bowie in 2014 and some people wanted to talk to me. People of different ages, places, genders, with a common love of Bowie's music. In fact, I talked to lots of random people in those weeks and months. Frankly, I would talk to anyone. Mine was a mouth made manic after silent grief.

Caring for pop music as I do and thinking of it as the primary way the world has opened up to young and not so young people for so many decades now, I had long worried how music like Bowie's would survive and whether it would form part of a differentiated and deep canon of culture. I have absolutely no doubt on that score anymore.

Whether you watched Bowie's breakthrough performance of "Starman" on BBC's *Top of the Pops* in July 1972 (I saw it on TV with my mum) simply doesn't matter. Bowie will live on for as long as there are people who feel that they don't really fit in the world, who feel that they somehow just fell to earth.

These are the people that R. D. Laing in *The Divided Self* (a favorite book of Bowie's) called the "ontologically insecure," those people with eccentric minds, for whom autonomy is not a fact, but a question, a search, a cry in the darkness, a sheer struggle to survive. Such people seem to be more numerous than ever. And more desirous than ever for the sad, sweet melancholy of music, which connects us like droplets of water across vast digital deserts.

Five years. Where are we now?

The first track on Bowie's 1972 album *The Rise and Fall of Ziggy Stardust and the Spiders from Mars* is called "Five Years." It sets an apocalyptic scene: The news has just come over that earth is dying and we have five years left to cry in. The narrator responds by pushing toward an experience of sensory overload, hearing and seeing everything at once until his "brain hurt like a warehouse, it had no room to spare." Everybody, all the fat-skinny people and the tall-short people, have to be somehow crammed inside his head.

And then things begin to get really odd: A girl hits some tiny children, a soldier with a broken arm fixes his stare at the wheels of a Cadillac, a cop kneels and kisses the feet of a priest. Then this:

> *And it was cold and it rained I felt like an actor*

Somehow, the overwhelming immediacy of the knowledge of the end of the world induces a feeling of unreality and isolation, the impression of the world as a film set and oneself as an actor in a movie. It is as if too much reality leads to depersonalization, the sense of living an illusion.

To Bowiephiles, this scenario is familiar, cropping up in countless songs over the half century that separates "Space Oddity" from "I Can't Give Everything Away," the last track on *Blackstar*. But it is perhaps most pronounced in the album *Diamond Dogs* from 1974, which was originally intended to be a musical based on Orwell's *1984*, another of Bowie's favorite books. *Diamond Dogs* begins with Bowie reciting "Future Legend," where a city not at all unlike Manhattan has become Hunger City. All social order has collapsed and crowds of Burroughs-like Wild Boys roam a destroyed landscape, where

> *Fleas the size of rats sucked on rats the size of cats*
> *And 10,000 peoploids split into small tribes*

And then, sliding into the title track, Bowie screams. A Stones-like guitar riff locks in and away we go.

But the track on *Diamond Dogs* that best reflects where we are now is "Candidate," which again presents a destroyed world that has faded into cinematic illusion:

> *My set is amazing . . .*
> *There's a bar at the end where I can meet you and your friend.*

In such a world of trumpery, in an unreal city, a candidate appears and says, "I'll make you a deal." With the fading of the ideal, everything becomes a deal.

Five years after Bowie's death, the dystopian world that his music describes seems closer than ever. The total sensory overload of the world, the intolerable pressure of reality, induces in us a feeling of unreality, of fakery, of deals and steals. The felt fragility of identity leads us to withdraw from the world into isolation, to a lonely place peopled only by virtual others, avatars and caricatures. Conspiracies compete to fill the vacuum of sense.

The only way we can survive in the face of this world is by retreating from it into our own private lockdowns and peering out suspiciously through windows and screens, feeling lonely and yearning for love. One might think that it is a world in which Bowie would have rather felt at home.

But Bowie would not have felt in any way sanguine or vindicated. Against the dead illusion, decayed reality, and vile bodies there is always the countermovement of imagination, pushing back against an unreal reality. There is Bowie's scintillating, permissive intelligence that speaks to us in our aloneness and reaches out to touch our aliveness. All we have to do is listen and give him our hands. As he says in "Rock 'n' Roll Suicide": You're not alone. You're wonderful.

JANUARY 9, 2021

ACKNOWLEDGMENTS

W E ARE GRATEFUL TO THE EDITORS OF THE NEW YORK TIMES Opinion section who generously gave The Stone a home for nearly 12 years; to Alex Ward and Caroline Que of the *Times*' licensing and book division who supported us and paved the way for all three Stone anthologies; to Anita Patil, Armando Arrieta, and Ian Carlino, at the *Times*' licensing division, who developed The Stone spinoff project The Big Ideas, where several of this book's essays originated; to the team at Liveright, led by the indefatigable and ever-faithful Bob Weil, and most especially our editor Haley Bracken, who took on this project in the midst of a global pandemic, and persisted through it all to consistently shape, sharpen, and refine the book into the gem of a volume we have here.

We are also indebted to two people who are no longer here with us to receive our gratitude. As we neared the completion of this volume, we sometimes joked that it should be subtitled *A Tale of Two Garys*, perhaps to lighten the sadness of their passing, but also because it was in some important sense true.

Gary Gutting, the beloved philosopher and emeritus professor at Notre Dame, the author of several books, and dozens of essays and interviews published at The Stone, was a model for this entire project. As one of The Stone's earliest contributors, he became a North Star for us as we navigated the wide and sometimes turbulent seas of public philosophy. His belief in the need for rigorous and civil public debate was the foundation on which most of our work was built. His death, in January 2019 at age 76, was a blow, and is now a felt absence. But both his writing and his spirit are pulsing through this book. It is not an exaggeration to say that it would not have come to exist without his encouragement, friendship, and guidance.

Gary Leib, the artist and animator, who died suddenly in March 2021, was a both a friend and muse. Importantly, Gary's animation work for The Stone, and his capacity for madcap creativity and humor in the presence of the profoundest philosophical concepts energized us and kept the flame of fun burning brightly in our meanderings in a discipline that takes itself *very* seriously. Even the profoundest among us could use a laugh now and then.

Finally, now that all is said and done, we'd like to thank each other: Good job, mate!

—Peter Catapano and Simon Critchley

CONTRIBUTORS

MARIANA ALESSANDRI is an associate professor of philosophy at the University of Texas Rio Grande Valley.

AVRAM ALPERT is a research fellow at the New Institute, Hamburg. His most recent book is *The Good-Enough Life*.

INI ARCHIBONG has designed products for a range of clients, including Hermès, Knoll, and Sé Collections. His work has been exhibited at numerous international museums.

STEPHEN ASMA is a professor of philosophy at Columbia College Chicago and a member of the Public Theologies of Technology and Presence program at the Institute of Buddhist Studies. He is the author of *Why We Need Religion* and *The Evolution of Imagination*.

ULRICH BAER is University Professor at New York University. His books include *The Dark Interval: Letters on Loss, Grief, and Transformation* (translator and editor), *Fictions of America: The Book of Firsts* (editor with Smaran Dayal), *What Snowflakes Get Right: Free Speech, Truth, and Equality on Campus*, and new editions of classics including *Frankenstein*, *Pride and Prejudice*, *The Great Gatsby*, *Mrs. Dalloway*, *The Sun Also Rises*, and others.

DAVID BEAVER is a professor of linguistics and philosophy at the University of Texas at Austin. He is the coauthor, with Jason Stanley, of the forthcoming *Politics of Language*.

DAVID BENATAR is a professor of philosophy and the director of the Bioethics Center at the University of Cape Town. His most recent book is *The Fall of the University of Cape Town*.

CATE BLANCHETT is a producer and Academy Award–winning actor.

PAUL BLOOM is a professor of psychology at the University of Toronto and Brooks and Suzanne Ragen Professor Emeritus of Psychology at Yale University. He is the author of several books, including *The Sweet Spot: The Pleasures of Suffering and the Search for Meaning*.

PAUL BLOOMFIELD is a professor of philosophy at the University of Connecticut and the author of *The Virtues of Happiness*.

COSTICA BRADATAN is the author, most recently, of *In Praise of Failure: Four Lessons in Humility*, and the religion and philosophy editor for the *Los Angeles Review of Books*.

ROBERT A. BURTON, a former chief of neurology at the University of California, San Francisco, Medical Center at Mount Zion, is the author of *On Being Certain: Believing You Are Right Even When You're Not* and *A Skeptic's Guide to the Mind: What Neuroscience Can and Cannot Tell Us About Ourselves*.

AGNES CALLARD, an associate professor of philosophy at the University of Chicago and the author of *Aspiration: The Agency of Becoming*, writes about public philosophy at *The Point* magazine.

AMBER ROSE CARLSON holds a doctorate in philosophy from Vanderbilt University, in addition to graduate degrees from Princeton Theological Seminary, the University of Notre Dame, and Texas A&M

University. Amber is currently working at the intersection of philanthropy and social justice advocacy.

JOSEPH P. CARTER earned his PhD in Philosophy of Science in 2018 from the University of Georgia. Now, he is the project coordinator for a reparations initiative called The Linnentown Project. He is also a political organizer and labor researcher in Athens, Georgia.

ADRIANA CAVARERO is a political philosopher, an honorary professor at the University of Verona in Italy, and the author, most recently, of *Surging Democracy: Notes on Hannah Arendt's Political Thought.*

ANDY CLARK is Professor of Cognitive Philosophy at the University of Sussex and the former director of the Cognitive Science Program at Indiana University, Bloomington.

GARY COMSTOCK is Alumni Distinguished Undergraduate Professor of Philosophy at North Carolina State University.

JOHN CORVINO is dean of the Irvin D. Reid Honors College and a professor of philosophy at Wayne State University and a coauthor of *Debating Religious Liberty and Discrimination*.

MEGAN CRAIG is an associate professor of philosophy and art at the State University of New York, Stony Brook, and the author of *Levinas and James: Toward a Pragmatic Phenomenology.*

SIMON CRITCHLEY is Hans Jonas Professor of Philosophy at the New School for Social Research in New York and the author of many books. He is the moderator of The Stone and coeditor of this book.

MONA ELTAHAWY is the founder and editor-in-chief of the newsletter FEMINIST GIANT. She is a public speaker on global feminism and the author of *Headscarves and Hymens: Why the Middle East Needs a Sexual Revolution* and *The Seven Necessary Sins for Women and Girls.*

ADAM ETINSON is a Senior Lecturer in the School of Philosophical, Anthropological, and Film Studies at the University of St. Andrews.

ELENA FERRANTE is the author of the four Neapolitan novels: *My Brilliant Friend*, *The Story of a New Name*, *Those Who Leave and Those Who Stay*, and *The Story of the Lost Child*.

ISKRA FILEVA is an assistant professor of philosophy at the University of Colorado, Boulder.

STANLEY FISH is a professor of law at Florida International University and a visiting professor at the Benjamin N. Cardozo School of Law. He is the author of many books and is currently at work on a book titled *Law at the Movies*.

PHILIP S. GARRITY holds a Master of Divinity degree from Harvard Divinity School and is currently pursuing a PhD in Clinical Psychology at Pacifica Graduate Institute. Since 2011, he has worked in the global health field with a focus on improving access to cancer and palliative care services for underserved communities in Latin America and Africa.

MICHAEL S. GAZZANIGA is the director of the SAGE Center for the Study of the Mind at the University of California, Santa Barbara, and the author, most recently, of *The Consciousness Instinct*.

BRIAN GREENE is the director of Columbia University's Center for Theoretical Physics and a cofounder of the World Science Festival. Portions of this essay were adapted from his latest book, *Until the End of Time: Mind, Matter, and Our Search for Meaning in an Evolving Universe*.

GARY GUTTING was a professor of philosophy at the University of Notre Dame and an editor of *Notre Dame Philosophical Reviews*. His book

Talking God: Philosophers on Belief (W. W. Norton, 2016) is based on interviews published in The Stone.

MARTIN HÄGGLUND is the Birgit Baldwin Professor of Humanities at Yale University and the author of *This Life: Secular Faith and Spiritual Freedom*.

ESPEN HAMMER is a professor of philosophy at Temple University and the author of *Adorno's Modernism: Art, Experience, and Catastrophe*.

CAROL HAY is a professor of philosophy at the University of Massachusetts Lowell and the author of *Kantianism, Liberalism, and Feminism: Resisting Oppression* and *Think Like a Feminist: The Philosophy Behind the Revolution*.

DANIEL M. HAYBRON, the Theodore R. Vitali C. P. Professor of Philosophy at Saint Louis University, is the author of *The Pursuit of Unhappiness: The Elusive Psychology of Well-Being* and *Happiness: A Very Short Introduction*.

EILEEN M. HUNT is a political theorist whose latest book, *Artificial Life After Frankenstein*, was published by Penn Press in late 2020.

PICO IYER is the author of many books, including *The Man Within My Head*, *The Art of Stillness*, and *Autumn Light*, a book on Japan.

MATTHEW JORDAN is a graduate student in psychology at Yale University.

JOHN KAAG is Donahue Professor of the Arts at the University of Massachusetts Lowell and External Professor at the Santa Fe Institute. He is the author, most recently, of *Sick Souls, Healthy Minds: How William James Can Save Your Life*.

ERIC KAPLAN is an Emmy Award–winning television producer and writer who has worked on *The Big Bang Theory* and *Futurama*, among other shows. He is the author of *Does Santa Exist: A Philosophical Investigation*.

GARRY KASPAROV is the chairman of the Renew Democracy Initiative and a former world chess champion.

SEAN D. KELLY is Teresa G. and Ferdinand F. Martignetti Professor of Philosophy and former chair of the Department of Philosophy at Harvard University. He is the author of numerous scholarly articles and the coauthor, with Hubert Dreyfus, of *All Things Shining: Reading the Western Classics to Find Meaning in a Secular Age*.

COLIN KOOPMAN is a professor and head of philosophy, as well as director of New Media and Culture, at the University of Oregon. He is the author of *How We Became Our Data* and other books.

CHRIS LEBRON is the author of *The Color of Our Shame: Race and Justice in Our Time* and *The Making of Black Lives Matter: A Brief History of an Idea*. He is an associate professor of philosophy at Johns Hopkins University.

MIN JIN LEE is the author of the novels *Free Food for Millionaires* and *Pachinko*, which was named a finalist for the National Book Award and runner-up for the Dayton Literary Peace Prize. Her writing has been featured in *The New Yorker*, the *New York Review of Books*, *One Story*, the *New York Times Book Review*, and the *Wall Street Journal*. She is the recipient of fellowships in fiction from the Guggenheim Foundation, the Radcliffe Institute of Advanced Study at Harvard, and the New York Foundation for the Arts. In 2019, she was inducted into the New York Foundation for the Arts Hall of Fame. She is a writer-in-residence at Amherst College and serves as a trustee of PEN America and a director of the Authors Guild. She is at work on her third novel, *American Hagwon*, and a nonfiction work, *Name Recognition*.

ESTHER LESLIE is a professor of political aesthetics at Birkbeck College, University of London, and the author, most recently, of *Liquid Crystals: The Science and Art of a Fluid Form*.

BERNARD-HENRI LÉVY is a French philosopher, filmmaker, and activist. He is the author of *The Empire and the Five Kings*.

MAXIM LOSKUTOFF is the author of the short story collection *Come West and See* and the novel *Ruthie Fear*.

T. M. LUHRMANN, a professor of anthropology at Stanford University, is the author of *How God Becomes Real*.

MICHAEL P. LYNCH is Board of Trustees Distinguished Professor of Philosophy and Provost Professor of the Humanities at the University of Connecticut. He is the author of *The Internet of Us*, *In Praise of Reason*, *Truth as One and Many*, and *Know-It-All Society*.

CLANCY MARTIN is a professor of philosophy at the University of Missouri, Kansas City, and the author of the novel *How to Sell*.

TODD MAY is the author of sixteen books of philosophy, including *A Decent Life: Morality for the Rest of Us*, *A Fragile Life: Accepting Our Vulnerability*, *A Significant Life: Human Meaning in a Silent Universe*, and *Nonviolent Resistance: A Philosophical Introduction*. He was also a philosophical adviser for the television series *The Good Place* and the adviser for showrunner Mike Schur's recent book *How to Be Perfect: The Correct Answer to Every Moral Question*.

ALISON McQUEEN is an associate professor of political science at Stanford University and the author of *Political Realism in Apocalyptic Times*.

CHRISTIA MERCER is Gustave M. Berne Professor of Philosophy at Columbia University, and the author of the forthcoming *Feeling the Way to Truth: Women, Reason, and the Development of Modern Philosophy*.

ERROL MORRIS is a writer and filmmaker. His latest film is *My Psychedelic Love Story*.

MARTHA C. NUSSBAUM is the Ernst Freund Distinguished Service Professor at the University of Chicago, jointly appointed in the Law School and the Philosophy Department.

MALKA OLDER, a faculty associate at Arizona State University, is the author of the Centenal Cycle trilogy, *...and Other Disasters*, and *The Mimicking of Known Successes*.

KELLY OLIVER is W. Alton Jones Professor of Philosophy at Vanderbilt University and the author of sixteen scholarly books, over one hundred articles, and three best-selling mystery series.

N. ÁNGEL PINILLOS is a professor of philosophy in the School of Historical, Philosophical and Religious Studies at Arizona State University.

REGINA RINI teaches philosophy at York University in Toronto, where she holds the Canada Research Chair in Philosophy of Moral and Social Cognition.

SONNY ROLLINS is a Grammy Award–winning saxophonist, a member of the American Academy of Arts and Sciences, and a recipient of the 2010 National Medal of Arts.

ALEX ROSENBERG is R. Taylor Cole Professor and Philosophy Department Chair at Duke University. He is the author of twelve books in the philosophy of biology and economics. W. W. Norton published his book *The Atheist's Guide to Reality* in 2011, and Lake Union published his novel *The Girl from Krakow* in 2015. The sequel, *In the Shadow of Enigma*, was published by Top Hat Books in 2021.

INGRID ROSSELLINI is the author of *Know Thyself: Western Identity from Classical Greece to the Renaissance*.

DORIS SALCEDO is a Colombian visual artist and sculptor who addresses the concept of memory and the forgotten in her installations. Her work has been exhibited at the Tate Modern, the San Francisco Museum of Modern Art, and the Guggenheim Museum.

CRISPIN SARTWELL teaches philosophy at Dickinson College in Carlisle, Pennsylvania. His most recent book is *Beauty: A Quick Immersion*.

MIKE SCHUR is a television producer and the former showrunner for the NBC series *The Good Place*. His book, *How to Be Perfect*, was supervised by philosopher Todd May.

ROY SCRANTON is the author of several books, including *Learning to Die in the Anthropocene: Reflections on the End of a Civilization* (City Lights, 2015) and the novel *War Porn* (Soho Press, 2016). He has written for the *New York Times*, *MIT Technology Review*, *Yale Review*, *The New Republic*, and other publications. He teaches at the University of Notre Dame.

KIERAN SETIYA is a professor of philosophy at the Massachusetts Institute of Technology, and the author of *Life Is Hard: How Philosophy Can Help Us Find Our Way*.

JONATHAN SHEEHAN is a professor of history and a cofounder of the Berkeley Center for the Study of Religion at the University of California, Berkeley.

LAURIE SHRAGE is a professor of philosophy at Florida International University.

SHAHZIA SIKANDER is a MacArthur Fellowship-winning visual artist. A traveling retrospective exhibition of her work, organized by the RISD Museum, was on display at the Morgan Library & Museum in New York and the Museum of Fine Arts, Houston, in 2021–2022.

ED SIMON is a staff writer for The Millions and a contributing writer at *Belt Magazine*. He is the author of several books, including *An Alternative History of Pittsburgh* and *Pandemonium: A Visual History of Demonology*.

JUSTIN E. H. SMITH is a professor of philosophy in the Department of History and Philosophy of Science at the Université Paris Diderot—Paris 7. He is the author of *The Internet Is Not What You Think It Is: A History, a Philosophy, a Warning*.

JASON STANLEY is Jacob Urowsky Professor of Philosophy at Yale University. He is the author of *Knowledge and Practical Interests, Language and Context, Know How, How Propaganda Works*, and *How Fascism Works*. He is the coauthor, with David Beaver, of the forthcoming *Politics of Language*.

GALEN STRAWSON is a professor of philosophy at the University of Texas at Austin, and the author, most recently, of *Things That Bother Me* (New York Review of Books, 2018).

WES STUDI is an actor. In 2019 he received an honorary Academy Award, the first Oscar awarded to a Native American actor.

JAMES TRAUB is the author of *What Was Liberalism: The Past, Present, and Promise of a Noble Idea*. He is currently writing a book about Hubert Humphrey.

BRYAN W. VAN NORDEN is James Monroe Taylor Chair in Philosophy at Vassar College. He is the author, most recently, of *Taking Back Philosophy: A Multicultural Manifesto*.

CHRISTY WAMPOLE is a professor of French at Princeton University and the author of *Rootedness: The Ramifications of a Metaphor, The Other Serious: Essays for the New American Generation*, and *Degenerative Realism: Novel and Nation in Twenty-First Century France*.

RIVKA WEINBERG is a professor of philosophy at Scripps College in Claremont, California.

AI WEIWEI (b. 1957, Beijing) lives and works in multiple locations, including Beijing, Berlin, Cambridge, and Lisbon. He is a multimedia artist who also works in film, writing, and social media.

GEORGE YANCY is Samuel Candler Dobbs Professor of Philosophy at Emory University. He has written, edited, and coedited numerous books, including *Backlash*; *Black Bodies, White Gazes*; *Look, a White!*; and *Our Black Sons Matter*, coedited with Maria de Guadalupe Davidson and Susan Hadley.

ROBERT ZARETSKY is a professor at the Honors College, University of Houston, and author of *The Subversive Simone Weil: A Life in Five Ideas* (Chicago, 2021) and *Victories Never Last: Reading and Caregiving in a Time of Plague* (Chicago, 2022).